MW00774392

Qurʾanic Hermeneutics

Also available from Bloomsbury

The Composition of the Qur'an, Michel Cuypers
Psychological Hermeneutics for Biblical Themes and Texts, edited by J. Harold Ellens
The Qur'an and Modern Arabic Literary Criticism, Mohammad Salama

Qurʾanic Hermeneutics

Between Science, History, and the Bible

Abdulla Galadari

BLOOMSBURY ACADEMIC
LONDON • NEW YORK • OXFORD • NEW DELHI • SYDNEY

BLOOMSBURY ACADEMIC
Bloomsbury Publishing Plc
50 Bedford Square, London, WC1B 3DP, UK
1385 Broadway, New York, NY 10018, USA

BLOOMSBURY, BLOOMSBURY ACADEMIC and the Diana logo
are trademarks of Bloomsbury Publishing Plc

First published in Great Britain 2018
Paperback edition first published 2020

Cover Images: (top) jvphoto / Alamy Stock Photo, (centre) Kenneth Sponsler / Alamy
Stock Photo, (bottom) belterz / istockphoto

A catalogue record for this book is available from the British Library.

Library of Congress Cataloging-in-Publication Data
Names: Galadari, Abdulla.
Title: Qur anic hermeneutics : between science, history, and the Bible /
Abdulla Galadari.
Description: London, England : Bloomsbury Academic, [2018] | includes
bibliographical references and index.
Identifiers: LCCN 2018009305 | ISBN 9781350070028 (hardback) |
ISBN 9781350070035 (epdf)
Subjects: LCSH : Qur'an—Hermeneutics. | Bible—Hermeneutics.
Classification: LCC BP130.2 .G35 2018 | DDC 297.1/22601—dc23 LC record
available at https://iccn.loc.gov/2018009305

ISBN: HB: 978-1-3500-7002-8
PB: 978-1-3501-5210-6
ePDF: 978-1-3500-7003-5
eBook: 978-1-3500-7004-2

Typeset by RefineCatch Limited, Bungay, Suffolk

To find out more about our authors and books visit
www.bloomsbury.com and sign up for our newsletters.

To the Truth
and all beings who are thirsty for knowledge and truth

Contents

Preface

This book is a product of years (and perhaps lifetimes) of work in search for truth and seeking the reality of God. I fully appreciate that some Muslims might find certain arguments made controversial, especially on the psychological state of Muḥammad. However, statements made are not meant to offend anyone, but a sincere search for knowledge and truth. Not a single disrespect is intended in any way.

I would like the reader to have an open mind. You do not need to agree to all, part, or any of the arguments. My intention is to provide observations without necessarily making assertions. I do not want to push any conclusion on you. I would love for you to draw your own conclusions based on these observations. The Qur᾽an, after all, frequently invites its audience to think, contemplate, ponder, and reflect upon its words. As such, if I achieve in making you do just that, then I would accomplish that goal, even if you end up disagreeing with me. We are all in a journey in pursuit of truth without any hidden agendas or blind convictions. I am fallible and when we put our minds together we can further understand and learn from each other what lies behind reality.

I hope you forgive my shortcomings and insanity.

Acknowledgments

I would like to extend my gratitude to everyone who helped me throughout my life. First, I would like to thank whatever Universal Force or Power that brought me into existence, and if I do not exist in reality, then whatever that made me think that I do.

I also like to thank all my family, who both genetically and environmentally reared me. I especially am appreciative to my late grandmother Zainab, who took me in her arms as a baby, showered me with her love, and raised me, as well my late grandfather Abdulla, who took me all around and taught me how to be human; my parents, Ibrahim and Afaf, and siblings, Hassan, Sarah, and Hind, who nurtured me and I grew up fondly with; my wife, Fatma, who supported me and endured my insanity.

I extend my appreciation to the many mentors, friends, and colleagues who shared with me their wealth of knowledge, such as Alhagi Manta Drammeh, Gabriel Reynolds, J. Harold Ellens, Ulrika Mårtensson, Gordon Newby, Linda Joelsson, Zohar Hadromi-Allouche, John Kaltner, David Penchansky, Reuven Firestone, Martine O'Kane, Luqman Zakariyah, Masoumeh Velayati, Hossein Godazgar, Michael Pregill, Holger Zellentin, Munʾim Sirry, and the late Andrew Rippin; as well as the many more whose presence alone provided me with insightful vibes.

I also wish to thank the anonymous reviewers who provided me with their invaluable feedback and supported the madness of this book. I would also like to thank my close friends Ahmad al-Khuraibet and Mansour al-Khouri who stand with me and support me even when my wild mind delves into the darkness of caves in search of a spark. I also want to acknowledge my gratitude to Ben and Diane Blackwell for wonderful discussions and their inspirational friendship.

In addition, I wish to thank the air breeze for allowing me to breathe the freshness; the sun for lighting our day; the rain for bringing forth living waters; the darkness for allowing us to see; the bees without whom we will have scarce fruits; the enemies, who are in dire need of our love; the all for everything its entirety provides; and the supreme existence in which nothing in reality exists except it.

Notes on Transliteration

Arabic

ء	ʾ	ر	r	ف	f
ا	a, ā	ز	z	ق	q
ب	b	س	s	ك	k
ت	t	ش	sh	ل	l
ث	th	ص	ṣ	م	m
ج	j	ض	ḍ	ن	n
ح	ḥ	ط	ṭ	ة, ه	h
خ	kh	ظ	ẓ	و	w, ū
د	d	ع	ʿ	ي	y, i, ī
ذ	dh	غ	gh		

The short vowelization at the end of a word is typically omitted.

I am using *The Study Qurʾan* (henceforth *TSQ*) as the main translation for the Qurʾanic quotations throughout the book, unless otherwise noted: Nasr, Seyyed Hossein, ed., *The Study Quran* (New York, NY: HarperOne, 2015).

Other languages

The book uses other languages, mainly Semitic and Greek. For Semitic terms, the transliteration follows similar to the Arabic with vowelization sometimes omitted. For Greek, it follows conventional methods.

1

The Science Behind Revelation

This book investigates a hermeneutical method for the Qur'an called intertextual polysemy. Since the method makes extensive use of intertextuality and polysemy, linking various words in the Qur'an with one another, as well as linking the Qur'an with the Bible, then it is important to understand why that is. Because the intertextuality and the use of polysemy and metaphor is complex, very much like jigsaw puzzle pieces in need of putting together, it brings us to an understanding of the high sophistication of Qur'anic linguistics. This book proposes three possibilities of how that came about: (i) Muḥammad was in an altered state of consciousness and the flow came naturally to him, according to our modern understanding of neuropsychology, (ii) the author(s) and redactors of the Qur'an applied a highly sophisticated interweaving of intertextualities, or (iii) there is a divine element that built this sophistication within the Qur'an, while perhaps Muḥammad was unaware of it, causing even him to be unable to comprehend what he is hearing of the Qur'anic words. Each one of these possible reasons gives us a different perspective, historical, literary, and theological respectively.

Personally, I lean more toward the first reason, which has a neuropsychological basis. This is because it offers us a possible reason with the least assumptions. The level of sophistication in the intertextual examples that are in this book seems unlikely to be the product of a highly erudite team of author(s) and redactors. It seems much more likely that this level of sophistication was produced by a single person than many working together. Since the third reason is theological, it requires the assumption of divinity, the ability of this divinity to communicate with humans, and a reason for such divinity to do so. As such, it becomes more of a philosophical exercise that can only be speculated upon. Therefore, I find that by applying Ockham's razor, the first reason is the simplest to answer why the Qur'an can perhaps have this high level of sophistication in its intertextualities.

To be clear, leaning toward the first reason, which uses our scientific knowledge of neuropsychology, does not necessarily mean I am a reductionist. If there is a divine or mystical element in the revelation and inspiration of the Qur'an, it is very much possible that it has occurred through a natural method of neuropsychology. As such, I am not dismissing divine origination of the Qur'an by accepting a scientific reason of what perhaps naturally occurred to Muḥammad. Today, we have scientific knowledge of what natural phenomena cause rainfall, which include the combination of atmospheric moisture, temperature, pressure, etc. The Qur'an frequently states that it is God that causes rain to fall (e.g., Qur'an 27:60, 29:63, 39:21). If we accept the scientific causes of rainfall, it does not necessarily mean that we dismiss God's role in it. It is very much possible that God causes the rain to fall through the means of natural laws, which, if there were a God, natural laws could have been enacted by God. Therefore, if we accept a scientific cause of what occurred in Muḥammad's mind during the time of his alleged revelation, it also does not necessarily mean that we are dismissing its divine origination, if any.

When using psychology, the book intentionally avoids psychoanalytic methods. Sigmund Freud and Carl G. Jung have placed their fingerprints on psychoanalysis, and Jung has used it extensively to describe religious experiences. However, psychoanalysis may be considered somewhat of a pseudoscience and speculative when compared to the advances in neuropsychology. There have been attempts to psychoanalyze Muḥammad, such as Duncan B. Macdonald[1] and Maxime Rodinson,[2] but psychoanalysis is not the methodology that this book probes. This book takes into account neuropsychological research as a basis to understand what might have gone through Muḥammad's mind. For the purpose of this book, I will not delve into the mind–body problem to distinguish between the mind and the brain. I only look at our understanding of neuropsychology, and whenever that science advances, then so would our understanding of the distinction between the mind and the brain, if any.

Assessing a psychobiography of Muḥammad is only good as his biography, which may not be without myth.[3] It must be clear, however, that due to limitations on the accuracy of these tales of Muḥammad's childhood and life, I will not use them to determine the cause of his psychological state of mind during his alleged mystical experience.[4] I will only use the traditional account of such mystical experience, and more precisely, the descriptions of Muḥammad in the cave. As such, I will not consider what kinds of childhood traumas and upbringing might have predisposed him to mystical experience, as to the most part not only are they unknown to modern historians, but were also unknown to early historians, who filled them with possible legends. I will only evaluate the narratives of what symptoms he appears to have had during such an experience. There have been previous attempts to write a psychobiography of Muḥammad in a polemical manner against him.[5] This book does not endorse a psychobiography for the propagation of a certain agenda, but for an objective understanding through an interdisciplinary nature. As such, it avoids pseudo-psychoanalytics in favor of neuropsychology. Also, it avoids the full historical tradition of Muḥammad that can be fuzzy in its accuracy, in favor of a single instant during his alleged mystical experience in the cave to derive his symptoms.

Since Muḥammad's experiences correlate with our modern scientific knowledge of the psychological basis of mystical experience and symptoms of an altered state of consciousness, it suggests that these narratives either may be true, or that whoever made up the descriptions of these narratives might have themselves achieved such mystical experiences and related their subjective experience to that of Muḥammad. In other words, the biographers who started the narratives of what happened to Muḥammad when he first claimed to receive revelations while in a cave may have themselves experienced them or saw or heard of individuals who had experienced them and retroactively suggested that this might have been what Muḥammad also experienced. Hopefully, using this constrained method of psychobiography would reduce its pitfalls and avoid its concerns, as outlined by William Runyan in *Life Histories and Psychobiography*.[6]

A psychological critique to help understand the Qur'an might be a new field in Qur'anic studies, but it certainly is not in the field of Psychological Biblical Criticism, in which it had flourished. Psychoanalyzing Biblical figures has come a long way in not only reading the text, but also what lies behind the text. J. Harold Ellens, Wayne G. Rollins, and D. Andrew Kille have pioneered this field in Biblical studies,[7] and perhaps time has dawned for it to enter the field of Qur'anic studies, as well.

This book makes use of various examples of intertextual polysemy for Qur'anic hermeneutics. Some of the examples used would be of great interest to scholars and students of Qur'anic studies, as it provides many Biblical contexts and subtexts for the Qur'anic arguments philologically. It will also be of interest to lay people who would like to understand what the Qur'an attempts to convey when arguing with Jews and Christians. As such, it may be of interest in interfaith dialogue. Since much of the Christology that the Qur'an argues with is based on the Gospel of John, then it is argued that the Qur'an is fully aware of the Gospel of John. However, unlike Emran el-Badawi's argument that the Qur'an is mainly engaging with the Aramaic Gospel traditions,[8] with the examples shown in this book, it is argued that even if the Qur'an is aware of the Aramaic Gospels, it attempts to interpret the Greek text, at least in the case of the Gospel of John, when it comes to its Christology.

I fully understand that to a reader, the first thing that may come up in their mind is the book's orientation toward an orientalist tradition that spurred Western scholarship on Islam and the Qur'an between the eighteenth and twentieth centuries. As such, I need to clarify that it is not positioned within such a scholarship. Many scholars of the orientalist tradition during such period, such as Aloys Sprenger (d. 1893), William Muir (d. 1905), William St. Clair Tisdall (d. 1928), David S. Margoliouth (d. 1940), Richard Bell (d. 1952), and Charles C. Torrey (d. 1956) were biased against Muḥammad and his religion, and most of whom were driven to show the superiority of their personal convictions. W. Montgomery Watt (d. 2006) seemed to have a debatably more balanced view of Muḥammad and his message.

What must be clear is that this book attempts to look at the human aspect of Muḥammad, his experience, and his work; it is in no way an attempt to demonize them. I am not an orientalist nor do I espouse oriental convictions. Chapters 5–7 of this book provides various examples on the Qur'anic text intertextualized with the Gospel of John to understand the Christology that is perhaps seen in both. The examples show that the Qur'anic text may not necessarily be against the Gospel of John's text. These examples show that the Qur'an is engaging with and interpreting the Gospel of John, in its own way, and not in the way that some Christian communities interpreted the Christology of the Gospel of John within the Qur'anic milieu. In other words, these examples do not assert an agenda to prove that the Christology of the Qur'an is very much Christian. They only show that the Qur'anic text is interpreting the Gospel of John and not discrediting it. As such, they should not be viewed that the purpose of this book is to show the superiority of the Christian faith over Islam. On the contrary, I personally equally apply skepticism to all, giving none a superiority over another.

The methodology applied in this book is interdisciplinary. It uses our modern knowledge of neuroscience and neuropsychology as a context for how the Qur'an could have possibly emerged. As such, the methodology is not purely historical. It provides a hypothesis of how the Qur'an might have emerged from a neuropsychological point of view, which would give reasons for how certain philological patterns can be found in the Qur'an, creating metaphor. As such, applying neuropsychology, linguistics, and Qur'anic studies in an interdisciplinary manner is not without its flaws: (i) the literary Qur'an may not be the best reproduction of Muḥammad's historical utterances; (ii) neuropsychology and how it explains semantic associations and metaphor is still an emerging science; and (iii) the historical accounts according to tradition as a basis of psychobiography are not without their own flaws. As such, there are various limitations that this study has, which would not be too different to that of Psychological Biblical Criticism.[9] This brings a need for further future research in this interdisciplinary field.

For the most part, much of what is found in this book is not a personal dogmatic conviction. Indeed, to be honest, I am as skeptical as anyone. For that reason, you will find that I try to carefully use words such as "perhaps," "maybe," and "possibly" to avoid making assertions. I have no intention to even state that the extrapolations made in this book are "the Qur'anic interpretation." There is no way to go back into history to see how the events unfolded. Even if we did, can anyone enter Muḥammad's mind to fully understand his intentions? Clearly, people's words can be misinterpreted and so are their intentions. This happens still today when we interact with people. I am certain that many people reading this book would also extrapolate what my intentions might be. Some might think I am driving a Christian scheme behind this work, especially when assessing Chapters 5–7. This is in no way my intention. The main reason behind Chapters 5–7 is to show that the Qur'an is *not* inconsistent, when on the one hand it asks the People of the Gospel[s] to uphold their scriptures (e.g., Qur'an 5:47), while on the other, still *seemingly* attacking its Christology. Perhaps this can be seen as a defense for the Qur'anic possible consistency within itself, without having to delve through the traditional abrogation (*naskh*) concept.

I have applied the methodology outlined in this book in other research that I do. The main one is by analyzing the Qiblah passages in the Qur'an with the Shemaʿ passages in Deuteronomy and its Talmudic commentary.[10] The paper in question provides what I think is even clearer evidence that this sort of methodology actually works than any of the examples outlined in this book. It also clearly shows how traditional Qur'anic commentators are not always credible, especially in issues pertaining to the Qur'anic engagement with the Bible or Biblical and Rabbinic literature. This might have been intentional by the commentators to avoid Judeo-Christian tradition when interpreting the Qur'an, or unintentional, due to these commentators' less than perfect knowledge of the literature. Equally, however, I am in no way suggesting that mine is any superior. We are all human and as any of us, we are all fallible.

As such, I would like readers to be cautious when reading this book and its examples. I will briefly describe my intentions, in order to avoid readers' speculation of what they might be. I am a searcher for truth, whatever it may be. My search is only as good as my mind and my research. Indeed, sometimes I will assume and speculate, and sometimes, I can provide harder evidence of why such a speculation is plausible. If, in the future, neuropsychology develops that the scientific process outlined here, of how the Qurʾan and its intertextual patterns might have emerged, by acquiring further understanding of how the minds of creative poets, artists, and scientists make ingenious associations, then indeed, the hypothesis may be falsified, and I will have no option but to reevaluate it. As I said, I have no dogmatic conviction. I am a searcher for the truth, whatever it may be. I am fully aware of other hypotheses out there on the origins of the Qurʾan and early Islam. I do not try to discredit them and prove the superiority of my hypothesis. In the end, this is just a hypothesis, some kind of *ijtihād*, to use an Islamic term. My other intention is at least to have people think outside the box, be creative, and, indeed, even to take them out of their comfort zones and question their own dogmas. I do that not to discredit their dogmas, but to make people think, contemplate, and ponder. I want to provoke thought in people's minds, to better make objective searches in our pursuit of humanity. I want people to also search for the truth due to their knowledge through the use of their minds, and not through the process of, "We found our fathers upon a creed, and we are surely following in their footsteps."[11] In this case, when it does come to the Qurʾan, this is what the Qurʾan asks us to do. Therefore, I earnestly appeal to the reader to have an open mind, to think, and to search for the truth; obviously I am not giving you a version of any truth, but a portal for us as humans to think and ponder. "Do they not contemplate the Quran? Had it been from other than God, they would surely have found much discrepancy therein."[12] "Do they not contemplate the Quran? Or do hearts have their locks upon them?"[13]

Background

Interpreting the Qurʾan, people tend to understand the historical and social context.[14] Nonetheless, when interpreting any piece of literature, it is important also to understand the context of the author or the scribes and editors. To understand how a person says or writes something, we need to dig deep into his/her psyche. In literary theory, this is called authorial intent, where the author's intent is sought to interpret his/her writing,[15] especially if it were metaphor.[16]

Whenever people say something, whether in speech or writing, there is always a chance that what is said is misunderstood, especially when what is intended is metaphoric.[17] This study attempts to investigate possible authorial intent of Muḥammad from Qurʾanic passages, but there are definitely limitations to this approach. There is no way to go into Muḥammad's mind or even ask him to validate the assumptions. Thus this study is not making any assertions, because in my humble mind, there is no way to make any kind of assertions in this world. I am even skeptical if my material existence actually exists. When I dream, I see myself, I feel, I see, I hear, I taste, I even talk, and move. However, is my dream a material existence or just an illusory projection of my mind? I do, sometimes, have lucid dreams where I know that I am dreaming. However, in many instances, I do not perceive that what I am experiencing is a dream. My mind is limited to its perception. Therefore, I may not even have a material existence: something that would be appreciated in Eastern philosophies. And so, if I cannot assert my own material existence, how will I be able to assert anything at all? As such, I would ask the readers to understand that this book is not to assert an argument or propagate any agenda. It is a humble attempt to seek and to provoke thought in people's minds to start a new path of inquiry in interdisciplinary Qur'anic studies.

Therefore, to clarify, the style of the book reflects my humble attempt to understand the Qur'an and its text. For that reason, the reader will see that I will sometimes state that perhaps current hypotheses of the Qur'anic origins and interpretations may be deemed valid or not valid. I will not make an assertion where an assertion is not due. Therefore, I understand that the reader may sometimes be confused when I claim that some scholar could be right in their views and perspectives. This is not to say that I agree 100 percent with their claims—nor would I want to dismiss them. We live in a world of possibilities. There are many possibilities and many hypotheses. Until I am certain, I shall continue to work, as Qur'an 15:99 states, "And worship thy Lord, till certainty comes unto thee."

Investigating Muḥammad's authorial intent would not be without bias due to the historicized sociological and cultural position of his race, class, gender, etc.[18] In other words, some people might suggest that seventh-century Arabia would not seem a place where this Muḥammad could have written with such an ingenious approach and with the intertextuality done with the Bible. The claim may even go further suggesting that such an approach was completely misunderstood for so many centuries by experts in linguistics, history, and hermeneutics. However, making such a claim would also mean that it would not be plausible for Copernicus to have reinvented how we look at our heliocentric solar system after so many centuries of highly celebrated experts in astronomy, mathematics, and physics, who had scientific, observational, mathematical, and empirical evidence for their geocentric models.

In the past decades, there has been a shift in Qur'anic studies, as revisionists attempted to reinterpret history about the origins of the Qur'an and Islam. Revisionists, such as John Wansbrough, Patricia Crone, and Michael Cook sought to critique traditional the historicity of Muslim accounts.[19] They have attempted to revisit the origins of the Qur'an and Islam from historical accounts beyond the Muslim traditions, by searching for clues from other sources who have interacted with Muslim communities. Fred Donner has argued that Muḥammad's message rooted itself within a monotheistic movement that included Jews and Christians, in which each was following their own revelation.[20] However, Donner proposes that it was only about a century later that the leaders of the community decided to distinguish themselves from Jews and Christians by stating that only the followers of the Qur'an would be part of its community, marginalizing Jews and Christians, and subsequently discrediting their scriptures altogether.[21]

Although many revisionists have been criticized, they do raise many interesting and valid points. In this book, I will tackle the issue between traditionalists and revisionists by being agnostic of both sides of the debate. Initially, I will assume the traditional account of Muḥammad's beginning of revelation while in a cave to try to identify his state of mind, to help us understand what he tries to convey in his message, if such an account were true. However, at the same time, I will not consider the traditional accounts of *tafsīr* at face value, and instead will attempt to contextualize it with Muḥammad's state of mind, during the time he claimed to be receiving his revelation. To understand Muḥammad's state of mind, I consider using contemporary psychological diagnostic techniques. I understand that such a diagnosis may seem to be absurd to many faithful Muslims. However, I am perhaps attempting to investigate the human aspect of Muḥammad's experience. Besides, if God reveals Its message through prophets, perhaps God uses scientific methods to bring forth revelation. Why should we consider a God, who is a wizard, when It can be seen as a scientist? Humans did not create the sciences. If God created this universe and provided its natural sciences and its natural laws, then why should we expect a God to break Its own laws? Therefore, I will initially attempt to completely investigate the human aspect of Muḥammad's experience. However, I must also be very explicit in the beginning that the diagnosis of Muḥammad's state of mind, as portrayed in this book, should in no way be interpreted that Muḥammad was insane or mentally ill. It also is in no way attempting to discredit a divine origin of the Qur'an that is uttered by Muḥammad. On the contrary, I attempt to show that Muḥammad is a human being of genius, who is highly creative, according to our knowledge of the psychology of creative individuals.[22]

Unfortunately, human societies stigmatize people who may seem mentally abnormal, perhaps experiencing psychosis or mental illness. Talking of geniuses having a mental abnormality is even taboo. Nonetheless, the studies on the psychology of creative and genius individuals tell us that major artistic pieces, spiritual insights, and major discoveries and breakthroughs in human history are highly dependent on intuition or a moment of epiphany, which occurs during what we may call abnormal mental states. As such, I prefer not to even call mental abnormality an illness or a disorder. Humanity should be proud to have genes that predispose individuals to such mental states, because they give birth to the most unique and creative insights that allow humanity to progress light years ahead than they would otherwise.

Although this book argues that Muḥammad might have been in a mental state of such high creativity and understanding it might unlock the mysteries of the words he uttered, the Qur'an, I will later provide multiple conclusions; one that would stand according to the assumption of Muḥammad's state of mind; another that would assume Muḥammad received revelation passively; yet another that would render the initial assumption of the traditional account of Muḥammad in a cave inaccurate, and provide a completely different scenario. In such a case, we may consider the literary study of the Qur'an and its intertextuality with the Bible, as this book will provide multiple instances of such, when considering the method of intertextual polysemy.

Through the examples that are portrayed in this book, especially in the areas where the Qur'an may be seen to be engaging with the Bible, I am arguing that the Qur'an does not attempt to nullify or abrogate previous scriptures. On the contrary, I show that the Qur'an is fully engaging with and attempting to interpret the Bible. There thus needs to be a distinction between the Qur'anic theology and Christology and how the later Muslim community's theology and Christology developed.

Psychology of religious experience

Heikki Räisänen states that describing the Qur'an as an expression of Muḥammad's religious experience is bound to offend Muslims.[23] It is for this reason that many scholars of Islam and the Qur'an avoid such language. Nonetheless, Räisänen feels that perhaps scholars may be forgiven if they apply the same methods to other scriptures.[24] Religious experience is not monopolized by Biblical figures. Mystics from across all religions and throughout history have claimed to have religious experiences.[25] The psychology of religious experience has also been widely studied from the perspective of various psychological schools of thought, such as those of Sigmund Freud and Carl Jung.[26] With modern understanding of the brain's neuroscience and cognitive functions, religious experiences have become a widely studied area in medicine.[27] The study of the evolutionary development of religion has a field of its own, neurotheology, which connects evolutionary biology, neuroscience, and the emergence of theology.[28] The parts of the brain that seem to have developed the human's hypervigilance, to ensure the species' safety from dangers and prey, also formed the mind's notion of causality.[29] The parts of the brain that are responsible for creativity and imagination also seem to be responsible for the evolution of neurotheology.[30]

Although Rhawn Joseph suggests that the belief of transmigration of souls and an afterlife has perhaps existed for over 100,000 years,[31] we do not really have definitive proof. He suggests that evidence of ancient burials may provide a case of such hominids having a belief of the realm beyond,[32] although he is aware that mortuary rituals of Neanderthals and early hominids are in no way proof of them having any sort of religious belief.[33] We do, indeed, have evidence that early modern hominids buried their dead.[34] Our Neanderthal cousins also buried their dead since at least the beginning of the Middle Palaeolithic.[35] Yet, these burial sites or burial rituals do not tell us more about what beliefs these individuals and communities had in regard to the afterlife. There is no reason to assume that burials should necessarily be associated with religious beliefs. These early hominids may have buried their dead out of respect or to stake a claim over land by having burial sites stand as signposts—'here lie our ancestors and so this is our land'[36]—or even perhaps simply to bury the repugnant smell of a decomposing body. This latter speculation may be criticized by archaeologists who have discovered that some early hominids had burial and mortuary rites that consisted of having tools and grave offerings next to the deceased.[37] Yet, these rituals may be caused by the emotions of grieving without necessarily assuming that there is a religious nature to it.[38] Early hominids might indeed have started to bury their dead to bury the repugnant smell of a decomposing body. As time passed and the hominids evolved to have higher emotional capacities, their mortuary rites might have evolved accordingly.

Piel and Stewart give examples of how some nonhuman animals, such as chimpanzees, elephants, and dolphins, pay attention to a dead body of a conspecific.[39] Rat burial and insect embalming, they suggest, are perhaps triggered innately with the release of polyamines of a decomposing body, in order to reduce the exposure to diseases or scavenging predators.[40] Nonetheless, this is not to completely discredit the capabilities of the brains of the early hominids to have experiences that may be regarded as religious.

Perhaps any brain that is capable of dreaming might also have the capacity to achieve what we might call a religious experience.[41] After all, some religious experiences are described as visions.[42] The brain becomes very active during the rapid eye movement (REM) stage of sleep, which is typically associated with dreams.[43] However, humans are not the only species who experience them. It has been suggested that animals have complex dreams and are able to retain and recall long sequences of events while they are asleep.[44]

The mind may typically dream things that have building blocks from what it has experienced in some way; for example, those who are congenitally blind have non-visual dreams.[45] This does not mean the mind cannot dream of flying, though the dreamer may have never flown before; the mind already understands the concept of flying. Congenitally blind individuals do not, for example, have visual hallucinations,[46] but may have mental imagery in accordance to their own visuospatial experiences.[47] In a study of dreaming experiences with congenitally deaf-mute and paraplegic persons, it has shown that the congenitally immobile individuals were still able to dream walking, though they have never walked before.[48] However, perhaps the reason is that their mind already understands the concept of walking, and so reconstructs it in a dream. Similarly, those who are congenitally deaf-mute do have dreams with communication and sometimes speak themselves,[49] perhaps because their mind already understands the concept of communication. Dreaming and the state of psychosis may have some sort of relationship.[50] Dreaming is related to the retrieval of stored memory, e.g., information and experiences in the brain that are reconstructed, though we acknowledge that understanding the source of dreams remains unknown.[51]

The neuroscience of religious and mystical experiences is by no means a way to materialize otherwise spiritual experiences or to discredit such experiences. Individuals who have these mystical experiences have mindful perceptions of what they are experiencing. If their mind plays a role in what they are perceiving, then understanding the neuroscience of their brains during such experiences is not sacrilegious. As Alexander and Andrew Fingelkurts state: "The result of such studies may (a) help to gain a better and deeper understanding of religious experience, (b) gain a better understanding of the doctrine of the image of God, and eventually (c) contribute to theological and philosophical conceptualisations. These studies will enhance human knowledge of how religious experience affects the mind, brain, body and behaviour."[52]

Rhawn Joseph, along with many neuroscientists, suggest that the core to religious experiences in human beings is perhaps the limbic system in our brains.[53] The limbic system supports numerous functions, including emotion, long-term memory, behavior, motivation, and olfaction.[54] Religious experiences ofter occur when a person might be in a heightened emotional state, including, but not restricted to, fear or anxiety, so the neurotransmitters in the limbic system may be a source of such experiences.[55] If Neanderthal burial sites show that they might have had emotional capacity as we do, and since this emotional capacity might be regulated in the limbic system(s), which could be the root of religious experiences, then it perhaps was possible that their minds had capacity to mystical experiences, causing religious beliefs to emerge, although no evidence exists to support this. Rhawn Joseph concludes:

> Indeed, it could be argued that the evolution of this neuronal spiritual, mystical, religious capacity is the consequence of repeated and exceedingly intense perceptual and emotional experiences with "God" and the spiritually sublime over many generations. Perhaps under the guiding influence of "God," or perhaps after repeated experiences with gods, spirits, demons, angels, and lost souls, *Homo sapiens* evolved these neurons, which enabled them to better cope with the unknown as well as to perceive and respond to spiritual messages that increased the likelihood of survival. A true scientist would not rule out such a possibility. Regardless of how or why, it is clear that there is in fact a scientific and neurological foundation of religious and spiritual experience. The reason for this is yet to be determined. Indeed, given the obvious role of the temporal lobe and limbic system in the generation and perception of myriad spiritual states, it also appears (at least at the level of metaphor) that the limbic system may well be the seat of the soul or may serve as the neural transmitter to God.[56]

Of course, this is not necessarily the conclusion of the reasons why humans might have evolved to have these experiences. As will be shown later, psychosis and creativity are genetically linked.[57] If high stress causes the limbic system(s) to become hyperactive causing low latent inhibition to those who are genetically predisposed,[58] then more likely than not, organisms with low latent inhibition and high intelligence have better chances of survival by being creative.[59] Since they are the survivors, this trait would have passed down through their genes to future generations.

Nevertheless, looking at the human aspect of Muḥammad's mystical, spiritual, and religious experience should not be interpreted as discrediting its divine origin or that Muḥammad was mentally ill. If we try to understand his mind and how his brain's neurons and chemistry might intervene in his perceptions, ultimately causing him to utter the Qur'an, then we may be able to better understand and unlock the message therein. Unlike other Muslims, who believe that the Qur'an is the verbatim Word of God, the Ismāʿīlīs believe that the words of the Arabic Qur'an is Muḥammad's translation of the spiritual truths and light that overcame him, during divine revelation.[60] They consider the divine language of the Qur'an is spiritual, and therefore, immaterial. Since they consider the words of the divine are inexplicable, Muḥammad had to translate it into the Arabic Qur'an, and then emphasize the esoteric and spiritual meanings that lie behind the Qur'anic text, which is there to lead to these spiritual truths. At least from such context, perhaps not all Muslims may feel offended. Yet, I would still like to reiterate that this book is in no way trying to offend the sensitivities of what Muslims may consider sanctities. Perhaps a person may look at the arguments in this book as scientific and textual evidence of the incredible linguistic ingeniousness of Muḥammad and the vocalizations he uttered, which has come to be known as the Qur'an.

The Ismāʿīlī concept of the Qur'an being spiritual and translated by Muḥammad is also a feature seen by other early Muslims. According to al-Zarkashī (d. 794/1392), there were three competing theories on Qur'anic revelation (*waḥy*), (i) the angel

Gabriel memorized it from *al-Lawḥ al-Maḥfūẓ* (the Preserved Tablet), where it was written in huge alphabets, each containing many esoteric meanings; (ii) Gabriel conveyed to Muḥammad the Qur'an in special meanings and Muḥammad translated it into Arabic based on, "193 brought down by the Trustworthy Spirit, 194 upon thine heart";[61] and (iii) that the Qur'anic meanings were given to Gabriel and that Gabriel translated it to the Arabic language.[62]

Nasr Hamid Abu Zayd leans toward the Qur'anic revelation (*waḥy*) as coming through a code used between God and the angel Gabriel through the *al-Lawḥ al-Maḥfūẓ* (the Preserved Tablet) and then between Gabriel and Muḥammad.[63] As such, Muḥammad's mind and the cultural context play a major role in transforming the meanings of the Qur'an, according to Abu Zayd.[64]

Abdulkarim Soroush, a contemporary Iranian intellectual, also espouses the consideration of the Qur'an being influenced by Muḥammad's mind and limitations.[65] He clearly states that Muḥammad had to translate the spiritual and formless into a language to be understood by people:[66] "Of course, this is all the more so when it comes to the language, the words, the terminology and the phrases. These are human vessels into which revelation is poured and they are all taken from the Prophet's mind and imagination to embrace and encase formless meanings."[67]

As such, the Qur'an being a product of Muḥammad's mind is not solely an orientalist view, but it has existed historically, according to al-Zarkashī;[68] this thought continues to exist today with contemporary Muslim thinkers. On neurotheology and Islam, Alireza Sayadmansour states:

> Neurotheology is multidisciplinary in nature and includes the fields of theology, religious studies, religious experience and practice, philosophy, cognitive science, neuroscience, psychology, and anthropology. Each of these fields may contribute to neurotheology and conversely, neurotheology may ultimately contribute in return to each of these fields. Ultimately, neurotheology must be considered as a multidisciplinary study that requires substantial integration of divergent fields, particularly neuroscience and religious phenomena. More importantly, for neurotheology to be a viable field that contributes to human knowledge, it must be able to find its intersection with specific religious traditions. For instance, Islam is powerful, growing religion that would seem to be an appropriate focus of neurotheology. After all, if neurotheology is unable to intersect with Islam, then it will lack utility in its overall goal of understanding the relationship between the brain and religion.[69]

Accordingly, this study intersects neurotheology with Islam, very early Islam, the emergence of Muḥammad, and the Qur'an.

Muḥammad's state of mind

According to traditional accounts, we have a story of Muḥammad who meditated in a cave in solitude.[70] He withdrew from friends and family, as he might have eaten meagerly or perhaps fasted during his seclusion.[71] He also apparently slept little in the cave and perhaps even less once he returned, as evidenced in the traditional account in Qur'an 73:2–4. Withdrawal from family and friends, loss of appetite, and a sleep disturbance could be precursors to a psychotic episode.[72] According to the traditional account in Qur'an 74:1,[73] a few nights later, something happened that appeared to make Muḥammad very anxious; he returned to his wife and asked her to cover him. Anxiety is also a symptom of a psychotic episode.[74] Muḥammad's mind enters a state that a modern psychiatrist would diagnose as an altered state. He hears a voice talking to him,[75] which would be typical for an auditory hallucination. He also sees what his mind describes as an angel,[76] which would include a visual hallucination.[77] His mind interprets these hallucinations to mean that he is a special person, a man on a mission, a messenger from God.[78] This description would be a delusion of grandiosity, where a person believes that he has been chosen for something special, or believes that he has some special powers or talents.[79] According to the Qur'an (i.e., Qur'an 17:79, 73:2–4) and the traditional account, Muḥammad appears to have slept little, which is a symptom of mania that may be linked to his grandiose delusion that he was a man on a divine mission.

> Isolation, food and water deprivation, increased or decreased sexual activity, pain, drug use, self-mutilation, prayer, and meditation are common methods of attaining mystical states of religious and spiritual awareness and have been employed worldwide, across time and cultures. These conditions also activate the limbic system as well as the overlying temporal lobe, thereby giving rise to hallucinations and the secretion of opiate-like enkephalins.[80]

Muḥammad comes down from the cave and starts uttering words that seem ingeniously poetic, but at the same time hold meanings that would be considered obscure. What he utters are poetic statements that appear to be erratic, jumping from one topic to another. This could be a form of thought disorder, although such a diagnosis is inconclusive.[81] Stanley Krippner et al. state, "For example, a person diagnosed with a mild thought disorder might write something viewed as gibberish in a mental hospital; but the same creative product might be viewed as beautiful poetry in a different context."[82] Whether or not the Qur'an is a product of a thought disorder, to a modern psychiatrist Muḥammad appears to have been affected by some sort of psychotic disorder.[83] However, Muḥammad may not necessarily have been in a state of psychosis, as he was able to cope and live a relatively normal functioning life filled with charisma. Nonetheless, the genes that predispose an individual to some kind of psychosis may be the same as those linked with creativity.[84] The fine line that divides psychosis from high creativity is high intelligence,[85] which Muḥammad would have possessed. Since mystical experience may be described as a psychosis-like state, then creativity is also associated with individuals with such experiences, given above average intelligence.[86] Also, if Muḥammad was able to produce a work like the Qur'an and memorize it wholly, it may also mean that he had high working memory.[87]

The key to a creative mind is low latent inhibition coupled with above average intelligence.[88] Typically, people's minds always treat familiar stimuli the same way each time. However, individuals with low latent inhibition treat a familiar stimulus as they would treat a new stimulus. This means they can easily redefine a familiar stimulus and give it a new association. Individuals with low latent inhibition coupled with average or below average intelligence might suffer from schizophrenia, as their mind will not be able to cope with the overstimulation from their environment.[89] However, individuals with high intelligence (and possibly sense of coherence)[90] would be able to cope with the overstimulation and become creative as they associate things that, typically, have nothing to do with each other and make creative associations between them.[91] Latent inhibition is linked with the state of the limbic system(s), which might be the root of religious experiences, as discussed earlier. The interaction between the temporal lobes, frontal lobes, and limbic system(s) promote creative drive and idea generation by activating dopamine to reduce latent inhibition.[92]

People with low latent inhibition, high intelligence, and high working memory master the art of symbology and, therefore, metaphor.[93] Alice Flaherty states, "metaphoric thought is nonetheless vital for creativity because metaphor depends on detecting analogies between phenomena previously thought unrelated."[94] As such, from a literary standpoint, people with low latent inhibition can become very creative in using metaphor in their speech or writing. Due to their creative ability of speaking in symbols, they are also capable of interpreting other people's metaphors. For example, a paranoid person may read hidden meanings in writings or people's speech, as they might think that these have symbolic meanings. A paranoid person will also see double meanings in people's actions, speech, and writings. However, a person with high intelligence has the ability to tune down the cluttering noise (overstimulation) from the environment by ignoring irrelevant stimuli.[95] They are able to make metaphors, and they also are able to interpret them.

If we assume that Muḥammad is the first person to have uttered the Qurʾanic passages, we need to understand Muḥammad's state of mind to understand the Qurʾan. He appears to have an altered state of consciousness that includes hallucinations, sometimes visual but mainly auditory. He also appears to have grandiose delusion that he is a man on a divine mission. He is highly intelligent and, therefore, a highly functioning individual with low latent inhibition, or simply, creative. He is capable of creating metaphors and interpreting them. Therefore, his work, the Qurʾan—if it is his to begin with—must be filled with symbology and metaphor with double meanings, as anyone in his state of mind would be capable of doing.

Muḥammad might have had such high intelligence that when his brain delved into a psychotic state, he did not fall into psychosis or mental illness, but instead became a person with high creativity linking seemingly unrelated ideas into a single formulation that he called the Qurʾan. To the believers, the Qurʾan becomes canonical scripture; to the nonbelievers of his time, Muḥammad was considered a lunatic.[96]

Psychology of creativity and metaphor processing

According to modern psychology, there is empirical evidence on the positive correlation between creativity and both schizophrenic-like positive schizotypal symptoms and hypomania.[97] Several studies have shown that even though individuals with high schizotypy may be partially impaired in pragmatic language processing,[98] they are not impaired with metaphor processing.[99] Semantic disinhibition is seen in individuals with high schizotypy.[100] In other words, individuals who score high on positive schizotypy determine unrelated words to be more closely associated with each other.[101] They also invent more imaginative associations to unrelated stimuli.[102] The neurological reasoning behind this is suggested to be the high positive schizotype individuals' reliance on the right hemisphere to process semantics.[103]

Individuals within the schizophrenic spectrum have what is known as loosened associations linguistically and semantically, which causes abnormal cognitive language functions.[104] Nonetheless, individuals with high intelligence within the spectrum have the ability to make creative associations, as discussed.

Within literary creativity and metaphor creation, it has been shown that creative writers are more likely to suffer from mental illness than control subjects.[105] They are prone to bipolar disorder, in which their highest creative states exist within their hypomanic or manic states.[106]

Decreased latent inhibition is a highlight of psychosis-prone "normal individuals"[107] and certain psychotic disorders[108] that Muḥammad appears to have experienced, according to the symptoms identified. Since Muḥammad's symptoms appear to be psychotic-like it is, therefore, highly likely that he experienced low latent inhibition. Low latent inhibition along with high intelligence, as discussed, would make him fall in the category of creative individuals, including those who can make creative semantic associations.[109] What this means is that people with low latent inhibition are more likely to bridge the gap of related semantic pairs, such as "cat" and "cheese," as used in the tests by Rominger et al.[110] These individuals can identify the relationship between those pairs with "mouse."

When it comes to psychotic disorders, such as schizophrenia, there is a much semantic and semiotic ambiguity, including when it comes to polysemy,[111] and the Arabic language of which the Qur'an is composed has much of it. Schizophrenics frequently create speech and dialogues with unusual semantic associations.[112] Individuals with schizophrenia and bipolar disorders also appear to sometimes speak poetically[113] with loose semantic associations.[114] To give a few examples, James Goss has researched and commented on schizophrenic discourse.[115] One of the examples come from Chaika who provides the following unusual and perhaps absurd utterances of a schizophrenic: "...My mother's name was Bill... and coo? St. Valentine's day is the official startin' of the breedin' season of the birds. All buzzards can coo. I like to see it pronounces buzzards rightly. They work hard. So do parakeets..."[116]

James Goss analyzes this unusual and seemingly absurd speech as something that a schizophrenic mind can formulate due to their loosened semantic associations, where he states: "Individuals with schizophrenia will often string ideas together based on loose semantic or formal associations such as taking the name 'Bill' and linking it to a bird's 'bill' which then leads to 'coo.'"[117]

James Goss also identifies how schizophrenics have this tendency to make wordplay through etymology and polysemy. Using an example cited from Lorenz:

> Contentment? Well, uh, contentment, well the word contentment, having a book perhaps, perhaps your having a subject, perhaps you have a chapter of reading, but

> when you come to the word "men" you wonder if you should be content with men in your life and then you get to the letter T and you wonder if you should be content having tea by yourself or be content with having it with a group and so forth.[118]

James Goss defines this as, "When asked to define 'contentment' this individual deconstructs the various constituent elements of the word and plays with the polysemy of these lexical fragments."[119]

James Goss continues by citing Wrobel on how schizophrenics connect things together through loose associations:

> In schizophrenia everything is interconnected, from itself everything results, every fact, even the most insignificant one (it could be a movement of a doctor's hand or a bird which alighted on a window-sill for a moment) are united into a monumental determined coincidence. In the world of schizophrenia, the accidental does not exist. Facts, objects, and phenomena of nature pulse with their unrelenting meanings. These meanings catch fire in a chain-like fashion, one from the other, like flames which consume everything all around.[120]

To this, James Goss describes the following: "Coincidental relationships can gain symbolic import for individuals with schizophrenia. In the flow of speaking and gesturing, poetic sparks string together loosely connected ideas. In schizophrenia, idiosyncratic poetic associations can overwhelm normative semiotic interpretation."[121]

Different kinds of psychological disorders, such as schizophrenia and bipolar disorder, though they may have different symptoms, can sometimes have similar neurological increases of dopamine levels in the brain that are associated with latent inhibition.[122] Mood, especially in bipolar disorders, seems to also play a role in how semantic associations are conceived.[123] The issue with Muḥammad, who might have experienced a manic episode (or at least hypomanic), and also several depressive episodes might suggest a certain kind of bipolar disorder, in which latent inhibition may also be decreased allowing the generation of loose semantic associations poetically.[124] During a manic episode, the brain goes into overdrive and would be able to construct creative semantic associations,[125] especially if the person is of above average intelligence. Hoffman states:

> The randomness of the model of manic cognition suggests that accessibility of memories is markedly enhanced due to jumps from one memory to another, though the stable generation of the correct nearest gestalt based on input information is impaired. This may account for the grandiose self-assessments of manics. Their minds might in fact be extraordinarily capable of accessing large numbers of gestalts. The price they pay, however, is a devastating instability of their mental constructions.[126]

With low latent inhibition, the use of wordplay, loose semantic associations, polysemy, etymology, etc. appear to have a neurological basis that suggest some sort of association with psychosis or altered states of consciousness. Given the discussion earlier on the relationship between creativity and altered states of consciousness mediated through the level of intelligence, along with the person's low latent inhibition allowing the person to make not just any semantic association, but those that are highly creative, this book will give examples of the patterns found in the Qur'an that when put into the context of the mental state of Muḥammad would seem natural. There are many examples that show metaphor-making and bursts of the best poetry and literary creativity do occur in the mental states described.

Muḥammad has had a mystical experience, which seems to have been mediated through his mental state. Language is but a symbol. His experience, however, as any mystical experience, is difficult to describe. Therefore, Muḥammad needs to use language, which is a symbolic medium of communication, to convey his mystical experience.

Understanding the Qur'an

If we imagine Muḥammad with the state of mind described, then the Qur'an must be filled with symbolism and hidden meanings. Muḥammad would have created these hidden meanings naturally. The Qur'an does provide us with clues that its meanings are perhaps obscured from the general public. "[77] Truly it is a Noble Quran[78] in a Book concealed (*maknūn*).[79] None touch it, save those made pure, [80] a revelation from the Lord of the worlds."[127]

Traditional exegetes, such as al-Ṭabarī (d. 310/923), suggest that the hidden book in the above passage is a heavenly Qur'an in the Preserved Tablet (*al-Lawḥ al-Maḥfūẓ*).[128] However, it is noteworthy to state that the term for concealed is "*maknūn*," which shares its root with "*akinnah*" that the Qur'an uses to describe the hearts of those who do not understand it.

> Among them are those who listen to thee, but We have placed coverings (*akinnah*) over their hearts, such that they understand it not, and in their ears a deafness. Were they to see every sign, they would not believe in it, so that when they come to thee, they dispute with thee. Those who disbelieve say, "This is naught but fables of those of old."[129]
>
> And when thou recitest the Quran, we place a hidden veil (*ḥijāban mastūrā*) between thee and those who believe not in the Hereafter.[46] And We have placed coverings (*akinnah*) over their hearts, such that they understand it not, and in their ears a deafness. And whenever thou dost mention thy Lord alone in the Quran, they turn their backs in aversion.[130]
>
> And who does greater wrong than one who has been reminded of the signs of his Lord, then turns away from them and forgets that which his hands have sent forth? Surely We have placed coverings (*akinnah*) over their hearts, such that they understand it not, and in their ears a deafness. Even if thou callest them to guidance, they will never be rightly guided.[131]
>
> They say, "Our hearts are under coverings (*akinnah*) from that to which you call us, and in our ears there is deafness, and between us and you there is a veil (*ḥijāb*). So do [as you will]; we shall do [as we will]."[132]

If the Qur᾽an suggests that its meanings may be obscured, then it would mean that the exoteric meaning may not always be the actual intended meaning. If the Qur᾽an is filled with riddles, then it is important to try to understand Muḥammad's state of mind while reciting those riddles.

Rarely do we find books that describe the method for its interpretation. However, the Qur᾽an does spell out a method for its interpretation, which is philological. Muḥammad created a code and provided the key to unlock it through the use of language. As Robert Bergen states, "Human language, being a code, possesses means by which an author's intentions may be conveyed to one who is privy to the code."[133] However, if someone is speaking in metaphors, how can we unlock the meanings?

First, we understand that Muḥammad's state of mind allows him to be symbolic and metaphoric in his speech, where he can associate things that appear to have no relation, and then make a creative relationship between them. He also has the ability to convey double meanings. Second, we have internal evidence from the Qur᾽an that its meanings are obscured and that the key to unlock it is perhaps philological.

Therefore, this book outlines a methodology for Qur᾽anic exegesis using intertextual polysemy in trying to imitate what is perhaps going in Muḥammad's mind during his highly creative state. There are various schools of Qur᾽anic exegesis and this book does not stand against any of them,[134] but it attempts to complement them with a different method. Gabriel Reynolds argues that since post-Qur᾽anic exegesis and biography of Muḥammad (*sîrah*) are full of assumptions, they are unreliable to contextualize the Qur᾽an.[135] I will choose a middle and moderate path in understanding all viewpoints, but post-Qur᾽anic literature cannot always be a fully reliable source for research on the Qur᾽an; instead, research should begin with the Qur᾽an's Biblical subtext, as argued by Reynolds. To study the history of Islam, an historical context may be important. However, with the Qur᾽an, textual analysis beyond its historical context as provided in Muḥammad's biography (*sīrah*) may provide us with a different view of the text, using what is called intertextual polysemy.

Thinking that the Qur᾽an is filled with metaphors with hidden meanings fascinated Muslims in the decades after Muḥammad's death. Throughout Islamic history, an esoteric exegesis of the Qur᾽an has developed among esoteric schools (*al-madāris al-bāṭiniyyah*). The most prominent, and the one that has survived throughout history, is the Ismāʿīlī school, which includes a shared heritage among Nizārī, Mustaʿlī (Bohra), and Druze communities. In Ismāʿīlī thought, the Qur᾽an has two characteristics: revelation (*tanzīl*) and hermeneutic interpretation (*ta᾽wīl*).[136] The characteristics of the Qur᾽an are mirrored in truth (*ḥaqīqah*) and law (*Sharīʿah*). The Sharīʿah is considered a symbol of the truth (*ḥaqīqah*), but not the truth itself. For this reason, there is a requirement for the Qur᾽an and Sharīʿah to be interpreted esoterically through allegorical, symbolic, and spiritual interpretations.

The purpose of the Ismāʿīlī methods of exegesis is not to deny the validity of the exoteric (*ẓāhir*), but to understand the significance of the exoteric (*ẓāhir*) in search for its spiritual truths (*ḥaqā᾽iq*).[137] When uttering the words of the Qur᾽an, which seem highly symbolic and poetic, Muḥammad must have meant something in his mind. It is this authorial intent that is being sought. As an example, the number of cycles (*rakʿāt*) in prayers are different among prayer times. The dawn (*fajr*) prayer only has two, while the evening (*maghrib*) prayer has three. It is unreasonable to believe the rituals were prescribed by the intelligent Muḥammad completely ad hoc and arbitrarily. There needs to be a reason behind it, which we may understand, if we understand Muḥammad's state of mind when prescribing these symbolic rituals. Even al-Ghazālī (d. 505/1111), who was against many of the esoteric schools, emphasized in his *Iḥyāʾ* that nothing is arbitrary in all the rituals prescribed as they must have a spiritual significance, which people may not yet be able to grasp.[138]

The Druze, who are an offshoot of the Ismāʿīlī, consider three stages of religious faith: (i) *islām* (surrender), as the exoteric (*ẓāhir*) is the door to (ii) *īmān* (faith), which is esoteric (*bāṭin*), and that in turn is the door to the ultimate goal, which is (iii) *tawḥīd* (unity).[139] Consequently, the Druze interpret the Qurʾan and Islamic rituals allegorically. Firro reports that in the Druze faith, the concept of *taʾwīl* is based on the correspondence between the exoteric (*ẓāhir*) and the esoteric (*bāṭin*).[140] To them, the apparent has a hidden, the literal has an inner, the external has an eternal, and the physical has a spiritual meaning that they represent. Perhaps with low latent inhibition and the ability to make creative metaphors, Muḥammad was able to ascribe double meanings in his utterances.

The Qurʾan describes heaven in great detail, as do the prophetic traditions (*ḥadīth*). In its descriptions of heaven, the literary style of the Qurʾan does not stipulate that it should not be taken literally. However, a tradition (*ḥadīth qudsī*) describes heaven as, "What no eyes had seen, no ears had heard, and no heart had contemplated."[141] If the description of heaven is to be taken literally, then how would it coincide with this tradition (*ḥadīth*), unless Muḥammad did not intend its description to be taken literally? Although many orthodox exegetes of the Qurʾan and the Bible agree on the existence of symbolic meanings, they consider the literary style of the text to be the determinant of whether it should be taken literally or symbolically. However, in the Qurʾanic description of heaven, this is not the case. Similarly, even the controversial debates between Muslim theologians about the anthropomorphism of divine attributes in the Qurʾan may not be taken literally, even though the literary style of the text does not necessarily indicate otherwise. Since the Qurʾan states there is nothing like unto God (i.e., Qurʾan 42:11), the anthropomorphism of the divine attributes is not understood literally, even though the textual literary style would not conclude it. Therefore, the literary style of the text alone cannot determine whether the text is describing something literally, spiritually, symbolically, analogically, etc., as many orthodox exegetes of scriptures, Biblical and Qurʾanic, believe. This is not to say that the literal meaning is invalid, but rather that there lies a reality beyond the literal meaning of the text. This would be in parallel to Muḥammad's state of mind, as described earlier: a mind capable of producing creative metaphor with double and hidden meanings.

Symbolic interpretation of the Qurʾan is not only found extensively in the esoteric schools, but it also exists within Shīʿī exegesis in general, including the Twelvers. In much of the Shīʿī exegesis, some Qurʾanic passages are interpreted as resembling symbolically the Prophet's household (*ahl al-bayt*). For example, ʿAlī ibn Ibrāhīm al-Qummī (d. 329/942), a prominent early exegete of the Twelver school, interprets the following verse, "There is no coercion in religion. Sound judgment has become clear from error. So whosoever disavows false deities and believes in God has grasped the most unfailing handhold, which never breaks. And God is Hearing, Knowing"[142] as meaning that the evil is symbolic to those who have betrayed the household of Muḥammad and that the trustworthy handhold is symbolic of ʿAlī ibn Abī Ṭālib, the first Imām.[143] Although al-Ṭabarsī (d. 548/1153), another later exegete of the Twelver school, does not share the same symbolic interpretation of the verse, symbolism in the Qurʾan identifying Muḥammad's household or their enemies is accepted among the majority of Twelver scholars.[144] In general, the Twelver school accepts symbolic interpretation of the Qurʾan, even if they are not directly associated with Muḥammad's household, and much of this interpretation is narrated from among the twelve imāms.

The esoteric exegesis is not only found within various Shīʿī schools of thought, but can also be seen in the majority of Sufi exegesis of the Qurʾan, even from within the Sunnī schools. The most mystical exegesis is that of Ibn ʿArabī (d. 638/1240), which although arguably Sunnī, reflects many aspects of the esoteric cosmology embedded within Ismāʿīlī interpretations.[145]

By using intertextual polysemy to interpret the Qurʾan, we might be able to resurrect a spiritual significance in its message. Muḥammad's state of mind is highly suggestive that he is creative in making relationships. If he had spent his youth looking for meaning and truth, orally traversing through different religions and spiritual traditions, then when his mind entered a psychologically altered state, he was capable of making creative associations and relationships with what he learned. If the other faiths were also symbolic and metaphoric, then perhaps he started to interpret them in his own way.

The Qurʾan has been heavily studied from early Islam up to the modern day with various perspectives through the lenses of multiple traditions. A whole array of studies, known as Qurʾanic sciences, developed through the history of Islam in an attempt to provide a systematic methodology for interpretation. Early Christian polemicists often argued that there were Jewish or Christian sources to the Qurʾan.[146] Orientalists have studied the Qurʾan in an attempt to have a scholarly view to understand its origins and roots from Judeo-Christian traditions. Within Qurʾanic sciences developed by early Muslim scholars, there has developed a set of systematic methodologies for understanding the Qurʾan through a process known as "*ijtihād*," which is an umbrella that encompasses Islamic studies, and not only Qurʾanic sciences.[147]

If one needs to study Islamic history, then a historical understanding of the Qurʾan, such as the circumstances of revelation (*asbāb al-nuzūl*), internal chronology, and transmission history would be imperative. However, the circumstances of revelation (*asbāb al-nuzūl*) may not in itself be accurate, as many contemporary scholars have suggested. The methodology of exegesis outlined in this book would not serve such a purpose. However, I will attempt to look at the Qurʾan from a different perspective, one that seems to be the only method explicitly sanctioned by the Qurʾan, which is linguistic in nature looking at the precise symbology used by the Arabic terms. Muḥammad's mental state allowed him to be very creative in formulating double meanings, which the Qurʾan suggests are based on philology.

Also, I argue that understanding intertextuality with other scriptures, such as the Bible, is also vital. The only two methods explicitly mentioned in the Qurʾan for its own exegesis is that God teaches the Qur'an and the significance of its language. Within classical Qur'anic sciences, interpreting the Qur'an by the Qur'an (*tafsīr al-Qur'an bil-Qur'an*) is one of the important methods for Qur'anic exegesis. The rationale is that if there is only one author of the Qur'an, and assuming that the author is consistent in the message therein, then it would seem obvious to use the author's works in one part to interpret another. If we adopt a Biblical method of exegesis, which goes beyond typology, then there is perhaps another aspect that needs to be studied, such as *sensus plenior*, but this will not be considered in this study.[148] This study focuses more on trying to understand Muḥammad's state of mind to interpret the Qur'an.

Hermeneutical factors

Most commentators agree that the knowledge of the Arabic definitions of the words are important to the understanding of the Qur'an, while others also argue the history of Islam is also crucial to putting the verses in the context of its revelation.[149] The history of Islam and the reasons of revelation (*asbāb al-nuzūl*) involve a methodology that is widely used by both classical and modern commentators, including those who use a thematic approach for Qur'anic interpretation. It is perhaps important to understand the reasons of revelation, but this approach should not restrict the interpretation solely to it, especially if there is doubt on its historical accuracy.[150] Nevertheless, some scholars argue that the fact revelation happened gradually over a period of twenty-three years is important to understand the interpretations of the verses.[151] Few scholars believe that interpretation of the Qur'an in isolation of the reasons of revelation is meaningless.[152] Also, some scholars like Nasr Abu Zayd argue that the knowledge of Arabic alone is not enough to understand the meanings of the Qur'an, because it has to be placed in its historical and cultural context open to reinterpretation at different times.[153] The issue with interpreting scriptures based on their social and textual context, even their lexical denotation, produces one major dilemma. The intention of Muḥammad is not to reproduce history. His mind was in an altered state making creative associations and producing metaphor with double meanings. As such, we need to interpret the Qur'an in accordance to such state of mind. Qur'anic studies are currently moving toward different hypotheses about the origins of the Qur'an. John Wansbrough, Andrew Rippin, Fred Donner, and Gabriel Reynolds suggest that the Qur'an perhaps originates from a Judeo-Christian context. However, others view the Qur'an as authored by Muḥammad, or according to believers, as the words of God revealed to Muḥammad. If we remove God from the formula, then it is important to understand what is going on in Muḥammad's mind when he started to recite the Qur'an. Muḥammad's state of mind and intention is the key to unlock the Qur'an. His mind was in a state that created creative associations and double meanings through the Arabic language, which the Qur'an often states is the key for people to understand it. These assumptions are what give birth to the method of intertextual polysemy. This book seeks to use authorial intent as spelled out by the Qur'an and through understanding Muḥammad's state of mind, because such a method is currently nonexistent in Qur'anic studies. I wish to repeat that I am in no way attempting to discredit the divine origin of Muḥammad's revelations. I only attempt to view the human side of it. Even if the origin of the Qur'an is divine, then perhaps it is divinely intended to have multiple meanings through the Arabic language, especially when the Qur'an states that sometimes God places veils on people's heart so that they may not understand it (e.g., Qur'an 6:25, 17:45–46, 18:57). If the Qur'an has a single exoteric meaning, then what kind of veils will hide its meaning, unless there are multiple meanings that are perhaps hidden? Maybe those veils could be called latent inhibition, in modern terms. As such, if it is assumed that Muḥammad had low latent inhibition, then perhaps he had the self-awareness that he is able to understand things that others do not, while getting frustrated and describing their hearts veiled. His adversaries claimed that he is mad (e.g., Qur'an 15:6, 37:36, 44:14, 51:52, 68:51). However, with his high level of intelligence, he is actually highly creative.[154] His adversaries may also seem aware that they do not understand or see what Muḥammad does. "They say, 'Our hearts are under coverings (*akinnah*) from that to which you call us, and in our ears there is deafness, and between us and you there is a veil (*ḥijāb*). So do [as you will]; we shall do [as we will].'"[155]

Meyer H. Abrams argued, in *Natural Supernaturalism*, that Romanticism was an attempt to secularize traditional theological concepts and stating about the intellectuals of the Romantic period, between the end of the eighteenth century and through the nineteenth century, seeking "in diverse degrees and ways, to naturalize the supernatural and to humanize the divine."[156] John H. Timmerman, a theologian, attacks such a notion by stating, "A vanity is any attempt to see divine mysteries exclusively in human terms," and, "any attempt to humanize the divine is a vanity, an emptiness."[157] I fully respect people's notions of divinity and divine mysteries. However, looking at things scientifically does not necessarily mean one is a materialist. If people use human endeavor to interpret holy books, then is science not also a human endeavor to interpret natural laws, which if created by God, were revealed much before any holy book we have in existence to date? If theologians seek to interpret God's words, then scientists are perhaps also theologians interpreting God's creation and that is if it indeed were created by God. If theologians say that God uses supernatural means to conduct Its affairs, we should still remember that this does not infer that natural means are ungodly.[158] For example, the Qur'an states a number of times that God generated Jesus through God's command with His word "be," and it is (*kun f-yakūn*) (e.g., Qur'an 3:47, 3:59, 19:34–35). Does that mean, according to the Qur'an, that Jesus was generated with an act of supernatural wizardry as an adult man? Or, did he still have to undergo natural fetal development in his mother's womb (i.e., Qur'an 19:21), then his mother had natural labor during childbirth (i.e., Qur'an 19:22), and that he was born a small baby (i.e., Qur'an 19:29)? I repeat this notion: natural is not ungodly.

The Qur'an several times suggests that Muḥammad is only human like anyone else, but is inspired (e.g., Qur'an 18:110, 21:7–8, 41:6). Perhaps this inspiration (*waḥy*) uses natural means to reveal a message.

Abu Zayd warned that if many Muslims take a strong hold of classical commentators as "the Qur'anic interpretation," who are placed in their social context, without taking into account how the natural sciences evolved through time, then much of science becomes religion, and much of religion becomes superstition.[159]

Literary analysis of the Qur'an

As the intertextual polysemy in the Qur'an is best described as caused by Muḥammad's state of mind, there is always a possibility that it is not. In fact Muḥammad's biography of what had happened in the cave may also not be an accurate historical account. As such, if this was not the cause for the intertextual polysemy that can be seen in the Qur'an, then one needs to consider other possible causes. A literary analysis of the Qur'an may provide us with some clues. If the Qur'an has its roots in Judeo-Christian oral or textual traditions, then it would not be surprising if the Qur'an uses specific terms that are meaningful within a Judeo-Christian context. The usage of polysemy in other examples of Chapters 5–7 and their intertextualities with the Bible might also constitute examples of how the Qur'an is using terms familiar to the Judeo-Christian context to form its arguments. Is the Qur'an possibly to be read as a Christian homily, as suggested by Gabriel Reynolds?[160] There is this possibility, although it may require making plenty of historical assumptions, which is not necessarily problematic. However, this would not give us a cause of why examples of inner-Qur'anic allusions using intertextual polysemy have unfolded, as seen in the examples of Chapters 3, 5, 6, and 7.

Nonetheless, there is a possibility that the textual author(s) and redactors of the Qur'an used these inner-Qur'anic allusions in a way similar to that perhaps used by Biblical authors and redactors, whenever they have applied inner-Biblical exegesis, as outlined by Michael Fishbane's method in *Biblical Interpretation in Ancient Israel.*[161] According to Fishbane, shared language and the use of unique or rare terminology increase the likelihood of an allusion. A word or a group of words appearing in a similar context also increase the likelihood of an allusion. There are many studies on the inner-Biblical allusions and exegesis with their relation to authorial intent.[162] Authorial intent of the Bible using textual analysis is widely studied.[163] The limitation of seeking authorial intent is that there could be biases and misinterpretations, on which scholars of Biblical studies concur,[164] but that does not mean we should dismiss it altogether, for the kinds of insights that it may provide.[165] If authorial intent of contemporary living individuals could be misinterpreted, and even that of those with whom we speak face-to-face, then imagine how it may be with historical figures, their speech, and writings.

The allusive technique that the scribes of the Hebrew Bible used to cite earlier parts of it might have also occurred within the Qur'an by its own scribes. Hitherto, this would not suggest a cause of why the Qur'an sometimes uses this technique in an allegorical method, as illustrated in the example of Chapter 8. Regardless, it is not impossible that such a technique was applied by the Qur'an's author(s), scribes, and redactors. Therefore, even if Muḥammad did not have an altered state of consciousness allowing him to seamlessly create polysemous intertextualities within the Qur'an or between the Qur'an and the Bible, there could be other literary causes for this to occur, which we cannot dismiss. It is only that Muḥammad's altered state of consciousness seems to provide us with a cause requiring the fewest assumptions, and one that would scientifically and biologically explain it. There can definitely be other causes for intertextual polysemy in Qur'anic hermeneutics. Whatever the cause may be is not the issue. The important matter is that intertextual polysemy in Qur'anic hermeneutics may be seen as a possible method to interpret the Qur'anic text.

2

Interpretation According to the Qur'an

In this chapter, I discuss the method of exegesis as spelled out by the Qur'an, which is my first argument. To understand Muḥammad's state of mind to perform some sort of hermeneutics, it is important to understand what methods of exegesis that the Qur'an suggests, as Muḥammad might have been providing a key so people could understand him. I argue in this chapter that the Qur'an only sanctions two methods for Qur'anic exegesis. The first is that God is the one who teaches the meanings of the Qur'an. The second is a linguistic approach, in which intertextual polysemy plays a major role, according to the Qur'an itself, as I will attempt to portray along with examples.

For centuries, the Qur'an has been studied to derive its meanings. Many schools of Qur'anic exegesis have developed throughout history ranging from literal interpretation to symbolic, from exoteric to esoteric, and from legalistic to metaphoric.[1] However, some of these methods are not necessarily mutually exclusive. For example, a literal interpretation of the Qur'an does not necessarily mean that it disregards symbolism. Looking at it from a linguistic perspective, language holds meanings. The words themselves are symbols, from which we derive meaning. They are not themselves the realities. For example, the word "apple" is just a symbol of what an apple actually is. Language is a symbolic form of communication, therefore we can only understand words symbolically. The Aristotelian understanding of language is defined thus: "Spoken words are the symbols of mental experience and written words are the symbols of spoken words."[2] Aristotle (d. 322 BCE) implies arbitrariness in the relationship between the linguistic symbol and the mental image formed by it.[3] Saussure, in "Nature of the Linguistic Sign," states that a linguistic sign does not truly give a relationship between a thing and its name, but between a concept and its acoustic image.[4]

Identifying a word (symbol) with a specific meaning is not usually an easy task. In linguistics, a word in isolation usually has no specific meaning unless it is used within a specific context.[5] However, in lexical semantics, words are defined independently of their context. The purpose of lexicons and dictionaries is to identify all the meanings that a word can be defined by regardless of its context. However, even in a specific context, this does not imply that a word cannot have multiple meanings even within that context. These concepts of understanding how to derive meaning from language and lexical semantics are important when analyzing any literature, including the Qur'an.

Qur'anic exegesis

According to some Muslim scholars, a scholar must possess certain qualifications to be considered capable of exegesis, such as knowing the different types of verses.[6] Although the qualifications required by Muslim scholars, both traditional and contemporary, may seem intriguingly excessive, it does not necessarily have a basis in the Qur'an.[7] We need to understand what Muḥammad intended to be the key to unlock his creative associations and symbolic metaphors. According to the Qur'an, there are two main criteria to understand the Qur'an, and only one of them is tangible. The first criterion, which is not tangible, is that it is God who teaches the Qur'an (e.g., Qur'an 55:1–2). The second criterion is repeated several times in the Qur'an, signifying the importance of understanding its Arabic language (e.g., Qur'an 12:2, 13:37, 16:103, 20:113, 26:195, 39:28, 41:3, 41:44, 42:7, 43:3, 46:12). The Qur'an states, "Truly We sent it down as an Arabic Qur'an, that haply you may understand/connect (*ta'qilūn*)."[8]

Many early methods of interpretation are heavily influenced by tradition, whether the sayings of Muḥammad, his companions, or other early individuals whom the author of the commentary deemed to have some knowledge of Qur'anic meanings.[9] Most traditional commentaries of the Qur'an use historic accounts for the circumstances or reasons of revelation (*asbāb al-nuzūl*) as part of understanding the context of the verses.[10] However, that method restricts the Qur'an to a historic event without taking into consideration Muḥammad's state of mind. Although traditional commentators of the Qur'an use history to understand its social and textual context, traditional scholars of the Qur'an do not consider it as a history book,[11] but a religious book with history.[12]

Al-Ṭabarī was an early Qur'anic exegete who used circumstances of revelation (*asbāb al-nuzūl*) as a method of Qur'anic exegesis. Since al-Ṭabarī was himself a historian, it was very natural for him to view the Qur'an through a historical lens. Some scholars, such as John Wansbrough, have argued that the Qur'an is not a reliable historical account, but one that needs to be viewed as a literary discourse.[13] Andrew Rippin attempts to shed light on the usage of the Qur'anic historical context according to traditional scholars, where he argues one of the fundamental usages of the circumstances of revelation (*asbāb al-nuzūl*) is not necessarily for juristic purposes, but rather connected to creating a narrative story around Qur'anic passages.[14] Some early scholars of the Qur'an, such as Muqātil ibn Sulaymān (d. 150/767),[15] al-Wāḥidī (d. 468/1075),[16] and al-Suyūṭī (d. 911/1505)[17] have written some detailed accounts of the circumstances of revelation in their Qur'anic exegesis. This has provided an understanding of the role of historical and social context in interpreting the Qur'an. However, anyone trying to extract historical meaning from the Qur'an would fall into the trap of their own presuppositions. The reception of the Qur'an in post-Qur'anic literature does not always provide us with an objective understanding of the Qur'an. There could be doubts involved in the circumstances of revelation (*asbāb al-nuzūl*) stories. Rippin states, "theory of the 'history reception' always presupposes most centrally that any work needs a reader to create meaning and that each reader will extract meaning appropriate to his own time, presuppositions and expectations."[18]

Traditional methods of Qur'anic exegesis, known as *tafsīr bil-ma'thūr*, are the most common method of interpretation in early and medieval Islam. They usually depend on a related prophetic tradition (*ḥadīth*) or sayings of the Prophet's companions for the interpretation of the Qur'an.[19] Although the traditional exegesis is considered mainstream, it still faces certain challenges, as follows:[20]

1. The Qur'an may hold meanings that are not always obvious. The Qur'an describes itself as a veiled book (*kitābin maknūn*) (i.e., Qur'an 56:78) and states that some people do not comprehend it (e.g., Qur'an 6:25, 17:46, 18:57). Therefore, it cannot be assumed that Muḥammad explained the vague parts of the Qur'an and any parts unexplained are to be considered evident. If the Qur'an is clear, then it would not describe itself as veiled. Also, if the Qur'an is clear, it would not suggest that some people will have difficulty comprehending it. Historically, the main use of prophetic interpretation has been for juristic purposes of Islamic Sharī'ah. The prophetic traditions used for Qur'anic interpretation do not always refer to a specific Qur'anic verse, but usually expound on the theme of rituals or legal rulings, such as the method of prayer, almsgiving, marriage, and divorce, etc.
2. The Qur'an often asks people to ponder its meanings. If the interpretation of the Qur'an was readily available or that the Qur'an is evidently clear, then it defeats the purpose of trying to contemplate its meaning (e.g., Qur'an 4:82, 47:24). Since the Qur'an often states that people should try to understand it using reason,[21] it opens the doors to plural interpretation that may not always be obvious.
3. Actually, much of the tradition that is used in early Qur'anic exegesis is not even prophetic but related to Muḥammad's companions or later followers. Interpretation through traditional narration assumes the interpreters are knowledgeable of the parts of the Qur'an that they are explaining. Ibn 'Abbās, for example, is a widely celebrated companion who interpreted the Qur'an. However, it is important to recognize that the interpretation of the Prophet's companions or early successors may still be viewed as their own personal opinions, and should not necessarily have any specific authoritative tone. Al-Bāqillānī (d. 403/1013) has shown that even the first two Caliphs, Abu Bakr and 'Umar, have disagreed with each other in many instances.[22] As such, it is important to understand that the companions never considered the things they say beyond their own mere opinions, which can very much be fallible. Although some Muslims may claim that the Prophet's companions had firsthand knowledge of the Qur'an from Muḥammad, and therefore, perhaps understood the Qur'an better than any other, such a claim is unfounded. The companions still disagreed with each other many times, proving that whatever opinions they had are just that, opinions. They cannot be taken for granted as "the interpretation" of the Qur'an, but only an opinion of what they thought the interpretation is. Accordingly, their interpretation can be as fallible as any other scholar. On the other hand, Shī'ī dogma states the infallibility of their imāms. I am not here to argue the infallibility dogma, according to Shī'ī doctrine.[23] However, even if we do accept it, there still exists a dilemma that the narrators are not themselves infallible, and therefore, there could always be some doubt as to the correctness of the narrations. Besides, the Muslim doctrine of infallibility of

prophets is not in itself necessarily Qur'anic. The Qur'an, and even prophetic traditions, shows that prophets have erred and committed sins.[24]

4. The reliability of the prophetic tradition is also brought into question.[25] James Robson argues that the prophetic tradition was not central to the early Muslim community in the time of Muḥammad. He suggests that although the tradition is presented as if it were preserved from early Islam, it actually emerged when the Qur'an gave no or insufficient guidance regarding new issues that arose in the community.[26] Tradition developed to become an authority in the Muslim community, and it was perhaps not even the intention of the authors who compiled books on these traditions.[27] Robson suggests that tradition does not portray Muḥammad for what he truly was, but portrays how his followers perceived him.[28]

In the Muslim community, due to the challenges facing traditional interpretation, several schools of Qur'anic exegesis emerged beyond the mainstream conventional method. These became known as rational approaches, including esoteric, linguistic, and scientific approaches.[29] As discussed earlier, a linguistic approach is the only tangible method that is clearly sanctioned by the Qur'an several times. If the Qur'an is the work of Muḥammad's mind, then he is providing the key that would allow us to understand his symbolism and references mentioned therein. He must have used a linguistic form of symbolism of creative associations that provide double or multiple meanings, which would be natural according to his state of mind. Linguistically, having more than one meaning in a word is called polysemy. Symbolic associations would infer intertextuality. Therefore, Muḥammad might have applied intertextual polysemy in constructing meaning in the Qur'an.

Understanding polysemy

Polysemy exists when a word has multiple meanings related to each other.[30] This definition is apparent from the nomenclature of the term, where "poly-" means many and "-semy" means meanings. This understanding of polysemy is important in Semitic languages, since the Semitic languages are constructed on root-based morphology (*mushtaqqāt*). This means that words in Semitic languages have roots that are typically three-lettered, in which morphologies of various meanings and understandings spring out.[31] Perhaps Muḥammad's state of mind allowed him to make creative associations using polysemy to sketch his thoughts into the Qur'an. One of the reasons for polysemy to exist is that it may hold not only a direct root meaning, but also an allegorical meaning.[32]

For example, the word "to write" is from the root "*k t b*." Different morphologies of this root would hold various meanings. A writer is called "*kātib*," a book is called "*kitāb*," a letter is called "*maktūb*," which literally means something written, dictating is called "*istaktaba*," a library is "*maktabah*," and an office is "*maktab*." However, defining those terms is not always semantically obvious, as it may sometimes be dependent on the context to understand what the term specifically refers to. For example, "*kitāb*" could be a reference to a book or sometimes even a contract, especially a marriage contract, and a "*kātib ʿadl*" would refer to a notary public. Those are just few definitions of the term and its morphologies.

Understanding etymology is also important to comprehend the root meanings. For example, the term "*katībah*" is a reference to an army battalion. The root of the term "*k t b*" actually means to join together in a group.[33] An army battalion is also a group of people who are joined together. Perhaps, it is because of this root meaning that it has taken the definition of the word writing, because writing is joining letters and words together in a group. Hence, having similar roots makes perfect sense once we understand its semantics and etymology.

Muqātil ibn Sulaymān was one of the first prominent scholars to deal with the topic of polysemy in the Qur'an in his books, *Kitāb al-wujūh wal-naẓāʾir* and *Al-Ashbāh wal-naẓāʾir*. Another early scholar dealing with polysemy is Abu al-ʿAbbās al-Mubarrad (d. 286/898) in his book, *Ma ittafaqa lafẓuhu wa ikhtalafa maʿnāhu min al-qurʾān al-majīd*. Other early works on polysemy include *al-Wujūh wal-naẓāʾir* narrated by Maṭrūḥ ibn Muḥammad (d. 271/884) from ʿAbdullah ibn Harūn al-Ḥijāzī, *al-Ashbāh wal-naẓāʾir* by al-Thaʿālbī (d. 429/1038), *Wujūh al-qurʾān* by Ismāʿīl ibn Aḥmad al-Ḍarīr (d. 430/1039), *Nuzhat al-aʿyun al-nawāẓir fī ʿilm al-wujūh wal-naẓāʾir* by Abu al-Faraj ibn al-Jawzī (d. 597/1201), *Wujūh al-qurʾān* by Aḥmad ibn ʿAlī al-Muqriʾ (d. 658/1260), and *Kashf al-sarāʾir ʿan maʿna al-wujūh wal-naẓāʾir* by Shams-ul-dīn ibn Muḥammad ibn ʿAlī al-ʿImād (d. 887/1482). These early and medieval works on polysemy usually tackle the issue of multiple meanings by defining them through their context.[34] Al-ʿIzz ibn ʿAbdulsalām (d. 660/1262) says, "The context guides to clarify the many and the likelihood of the possibilities, and specifies the clarities."[35] However, once a word is defined through context, it loses its lexical semantics. Also, there could be multiple contexts understood from a passage, which will have various meanings, even contextually. If the Qur'an has a spiritual context that is different from its direct literal context, then the terms may have multiple meanings, one dependent on the direct literal context of the passage, and another on the fuller spiritual context of the Qur'an. This could be a case of applying the theory of *sensus plenior* (fuller sense) in scriptures.

Al-Suyūṭī discusses in *al-Itqān fī ʿulūm al-Qurʾān* the use of polysemy in the Qur'an.[36] He refers to the prophetic tradition (*ḥadīth*) (quoted in Muqātil's *al-Ashbāh wal-naẓāʾir*) stating under the authority of Abī al-Dardāʾ, "A man is not a *faqīh* in all *fiqh* unless he sees the Qur'an in many faces (*wujūh*)."[37] Al-Suyūṭī explains from this tradition the importance of understanding polysemy.[38] He continues to say that some suggest that this prophetic tradition is meant for the understanding of esoteric symbolism, not just the exoteric interpretation.[39] Al-Suyūṭī also adds that ʿAlī ibn Abī Ṭālib was told by Ibn ʿAbbās not to argue with the *khawārij* by the Qur'an since the Qur'an has many faces (*ḥammāl dhu wujūh*),[40] but instead to argue by the Sunnah.[41]

Evidently, classical scholars realized the importance of polysemy in Qur'anic discourses, and the possibility that a Qur'anic passage might have multiple meanings due to the polysemy.[42] Therefore, the role of intertextual polysemy may include determining different contexts in which the different meanings of the terms may still hold validity. Once the text is freed from its *Sitz-im-Leben* (site in life), it opens the doors to multiple interpretations.[43] Aḥmad Al-Maʿtūq states that although polysemy has been discussed by many grammarians of the Arabic language, they mostly give examples without identifying a specific methodology.[44] Perhaps the complexity of the methodology makes it difficult to define polysemy with a specific method.

There are always arguments that one needs to interpret a text based on its context. However, what is the context of scriptures, which are perhaps intended as spiritual guidance using symbolism that self-identify with hidden meanings? Polysemy might play a major role in the textual hermeneutics of scriptures. We can always look at a text and figure out how an audience might interpret it without necessarily going into the texts that respond to it.[45] The issue of polysemy in hermeneutics is not only recognized in Qur'anic interpretation, it is also found in other traditions, such as rabbinic interpretations.[46] In the midrash, polysemy provides various senses of a word in scriptures.[47] Stern makes a detailed analysis of the notion of scriptural polysemy used in rabbinic literature.[48] Scriptural polysemy played a significant role in interpretation in Judaism with the allowance of multiplicity and plurality in meaning. Stern states:

> Polysemy in midrash, then, is to be understood as a claim to textual stability rather than its opposite, an indeterminate state of endlessly deferred meanings and unresolved conflicts. In fact, midrashic polysemy suggests more than just textual stability; it points to a fantasy of social stability, of human community in complete harmony, where disagreement is either resolved agreeably or maintained in peace.[49]

The rabbis view scripture as dictating its own polysemous reading.[50] Multiple interpretations were not only based on scriptural polysemy, but also in the distinction between literal or manifest meaning and allegorical or deeper sense. The latter was mainly utilized by the likes of Philo of Alexandria (d. 50 CE), where it is subdivided into categories of the naturalistic, the ethical, the metaphysical, or the mystical.[51] These subcategories were developed in medieval Christian exegesis as the four senses of scriptures.[52] The four senses of scriptures trace their origins back to Origen (d. 254 CE), Philo, and eventually the Stoics.[53] However, the notion of the four senses of scriptures is mainly a hierarchy in the different levels of meaning that could be ordered in ascending order of significance,[54] and not necessarily a polysemous approach, which Philo extensively used. Perhaps some Muslims have approached the Qur'an in a similar way, especially giving birth to the esoteric (*bāṭiniyyah*) schools. However, given Muḥammad's state of mind, he might have been able to easily make metaphor and multiple meanings in his speech by playing with polysemous words.

Paul Ricoeur defines polysemy as, "simply the possibility of adding a new meaning to the previous acceptations of the word without having these former meanings disappear."[55] Ricoeur has written extensively on hermeneutic phenomenology and the role of polysemy. He argues that language is polysemous, containing multiple meanings, and it is the context of the author and the audience that gives it univocality.[56] However, there might be multiple contexts in which a text may be read. Condit et al. have even argued that polysemous audience responses may possibly interpret texts differently if they were in a different context.[57] For example, an audience may respond to a survey differently than in a live discourse asking the same question.[58] Nonetheless, I think with Muḥammad's state of mind, his creative linguistic associations might easily be regarded as a play on words and polysemy.

Understanding intertextuality

Sometimes, it is possible that an author of a literary piece intentionally uses polysemy as part of its rhetoric style. We can assume that the Qur'an might use polysemy as an intentional portrayal of its rhetoric. Although the role of polysemy in early Qur'anic scholarship is well studied by various exegetes and linguists, especially between the different grammar schools of al-Kūfah and al-Baṣrah, another form of exegesis may be required besides understanding the lexical polysemy of Qur'anic text. Twice when the Qur'an emphasizes its Arabic language, it uses the term "*ta'qilūn*," as seen here:

> Truly We sent it down as an Arabic Quran, that haply you may understand (*ta'qilūn*).[59]

> Truly We have made it an Arabic Quran, that haply you may understand (*ta'qilūn*).[60]

As seen in the translation, the term "*ta'qilūn*" is assumed to mean "to understand." However, this term is also polysemous. The root of the term is "*'a q l*," which holds various meanings. The term "*'aql*" is the brain or mind, "*i'taqal*" is to arrest someone, "*mu'taqal*" is an arrested person or a prison, "*'iqāl*" is the black ring worn as part of a traditional man's headdress in modern Arab cultures, "*'uqlah*" is a knot, and "*'uqunqulah*" is a rope.[61] Although it appears those various meanings are distinct, it again comes back down to understanding the lexical semantics and etymology of the root term "*'a q l*." The root meaning is to tie, such as tying a knot. Since the "*'iqāl*" is twisted and tied, it gets its name from that. The same goes for a rope. Also, when arresting someone, they are usually tied or locked in prison, and hence, the same morphologies of the root "*'a q l*" are used for arresting someone or a prison. Because the brain is capable of connecting things to make sense of them and understand them, it is also called "*'aql*," as connecting is like tying things together and connecting them. When we read the word "apple," our mind connects the word with the actual fruit. Hence, it ties the word (the linguistic sign) with the visualization of the fruit and its mental image, and as such the mind understands the meaning once they are tied together or connected. Now that we know the lexical semantic of the root term for "*'aql*," we may have a different understanding of the term "*ta'qilūn*" used in those two verses. It could be understood as an instruction that the Arabic Qur'an requires us to connect the Arabic words together. Also in Hebrew and Aramaic, the term "*'arab*" means to mix and to combine, mixed races, or confusion and disorder.[62] As such, when the Qur'an describes itself to be "*'arabī*" and requires people to "*ta'qilūn*," then it may describe itself to be mixed or disordered and requires people to make the connections. As such, I may translate the passages as:

> We have sent it down as an Arabic (mixed) Qur'an, in order that you may connect (*ta'qilūn*).[63]

> We have made it a Qur'an in Arabic (mixed), that you may connect (*ta'qilūn*).[64]

From the context, this definition might be possible, as the context does not always provide us with an exclusive definition for a term. It may even be part of the Qur'anic rhetoric. Muḥammad might be giving us a key to unlock his creative associations. If we connect the Arabic words with what we think they mean, we would understand and comprehend them. However, it is also possible to understand that connecting the Arabic words may also mean some sort of intertextuality. Hence, those two verses might be considered an invitation to use some sort of intertextuality so we may be able to understand and learn wisdom.

Intertextuality is a broad term and could mean different things to different people. Personally, I hesitate to define it because, by doing so, I may inadvertently confine it and restrict it to a specific notion. With a few examples that will be seen in the following chapters, a better understanding of the extent of intertextuality and its role in Qur'anic exegesis may be realized.

Qur'anic hermeneutics

Arabic roots

Taking into consideration Muḥammad's state of mind and his ability to make creative associations, which may be understood through intertextual polysemy, the proposed method for Qur'anic exegesis is defined through the understanding of the root meanings of the Arabic words, since many Arabic roots are polysemes, i.e., having different meanings that are related. To remind the reader, the Qur'an emphasizes the understanding of the Arabic language to understand its meanings (e.g., Qur'an 12:2, 13:37, 16:103, 20:113, 26:195, 39:28, 41:3, 41:44, 42:7, 43:3, 46:12). The method identifies how the same root is used in other passages of the Qur'an, known as intertextual polysemy through understanding the lexical semantics of the term. It is also useful to relate the root words and their usages, not only within other passages of the Qur'an, but also with the Bible, which the Qur'an sometimes intends to engage with.

Words as symbols of spiritual realities

To talk about Qur'anic hermeneutics, one needs to understand what it represents to the community. The community that received the Qur'an considered it a divine symbol of the very Word of God. Since the Qur'an is made up of words of a language, then it is imperative to understand its language and representation.

According to the Muʿtazilah, language is a human invention because relating sound to a meaning is a social convention,[65] an idea which resembles that of a Saussurean approach. On the Muʿtazilah concept of language, Nasr Abu Zayd states, "Language never refers directly to reality, but reality is conceived, conceptualized, and then symbolized by the sound system."[66] Since language is a human invention, the Muʿtazilah considered the Qur'an created, as it cannot be eternal since the Arabic language was not eternal.[67] To them, there was a bridge between human reason and the divine word.[68] The Ashʿarī school of theology held a different ideology in which language is not a human invention but a divine gift to humans, as they take Qur'an 2:31, which refers to God teaching Adam all the names, to be a literal teaching of language.[69] The Muʿtazilah preferred a metaphorical meaning of this verse.[70] According to the Ashʿarī view, therefore, the connection between the signifier and the signified is divinely stated, and not an evolution of a social convention.[71] According to the Book of Genesis, language appears to be a human invention.

> [19] Now the Lord God formed out of the ground all the wild animals and all the birds in the sky. He brought them to the man to see what he would name them; and whatever the man called each living creature, that was its name. [20] So the man gave names to all livestock, the birds in the sky and all the wild animals.[72]

According to Philo of Alexandria, even if God did not do the naming, It still knew beforehand what the man would name them.[73] However, Philo was heavily influenced by the Stoics, who were naturalists and considered the names in a language not as arbitrary, but as innate in nature of the human who made the original names.[74] Aristotle argues, "Speech is the cause of learning ... not on its own account but by convention; for speech consists of words, and every word is a symbol."[75] Johann Süssmilch (d. 1767) published a thesis in 1766, *Versuch eines Beweises, daß die erst Sprache ihren Ursprung nicht vom Menschen, sondern allein vom Schöpfer erhalten habe*, arguing that language was a gift from God. Herder (d. 1803) wrote his *Essay on the Origin of Language* (*Abhandlung über den Ursprung der Sprache*) in 1772 to disprove Süssmilch by arguing that language is instead a human invention.[76] The diversity of language and its evolution as a phenomenon strongly suggests that language is a human invention.[77]

Literacy in ancient cultures was very limited;[78] many ancient religions were perhaps taught through visualization and illustration, since literacy was reserved to an elite few, if a written language existed at all in that particular culture. Spiritual teachers had to use visual forms as metaphors and symbols for what they were trying to teach in the spiritual realm. The use of forms and images in religion was, therefore, necessary for these ancient cultures. It is not always obvious whether the spiritual teachers considered these symbols as sacred, or that after a time, future generations, who inherit the religion, take the forms and images of the religion to be sacred symbols, while perhaps forgetting the deeper meanings they were meant to portray. This is how idolatry might have acquired its negative connotation. Hence, in these cultures, intense meditation and contemplation upon those images are necessary in trying to identify what those different images are trying to teach about spiritual aspects.[79] Among widely known scholars in religious symbolism are Joseph Campbell and Mircea Eliade, who have recognized the importance of symbolism and imagery in religious cultures throughout human history.[80] Eliade discusses how myth and symbolism are widely used in various religious cultures to further the understanding of their metaphysical denotations.[81] Symbolic imagery and myths in various religious cultures are considered an anthropological understanding of the divine. They are understood as worldly metaphors for the nature of the divine. Since the divine is unknown, people use things in the physical realm to comprehend the spiritual realm.

Possibly, many of the great spiritual teachers of the ancient past founded religions that might be considered idolatrous, which may be defined as the veneration of a symbol. However, their intentions were very pure; they tried to explain the unknown divinity by using forms and images that were known to people, since the written word (literacy) was not easily accessible to the general public. This could be viewed in the religions of Ancient Egypt or Greece, or even the forms of animalism that might exist to this day. After all, even in Islam, the veneration of the Ka'bah would make it seem like idolatry to those who might otherwise be ignorant of the faith. As such, those who are ignorant of ancient religions, including the faith of pre-Islamic Arabs, may also accuse it of idolatry for venerating what otherwise should have been only symbols. In many religions, those forms and images were never intended to be taken literally, but rather as means of understanding deeper spiritual realities, just like the Ka'bah. Muslims do not consider God to be literally residing within the Ka'bah, it just symbolizes the House of God. For example, 'Umar ibn al-Khaṭṭāb stated about the Black Stone (in the Ka'bah) that it is only a stone that does nothing, and that if he had not seen the Prophet kissing it, he would not have done so.[82] Seemingly, 'Umar considered the Black Stone as a symbol, but perhaps not even a sacred symbol. It is not obvious whether Muḥammad intended it to be a sacred symbol or not, at least to 'Umar. Campbell suggests that since God is a mystery, then the divinity may only be defined through metaphor.[83] He argues that when a religious symbol is misinterpreted by mistaking its denotation for its connotation, the message embedded in that symbol is lost.

Some religions, such as Judaism and Islam, were founded upon the basis of literacy and the written word. Nonetheless, the foundations of those religions are still based on explaining the unknown divinity with words and language that are known to people. As some cultures have taken forms and images as sacred symbols of divinity, others have taken the written word as the sacred Word of God. With cultures that employ images and forms as symbols of divinity, the divinity is understood as an abstraction that is beyond the symbol, and can never be contained or restricted by that symbol.[84] However, the physical symbol merely tries to explain the spiritual reality of the divine. Similarly, in cultures with the written Word of God, it may also be understood that the word is a symbol for understanding deeper realities of divinity, while the divine itself cannot be fully contained within words. Naturally, in the heightened state of mind of Muḥammad, he is trying to convey his experience and the voice he hears, which he interprets as spiritual, into meaningful words (symbols). Campbell and Eliade have also considered the symbolism attained from within religious language.[85] They consider words as symbols with deeper meanings. Dupré argues that although religious expression is symbolized through ritual, the symbolic usage of words is also of great significance in religious expression.[86]

Similar to the concept of visual images and forms, scriptures use words that need to be further contemplated and analyzed. In cultures with images, the emphasis is on understanding the deeper meanings of the forms and images. However, in cultures with scriptures as the symbol of divinity, the deeper meanings of the language of the words contained in scriptures must be emphasized. In these cultures, there are no images to meditate upon for their various forms and meanings, but it is rather the language itself that is of great importance. As a spiritual teacher, Muḥammad, instead of using forms and images as symbols of divinity, uses words. The Qur'an places great emphasis on the understanding of the language through which it was recited or written, providing the necessary evidence that a linguistic approach for Qur'anic hermeneutics is vital.

Language is a symbol for a reality. It is, therefore, at some level of metaphor. Hence, it is not polysemy that creates the metaphor, but language is inherently symbolic and, therefore, metaphoric. Ricoeur gives a relationship between polysemy and metaphor by stating:

> Metaphor is not polysemy. Semic analysis produces a theory of polysemy directly, and only indirectly a theory of metaphor, to the extent that polysemy attests to the open structure of words and their capacity to acquire new significations without losing their old ones. This open structure is only the condition of metaphor and not yet the reason for its production.[87]

Language is a sign used in speech to convey a form of communication. An apple, whether phonetic or written, is just a sign that signifies the mental image of what an apple is in reality. Saussure defined language as a sign system, which is typically presented in binary terms as signifier and signified or sound-image and concept. The key concept in Saussure's work is the definition of language as nothing other than an arbitrary sign-system. In his *Course in General Linguistics*, Saussure states, "Language is a system of sign that expresses ideas, and is therefore comparable to a system of writing, the alphabet of deaf-mutes, symbolic rites, polite formulas, military signals, etc."[88] According to Saussure, it is important to take the community into account because the community defines the meaning.[89]

Robert Bergen highlighted some basic assumptions when trying to understand authorial intent through discourse criticism: (i) language is a code; (ii) most of the communication process occurs at the subliminal level of human consciousness; (iii) subliminal factors in human communication contain data essential for making judgments about authorial intention; (iv) the language code is genre-specific; and (v) though the specifics of each language code are unique to a given language, a common set of principles governs the structuring and application of the language code in all languages.[90]

The problem with this definition when applied to the Qur'an is to understand which community defines its meaning. If the Qur'an suggests that it is a hidden book with obscure meanings that are veiled from the general public, then defining the community that would make sense of the Qur'an may be difficult. Muḥammad is in a heightened state of mind and at first is surprised why people do not see the creative associations that he sees in his recitation of the Qur'an. What he sees comes naturally to him. Muḥammad perhaps concludes that only a few people understand what he means and are capable of interpreting these creative associations that he is capable of making, as the Qur'an seems itself aware that it is a hidden book.

Which Arabic is the Qur'anic Arabic? Did Muḥammad intend a specific dialect of Arabic in the Qur'an, or were his creative associations making use of polysemy through various dialects of Arabic? It is reported that the fourth caliph, ʿUthmān ibn ʿAffān, requested the Qur'anic scribes to write the Qur'an in the language of Quraysh, as he states that the Qur'an was revealed in their language.[91] However, this definition of the language of the Qur'an is based on the logic of 'Uthmān and it does not necessarily describe with certainty what Muḥammad intended. Actually, the Qur'an challenges its audience, even Quraysh at the time, to fully comprehend the language used in the Qur'an. If the meaning of words in a language is defined by the community that uses it, then in the case of the Qur'an, it states that the community receiving it does not even understand it. Contrary to the definition of Saussure, it appears that a single author has made an arbitrary sign with meaning independent of the community, and that is especially evident in the disjoined letters (*muqaṭṭa'āt*) in the beginning of some chapters of the Qur'an. Another possibility is to understand that the Qur'an uses the form of polysemy for the community to connect their meanings together or to form a metaphoric understanding of the meanings. A similar concept can be understood from the text of the Gospels, where Matthew reports that Jesus Christ states that he speaks in parables so that the general public would not understand him and only the disciples (his audience) would understand him (e.g., Matthew 13:10–11, 13:34–35).

Allegory in the Qur'an

The study of allegory (*majāz*) in the Qur'an is important in understanding the rhetoric of this body of literature. The allegorical sense's counterpart is the literal (*ḥaqīqah*) sense. However, the term "*majāz*" in the early texts on this study in the Qur'an does not always define it as allegory, since some are more subtle definitions than metaphor.

One of the earliest books on *majāz* in the Qur'an[92] is by Abū 'Ubaydah Mu'ammar ibn al-Muthannā (d. 209/824) known as *Majāz al-Qur'ān*.[93] In his book, he shows how words and terms describe things that are not literal. However, Abū 'Ubaydah did not use "*majāz*" as a counterpart of "*ḥaqīqah*." The definition of "*majāz*" being the counterpart of "*ḥaqīqah*" appears to be developed in later Muslim medieval scholarship. Wansbrough argues that the term "*majāz*" by Abū 'Ubaydah may be best understood as periphrastic exegesis.[94] Almagor argues that in some instances this definition is not true, as in the cases of pleonasm and lexical explanations.[95] She explains that the term "*majāz*" is rooted in "*jāza*," which means to be allowable.[96] Also, the term "*jāza*" is rooted in the meaning to pass. This could be used as a definition that indirectly means something different than its literal sense. As such, this states that a word allows for more than one meaning. Abū 'Ubayda rarely used "*majāz*" as figurative language.[97] Heinrichs concludes that the definitions of "*majāz*" evolved throughout Muslim history, and they may not always mean the same thing.[98]

Al-Sharīf al-Raḍī (d. 1306/015) wrote two books on metaphor, *Talkhīṣ al-bayān fī majāzāt al-qur'ān* and *al-Majāzāt al-nabawiyyah*. However, there is a difference in the approaches between Abū 'Ubayda and al-Raḍī. Abū 'Ubayda describes a systematic study of "*majāz*," but it was not a study of metaphoric language as it was adopted by al-Raḍī. Abu-Deeb states:

> Abū 'Ubayda is a *rāwiya*,[99] a genealogist, a historian, and a linguist, who wrote his book in response to a specific challenge. Al-Raḍī was a poet and a Shī'ite *imām*,

well immersed in *bāṭinī* interpretation an contemplation of what lies beyond the surface of discourse in all its forms, from an oral text like *ḥadīth* of the Prophet, to a tightly composed, written text, like the Qur'ān.[100]

Abu-Deeb provides an overview of the approaches on "*majāz*" by Abū 'Ubayda and Sharīf al-Raḍī.[101] Ibn Taymiyyah (d. 728/1328) suggests that the usage of the term "*majāz*" by Abū 'Ubayda has nothing to do with its later use as a counterpart of a literal sense (*ḥaqīqah*).[102] Abdul-Qāhir al-Jurjānī (d. 471/1078) wrote a book on figures of speech called *Asrār al-balāghah*, where he gives some examples of "*majāz*" in the Qur'an.[103] Al-Jurjānī defines "*majāz*" as a word with meaning that extends beyond its original position.[104]

Besides al-Jurjānī, other early scholars also looked into the sciences of allegory in Arabic, such as Ibn Jinnī (d. 392/1002),[105] al-Tha'ālbī,[106] al-Zamakhsharī (d. 538/1143),[107] and al-Yāzijī (d. 1324/1906).[108] The Mu'tazilī school of theology interprets Qur'anic anthropomorphism of God's descriptions as metaphors.[109] Meanwhile, the Ash'arī school of theology maintains literal understandings of the words, with the "*bi-lā kayfa*" understanding.[110] According to the Ash'arī school of theology, if there is no explicit evidence that a term needs to be taken metaphorically, then it should not be taken as such.[111] Some have considered the metaphoric and allegorical meanings in the Qur'an to be unacceptable.[112] Even after the Mu'tazilah disappeared, after being persecuted and fading away, their theological successors, such as the Shī'ah, continue to accept allegorical interpretations of the Qur'an.[113]

Avicenna (d. 427/1037) uses allegory in his philosophical treatises and narratives, such as the story of Ḥayy ibn Yaqẓān. In some instances, he provides allegorical interpretations of select verses from the Qur'an.[114] Al-Ghazālī uses the following law of allegorical interpretation.

> Now listen to the law of allegorical interpretation: ... all concur in subordinating the exercise of allegorical interpretation to having demonstrated the impossibility of a plain meaning. The first literal sense ... embraces all other modes of existence, but when it fails, we have recourse to sensible existence, so that if we can affirm this, it will embrace the modes which follow. If not, we will have recourse to imaginative or rational existence, and only when these cannot obtain will we finally turn to metaphorical or figurative existence.[115]

Al-Ghazālī argues that the Muslim leaders of the first generation avoided using allegorical interpretations for the fear that they might shake popular faith.[116] Nonetheless, some Sufis and sectarians, such as the Shī'ah, considered every Qur'anic passage to have an exoteric (*ẓāhir*) and esoteric (*bāṭin*) interpretation,[117] which is typically called *ta'wīl*. Averroës (d. 595/1198), in *The Decisive Treatise*, writes on the issues pertaining to the apparent and allegorical interpretations of the Qur'an, and he states the following:

> The reason an apparent and an inner sense are set down in the Law is the difference in people's innate disposition and the variance in their innate capacities for assent.

> The reason contradictory apparent senses are set down in it is to alert "those well grounded in science" to the interpretation that reconciles them. This idea is pointed to in His statement (may He be exalted), "He it is who has sent down to you the Book; in it, there are fixed verses . . ." on to his statement, "and those well grounded in science." . . . It has been transmitted that many in the earliest days [of Islam] used to be of the opinion that the Law has both an apparent and an inner sense if he is not adept in knowledge of it nor capable of understanding it.[118]

Averroës argues that demonstrative truth and scriptural truth cannot conflict, and whenever they do, scripture must be interpreted allegorically. Perhaps this principle of allegory by Averroës may also hold true—if scriptures contradict, then it may be a reason to resort to allegory to reconcile between them. Aḥmad ibn Ḥanbal (d. 241/855)[119] apparently uses a similar logic when arguing that the plurality used in the Qur'an for God, such as "We are with you,"[120] is metaphoric (*majāz*).[121] Here, Ibn Ḥanbal accepts the existence of metaphor in the Qur'an but warns that the followers of Jahm ibn Ṣafwān (d. 128/746) (i.e., the Muʿtazilah) had used the metaphorical senses of the Qur'an to argue against mainstream understandings.[122] Ibn Taymiyyah suggests that the dichotomy between literal and allegorical senses of the Qur'an was introduced by the Muʿtazilī school of theology.[123] There is no doubt that allegory and metaphor in the Qur'an are accepted by consensus from literature. However, the main argument by traditional scholars is like Ibn Ḥanbal's argument that sectarians would use the metaphorical meanings of the Qur'an to suit their needs, which the traditional scholars would consider devious.

The study of the disjoined letters influences the understanding of the Qur'anic language. If the philosophy of language is to convey the meaning of the text to the audience and this synergy is what makes meaning in language, then who is the audience that will make meaning out of the disjoined letters of the Qur'an?[124] If it is a message from Muḥammad to the people, while he is the only person who made up these words, then it is counterintuitive that the role of language considers the existence of a community that would make meaning out of arbitrary words, as defined by Saussure. Otherwise, Muḥammad could have made these as secret meanings to a select few of his followers, who would otherwise be considered the audience.[125] What can be concluded from the disjoined letters in the Qur'an is that its meaning cannot be taken primarily exoterically. As such, allegory and metaphor are undeniably in existence in the Qur'an. Also, this proves that the social and historical community that received the Qur'an may not be the only context in which the Qur'anic language needs to be understood. More important is to try to understand Muḥammad's state of mind to determine what he might have meant.

Commenting on Qur'an 3:7, Muḥammad Asad suggests that the Qur'an is explicit that some of its interpretations are supposed to be allegorical.[126] Bringing forth various arguments of what is allegorical in the Qur'an and what is to be taken in its literal sense is unclear. For example, the disjoined letters (*al-muqaṭṭaʿāt*) in the Qur'an, if taken literally, only mean that they are simple alphabets, without necessarily any specific meaning attached.[127] However, since the Qur'an challenges its audience to understand its meanings, perhaps it is an attempt to prove that these are not to be taken literally, but they need to be further extrapolated to be understood more deeply metaphorically. Unlike many other passages in the Qur'an in which the exoteric and esoteric meanings may both be valid, the disjoined letters are not meaningful exoterically, therefore their primary role perhaps is that of a metaphor.[128] It is narrated that the first caliph, Abu Bakr, stated, "To every book is a secret, and the secret of the Qur'an is in its disjoined letters."[129] If the disjoined letters are considered a secret, it can only mean that its exoteric meaning is not the intended meaning. Therefore, there is a place of allegory and metaphor in the Qur'an. Some Sufi understandings of the disjoined letters are summed up by Abu al-ʿAbbās (d. 1224/1809) considering them symbols that the general public would not immediately understand.[130] Undoubtedly, allegory is in existence in the Qur'an and clues of it are found in various parts of the Qur'an (e.g., Qur'an 6:25, 17:46, 18:57, 41:5, 56:77–80):[131]

Root-based morphology

As discussed earlier, the Semitic languages are root-based systems of lexical semantics. This challenges commentators in the interpretation of texts from scriptures due to the existence of semantic polysemy. The interpreter may find it difficult to identify and define which sense of the word is meant by the author. Determining whether the word is only meant in one form of its morphological definition, or in some or all of its forms, creates an enormous challenge. It is possible that, for this reason, the Qur'an emphasizes the significance of understanding its language. In addition, Islamic scholars do not consider Qur'anic translations to be the translation of the Qur'an, but merely an approximate interpretation of the Qur'an.[132]

Classical commentators of the Qur'an have realized the polysemic nature (*al-ashbāh wal-wujūh*) of the Qur'an. As discussed, al-Thaʿlabī (d. 427/1035)[133] and Ibn al-ʿImād[134] are examples of notable scholars who have studied the nature and sense of polysemic semiotics within the Qur'anic text. Classical scholars have identified polysemy in Qur'anic texts as semiotics (*ashbāh*) or different faces of the word (*wujūh*), quoting Qur'an 3:7 and 39:23. Al-Suyūṭī quotes Abu al-Dardā' as stating that a person does not understand *fiqh* unless he ascribes different faces to the Qur'an (*wujūhan*).[135] Some contemporary Islamic scholars, such as Mulla Ṣadr, have also allowed the analysis of Qur'anic keywords in a polysemous method for interpretation, as it reveals its linguistic eloquence.[136]

The methodology proposed, intertextual polysemy, is a linguistic approach through lexical semantics in an attempt to understand the written word. The roots of the words are analyzed in their various forms to ascertain the diverse meanings of the polysemes rooted in the word. The various Arabic, Hebrew, and Aramaic meanings of the Semitic words are identified to understand the word fully along with its polysemes. The words are then compared in their usage within the Qur'an and perhaps the Bible and Biblical literature to identify how scriptures have used the words with their various forms or polysemes, as perhaps the Qur'an is engaging with the Bible. A comparison of etymological usage of the words between the Bible and the Qur'an is analyzed to provide further scrutiny of the meanings of scriptures. As a supplement, a comprehensive database of Qur'anic commentary, which includes a wide variety of Qur'anic commentators from different Islamic traditions, are also consulted to view the commentary and interpretation of several scholars for the verses of the Qur'an.[137]

The fallacy of the root and etymological fallacy

To keep it in the reader's mind, I must be clear that I do not necessarily argue in favor of an etymological supremacy. More specifically, the main core of the methodology I use is not necessarily etymology, but intertextual polysemy, although etymology is still an important factor to further utilize intertextual polysemy. Languages evolve with time giving birth to polysemous terms, some of which are divergent from the root meaning.[138] As such, it is imperative to understand the etymology of the words and its various morphological permutations.

Varro (d. 27 BCE), in *De Lingua Latina*, considered that the ultimate origin of a word is of little significance.[139] However, Socrates argues that unless one knows the principles of what the origin of a word means, then it is impossible to understand the meanings and evolution of its derivatives.[140] How the ancients considered the origin of language is divided into two schools: the natural and the conventional.[141] The natural origin suggests that the primitive humans gave names to things inspired by an innate or psychological effect. The conventional origin is similar to that of Saussure, in which the symbolic names given to objects are arbitrary. As a conventionalist, Aristotle argues, "No name exists in nature, but only by becoming a symbol."[142]

Even if we adopt a Saussurean understanding of language, in which meaning is shared by a community, words must have been created by a single person who has such an authority to impose this meaning onto the community. The origin of a word must have been started at some point by some person. Such an authority does not necessarily mean political or otherwise, but the ability to make an effect on the community. Plato (d. 347 BCE) considered language a human invention, in which much of it is conventional.[143] However, even when looking at the Arabic language, if it were true that the origin of the words is conventional, their derivatives may be highly associated with its etymology. This brings forth the case of polysemous terms, in which even if the etymology is arbitrary, their morphological derivatives are highly associated with the original symbol desired from the root meaning. This would be true especially in Semitic languages, which are highly polysemous. However, William Sidney Allen suggests that development of language, which is different in study than its origin, is speculative due to the lack of material for historical treatment of the subject.[144]

Understanding the development of language from etymological roots was a popular study in antiquity. Allen argues that ancient studies of etymology are grounded on an insecure basis, especially on the concept of *composito* (etymology by contraction), in which a word is derived from two or more component words.[145] He brings forth examples from words, in which a suffix could be misunderstood as a second word combined with another to make meaning. Allen calls ancient etymology unscientific, in which a single syllable or even letter were commonly used to establish an etymological connection. Nonetheless, if these particular methods are what make etymological studies inaccurate, then it cannot be applied to etymological studies in

Semitic languages, such as Arabic. Due to having root-based morphologies, Arabic etymology does not stem from a combination of two or more words, but is based on the morphological permutations of a single root word. Another distinction between Semitic languages and many others in the study of etymology is the understanding of what came first, the noun or the verb.[146] According to Allen, the study of language development and etymology in antiquity saw a debate about what came first.[147]

Several scholars, both traditional and contemporary, have issues with the usage of certain methods of a linguistic approach. Plato, Quintilian (d. 100 CE), Sextus Empiricus (d. 210 CE), and Augustine (d. 430 CE) criticized the overuse of etymology, though they did not completely deny the use of etymological inquiry.[148] Traditionally, some scholars, such as Ibn Durustawayh (d. 347/958) in his *Sharḥ al-faṣīḥ*, reject the notion that the Arabic language contains polysemy, and therefore, the sharing of a common etymological root. Ibn Durustawayh gives reasons why he thinks polysemy needs to be clear in the Arabic language. One reason is that God created language to have clear meanings, and if a word has multiple meanings then it is against how God intended it.[149] He also notes that the morphological permutations of a root term having different meanings are not evidence of polysemy, but that different meanings would have different morphological permutations and are not the same.[150] Ibrāhīm Anīs (d. 1399/1977), a prominent grammarian in the twentieth century, agrees with Ibn Durustawayh that polysemy occurs when a single word has two different meanings, and not that one that is the etymology of the other, in which the other is considered a metaphor derived from that etymology.[151] Abū ʿAlī al-Fārsī (d. 377/987), an early grammarian, took a moderate stance on the role of polysemy in the Arabic language. He did not deny it, as Ibn Durustawayh, nor did he exaggerate its existence. Nonetheless, he did not define a specific etymology to the polysemes, but argued that it is because different tribes use a term for different meanings that the Arabic language evolved to include all these meanings, and not that they necessarily share a root etymology.[152] However, the opinions of Ibn Durustawayh and Ibrāhīm Anīs on polysemy go against how most classical grammarians, such as al-Suyūṭī, have defined polysemy and its special existence in the Qur'an.[153] It would also appear to go against the prophetic tradition that the Qur'an has different faces, as discussed earlier. Al-Suyūṭī suggests that it is natural for polysemy to occur because words are limited, while meanings are countless.[154] Therefore, it is only natural for polysemy to be born and to evolve with time.[155]

In more recent times, James Barr argues against the use of certain semantic methods for theological interpretation of scriptures that he believes distorts the state of the intended meaning of the word.[156] It must be noted that he is more concerned with the relationships between Hebrew and Greek words than those within the same language, although he does examine some examples of differences within the same language. Andrzej Zaborski[157] and Walid Saleh[158] also argue against the extent of the use of etymology in Qur'anic interpretation, although not by completely ignoring it. Saleh's main issue is in the assumption that the Arabic language might have borrowed words from another Semitic language, such as Hebrew, Aramaic, or Syriac. However, in the study of language, we must understand that a word in a language that shares the same family of another language may not necessarily be borrowing a word from the other language. The concept is usually simpler than a mere borrowing from another language in the same family. Since both languages share the same family group and origins, then those words could have evolved within the two languages, without having either of them borrowing from the other. They may be considered as having evolved from a similar ancestral protolanguage.

To examine an old example, Saleh correctly assumes that the term "*ḥanīf*" is probably one of the most widely debated words in terms of its etymology and meaning.[159] In Syriac, the meaning of the root "*ḥ n p*" is an idolater, something that Rippin states is what scholars generally accept as the roots of the Arabic word.[160] Rippin quotes Beeston[161] that the Arabs in Ḥijāz might have adopted a Najrānite word, which came by way of Syrian missionaries to designate all non-Christians, whether polytheists or monotheists. While Saleh agrees with Rippin that the term "*ḥanīf*" can only be understood in its Qur'anic context and that the etymological analysis of the word would not lead us anywhere, I find these statements very generalized. There can be an etymological link of how to understand the term "*ḥanīf*" in the Qur'an when we first understand the term's polysemous nature.

To analyze the term "*ḥanīf*" from its polysemous and etymological point of view, we must understand its root meanings. The term is usually understood as someone who is upright, according to its assumed Qur'anic context. However, it also means someone with a crooked leg.[162] The term for water tap is "*ḥanafiyyah*," sharing the same root, because a water tap is typically crooked. The root of the term, even in Arabic, is something crooked.[163] Therefore, let us not assume that the word was simply borrowed from Syriac and that the Syriac definition means heathen, or in other words "a person whose thoughts are crooked from ours," in a Christian Syriac context. In the context of the Arab idolaters, the Muslims or monotheists hold a crooked belief from the mainstream ideology, and therefore they would be called "*ḥanīf*" too. Similarly, Abraham had lived with idol-worshippers and his thoughts were crooked (*ḥanīf*) from their mainstream thought. If a person is crooked from the mainstream people who are crooked, then it could be that the person is considered upright. A prophetic tradition states that, "Islam started strange and will return back strange as it started. So, blessed are the strangers."[164] This prophetic tradition implies that Islam is not mainstream, and therefore crooked (*ḥanīf*) from the mainstream. The root meaning of crooked for the term "*ḥanīf*" is as much Arabic as it is Syriac, while not assuming that either has borrowed it from another, but that they share the same ancestor, in which this word perhaps had independently evolved in each language.

Analyzing the etymology of a word is to understand its root meaning, and not necessarily to assume a cross-cultural borrowing of a word from a different language to another. It would be somewhat safe to assume that the majority of the Semitic roots share a similar ancestor. Therefore, that Semitic languages share similar roots is not necessarily evidence that one has borrowed from another, but more correctly it is understood that the root term has perhaps evolved independently within each of the sister languages from a common ancestor. Hence, those who argue against the use of etymology for Qur'anic terms seem to generalize their statements. They are perhaps defensive against misuse of etymological analysis of terms, but misusing etymology is not enough to condemn an objective use of etymology. Although Zaborski[165] and Saleh[166] agree that etymology is not the best method to understand the Qur'an, they had to refute methods that seem to be false. However, this should not be a reason to generalize the statement that etymology is not a good way to understand scriptures. If we understand the polysemous nature of root terms and their morphologies, etymology is both necessary and beneficial.

James Barr, in *The Semantics of Biblical Language*, argues fervently against what he assumes are devious and dubious methods of Biblical interpretation using etymological approaches. Although Barr brings some good understandings of the pitfalls of a linguistic approach, he still has some issues with his arguments. For example, he states that in Pauline writings, the Greek term "*sarx*" is used for flesh and "*sōma*" for body, while the Hebrew only uses "*bashar*" for both.[167] He assumes that the way of thinking of the Greeks in the past had to differentiate between flesh and body, while the Hebrews did not delve into philosophical questions that required such a term to be differentiated. However, the Hebrew has several words for body and flesh, and not just one in Biblical language (e.g., *gewiyah*, *gawph*, *leḥum* all which correspond to the Arabic *juwa*, *jawf*, and *laḥam*), although he is correct to state that the Septuagint has at various instances translated the term "*bashar*" into the Greek "*sarx*" and at other times into "*sōma*." Perhaps the two terms can sometimes be synonymous, though not necessarily always. Besides, in the analysis of a linguistic approach, we must realize that the language of an original text should not be compared with a translation. Although a translation may provide a good approximation of the meaning, it would not hold the same credibility as the original language, in which the author might have specifically intended a certain word to be used. Hence, the translators of the Septuagint should not be always considered a reference for the Greek New Testament, although to a great extent it could be used for such, especially since the majority of the New Testament authors were thinking in Hebrew (Aramaic) and possibly translating in their minds the Hebrew (Aramaic) words into Greek.

Nonetheless, Barr assumes that a language is not always necessarily a reflection of the thoughts of people in a particular culture.[168] I agree with this concept. However, Barr argues what he considers the root fallacy, which is an extensive reliance of understanding root meanings of the Hebrew language.[169] Since I argue in favor of understanding its roots, polysemous nature, and morphologies, then I must disagree with Barr. Barr provides an example where he doubts that the Hebrew words for bread (*laḥm*) and war (*milḥama*) have any significance in sharing the same root.[170] This again proves the misunderstanding of root meanings of Semitic languages. The term is polysemous and one of the meanings of "*laḥm*" is to join,[171] which is very similar to that of its corresponding Arabic cognate, "*laḥm*."[172] Something that joins together is called "*yaltaḥim*." As such, the term for welding is called "*liḥām*," as it joins two objects together.[173] When skin is wounded, it joins itself back, usually creating scar tissue. Bread is the joining of flour together. Flour is separate pieces joined together (*laḥm*) into dough to make bread.[174] A battle is when two or more forces collide with each other and therefore joined together (*milḥama*) or also a reference to swords cutting off flesh (*milḥama*). The standard understanding of the Semitic language is that when we want to understand the polysemous nature of words, it is important that we understand the root meanings. Suggesting that apparently completely different meanings are derived from the same root is meaningless or abstract is the naïvety of Semitic linguistics.[175] This is similar to the previous example shown between writing (*kitābah*) and an army battalion (*katībah*) sharing the same root meaning. Barr suggests that the etymology of a word is only useful to understand the history of a word, but may not necessarily be a guide of how to understand a word in its present form.[176]

The Qur'an challenges its audience to be as eloquent as itself. It challenges its audience to be fully versed in deeply understanding its Arabic language to fully appreciate it and understand its meanings. The Qur'an portrays that its audience, even at the time of Muḥammad, did not fully comprehend its language and meaning. The Qur'an shows that although it is in Arabic and revealed among Arabs, they still had difficulty understanding it.

> [2] A revelation from the Compassionate, the Merciful, [3] a Book whose signs have been expounded as an Arabic Quran for a people who know, [4] as a bringer of glad tidings, and as a warner. But most of them have turned away, such that they hear not. [5] They say, "Our hearts are under coverings (*akinnah*) from that to which you call us, and in our ears there is deafness, and between us and you there is a veil (*ḥijāb*). So do [as you will]; we shall do [as we will]."[177]

This means that the mainstream understanding of the words in the Qur'an may not necessarily be a full and correct understanding of the Qur'an: a good example of this is the use of the disjoined letters (*muqaṭṭa'āt*) in the beginning of some Qur'anic chapters. Muḥammad seems to have intended to use obscure meanings of words, while creatively reciting the Qur'an, thinking it may be obvious to people other than himself. However, when he saw that people did not understand his creative associations using the Arabic language, he said that the general public would not fully understand the Qur'an. If at the time the Qur'an was first recited, there was difficulty in understanding its language and meaning, then it should not be at all surprising that we have difficulty even today. In many instances, Barr suggests that current speakers of a language when using a word are usually unaware and care less of its etymological meaning in the past.[178] If we are to assume scriptures to be literature without any divine significance, Fishbane illustrates with plentiful examples how Biblical authors had a great deal of awareness of previous Biblical literature, while using words selectively showing their full awareness to form what is known as inner-Biblical exegesis.[179] As such, understanding the root meanings and etymology is not only important, but perhaps necessary to fully appreciate the meanings of the Qur'an.[180]

Arabic and the Qur'an

Within the methodology of intertextual polysemy proposed in this book, not only are the Arabic terms analyzed, but they are also compared with other Semitic languages, such as Hebrew and Aramaic, as the term "'*arabī*" does not necessarily specify a single standard language of the Arabs. What does the Qur'an mean when describing itself as "'*arabī*?" The term may mean various languages of Arabia, some of which could be closer to Hebrew and Aramaic, while others could be closer to Ethiopic (Ge'ez). This provokes a question about the pursuit of polysemy. Muḥammad Bakr Isma'īl defines polysemy as an Arab tribe using the same term for a different meaning than that used by another tribe, and so there is vagueness in its meaning.[181] Muḥammad might have been aware of various Arabic dialects and perhaps Semitic languages. When Muḥammad entered a heightened state of creativity, he might have associated meanings from across the Arabic spectrum.

The term "*ʿarabī*" in the Qur'an is typically understood to mean the Arabic language. However, we need to further analyze what the term "*ʿa r b*" actually means, as it is a term that is itself polysemous. According to *Lisān al-ʿarab*, the term "*ʿarab*" means the Arabs or the dwellers of the desert,[182] which has the same definition in Hebrew and Aramaic.[183] However, *Lisān al-ʿarab* also mentions that the Arab tribes did not all have a single standard Arabic language, their languages were diverse.[184] Hence, we should not assume that the Arabic Qur'an is specifically the language of Quraysh, as ʿUthmān ibn ʿAffān stated.[185] There is no Qur'anic basis that its language is specifically that of Quraysh. Assuming that the traditional account is correct and Patricia Crone's account that Islam rose in northern Arabia is incorrect,[186] then Muḥammad lived in Makkah, which is in central West Arabia, where Arabs from various parts of the peninsula flocked for pilgrimage. Also, perhaps being at the center of the trade route of merchant caravans traveling between South and North Arabia, he was likely aware of the various Arab tongues spoken by different tribes. Also, according to prophetic tradition, Muḥammad allowed the Qur'an to be read in various ways.[187] Therefore, there is no specific form that is exclusive. This also shows that the Arabic language was not a specific single language, but that various tribes had a different language, while some might be closer to other Semitic languages, such as Aramaic or Hebrew.

We need to look closer at the meaning of "*ʿarab*." The term has various meanings that are not always related. As such, the *Theological Dictionary of the Old Testament* (*TDOT*) cautions that since the root has many unrelated meanings that it should not be considered to all have been derived from the same etymological root.[188] The term "*ʿarabah*" means a boat, while "*taʿrīb*" is cutting palm leaves.[189] The term "*ʿurbūn*" is the contracted sale value or a deposit,[190] which is similar to its definition in Hebrew and Aramaic,[191] stemming back to the Akkadian usage from the Alalakhi texts to mean pledge or surety.[192] Also, the term means to be sweet (e.g., Psalm 104:34; Hosea 9:4; Sirach 40:21) or pleasure, with its etymological meaning also found in South Semitic, mainly Old South Arabic and Arabic dialects.[193]

Since the term for "*ʿarab*" also means to be pleasant,[194] it is interesting, because the term "*ʿajam*," which is typically used as non-Arab by the Arabs,[195] also means to grieve in Hebrew and Aramaic,[196] and therefore, would act as an antonym to "*ʿarab*." Nonetheless, one must not jump to conclusions. According to *Lisān al-ʿarab*, one of the meanings of "*ʿajam*" is to be of unclear speech, and perhaps for that reason the Arabs called those who are not Arabs "*ʿajam*" as their speech is unclear to them.[197] Yet, *Lisān al-ʿarab* also states that the term "*ʿajam*" means one whose speech is unclear, even if they were Arabs.[198] Hence, its root meaning is not necessarily an antonym of Arab, but an antonym of clear speech (*faṣāḥah*).

In addition, in Hebrew and Aramaic, the term "*ʿarab*" means to mix and to combine, mixed races, or confusion and disorder.[199] The usage in this meaning is attested in Exodus 12:38 and in various other places in the Hebrew Bible. It has also been used in the sense of weaving, which is perhaps due to mixed fabric woven from different yarns (e.g., Leviticus 13:48).[200] In the Dead Sea Scrolls, the term is also used in the meaning of mix, confuse, or intermingle (e.g., 11QT19 45:4). If the term for "ʿ*arab*" also means mixed races, then this might describe ancient Arabia, in which tribes could have been mixed between different Semitic tribes. As such, when the Qur'an states that it is in clear (*mubīn*) "ʿ*arabī*" and not "ʿ*ajamī*" (i.e., Qur'an 16:103, 41:44) it might mean that its language is clearly "ʿ*arabī*," whatever "ʿ*arabī*" means. It could mean clearly mixed (ʿ*arabī*) in need of connecting (*taʿqilūn*). These are just few non-exhaustive examples of what the term "ʿ*arab*" means.

According to a prophetic tradition, it is narrated that Muḥammad said, "Five prophets from the Arabs are Muḥammad, Ishmael, Shuʿayb (Jethro), Ṣāliḥ, and Hūd."[201] Here, the meaning of Arab is those living in the desert, and not even necessarily describing a single ethnic group or language. Ishmael is presumed to have a Hebrew father and an Egyptian mother but lived among the Arabs in the desert. Though a Semite, he was not himself ethnically an Arab. Shuʿayb, on the other hand, was a Midianite in North of Arabia. What is the Midianite language? It cannot necessarily be assumed to be standard Arabic. We do not have much knowledge of their language. However, given the geographic location of Midian, then it might be assumed that it could have been close to Aramaic. Rofé suggests that the Canaanite language is close to the Midianite language,[202] which means that the Midianite language might have had its own distinct features, though it is a Semitic language.

If, according to tradition, Madā'in Ṣāliḥ is the place where Ṣāliḥ preached, then he would be a Nabataean in North of Arabia. If Patricia Crone and Michael Cook's theory that Muḥammad was from northern Arabia is correct, then his Arabic might have been Nabataean.[203] North Arabic might be represented by Classical Arabic and other pre-Islamic dialects, such as Lihyanite, Thamudic, and Safaitic. However, there are various hypotheses on the Nabataean language. Beyer suggests that it is close to Achaemenid Imperial Aramaic.[204] Healey notes that Nabataeans are believed to have used Arabic in everyday life, but that their vocabulary is clearly Aramaic with loanwords from languages such as Greek and Persian.[205] He states, "There are four other, more or less contemporary Aramaic dialects, Palmyrene, Hatran, Nabataean and Jewish Aramaic, which can be compared with Syriac."[206] Healey continues: "The most distinctive feature of Nabataean by comparison with all other Aramaic dialects of the period is its Arabic colouring or, to be more precise, colouring from an Arabian language allied in some way to what became Classical Arabic."[207]

Some scholars believe that Nabataean seems to be likely Aramaic that was slowly influenced by Arabic, as its vocabulary was slowly being replaced by Arabic loanwords.[208] If the language of Ṣāliḥ is Thamudic, which is a dialect of Arabic,[209] then it would still be different to Classical Arabic, which was only standardized in the eighth century.[210] It might still have had some of its Nabataean ancestral resemblance, which would have been close to Aramaic.[211] Healey states, "there is evidence of a difference between the Arabic in the background of the Nabataean texts and Classical Arabic, both in vocalism and in morphology—the Arabic behind Nabataean had already lost case endings. This seems to imply that the dialect behind the Nabataean inscriptions is a more developed form of Arabic than Classical Arabic."[212]

According to tradition, Hūd lived in Yemen, South of Arabia, which included languages such as Ancient South Arabian, Sabaean, and Mehri. Through an analysis of modern dialects, it is suggested that although they may have been influenced by Classical Arabic, they still resemble, in some ways, their ancestral ancient languages. This suggests that the languages of Ancient South Arabia, while they may have had a close resemblance to Classical Arabic, were still distinct.[213] With Shu'ayb and Ṣāliḥ situated in North Arabia, while Hūd was situated in South Arabia, Muḥammad lived in Makkah, which is in central West Arabia, perhaps with a language influenced by both the north and the south. This would be especially true since Makkah was perhaps a destination of many of the Arabs in the peninsula, as it might have been a stop on the trade route between South and North Arabia.[214]

So it comes to question of what is meant by Arabic. Which Arabic are we talking about? Is the Arabic of the Qur'an specifically that of Quraysh, as 'Uthmān assumed, or is it more general to the dwellers of the desert, with their various forms of the Semitic languages? It seems that Muḥammad did not mean by the term "Arab" specifically Quraysh, but a more general term meaning the dwellers of the deserts of Arabia, who had various languages, some of which were possibly closer to Hebrew and Aramaic in North Arabia, while others were different and even possibly closer to Ethiopic in South Arabia.

Since Classical Arabic was only standardized in the post-Qur'anic era of the eighth century, it cannot be presumed that this is the language of the Qur'an. The Arab grammarians, who standardized the Arabic language based on the Qur'anic discourse in the eighth century did not always agree, especially among those between the grammar schools of al-Kūfah and al-Baṣrah.[215] The term "*'arabī*" in the Qur'an is not the Classical Arabic standardized in a post-Qur'anic era. Nor is the term specific to the Arabic of Quraysh. It can simply mean the languages of the dwellers of the desert (*'arab*), which would include many various forms of Semitic languages. Abū 'Ubayda is noted to say, "Whoever pretends that there is in the Qur'an anything other than the Arabic tongue has made a serious charge against God."[216] However, what is the Arabic tongue that the Qur'an refers to? Why should it be restricted to the tongue of Quraysh or even why should it be restricted to what grammarians of the eighth century assumed? This assumes that the Arabic of the Qur'an is restricted to these opinions based on dogmas and not facts, as noted by Kopf.[217] Since the Qur'an itself does not specify what it means by the term "*'arabī*," then one can only think that the term may simply refer to the dwellers of the desert and their languages.[218] Otherwise, it might mean its definition of mixture, as the Qur'an is mixed (*'arabī*) in need of making connections (*ta'qilūn*) to make sense out of it.

The methodology

Being in a heightened state of mind, Muḥammad was able to make creative connections using language as a symbol. I attempt to decipher his state of mind and read the Qur'an based on his state of mind. Although I have stated that the proposed approach of hermeneutics is linguistic using intertextual polysemy and tried to show the significance of such style, it is important to briefly describe this method in a systematic manner, so that it can be understood clearly.

The method can be summarized as follows:

1. Keywords of a passage are taken back to their root meanings in the Arabic language. Possible meanings from the root's morphological permutations are taken into account. The lexical semantics are taken from Arabic definitions, but also from other sister Semitic languages, such as Hebrew and Aramaic for the reasons described in the previous section. The reason is, we cannot fully rely on medieval lexicons to understand the Qur'an, as a word might have evolved as a reaction to its use in the Qur'an, instead of its actual etymological meaning at the time of Muḥammad. It is assumed that the Semitic languages have a common ancestor, in which the root meanings of the words could have evolved in each descendent language. Also, medieval Arabic lexicons may define Qur'anic terms as a way of interpreting (*tafsīr*) the Qur'an, and not the actual meaning of the word as it was intended. As such, comparing the Arabic definitions with their Semitic cognates, such as Hebrew and Aramaic, may provide us with a more reasonable knowledge of the possible meanings of the word without it being tainted specifically as a way of interpreting the Qur'an by medieval lexicographers. Some might argue why Hebrew and Aramaic lexicographers may have retained certain meanings of an Arabic Qur'an, while the Arabs may have not. The counterargument is that the literary history of several literary Semitic texts, such as Akkadian, Ugaritic, Hebrew, and Aramaic by far surpasses that of the Arabic language and are attested during the pre-Islamic era, since Arabic literary history is mainly post-Qur'anic.[219] As such, it is conceivable that some Arabic words and meanings used during the time of the Qur'an might have had some associations with the Hebrew and Aramaic terms, but the Arabic meanings of these terms could have been lost in the post-Qur'anic era. As such, I would also argue that perhaps the definitions of the Hebrew and Aramaic words in defining Biblical language may also be compared with the Arabic words to ensure that definitions that may have been lost in its Hebrew or Aramaic use are still taken into consideration as possible intended meanings in the past. To ensure that an etymological usage of the meanings of the roots are all taken into account, the lexical semantics of the term and its morphological permutations are taken into consideration, along with possible permutations in the change of letters in the sister languages. For example, the word for remembrance is "*dhikr*" in Arabic sharing the same root for male, which is "*dhakar*." However, to ensure that the lexical semantics that need to be analyzed would include the term "*dakar*" in Hebrew and Aramaic, which means male, but also includes the term "*zakar*" in Hebrew, which corresponds to "*dhikr*" in its definition for remember. This is what I mean by taking care of various corresponding morphological permutations. Another major consideration would include terms with the letter "*ḥā*'" or "*khā*'," as their corresponding terms in Hebrew and Aramaic are undifferentiated. Hence, it is sometimes imperative to take into consideration the lexical semantics of the term to include both permutations of those letters. A similar issue would be permutations of letters that include "*tā*'" and

"*thā*'," "*dāl*" and "*dhāl*," "*sīn*" and "*shīn*," "*ṣād*" and "*ḍād*," "*ṭā*'" and "*ẓā*'," or "*'ayn*" and "*ghayn*," as similarly the corresponding Hebrew and Aramaic terms are not always differentiated, when compared to their corresponding Arabic terms. This is also to keep in mind that these letters were undifferentiated in the written Arabic script during the time of Muḥammad and in the earliest Qur'anic manuscripts, including the presumed 'Uthmānic codex.[220] However, not all undifferentiated early Arabic scripts are necessarily taken into consideration, as they correspond to different Hebrew and Aramaic alphabets, such as the "*bā*'" corresponding to "*beth*," "*jīm*" corresponding to "*gimel*," "*rā*'" corresponding to "*resh*," and "*zayn*" corresponding to "*zayn*." Nevertheless, certain morphological anomalies can occur between "*dhāl*" corresponding to "*zayn*," as in the case of "*dhakar*" and "*zakar*" stated above, and between "*thā*'" corresponding to "*shīn*," as in the case of "*thiql*" and "*shekel*." Nonetheless, the examples in the next chapter are purely from the Qur'an and correspond to undebatable Arabic definitions. This is to ensure that the methodology remains valid even if other sister languages are not taken into account. Later examples in the book will include a comparative analysis of lexical semantics within Hebrew and Aramaic, which is sometimes necessary to ensure that all possible etymologies and polysemous permutations are taken into account, while also providing a gateway for a comparative textual analysis with the Bible and Biblical literature.

2. Once all possible meanings from the point of view of lexical semantics are taken into account, then intertextuality becomes important. The intertextuality has two forms. The first compares and analyzes how the term and its various morphological permutations are used within the Qur'an and other scriptures. The second form is not always obvious. It involves the intertextuality of comparative meaning or the homophone of the term being analyzed, and not necessarily one that would share the exact same root. An example would be analyzing the term for father, which is "*ab*." The root term for this word might include "*awb*," "*ayb*," or "*aby*." Arab Christians, for example, use the term "*āb*" for God the Father, which could be rooted in either "*awb*" or "*ayb*." Nonetheless, the term "*aba*," which also corresponds to the Aramaic "*aba*," could be rooted in the term "*aby*" or "*abw*." Hence, these would be cases in which a full array of possible root meanings is taken into consideration in the analysis. An example of homophone intertextuality would include terms such as "*qirān*," which literally means joining, but is usually understood as marriage or partnership, and comparing it with "*Qur'an*." Although the term "*qirān*" is rooted in "*qaran*," while the term "*Qur'an*" is rooted in "*qara*'," they are morphologically similar in nature. The second form of intertextuality is not as strong as the obvious first, where sharing the same root is more evident and simpler to compare. Nonetheless, the second form may sometimes provide us with interesting insights during intertextual analysis, and hence, cannot always be ignored.

The above provides a brief systematic description of the approach of intertextual polysemy. However, with examples in the following chapters, a clearer understanding of how they are applied can be more visibly appreciated.

Critique of the methodology

The methodology outlined for the method of intertextual polysemy appears not to be too different to that of Christoph Luxenberg's proposed methodology,[221] but also holds major differences. Luxenberg's thesis follows that of Günter Lüling that the origin of the Qur'an is dated earlier than originally thought (i.e., pre-dates the traditional dates of Muḥammad) in what he calls the Ur-Qur'an.[222] This is different to John Wansbrough's thesis that the Qur'an is to be dated much later than initially thought.[223] Luxenberg's thesis is that the Qur'an stems from a Syriac Christian liturgy. I am in no way suggesting that the Arabic Qur'an somehow is mostly Aramaic in disguise. The language of the Qur'an is Arabic, which may encompass the many dialects and tongues of those living in the desert.

Fundamentally, I am not even assuming the Qur'anic origins to have come from anyone besides Muḥammad. I am assuming that Muḥammad is the author, and that the Qur'an is formulated in Muḥammad's mind, whether or not through divine intervention. Looking into cognate roots and meanings in other Semitic languages is not to assume that it was written in another language later adopted by the Arabs, but to assume that perhaps some Arabic meanings evolved during post-Qur'anic era that may have existed within the Arabic language during the time of the Qur'an. If we discover Arabic literature texts that pre-date the Qur'an, then we can test if any of the meanings are attested within the Arabic language or not. Also, the Qur'an does engage with the Bible in many instances, and therefore, it is possible that Muḥammad is attempting to use terminologies that are familiar to Jews and Christians; not that he adopted them from an original Syriac text and transformed it to a Qur'an. This can be especially seen how the term "*qiblah*," understood as the direction of prayer, appears to have been purposefully used to allude to the *Shema'* passages in Deuteronomy, which the Talmud calls "*kabbalat 'ol malkhut shamayim*," as I have discussed in an article.[224]

Luxenberg has many scholarly opponents and few who might agree, at least partially, with his views, such as Gabriel Reynolds.[225] I admit that using the methodology outlined in this book, or that adopted by Luxenberg, is not without its flaws. However, no methodology is without its flaws. The main flaw of the method outlined here is that any term may be used to mean almost anything to fit one's predispositions. Gerald Hawting has made this point early on Lüling's theories.[226] However, in using Semitic languages that attest to various meanings of the terms used in the Qur'an is not to assume that the text had Syriac origins. As stated earlier, Arabic and its sister languages come from a common ancestor of Proto-Semitic. Therefore, not every term found in Arabic and Hebrew or Aramaic is a loanword, but has come down through a common ancestral language. Therefore, it is essential to use Michael Fishbane's process of looking into patterns.[227] A single word may not alone be evidence of intertextuality, but the existence of a pattern in the use of terms along with their contextual neighboring terms may be essential to provide evidence that such a reading is plausible.

I agree that some of the extrapolations made in some of the examples in this book are speculative. However, when there are several examples that prove that such a method is a possibility, such as that outlined on the "*qiblah*," as discussed,[228] then it does give some plausibility to this method, where other methods have failed. However, this method, like any other, is not foolproof. Therefore, I do request readers to proceed with caution. Do look at how the method is applied and make a distinction between what can be asserted, and extrapolations that are merely opinions of what the underlying metaphor might be. We can sometimes easily assert that a pattern does exist through intertextual polysemy, but why it exists and what message is it trying to convey may be a matter of opinion only.

The methodology outlined in this book is fundamentally different to the apparent intentions of the likes of Lüling and Luxenberg. Unlike Lüling and Luxenberg, I can make no assertions. I walk behind Socrates' fabled claim in Plato's *Apology*, which I rephrase as, "The only thing I know is that I do not know anything." I have absolutely no polemical intentions. The method outlined in this book is purely textual analysis of a comparative nature, which to the most part shows that the Qur'an is consistent in the areas where it appears to sometimes be self-contradicting, as will be seen in some of the examples.

Another main critique is that this book does not delve into the theological or historical reverberations that can be echoed from the observations made. The reasons for that are manifold, but one is simply a matter of space. Another reason is to avoid any assertions and to allow the readers to form their own conclusions. As stated in Chapter 1, one of the major intentions behind this research and its findings is to open new inquiries in the field and to incite insightful and thought-provoking dynamics in people's minds. Together, we can better understand reality.

3

Examples of Intertextual Polysemy from Qur'anic and Arabic Perspectives

This chapter gives a few examples of the application of intertextual polysemy for Qur'anic hermeneutics. These examples represent two forms of analysis. The first is that analysis can be done independently from other scriptures. The second aspect is a comparative analysis between the Qur'an and the Bible. The reason behind this is to show the extent of intertextuality between the Qur'an and itself, as well as between the Qur'an and the Bible. More examples of intertextual polysemy between the Qur'an and the Bible will be discussed in Chapters 5–7. This means that Muḥammad, in his creative state of mind, made associations between his sayings in Arabic and engaging with the Bible, which he likely had access to and expected his audience to be well-versed in, to further understand his sayings.

Intertextual polysemy between the Qur'an, itself, and the Bible

According to Muslim tradition, the first passages of the Qur'an revealed to Muḥammad were the first five verses of sūrah al-ʿAlaq.[1] I find these presumed first Qur'anic passages to be interesting because they talk about the creation of the human from a "clinging." Although we may infer what the clinging is, it does not answer why such a clinging is so important that it is traditionally considered the first chapter revealed in the Qur'an. Why does the Qur'an specify the clinging as the means of human creation? Why does it not state that the human is created from sperm (*nuṭfah*) or clay (*turāb*)? Are these simply rhyming words? If so, then why not choose words in the rest of the verses that rhyme with sperm (*nuṭfah*) or clay (*turāb*)? Stating that the human is created from a clinging, which is assumed to be the clinging of a fetus in its mother's womb, must serve a purpose for Muḥammad. Traditionally, the first passages revealed in the Qur'an are believed to be the following:

> 1 Recite (*Iqra'*) in the Name of thy Lord Who divided (created),[2] 2 divided (created) man from a clinging (*ʿalaq*).[3] 3 Recite! (*Iqra'*) Thy Lord is most noble, 4 Who taught (*ʿallam*) by the Pen, 5 taught (*ʿallam*) the human[4] that which he knew not.[5]

The first verse of the chapter of the Clinging (*al-ʿAlaq*) talks about the Qur'an, its revelation and proclamation, and its creation (or division). The second verse discusses the creation (or division) of the human being from a clinging (*'alaq*).[6] Qur'anic exegetes consider the clinging described in the second verse to be that of a fetus in its mother's womb.[7] Verses 3–5 reiterate the proclamation of the Qur'an (*iqra'*) and portray how God teaches the human being things that the human being did not know before.

To me, the mystery of the first Qur'anic revelations lies within understanding the significance of the creation of the human being from a clinging (*'alaq*) in the womb. Although Qur'anic commentators are capable of answering what the clinging is, they fail to answer the question of why this clinging is so significant that it is traditionally in the first verses of the Qur'an and the chapter is even named after such clinging. Using intertextual polysemy, the answer to that question may be simple and the Qur'an may be giving a very informative interpretation of the meanings behind the clinging.[8] Roots of the keywords in the first passages of the chapter of Clinging (sūrah al-'Alaq) are to be compared with the first passages of sūrah al-Raḥmān, as part of the intertextuality: "[1] The Compassionate (*al-Raḥmān*) [2] taught (*'allam*) the Quran; [3] divided (created) man; [4] taught him (*'allamahu*) speech (the clarity) (*al-bayān*)."[9]

From the first passages of sūrah al-Raḥmān, the root keywords may be compared with those of sūrah al-'Alaq. There are six points of intertextuality:

1. The second verse of sūrah al-Raḥmān states that God teaches the Qur'an, sharing the same root of the word Qur'an, "*iqra'*" when compared with the first and third verses of sūrah al-'Alaq, and it is stated that God teaches the proclamation of the Qur'an.
2. The first verse of sūrah al-'Alaq states to read or to proclaim in the name of the Lord. The first verse of sūrah al-Raḥmān uses one of the names of God (the Lord), which is the Most Compassionate, or *al-Raḥmān*.[10]
3. The third verse of sūrah al-Raḥmān uses the term for the creation (or division) of the human being, "*khalaq*," which may be compared with the same words used in the first two verses of sūrah al-'Alaq.
4. The third verse of sūrah al-Raḥmān also uses the term for the human, "*al-insān*," which corresponds to the same term used by the second and fifth verses of sūrah al-'Alaq.
5. The fourth and fifth verses of sūrah al-'Alaq describe God teaching, "*'allam*," which can also be seen in the second and fourth verses of sūrah al-Raḥmān.
6. The fourth verse of sūrah al-Raḥmān explains, in a similar way to that of sūrah al-'Alaq, that God teaches the human being things that he knew not or the "*bayān*."

The first passages of sūrah al-'Alaq and sūrah al-Raḥmān seem to be entwined with and interrelated to each other. According to Michael Fishbane's technique,[11] this would mean that those two passages allude to each other, or at least the latter alludes to the former, whichever came first. Unfortunately, the traditional methods of Qur'anic hermeneutics would not have revealed the interrelationship of the roots of the keywords between the passages. However, understanding this relationship seems to be essential for Qur'anic interpretation, as the Qur'an is not only trying to explain what the clinging (*al-'alaq*) really means, but it is also portraying the significance of why this clinging (*al-'alaq*) is revealed in the traditionally first revelations of the Qur'an.

Since the binding relationship between sūrah al-ʿAlaq and sūrah al-Raḥmān is firmly established, then it can be seen that sūrah al-ʿAlaq is not simply speaking of the creation (*khlq*) of the human being as a clinging fetus in the mother's womb or even the division (*khlq*) of the fetus from the womb during birth. The term for womb is "*r ḥ m*," which shares the same root as the first verse of sūrah al-Raḥmān, naming God as the Most Compassionate (*al-Raḥmān*), after which the whole chapter is named. From this method of Qur'anic hermeneutics, the Qur'an may seem to use inner-Qur'anic allusion to interpret itself. Sūrah al-ʿAlaq is not talking of the creation of the human being as a clinging fetus in its mother's womb (*r ḥ m*), but speaking about the creation of the human being as the human clings unto God (*al-Raḥmān*). The portrayal of the fetus clinging in the mother's womb in the physical realm is used as a metaphor for the clinging unto God (*al-taʿalluq bil-Raḥmān*). It might be for that reason that sūrah al-Raḥmān is traditionally called the Bride of the Qur'an,[12] because it attempts to describe the womb that teaches the human being the Qur'an, as in the chapter of the Clinging (sūrah al-ʿAlaq). Here, it may be seen that the final redactors of the Qur'an wanted these two passages to allude to each other, or that Muḥammad, in his high state of creativity, associated things that appear to be unrelated through a polysemous manner to create metaphor. According to a prophetic tradition (*ḥadīth*): "The Prophet states, 'No one enters heaven (*al-jannah*) with his works,' so he was asked, 'Not even you?' and he replied, 'Not even me, unless my Lord encompasses me with mercy (*raḥmah*).'"[13]

In an Islamic context, God's heaven (*jannah*) is portrayed in His mercy (*raḥmah*). According to the method of intertextual polysemy, this understanding of heaven and God's mercy is interesting. As a fetus (*janīn*) is in the mother's womb (*rḥm*), so is heaven (*jannah*) in God's mercy (*raḥmah*). The terms fetus (*janīn*) and heaven (*jannah*) share the same root, as do the terms womb (*rḥm*) and mercy (*raḥmah*). The Qur'an uses the physical conception and birth of human beings as a metaphor for their spiritual birth through their clinging unto God.

The mother's womb feeds the fetus through the umbilical cord into its navel, which is called "*surrah*." The root of the word for the navel, "*surrah*," is embedded in the term "*srr*," which means secret.[14] The term for belly is "*baṭn*," which shares the same root as the term "*bāṭin*" describing the inner or hidden meanings.[15] Perhaps Muḥammad is trying to show a metaphorical analogy that as the fetus clings unto the mother's womb to be fed through its navel (*surrah*) in their bellies (*baṭn*), so are those who cling unto God fed with divine mysteries (*asrār*) of the inner meanings (*bāṭin*) of life. This is perhaps what sūrah al-ʿAlaq and sūrah al-Raḥmān explain: it is God who teaches the human being knowledge that he did not know before. How does God teach that knowledge, according to the Qur'an? The knowledge is taught as the human being clings unto God as a fetus clings unto a mother's womb. This appears to be the first message that the Qur'an tries to explain, in its presumed first passages. This might be paralleled with the teaching of being born from above, as narrated in the Gospel of John:

> 3 Jesus replied, "Very truly I tell you, no one can see the kingdom of God unless they are born again." 4 "How can someone be born when they are old?" Nicodemus asked. "Surely they cannot enter a second time into their mother's womb to be

> born!" 5 Jesus answered, "Very truly I tell you, no one can enter the kingdom of God unless they are born of water and the Spirit. 6 Flesh gives birth to flesh, but the Spirit gives birth to spirit. 7 You should not be surprised at my saying, 'You must be born again.' 8 The wind blows wherever it pleases. You hear its sound, but you cannot tell where it comes from or where it is going. So it is with everyone born of the Spirit."9 "How can this be?" Nicodemus asked. 10 "You are Israel's teacher," said Jesus, "and do you not understand these things? 11 Very truly I tell you, we speak of what we know, and we testify to what we have seen, but still you people do not accept our testimony. 12 I have spoken to you of earthly things and you do not believe; how then will you believe if I speak of heavenly things?"[16]

Using intertextual polysemy for Qur'anic hermeneutics provides insight by not only answering the question "what" is stated by the Qur'an, as the majority of Qur'anic scholars and commentators try to explain in their interpretations, but more importantly answers the question "why." Here, understanding Muḥammad's state of mind in making creative associations and producing metaphor tells us what could be his intentions in making the Qur'anic statements. Although they may seem erratic, they are not an example of a thought disorder, but they are creative pieces.

Comparing Islamic ruling with the text: divorce

In this example, intertextual polysemy is used to compare Islamic Sharī'ah with the text of the Qur'an. The story of Moses' meeting with a mystical character, presumably al-Khiḍr in sūrah al-Kahf (Chapter of the Cave),[17] is a story filled with mystery, as the outer actions are not evidence of their inner meanings. It is mysterious in such a way that even Moses could not easily comprehend the events that were going on during his meeting with the mystical figure. Nonetheless, if I claim a hypothesis that one of the intentions of the Qur'an's creative associations in the story is its relationship with the Islamic ruling of divorce, then it may not be easily perceived, because such an association is not obvious in the story. However, when using intertextual polysemy, it may be seen that such a relationship may be valid, given Muḥammad's state of mind.

The story of the meeting between Moses and the mystical figure, presumably al-Khiḍr, provides insight into the possible Qur'anic eloquence in the precise usage of terms. The passages relate that al-Khiḍr and Moses travel through three different journeys together. At the start of each journey, the Qur'an uses the term "*inṭalaqā*" (i.e., Qur'an 18:71, 18:74, 18:77), which means that they both proceeded or traveled.[18] However, the root of the word is "*ṭalaq*," which shares the same root as divorce (*ṭalāq*).[19] According to the Qur'an, after the third divorce, the man and the woman may no longer reconcile with each other, unless the woman had married and divorced a different husband (i.e., Qur'an 2:229–230).[20]

According to the story of al-Khiḍr and Moses in those passages, they used the term "*inṭalaqā*" for each of their three journeys. After the third "*ṭalaq*" (travel or divorce), they separated without reconciliation, in accordance with the rules of divorce (*ṭalāq*) in the Islamic Sharīʿah, as per the Qur'an. This is perhaps a way that the Qur'an subtly introduces a spiritual message within it as part of its creative style. Conventional methods of exegesis would not provide us with such insights. Hence, the method of intertextual polysemy is not necessarily replacing conventional methods, but one that might complement it by providing innovative perspectives through understanding Muḥammad's state of mind and authorial intent within a linguistic approach, which is the only tangible method emphasized and sanctioned by the Qur'an.

Zechariah and a son[21]

Zechariah is made of two words put together, "*zakar*" and "*Yah*." In Hebrew, "*zakar*" means remember, male, or male organ, as it is cognate to the Arabic "*dhakar*." The word "*Yah*" means God (*Yahweh*). Hence, Zechariah means God has remembered or the remembrance of God. The chapter of Maryam in the Qur'an begins with the story of Zechariah using "*dhikr*" (remembrance) of God for his servant Zechariah (remembrance of God). "A reminder (*dhikr*) of the Mercy (*raḥmah*) of thy Lord unto His servant, Zachariah..."[22]

According to the Qur'an, God granted Zechariah a son. The term "*dhikr*" is related to the male organ. The term for mercy (*raḥmah*) shares the same root as womb (*raḥm*). What is the significance of this? To make a child, or create the human, the sperm fertilizes the ovula, and then it splits into a new creation. This means that the male organ (*dhakar*) flows with sperm that enters the womb (*raḥm*), just as the story of Zechariah starts in the above verse. This is a simple example of the use of intertextual polysemy in the Qur'an.

4

The Relationship Between the Qur'an and the Bible

There seems to be an apparent contradiction within the Qur'an, when one views traditional exegesis of the Qur'an from classical exegetes (*mufassirūn*) in their attempt to interpret the relationship between the Qur'an and the Bible. The assumption is that since Muḥammad's state of mind allows him to make creative associations, he not only made such associations within the Qur'an, but also between the Qur'an and the religious milieu of his time. In some instances, the Qur'an talks well of the Bible, including the Gospel[s][1] (e.g., Qur'an 5:47, 5:66, 5:68), while apparently attempting to have a distinct theology from Christianity, such as the notion of Jesus Begotten of God, according to the Gospel of John. Although this book argues that Muḥammad had experienced an abnormal psychological state of mind, his high intelligence protected him from mental illness so he would not have changed his ideas frantically. There does seem to be a change of style as the Qur'an progressed, as can be seen between early Makkan, later Makkan, and Madinan sūrahs. Also, the topics might have changed. However, there is no reason to think, in understanding its themes, that the Qur'an is not homogeneous. What I mean is that it seems if there was an intelligent Muḥammad, then he would not have had included contradictory statements. If there is an apparent contradiction, we might need to analyze these to further understand Muḥammad's intent, given his state of mind.

Why would the Qur'an ask Christians to follow the Gospel[s] (i.e., Qur'an 5:47) if the Qur'an opposes its theology? If we are to think that perhaps those were different periods of Muḥammad's message, then why did he not have the passages that speak well of the Gospel[s] struck from the Qur'an? Classical Muslims scholars attempted to make sense of this with the concept of abrogating and abrogated verses (*nāsikh wa mansūkh*), where latter verses have abrogated former verses that may contradict.[2] Perhaps this concept of abrogation is an easy way out of a more scholarly investigation of the apparent contradictions in the Qur'an. With an intelligent Muḥammad, who seems to be capable of making creative associations, it is highly unlikely that he would keep a Qur'an that contradicts itself. As such more investigation on these apparent contradictions needs to be made, and that is what the next chapter will show in its examples, where these apparent contradictions might be viewed with a different perspective using intertextual polysemy than that which may be obtained from classical exegetes. Perhaps Muḥammad was more creative in the precise usage of words in the Qur'an in an attempt to fully engage with the Bible.

Moch Ali shows some examples of how intertextuality in the polysemous and etymological usage of Abrahamic scriptures provides a linguistic understanding of the intended meanings of the words.[3] He has mainly used the Hebrew Bible and Aramaic Gospel for intertextuality and literary criticism with the Arabic Qur'an to identify the Semitic roots in the verses of the Qur'an that appear to be citing other scriptures. He considers the linguistic criticism of scriptures as a reference of their common origin and heritage of their sacred discourses. Gabriel Reynolds argues in *The Qur'ān and Its Biblical Subtext* that the Qur'an should not be interpreted through medieval commentaries (*tafsīr*) and biography (*sīrah*) of Muḥammad, but it should be interpreted through Jewish and Christian sources that pre-date the Qur'an.[4] Reuven Firestone also argues the same concept by stating, "In fact, it [the Qur'an] contains so many parallels with the Hebrew Bible and New Testament that it could not possibly exist without its scriptural predecessors as subtexts."[5] However these contemporary scholars are not unique in their view. Before them, John Wansbrough considered the Qur'an as a literary text independent from the historical context given to it by Islamic tradition.[6]

Other Western scholars such as Theodor Nöldeke, Tor Andrae, and Karl Ahrens examined influences of other religions on the Qur'an, and did not completely reject the use of historical literature from traditional medieval Muslim scholars. On the other hand, Wansbrough considered Islamic history as mentioned in traditional Qur'anic commentaries and biography (*sīrah*) of Muḥammad to be a reconstruction that evolved in post-Qur'anic Islam.[7] Hence, Islamic history is a later literary development. Wansbrough suggests that the Qur'an uses Biblical allusions and imagery for homiletical purposes, something that Reynolds argues fervently.[8] As a matter of academic debate, it does seem highly likely that the commentators (*mufassirūn*) attempt to fill in the gaps to make sense of the Qur'an, while this filling is plagued with assumptions and opinions rather than real facts. For example, in the Qur'anic passage of the crucifixion, the commentators (*mufassirūn*) had to fill the gap of what the Qur'an means by "but it appeared so unto them (*shubbiha lahum*)."[9] The *mufassirūn* had to find stories to fill this gap by suggesting that Jesus had one of his disciples look like him and take his place in the crucifixion, or otherwise it was Judas who betrayed him taking his likeness.[10] If these stories were facts, then the *mufassirūn* would not have brought up the differing opinions among Muslim narrators of what this passage means. These stories seem to have been developed later, and since the *mufassirūn* wrote various opinions on the subject, these are in themselves proof that the interpretations are no more than mere opinions.

Abraham Geiger revolutionized Western scholarship on Islam by looking at the various possible borrowings that Muḥammad had made from earlier faiths, mainly Judaism.[11] He considered Muḥammad to have had Jewish informants who reported to him Biblical narratives through the midrash, which is the reasoning that Geiger gave for why some Qur'anic narratives deviate from the Biblical ones. Geiger was not the first orientalist to show the mentorship Muḥammad had from Jewish informants who narrated to him Biblical stories via the midrash. Petrus Alfonsi (d. 1140) also credited the Talmud as a likely source of the Qur'an and said that Muḥammad regarded the work of sectarian Jews and Christians, such as Samaritans, Nestorians, and Jacobites, to etch together the Qur'an.[12]

According to Geiger's ideology, Christianity and Islam have the concept that they supersede previous religions, while Judaism is original and was not influenced by previous faiths. Nonetheless, there might have been Ancient Egyptian influence in shaping Judaism, such as in the establishment of priesthood, circumcision,[13] and the prohibition of pork.[14] Therefore, one might say that Judaism borrowed from Ancient Egyptian religion in the way that Muḥammad borrowed from Judaism and Christianity. However, Steven Wasserstrom convincingly shows that the relationship between Judaism and Islam is far too complex to be simply called mere borrowing.[15] As Wasserstrom puts it, "The model of 'influence and borrowing,' by means of its over-emphasis on genetic origination, may in fact obscure insight into a mature interreligious sharing."[16] Zayd ibn Thābit, who traditionally is considered one of the Prophet's scribes and who wrote down the Qur'an, did, according to one tradition cited by Ibn Sa'd (d. 230/845), study Hebrew and/or Syriac, as well the Jewish texts,[17] thereby making this kind of interwoven textual allusion to Jewish literature in the Qur'an a possibility.[18]

Ever since Geiger, the main position that Western scholars have taken on Islam is that Muḥammad had borrowed concepts from earlier faiths and sewed them together into a new religion and jurisprudence. Western scholars became obsessed with the so-called borrowing that Muḥammad had allegedly made from earlier religions. Torrey continued to argue the borrowing of Muḥammad from Judaism.[19] Jeffery, for example, gives us the view that it is not only the concepts that were possibly borrowed, but that the Arabic terms in the Qur'an are actually borrowed from Hebrew or Aramaic terms.[20] Nonetheless, to assume that the Arabic language uses Hebrew or Aramaic loanwords is in itself naïve. Arabic, along with it sister languages, descend from a common Semitic ancestor. Hence, the similarities between the Arabic and Hebrew or Aramaic words should not always be viewed as a case of borrowing from one another, but that the terms evolved independently in each respective language. It is as if saying that the French *bonjour*, meaning good morning, is borrowed from the Italian *buongiorno*. Such a claim would be absurd. Since both French and Italian are Latin based, the terms evolved in each language independently from the common Latin ancestor. Catherine Pennacchio makes a note of the Arabic borrowing from Syriac, in which Jeffery's borrowing concept cannot be taken for granted without first applying modern linguistic analysis of the terms.[21]

Gordon Newby argues that Muḥammad's companions do occasionally ask for clarifications on the meaning of some terms, but when it comes to typical terms such as prayer (*ṣalāt*) they do not ask what the term means, but they are more prone to ask how to perform them.[22] Thus, it proves that the terms were understood by the Arab companions of Muḥammad, and therefore they cannot be considered as foreign words. Even if Muḥammad was aware of Hebrew and Aramaic, he nonetheless preached in Arabic. Since the Qur'an is a unique Arabic text, in which earlier Arabic literature or manuscripts are rare, then it is difficult to identify which terms were used in pre-Qur'anic Arabic; however, that does not necessarily mean that the Qur'an borrowed terms from other languages, where it can be more adequately considered that such terms may be in engagement with terms used in other religions. Richard Bell (d. 1952) described the possible influences that the religious communities in Arabia had on Muḥammad and the Qur'an.[23]

To call the similarities between Islam and other religions as mere borrowings is naïve. They can be more appropriately called engagement. It seems more likely that the Qur'an is engaging with other religions and part of their receptive audience. As such, the intertextuality does not mean borrowing but engagement. The Qur'an is not repeating like a parrot what is found in other religions, but it is part of the reception literature of the Bible. As Pregill puts it, "we cannot justifiably claim that the Quran [*sic*] is the product of a simple, direct dependence on narratives from the canonical Bible slavishly copied in a straightforward and unsophisticated fashion."[24]

There is no doubt that earlier religions influence a new one. The reason could be that a new religion must develop some sort of legitimacy in persuading followers from different backgrounds to convert. Judaism might have been influenced by Ancient Egyptian religions, as well as Sumerian myths, to name just two sources.[25] During the Israelite exile in Babylon, it seems likely that Judaism became influenced by Zoroastrianism in ideas such as dualism and eschatology, which did not necessarily exist in the Torah.[26] Hence, the Hebrew Bible evolved based on the various influences it had from the diverse religions that surrounded it. Christianity was heavily influenced by Judaism, in such a way that it could be considered an offshoot of it, while at the same time the early Church might have been also influenced by pagan folklore.[27] It would not at all be surprising that influences might have helped shape the Qur'an, but that would not necessarily constitute borrowing materials, as it would be more precisely portrayed as engaging with them.

Using other scriptures for Qur'anic exegesis may seem unconventional to a confessional audience, but it is not truly unwarranted. There are reasons to make such an argument, which would include the following:

1. The Qur'an refers to earlier scriptures and explicitly engages with them. Sometimes the Qur'an even requests that other scriptures be read while engaging with it, as in Qur'an 3:93 and 10:94. Therefore, to better understand what the Qur'an is referring to, it is imperative and intuitive to use the references from other scriptures to fully comprehend the meanings that the Qur'an attempts to convey.
2. Early Muslim scholars and exegetes, such as Muqātil ibn Sulaymān,[28] al-Thaʿlabī,[29] and others have used what is known as Israelite traditions (*isrāʾīliyyāt*), which would include Jewish and Christian sources.[30] Although there is criticism in using those traditions by exegetes,[31] such as Ibn Kathīr (d. 774/1373), it is not a shared criticism among all exegetes. Many exegetes have used traditions narrated by Wahb ibn Munabbih and Kaʿb al-Aḥbār, who could be considered the earliest Muslim Biblical scholars.[32] Also, the Bible had been heavily used for Qur'anic exegesis by al-Biqāʿī (d. 885/1480), which will be discussed in more detail later in this chapter.
3. The Qur'an considers itself verifying earlier scriptures (*muṣaddiq*) and a witness (*muhaymin*) to them (e.g., Qur'an 5:48). It is important to further understand the other scriptures and their relation to the Qur'anic engagement with them.

Although the method of interpreting the Qur'an not only through itself, but also through other scriptures may be nontraditional in some sense to Muslims, it is not without merit. Many of the Muslim exegetes, such as al-Rāzī (d. 606/1210) and Ibn

Kathīr have utilized Israelite traditions (*isrā'īliyyāt*) in their interpretations of the Qur'an, though not without self-criticism in doing so.[33] The Israelite traditions used by traditional Muslim commentators include the usage of Biblical stories or other sources of Jewish traditions, such as the Oral Law or Jewish and Christian pseudepigrapha and apocrypha.[34]

One of the earliest examples of the usage of "*isrā'īliyyāt*" are the narrations of Ka'b al-Aḥbār and Wahb ibn Munabbih. Ka'b was a Jewish religious teacher who converted to Islam within a decade of the death of Muḥammad, and therefore, naturally narrated many of the Jewish views that are discussed by the Qur'an. He was a contemporary of many of Muḥammad's companions. As such, many of the earlier commentators of the Qur'an have used his narrations about the Bible and Jewish traditions, such as al-Ṭabarī and Ibn Kathīr.

Although Ka'b al-Aḥbār and Wahb ibn Munabbih are celebrated for being two of the first Biblical scholars in Islam, their introduction of "*isrā'īliyyāt*" has brought a wide range of criticism.[35] Some Muslim scholars believe that the introduction of Jewish traditions into Islam undermines the purity of the Islamic message.[36] Ibn Taymiyyah has been suspicious of Qur'anic interpretation through "*isrā'īliyyāt*."[37] Comprehensive literature in the usage of "*isrā'īliyyāt*" in Qur'anic interpretation has been compiled by Na'nā'ah[38] and al-Dhahabī.[39]

Meir Kister has compiled a study of the prophetic tradition, "Narrate from the Children of Israel and there is no objection,"[40] as a permission to use "*isrā'īliyyāt*."[41] He states that the main arguments against "*isrā'īliyyāt*" among Muslim scholars are the credibility and reliability of the source, as scholars such as Zayn al-Dīn al-'Irāqī and Ibn al-Jawzī presume that many Jewish sources of "*isrā'īliyyāt*" are storytelling that, while providing good morals in their preaching and teaching styles, are fiction or caused by fabrication, and therefore they should not be used in the interpretation of the Qur'an.[42] However, these kinds of arguments shed some required understanding on the study of "*isrā'īliyyāt*." It is imperative to know the sources of such traditions, as to whether or not they are from earlier scriptures, Talmud, apocrypha, pseudepigrapha, or other sources.[43] In other words, not all of "*isrā'īliyyāt*" are supposed to be given equal weight for their credibility. To Muslims, a story from Jewish pseudepigrapha should not be considered equal in importance to a story found in scriptures. However, it is apparent that early and medieval Muslim scholars were perhaps not using the same methods on "*isrā'īliyyāt*" as they used in prophetic tradition to discern the chain of transmission (*sanad*) and content (*matn*) of *ḥadīth* to understand whether it is strong or weak.

Ibn Kathīr has utilized "*isrā'īliyyāt*" in his exegesis of the Qur'an, but not without any critical comments, following in the footsteps of his mentor Ibn Taymiyyah. As such, even when he brings forth the prophetic tradition that permits the usage of "*isrā'īliyyāt*," he continues to say that the "*isrā'īliyyāt*" are only meant to bear witness to the credibility of other Islamic sources, but they are not meant to be used independently as a reliable source.[44] In general, Ibn Kathīr categorizes "*isrā'īliyyāt*" into three classes, (i) those that attest the validity of the Islamic sources, (ii) those that contradict the Islamic sources, and (iii) those that neither attest nor contradict the Islamic sources.[45]

Abd Alfatah Twakkal shows that Ibn Kathīr's stance against "*isrā'īliyyāt*" not only displays his prejudice against what he believes are Jewish sources, but his belief that some earlier Islamic sources from Muḥammad's companions have been corrupted by Jewish influences.[46] An example of this is given in Ibn Kathīr's exegesis on Abraham's sacrificial son (i.e., Qur'an 37:102–107). As is evident from Ibn Kathīr's commentary, the debate within the Muslim community as to whether Abraham's sacrificial son was Ishmael or Isaac is an old one. He attempts to affirm that it was Ishmael.[47] Although he states that some Muslims, including prominent companions of Muḥammad, such as ʿAbdullah ibn Masʿūd, Ibn ʿAbbās, and ʿAlī ibn Abī Ṭālib, state that Isaac was the sacrificial son, he dismisses the companions' understanding as the effect of Jewish influences through Kaʿb al-Aḥbār, without sufficient evidence to support his own claim. Therefore, it remains his opinion to circumvent any sort of possible "*isrāʾīliyyāt*" in his assumptions. Al-Ṭabarī, on the other hand, shows in his exegesis that the sacrificial son is Isaac, with only few references to the possibility of him being Ishmael.[48] Since Ibn Kathīr is a later exegete, one might question whether the story relating Isaac as the sacrificial son is a possible Jewish influence or if Ishmael as the sacrificial son is a possible later Muslim addition that did not necessarily exist in early Islamic thought. This is especially important since the majority of the companions affirmed that it was Isaac, such as ʿAbdullah ibn Masʿūd, al-ʿAbbās, Ibn ʿAbbās, and ʿAlī ibn Abī Ṭālib according to majority of commentators,[49] including Abū Hurayra according to al-Samarqandī (d. 373/983)[50] and ʿUmar ibn al-Khaṭṭāb according to al-Rāzī,[51] al-Qurṭubī (d. 671/1273),[52] and al-Ṭabarānī (d. 360/970).[53] Reuven Firestone suggests that the early Islamic community understood the intended sacrificial son to be Isaac, but the later Muslim community wanted to distinguish themselves from Judeo-Christian influences.[54] We will come back to this point in the next chapter.

Twakkal continues to provide examples wherein Ibn Kathīr does not accept Kaʿb al-Aḥbār's interpretation due to its possible Jewish sources (*isrāʾīliyyāt*) in favor of his opinion.[55] In another example, Twakkal shows that Kaʿb was criticized by Ibn Masʿūd or Ibn ʿAbbās for saying that the heavens revolve around the shoulder of an angel, when he should have rightly said that it is God that revolves the heavens.[56] However, this brings forth a very important aspect in the study of "*isrāʾīliyyāt*." As stated earlier, it is important to understand further the source of "*isrāʾīliyyāt*," on whether the criticism is against Biblical literature or other forms of Jewish literature. The revolution of the heavens on the shoulder of an angel is neither based on Jewish scriptures nor is it from the Talmud or the Oral Law. However, there is a possibility that this tradition is from the Book of Enoch (i.e., Enoch 82), which does describe the revolution of the heavens and the stations of angels who are entrusted with the heavenly motions.[57] Evidently, Muslim commentators did consider "*isrāʾīliyyāt*" as a possible mode for Qur'anic interpretation and as such started the whole concept of using other scriptures to interpret the Qur'an.

Muḥammad and the Bible

The relationship between Muḥammad and the Bible is interesting to note. We understand this relationship mainly based on the Qur'anic passages that engage with the Bible, whether through reference or allusion. Since Muḥammad, in his psychological state of mind at the time, wanted to prove his legitimacy as a prophet of the same God as the Bible's, then it seems natural that he would talk about the Bible and allude to it. Along with his state of mind in making creative associations, we perhaps may be able to see Biblical allusions in the Qur'an. However, what is the Qur'an's main stance on the Bible? Is it positive as some Qur'anic passages state (e.g., Qur'an 5:66, 5:68) or is it negative, as some medieval Muslim scholars have argued on the concept of corruption (*taḥrīf*).[58] This would be a contradiction, and instead of taking the easy way out by arguing that the latter passages abrogated the former (assuming we even know the chronological order of the Qur'an), we need to further analyze such a contradiction.

The corruption of scriptures has always been a debatable topic among Muslim scholars, whether it involves the changing of the words of scriptures or altering the meanings (*taḥrīf al-ma'na*).[59] On the issue of "*taḥrīf*," a tradition attributed to Wahb ibn Munabbih relates, "The Torah and Gospel as revealed by God did not change a single letter, but they go astray in meaning and exegesis and books they were writing from themselves and saying this is from God and it is not from God. However, God's books are preserved and do not change."[60] Al-Bukhārī (d. 256/870) says in his *Ṣaḥīḥ* on the issue of "*taḥrīf*," "and not a person can remove a wording in a book of God's books, but they *yuḥarrifūnahu*, change its meaning to something other than its meaning."[61] Ibn Qayyim al-Jawziyyah (d. 751/1350), on his remark regarding Qur'an 3:93, suggests that the verse of stoning in the Torah would have been changed if the Jews could have changed it.[62] This is evidence not that the Torah is changed, but that its meanings might have been changed.[63] The idea that the Jews and Christians corrupted the text of scriptures is possibly a misunderstanding and a misreading of the Qur'anic intention.

At times the Qur'an states that Jews or the People of the Book make statements that may not necessarily be found in Biblical scriptures but rather in the Talmud (e.g., Qur'an 5:32).[64] The Talmud gives a rabbinic commentary on Biblical scriptures, and it may further allow an understanding of Qur'anic statements and arguments about Jews or the People of the Book.[65] Besides, the use of the Bible to further understand the Qur'an is not simply based on the prophetic tradition (*ḥadīth*) that permits it, "*Ḥaddithū 'an banī Isrā'īl wa la ḥaraj* (Narrate from the Children of Israel and there is no objection),"[66] but it is also stated clearly in the Qur'an in two separate but identical verses: "We sent no messengers before thee, save men unto whom We revealed—ask the people of the Reminder, if you know not. . ."[67]

Some medieval Muslim scholars have used the above verses as an indication by the Qur'an that they should seek the opinions of Islamic scholars on issues that they do not understand.[68] However, it seems that it actually requires people to ask the People of the Book if they do not have knowledge about the stories of the prophets that came before Muḥammad. This seems a possibility in Qur'an 16:43–44, as it describes the term "*dhikr*" to be the "*bayyināt*" and "*zubur*," which would mean that "*al-dhikr*" would also include the Psalms. The consensus of Muslim exegetes of various sects, such as al-Ṭabarī,[69] Ibn Kathīr,[70] al-Qurṭubī,[71] al-Rāzī,[72] al-Ṭabarsī[73] and many others, is that these verses provide an indication that one should ask the People of the Book about the prophets that came before Muḥammad. Therefore, it is not simply a prophetic tradition that permits it, but the Qur'an itself also expects it from its audience to use Biblical literature to further understand the Qur'an.

Burhān al-Dīn Al-Biqāʿī, a fifteenth-century CE Muslim scholar, used the Bible to interpret the Qurʾan and wrote an extensive treatise in defense of his approach called *al-Aqwāl al-qawīmah fī ḥukm al-naql min al-kutub al-qadīmah* (*The Just Sayings in the Ruling Regarding Quoting from Ancient Books*).[74] Walid Saleh has made a study of al-Biqāʿī's defense of using the Bible to interpret the Qurʾan.[75] In al-Biqāʿī's time, his thought on using the Bible to interpret the Qurʾan was a revolutionary idea that was controversial among his contemporary scholars.[76] Many Muslim scholars have quoted the Bible in an attempt to prove it wrong or to prove the prophecies in favor of Muḥammad.[77] However, al-Biqāʿī did not use it as such polemical perspective. He extensively quoted the Bible as part of his Qurʾanic exegesis, which is perhaps the first time that a Muslim scholar used the Bible extensively for exegesis,[78] beyond those done by Wahb ibn Munabbih and Kaʿb al-Aḥbār. Not only did he quote the Bible, but he did so without paraphrasing, which was the usual method used by other Muslim scholars in their polemic writings.[79] Many of his opponents considered the usage of the Bible to interpret the Qurʾan to be sacrilegious. However, al-Biqāʿī was able to get the support of *muftīs* and judges of Cairo,[80] where he lived.[81]

Although al-Biqāʿī extensively quotes the Bible in his interpretation of the Qurʾan, he was not very sympathetic to the Jewish and Christian faiths.[82] However, he did not find it paradoxical to use the Bible, while not necessarily accepting Jewish and Christian dogmas. In al-Biqāʿī's first defensive argument for using the Bible to interpret the Qurʾan, he uses the Qurʾanic text that sanctions such actions:[83] "All (*kul*) "*al-ṭaʿām*" (food)[84] was lawful unto the Children of Israel, save what Israel had forbidden for himself, before the Torah was sent down. Say, 'Bring the Torah and recite it, if you are truthful.'"[85]

Al-Biqāʿī continues to argue that just as polemics quote the Bible, the interpreter could also do the same.[86] As is evident from the preface of his treatise, al-Biqāʿī did not want to defend his usage of the Bible to interpret the Qurʾan, because he found it unnecessary. Al-Biqāʿī believes that the legitimacy of this use is obvious from the Qurʾan and early Islamic history, in which the Bible was quoted.[87]

In his arguments, al-Biqāʿī shows how his works were well received by many contemporary scholars. He also compares his works with other very controversial works, such as the commentary on the Qurʾan of al-Zamakhsharī, who was a Muʿtazalite, Ismāʿīlī works like the *Epistles of the Pure Brethren* (*Rasāʾil ikhwān al-ṣafāʾ*), and Ibn ʿArabī's *Bezels of Wisdom* (*Fuṣūṣ al-ḥikam*), which he considers were not as severely attacked as his own, though may be considered heretical in nature.[88] He finds it unfair, therefore, that his works are attacked, which he believes is based purely on personal grudges against him. Besides using the Qurʾanic verse in his argument against those who opposed him, he even cites prophetic tradition, in which Muḥammad requested the Jews to bring forth the Torah and judged them in accordance with the Torah, such as the dispute case of the punishment for adultery, as recorded by many of the prominent commentators of the Qurʾan for the circumstances of revelation (*asbāb al-nuzūl*) of the following Qurʾanic verses:[89] "And how is it that they come to thee for judgment, when they have the Torah, wherein is God's Judgment? Yet even after that, they turn their backs. . ."[90]

Al-Biqāʿī considers that since the Qurʾan ordains using the Bible, and Muḥammad practiced that which is ordained in the Qurʾan, then the primary sources of the legal texts of Islam have made such a method legally binding.[91] Therefore, he argues that it is not up to any scholar to shed doubt on the legality of quoting the Bible. Al-Biqāʿī continues to use arguments from other scholars that support his use of the Bible, as Walid Saleh states:

> The first scholar whom al-Biqāʿī quotes is Muḥammad b. Yūsuf al-Kirmānī (d. 786/1384), one of the commentators on the collection of ḥadīth by al-Bukhārī (the most authoritative hadith collection in the Sunnī tradition). Al-Kirmānī is quoted as saying that Muslims were simply in no position to determine what was corrupted of the Jewish and Christian scriptures and what was not. Thus Muslims should not reject them for fear they might be rejecting the Word of God.[92]

Al-Biqāʿī continues to argue in favor of Muslims using the Bible, because from a legalist perspective there are definitely parts of the Bible that are not corrupted; at the very least, the Qur'an can be used as a comparative tool to judge the authenticity of the Bible. He also brings up the subject of the authenticity and corruption of the Bible. He states that there exists a wide range of debate that can be divided into four camps, (i) all of the Bible is corrupt, (ii) the majority of the Bible is corrupt, (iii) a few parts of the Bible are corrupt, and (iv) none of the Bible is corrupt, but the followers simply misinterpreted parts thereof (*taḥrīf al-maʿna*).[93] Al-Biqāʿī states that followers of the first camp are arrogant and excessive and in obvious contradiction of the Qur'an and Sunnah.[94] He argues against the second camp in a similar manner.[95] He finds himself in the third camp in which he states that al-Shāfiʿī (d. 204/820) also belongs to, as well as the prominent scholar Ibn Ḥazm (d. 456/1064).[96] As many of his contemporary opponents argued in accordance with jurist consensus (*ijmāʿ*) to prohibit reading the Bible, he argues that because many of the prominent early and contemporary Muslim scholars of his time used the Bible, especially in their polemic treatises, then using the Bible should be permissible.[97] He even states that although the Qur'an is used as the criterion to compare the authenticity of the Bible, on matters of which the Qur'an is silent it would still be permissible to accept the Biblical text, as denying it could bring an error against the Muslim, who might be denying the words of God.[98] He categorizes Biblical texts into three groups (i) those that are confirmed by the Qur'an may be quoted as proof (*ḥujjah*) of the Qur'an, (ii) those whose status cannot be determined may be quoted for purposes of exalting (*targhīb*) the wisdom of the Bible, and (iii) fabricated materials, which may be quoted to caution people against it.[99] In actuality, al-Biqāʿī states that he avoided Jewish and Christian lore (*isrāʾīliyyāt*) in his method of Qur'anic interpretation, which many others before him had actually introduced. He limited himself only to the use of the Bible. Al-Biqāʿī confirms that he quotes God whenever he quotes from the Bible. He compares the Bible with divine traditions (*ḥadīth qudsī*) that have come through narrations (*tawātur*).[100] He even mentions that the whole prophetic tradition cannot be considered fully reliable, and yet jurists use it to obtain legal edicts. Therefore, Saleh deduces that al-Biqāʿī may have considered the Bible to be as reliable as prophetic tradition, which is not without corruption, though still a basis of Islamic legal rulings.[101]

Besides al-Biqāʿī's controversies with contemporaries in using the Bible to interpret the Qur'an, he was a very controversial figure who was critical of many of the Sufi works, especially in his statements against the Sufi poet Ibn al-Fāriḍ (d. 632/1235), which caused him to go into self-exile in Damascus. Similarly, he was very critical of al-Ghazālī's works and philosophy, while al-Ghazālī also belonged to the Shāfiʿī school of jurisprudence.[102] Guo has discussed more controversies between al-Biqāʿī and Sufis in his chronicle of al-Biqāʿī.[103] Chodkiewicz has also portrayed al-Biqāʿī's strong opposition against Ibn ʿArabī.[104]

Muḥammad and exclusivism and corruption (*taḥrīf*)

Exclusivism or not?

The major proof within the Qur'an that exclusivists use is the passage that states that God only accepts "*islām*" as a religion.[105] This verse, which apparently preaches exclusivism, is actually quite interesting because it is explicitly instilled with the belief of other scriptures:

> 83 Do they seek other than God's religion, while whosoever is in the heavens and on the earth submits (*aslam*) to Him, willingly or unwillingly, and unto Him they will be returned? 84 Say, "We believe in God and what has been sent down upon us, and in what was sent down upon Abraham, Ishmael, Isaac, Jacob, and the Tribes, and in what Moses, Jesus, and the prophets were given from their Lord. We make no distinction among any of them, and unto Him we submit (*muslimūn*)." 85 Whosoever seeks a religion other than *islām* (submission), it shall not be accepted of him, and in the Hereafter he shall be among the losers.[106]

Although these passages seem explicit in believing in other scriptures, and therefore, we can infer the ability to use them for Qur'anic interpretation, exclusivists will argue the concept that other scriptures have been corrupted (*taḥrīf*). Hence, I will first argue the definition of "*muslim*" in the Qur'an, and then I will argue the concept of corruption (*taḥrīf*) to make my case that the use of other scriptures to interpret the Qur'an is not only allowable, according to the Qur'an, but it expects it from its audience.

Many Muslim scholars and Qur'anic commentators, as shown earlier, understand the term "*islām*" in the Qur'an, as the religion known today as "Islam," which is an understandably obvious interpretation. However, is the Qur'an defining "*islām*" as the message and dispensation of the religion known as "Islam," or does the Qur'an provide a different understanding for the term "*islām*?"[107] Ibn Ḥazm brings the interpretation of "*islām*" in Qur'an 3:85 as the rituals and beliefs that are associated with the religion known as Islam.[108] On defining "*islām*," he states that it requires complete submission to God.[109] He assumes that the term "*islām*" in the Qur'an may hold various meanings, where sometimes it is different than "*īmān*" (faith),[110] which is based on Qur'an 49:14, while at other times he suggests that it is the same as "*īmān*" (faith), which is based on Qur'an 49:17.[111] However, to think that the Qur'an uses different meanings for the same term only two verses apart may seem unusual, unless Ibn Ḥazm is actually extrapolating the meaning even though it should not be so.

The term "*islām*" is mentioned in several places in the Qur'an (e.g., Qur'an 3:19, 3:85, 5:3, 6:125, 39:22, 61:7). The Qur'an also uses terms that are rooted in the word "*islām*," such as "*muslim*," "*aslam*," or other words from the same root while not necessarily being interpreted as the followers of the religion known today as Islam. Scholars, such as Robson, define the term "*islām*" from a broader sense as the resignation to God, and not simply the religion known today as Islam.[112] Izutsu defines the terms "*islām*" and "*muslim*" in the Qur'an as the surrender to God.[113]

The Salafist viewpoint of exclusivism may be traced back to Ibn ʿAbdulwahhāb's (d. 1206/1792) writings on Qur'an 3:85. In one of his letters, Ibn ʿAbdulwahhāb states that the meaning of "*islām*" in this verse is the religion known today as Islam, which has five main pillars:[114] to witness there is only one God and that Muḥammad is His messenger, to pray five times a day toward Makkah, to give alms, to fast during the month of Ramadan, and to make the pilgrimage once in a lifetime, if capable. Ibn ʿAbdulwahhāb, in *Kashf al-Shubuhāt*, defines the term "*islām*" in Qur'an 3:85 as monotheism (*tawḥīd*).[115] This definition is even more disturbing because according to Ibn ʿAbdulwahhāb's theology, he usually refers to his form of Islam as "*tawḥīd*," which brings any other Islamic form outside his definition of "*islām*." His writings make his followers exclusivists to the point that they may reject any other interpretation of Islam.[116]

The term "*islām*" has various meanings.[117] Among the various meanings, it means to submit and to surrender.[118] It also means stairways and peace.[119] The Qur'an calls Abraham a *muslim*, and that Abraham taught that to his children and his children's children (e.g., Qur'an 2:127–133, 4:125, 22:78, 37:103). What made Abraham a *muslim*? Was it that he had done all the five pillars of Islam that would have made him a *muslim*? It cannot be. He was a *muslim* even before he knew where the Kaʿbah in Makkah is. Therefore, the criteria that made him a *muslim* does not necessarily move in parallel with the religion known today as Islam.

Noah is considered a *muslim*, according to the Qur'an (i.e., Qur'an 10:72). The Qur'an also notes that the sorcerers of Moses, once they were defeated in a contest with him, became *muslims* (i.e., Qur'an 7:126). The Qur'an says that Moses requested the Children of Israel to become *muslims* (i.e., Qur'an 10:84). The Qur'an also shows that when Pharaoh was drowning, he too declared to have become a *muslim*, while the Qur'an then shows that it was only when his drowning was imminent did he realize the true God (i.e., Qur'an 10:90–92). Even when Solomon sends a message to the Queen of Sheba, he requests her and her people to become *muslims* (i.e., Qur'an 27:31, 27:38, 27:42, 27:44). Lot's household is even called by the Qur'an a *muslim* household (i.e., Qur'an 51:36). According to the Qur'an, Jesus' disciples call themselves *muslims* (i.e., Qur'an 3:52, 5:111). The Qur'an also shows that the religion of God is for people to become *muslims*, since everyone in the heavens and the earth is a *muslim*, willingly or unwillingly (i.e., Qur'an 3:83). The Qur'an also calls all the prophets to the Children of Israel *muslims* (i.e., Qur'an 5:44). Ibn Taymiyyah, in his statements on Qur'an 3:85, makes note that all religions and prophets were in the guise of "*islām*."[120] He defines the term "*islām*" as sincerity to God combined with generosity and good works with faith, in which Ibn Taymiyyah quotes a passage in Qur'an 2:62 that accepts other religions when describing the term "*islām*" in Qur'an 3:85.[121] It is evident that Ibn Taymiyyah in his *al-Īmān* does not consider Qur'an 3:85 abrogating Qur'an 2:62.[122] Nonetheless, Ibn Taymiyyah does state that the term "*islām*" in Qur'an 3:85 means the good works and not just faith.[123] It seems Ibn Taymiyyah in here agrees with the Epistle of James that faith without works is dead (i.e., James 2:14–26).

Ibn Abī al-'Izz (d. 792/1390) in his famous *Sharḥ al-'aqīdah al-ṭaḥāwiyyah* depicts that the term "*islām*" in Qur'an 3:85 does not mean the religion known today as Islam.[124] He narrates the prophetic tradition (*ḥadīth*), "We the prophets are of one religion."[125] Ibn Abī al-'Izz continues to state that the religion of "*islām*" in Qur'an 3:85 is general in every age, but the laws (revealed to each prophet) are different, in which he quotes Qur'an 5:48.[126] He states that the religion (of *islām*) are the laws given to people in the tongues of messengers.[127] Hence, he does not interpret the term "*islām*" in Qur'an 3:85 as the religion known today as Islam, but the religion of every prophet and messenger. On the one hand, we have scholars like Ibn Abī al-'Izz who prove their arguments from the Qur'an, while on the other we have scholars like Shams al-Dīn al-Safārīnī (d. 1188/1774), who state that Qur'an 3:85 refers to the religion known today as Islam. Their argument is that this passage abrogates all others that show pluralism without sufficient Qur'anic evidence for such an argument.[128]

When looking at it from an overall perspective, it seems obvious that the term for *muslim* used in the Qur'an does not necessarily mean a follower of the religion known today as Islam. Fred Donner suggests that the Qur'anic terms "*islām*" and "*muslim*" are different than how they later became associated with the current distinct religion of Islam.[129] The term for *muslim* used in the Qur'an may be understood as anyone who has surrendered his soul to God and submitted to the Will of God. If the Qur'an uses the term for *muslim* so loosely to mean anyone who has surrendered to God, why would some Qur'anic scholars and commentators insist that the term "*islām*" in the Qur'an specifically refers to the religion known today as Islam? Since the terms "*islām*" and "*muslim*" come from the same root word and carry the same meanings, and since a *muslim* is one who has espoused "*islām*," then it is possible that the term "*islām*" would be applicable to anyone who surrenders to God. Therefore, it may not necessarily be defined as the religion known today as Islam.

Abraham, the patriarchs, the prophets, etc. are called *muslims* by the Qur'an, because seemingly they have all surrendered to the Will of God. Therefore, their religion may be considered as "*islām*." The Qur'an does not consider itself ushering a new religion, but it considers itself as a reformation in an attempt to resurrect the same pure religion of Abraham (e.g., Qur'an 2:130–136, 3:95, 4:125, 6:161–163, 16:123, 22:78). However, what made Abraham and the prophets *muslims*? The Islamic laws and method of prayers and fasting are not the same as those of the previous religions. The Qur'an even shows that there are differences in the divine laws prescribed to different people (i.e., Qur'an 5:48), as Ibn Abī al-'Izz argues.[130] Since the religion known today as Islam is not what the Qur'an intended to be interpreted for the term *muslim* in the Qur'an, then consequently, the term "*islām*" in the Qur'an may not necessarily be interpreted as the religion known today as Islam either. There needs to be no double standard in defining the terms "*islām*" and "*muslim*" in the Qur'an, from a grammatical and linguistic point of view.

The verses in the Qur'an that are referred to as proof of an exclusivist ideology (i.e., Qur'an 3:19, 3:85) seem to be misinterpreted by some scholars and commentators if they define it specifically as the religion known as Islam, which is a definition that perhaps was not espoused by the early Muslim community.[131] The term *muslim* does not necessarily mean followers of Islam as known today, but the Qur'an uses it generally to mean those who have surrendered and resigned to the Will of God. There is no reason to define "*islām*" from a textual or contextual basis as the religion known today as Islam, when the Qur'an uses it in a more generic perspective.

If one assumes that the Qur'an preaches an exclusivist ideology, then various passages will seem to oppose such an understanding. Diversity, as a topic, is referred to in the Qur'an, such as that in the following verse: "O humankind![132] Truly We divided (created)[133] you from a male and a female, and We made you peoples and tribes that you may come to know one another. Surely the most noble of you before God are the most reverent of you. Truly God is Knowing, Aware."[134]

In interpreting this verse, Asani states, "the divine purpose underlying the creation of human diversity is to foster knowledge and understanding, to promote harmony and cooperation among peoples."[135] Classical commentators (*mufassirūn*) interpret this verse mainly on the theme of marriage and knowing ancestral descent,[136] which is an understanding based on the verse opening with the issue that people are divided male and female. However, even if we do consider this verse to be discussing diversity, it seems more appropriate to recognize that it discusses ethnic diversity rather than religious diversity. As such, we cannot necessarily use it to portray religious pluralism in the Qur'an. However, when it comes to discuss religious issues with the People of the Book,[137] the Qur'an seems to offer a pluralist view: "And dispute not with the People of the Book, save in the most virtuous manner, unless it be those of them who have done wrong. And say, 'We believe in that which was sent down unto us and was sent down unto you; our God and your God are one, and unto Him are we submitters (*muslimūn*).'"[138]

The following passage in the Qur'an seems to portray a pluralist view without espousing the notion of exclusivism. It states that some of the People of the Book are believers: "You are the best community brought forth unto humankind,[139] enjoining right, forbidding wrong, and believing in God. And were the People of the Book to believe, that would be better for them. Among them are believers, but most of them are iniquitous."[140] In this verse, the Qur'an distinguishes between those who are believers from those who are perverted. It does not make them all equal. Classical exegetes, however, identify the believers among the People of the Book as those who convert to Islam.[141] The exegetes are making an assumption that the Qur'an here talks about converts, when there is nothing from the text that makes such a claim. The Qur'an continues to differentiate between the believers and unbelievers from among the People of the Book:

> 112 They shall be struck with abasement (*ḍuribat ʿalayhim al-dhillah*) wherever they are come upon, save by means of a rope from God and a rope from mankind. And they shall earn a burden of wrath from God, and they shall be struck with indigence (*wa bāʾū bi-ghaḍab min Allah wa ḍuribat ʿalayhim al-maskanah*). That is

because they used to disbelieve in God's signs and kill the prophets without right. That is for their having disobeyed and transgressed (*dhālika bi-annahum kānū yakfurūn bi-āyāt Allah wa-yaqtulūn al-anbiyā' bi-ghayr ḥaqq, dhālika bimā 'aṣaw wa-kānū ya'tadūn*). 113 They are not all alike. Among the People of the Book is an upright community who recite God's signs in the watches of the night, while they prostrate. 114 They believe in God and the Last Day, enjoin right and forbid wrong, and hasten unto good deeds. And they are among the righteous. 115 Whatsoever good they do, they will not be denied it. And God knows the reverent.[142]

The above passages also do not provide any hints that it is meant for converts from other faiths to Islam. Actually, it defines faith as in the belief in God and the Last Day. It does not at all show that the People of the Book need to even believe in Muḥammad per se. There is another passage with a strong relationship to the above with intertextuality of the parallel keywords and terms used in both:

61 And when you said, "O Moses, we shall not endure one food, so call upon your Lord for us, that He may bring forth for us some of what the earth grows: its herbs, its cucumbers, its garlic, its lentils, its onions." He said, "Would you substitute what is lesser for what is better? Go down to a town, and you will have what you ask for." So they were struck with abasement and poverty, and earned a burden of wrath from God. That is because they disbelieved in the signs of God, and killed the prophets without right. That is because they disobeyed, and were transgressors (*wa-ḍuribat 'alayhim al-dhillah wal-maskanah wa-bā'ū bi-ghaḍab min Allah, dhālika bi-annahum kānū yakfurūn bi-āyāt Allah wa-yaqtulūn al-nabiyyīn bi-ghayr al-ḥaqq, dhālika bimā 'aṣaw wa-kānū ya'tadūn*). 62 Truly those who believe, and those who are Jews, and the Christians, and the Sabeans—whosoever believes in God and the Last Day and works righteousness shall have their reward with their Lord. No fear shall come upon them, nor shall they grieve.[143]

Clearly, the keywords in Qur'an 3:112 are parallel to and almost verbatim to the same keywords in the end of Qur'an 2:61. Qur'an 2:62 shows that Jews, Christians, and the Sabians, who believe in God and the Last Day and work righteousness (parallel to Qur'an 2:114) are acceptable and will not be rejected. This passage is related to even another:

68 Say, "O People of the Book! You stand on naught till you observe (*tuqīmū*) the Torah and the Gospel, and that which has been sent down unto you from your Lord." Surely that which has been sent down unto thee from thy Lord will increase many of them in rebellion and disbelief. So grieve not for disbelieving people. 69 Truly those who believe, and those who are Jews, and the Sabeans, and the Christians—whosoever believes in God and the Last Day and works righteousness, no fear shall come upon them, nor shall they grieve. 70 We indeed made a covenant with the Children of Israel, and sent messengers unto them. Whensoever a messenger brought them what their souls did not desire, some they would deny and some they would slay.[144]

It is clear that Qur'an 5:69 is parallel to Qur'an 2:62. There are other points of intertextuality around these two passages. For example, Qur'an 5:60 and 2:65 both talk about those who have become apes. Also, Qur'an 5:70 and 2:63 both refer to the covenant (*mīthāq*) that God had made with the Children of Israel.[145] Another point of intertextuality between these verses is with the passages in the Qur'an that reject exclusivism of the Jews and Christians:

> [111] And they said, "None will enter the Garden unless he be a Jew or a Christian." Those are their hopes. Say, "Bring your proof, if you are truthful." [112] Nay, whosoever submits his face (*aslam wajhahu*) to God, while being virtuous, shall have his reward with his Lord. No fear shall come upon them; nor shall they grieve. [113] The Jews say, "The Christians stand on nothing," and the Christians say, "The Jews stand on nothing," though they recite the Book. Likewise, did those who know not speak words like theirs. God will judge between them on the Day of Resurrection concerning that wherein they differed.[146]

The above verses reject the exclusivist beliefs that some Jews or Christians may advocate. Instead, the Qur'an continues to state that anyone who submits to God using the term "*aslam*," which shares its root with the term "*islām*," and does righteousness, shall neither fear nor grieve, using the same terminology used in Qur'an 2:62 and 5:69.[147] Hence, one may interpolate that the believers, the Jews, the Christians, and the Sabians who surrender to God and do righteousness are within the fold of the term "*islām*," and therefore, they shall neither fear nor grieve. Qur'an 2:113 also continues to reject the notion that Christians have nothing or that the Jews have nothing. It states that those who have no knowledge agree to such a concept. This implies that those who know would not say that the Jews have nothing or that the Christians have nothing. Therefore, the Jews and the Christians are onto something when it comes to their scriptures, in which the Qur'an continues to state the following verse: "Those unto whom We have given the Book and who recite it as it should be recited are they who believe in it. And whosoever does not believe in it, they are the losers."[148]

The above verse would not be stated if the scriptures of the Jews and Christians are corrupted. Also, another point of intertextuality between Qur'an 2:111–113 and Qur'an 5:68–70 is the terms for "nothing" (*laysat 'ala shay'*). Qur'an 2:113 shows that Christians claim that the Jews stand on nothing while the Jews claim that the Christians stand on nothing, while they both read the scripture. Qur'an 5:68 indicates that neither the Jews nor the Christians are on anything (*lastum 'ala shay'*), unless they adhere to the Torah and the Gospel[s]. It must be noted that the Qur'an here does not show any indication that the Jews and Christians must adhere to the Qur'an, but they must adhere to their scriptures respectively. Even before Qur'an 5:68, the Qur'an mentions that the Jews and Christians needed to adhere to their scriptures: "Had they observed (*aqāmū*) the Torah and the Gospel and that which was sent down unto them from their Lord, they would surely have received nourishment from above them and from beneath their feet. There is a moderate community among them; but as for many of them, evil is that which they do!"[149]

Qur'an 5:66 and 5:68 also use the terms "*aqāmū*" and "*tuqīmū*" respectively, which will be seen as significant in the discussion in the next section that describes the term "*taḥrīf*." The significance of these terms, as will be seen, is that "*taḥrīf*" means bent or crooked, as in "*inḥirāf*" or "*munḥarif*,"[150] while the term "*tuqīmū*" means to straighten.[151] Hence, the terms are antonyms, and as such, the Qur'an perhaps requires the Jews and Christians not to bend and sway away from the Torah and Gospel, but instead to straighten up and stand fast upon them.

Corruption (*taḥrīf*) of scriptures

Another issue that brings forth the exclusivism in Islam is due to the understanding by some early Muslim scholars that previous scriptures have been corrupted.[152] Ṣāliḥ al-Hāshimī (d. 668/1269) argues incessantly on the issue of "*taḥrīf*" in the Bible in *Takhjīl man ḥarraf al-tawrāt wal-injīl*, but it is filled with bias against Jewish and Christian dogma.[153] The Muslim concept of the corruption of the Bible is old. In the eighth century CE, it is reported that the Abbasid caliph al-Mahdī stated that the corruption of the Bible is common knowledge during his debate with the Nestorian patriarch Timothy I.[154] However, there is a clear division between what is common knowledge in the eighth century CE and what is actually based on the Qur'an, during the time of Muḥammad. There is a *ḥadīth* that is not attributed to the Prophet, but stated by Ibn ʿAbbās, as follows:

> O community of Muslims, how do you ask the People of the Book and your book which was revealed to His Prophet blessings and peace be upon him is a newest report about God. You read a book that has not been distorted, but the People of the Book, as God related to you, exchange that which God wrote, changing the book with their hands. They said it is from God to traffic with it for a miserable price. Would not the knowledge that has come to you stop you from asking them? No, by God we have never seen one of them asking about what has been revealed to you.[155]

This declaration contradicts the Qur'an.[156] Ibn ʿAbbās states that Muslims should not ask the People of the Book. In contrast, the Qur'an requires that the People of the Book be asked about previous prophets (i.e., Qur'an 16:43–44, 21:7). The context of the Qur'an is apparent: it refers to the People of the Book who need to be asked about previous prophets, and classical exegetes, such as al-Ṭabarī, agree.[157]

There are various schools among medieval Muslim scholars on the issue of corruption (*taḥrīf*) of scriptures: (i) those who believe that the whole text is corrupted, (ii) those who believe that part of the text is corrupted, and (iii) those who believe that the words remain intact and corruption is only in the meanings.[158] Traditionally, the term "*taḥrīf*" is divided between "*taḥrīf al-lafẓ*" (distortion in words) and "*taḥrīf al-maʿna*" (distortion in meaning). Tarakci and Sayar consider that the earliest usage of the term in Islam is "*taḥrīf al-maʿna*" (distortion in meaning).[159] *Al-Radd al-jamīl*, attributed to al-Ghazālī,[160] uses the concept of distortion in meaning when explaining "*taḥrīf*."[161]

The concept of misinterpreting scriptures is not new with the advent of the Qur'an. Early Christians in general and particularly Syrians considered the Jews to be heretics who completely misinterpreted the Hebrew Bible.[162] Reynolds suggests that Syriac Fathers were concerned with spiritual interpretations of the Hebrew Bible for purposes of typology.[163] Since the Jews did not interpret the Hebrew Bible in the same way, they would have accused them of misinterpretation. Reynolds continues with examples showing how Christians during pre-Islam accused the Jews of misinterpreting the Hebrew Bible.[164] Perhaps it is for that reason Qur'an 2:113 states that the Jews accuse the Christians to stand on nothing, while the Christians accuse the Jews to stand on nothing, although they are reading the same scripture. Consequently, it must be noted that the Christians did not necessarily accuse Jews of changing the words in scriptures but simply misinterpreting them, which would adhere to the definition of "*taḥrīf al-maʿna*." Al-Ṭabarī implies that corruption of scriptures is more likely in the meaning of the words and not necessarily the changing of the words.[165]

The term "*yuḥarrifūn*" is mentioned four times in the Qur'an (i.e., Qur'an 2:75, 4:46, 5:13, 5:41). According to *Lisān al-ʿarab*, the term "*taḥrīf*" means the distortion of meaning.[166] From a linguistic point of view, the term "*taḥrīf*" does not mean changing the words of scriptures, but being crooked like "*inḥirāf*,"[167] as also stated by al-Ṭabarī.[168] Changing the words for another is known as "*tabdīl*." The Qur'an specifically says that the words of God cannot be changed by people, and it may only be God who has such authority (e.g., Qur'an 10:15, 16:101). In neither of these Qur'anic verses does it show that God had changed the previous revelations. Some traditional exegetes do not even show that such an interpretation was considered for these two verses.[169]

Many Muslims believe that the words of the Qur'an are preserved and cannot be changed, due to an explicit promise (i.e., Qur'an 15:9). However, even in that promise, the term used for scripture, which classical Muslim exegetes, such as al-Ṭabarī and al-Ṭabarsī, interpret as the Qur'an, is "*al-dhikr*."[170] Although the Qur'an uses this term many times to refer to itself, it does use this term several times to mean other scriptures as well, such as the Torah (e.g., Qur'an 16:43–44, 21:7, 21:105).[171] According to the Qur'an, no one can change (*tabdīl*) God's words.

> Surely messengers were denied before thee, and they bore patiently their being denied and persecuted till Our help came to them. None alters (*mubaddil*) the Words of God, and there has already come unto thee some tidings of the messengers.[172]
>
> The Word of thy Lord is fulfilled in truth and justice. None alters (*mubaddil*) His Words, and He is the Hearing, the Knowing.[173]
>
> For them are glad tidings in the life of this world and in the Hereafter. There is no altering (*tabdīl*) the Words of God. That is the great triumph.[174]
>
> Recite that which has been revealed unto thee from the Book of thy Lord. None alters (*mubaddil*) His Words. And thou wilt find no refuge apart from Him.[175]

The Qur'an even shows that there were attempts to change the words of God, but those attempts have met with failure. "Those who stayed behind will say when you set out to capture spoils, 'Let us follow you.' They desire to change (*yubaddilū*) the Word of

God. Say, 'You will not follow us; thus has God said before.' Then they will say, 'Nay, but you are jealous of us.' Nay, but they have not understood, save a little."[176]

Since the words of God cannot be changed (*tabdīl*), when the Qur'an speaks of the People of the Book, it uses the term "*taḥrīf*." Linguistically, the term "*taḥrīf*" does not mean changing the words, but more precisely, it is the antonym of being upright, which is being crooked (*munḥarif*). Perhaps this means that the words are kept unchanged, but their meanings are interpreted in a crooked manner. Also, when the Qur'an speaks of Jews "*yuḥarrifūn*," it does not generalize it to all the Jews, but specifies that some of the Jews resort to that:

> Do you hope, then, that they will believe you, seeing that a party of them would hear the Word of God and then distort it (*yuḥarrifūn*) after they had understood it, knowingly?[177]
>
> Among those who are Jews are those who distort (*yuḥarrifūn*) of the word, and say, "We hear and disobey," and "Hear, as one who hears not!" and "Attend to us!" twisting their tongues and disparaging religion. And had they said, "We hear and obey" and "Listen" and "Regard us," it would have been better for them and more proper. But God cursed them for their disbelief, so they believe not, save a few.[178]
>
> Then for their breaking of their covenant, We cursed them and hardened their hearts. They distort (*yuḥarrifūn*) the Word, and have forgotten part of that whereof they were reminded. Thou wilt not cease to discover their treachery, from all save a few of them. So pardon them, and forbear. Truly God loves the virtuous.[179]
>
> O Messenger! Let them not grieve thee, those who hasten unto disbelief, those who say, "We believe" with their mouths, while their hearts believe not, and those who are Jews, who listen to lies and to others who have not come to thee. They distort (*yuḥarrifūn*) the word, saying, "If you are given this, then take it, but if you are not given this, then beware!" For whomsoever God desires that he be tried, thou hast no power to avail him aught against God. They are those whose hearts God desired not to purify. Theirs is disgrace in this world, and in the Hereafter they shall have a great punishment.[180]

In all of the above instances, the Qur'an speaks of some of the Jews and not the Christians. Haggai Mazuz suggests that perhaps the Qur'anic accusation against some Jews is a reference to some sort of homiletic Talmudic interpretation of scriptures.[181] He states that there are at least seventy instances in which the Talmudic sages change one word or more to interpret Biblical verses in the Babylonian Talmud by changing the vocalization of a word to arrive at a specific interpretation.[182] Mazuz gives as an example how the word "these" (*elleh*) in Leviticus 26:23 is changed to "*alah*" a curse associated with oaths.[183] In other cases the Talmudic sages sometimes split a word into two, with Mazuz giving an example the word "delayed" (*bōshesh*) in Exodus 32:1 to become "the sixth [hour] had come" (*bāū shesh*).[184] The Talmudic sages also sometimes change a word by adding, subtracting, or moving a letter, with Mazuz giving an example the word "roses" (*shōshanīm*) changed to "they that learn" (*she-shōnīm*).[185] Mazuz suggests that perhaps the Qur'an rejects these kinds of homiletic interpretations.[186]

Also, the term "*ḥ r f*" may be seen to mean language (or dialect).[187] This meaning is perhaps attested by the prophetic tradition (*ḥadīth*) that states, "Gabriel recited me [the Qur'an] on a dialect (*ḥarf*), and I continued to ask for more until he finished to seven dialects (*aḥruf*)."[188] There is a possibility, therefore, that the term "*yuḥarrifūn*" could mean translating the words from one language (or dialect) to another,[189] which would perhaps point to rabbinic targums.[190] The rabbinic targums were explanations of the Hebrew Bible usually in the spoken language of the people, such as Aramaic, which at the time was replacing Hebrew.[191] However, the dating of written targums is a highly debatable matter.[192] Martin McNamara notes several examples, in which the Biblical text is changed in the targum. In one example about the respect due to the Elders of Israel, he states: "According to a later rabbinic dictum one should not speak disparagingly of the righteous, meaning by this the worthies of Israel. The tendency to change the biblical [*sic*] text itself, or rewrite it in translation, in order to remove or tone down passages detrimental to the reputation of the elders of Israel is already attested in pre-Christian times."[193]

The root "*ḥ r f*" also means an edge or to sharpen.[194] It is perhaps from this etymological root that the term has taken to mean a craft (*ḥirfah*).[195] However, it might also be caused by its etymological root meaning to bend, as a craftsperson bends things to create or build something.[196] In Hebrew and Aramaic, the term is sometimes used to mean insult, abuse, or slander (e.g., Psalm 57:3, 74:10, Proverbs 14:31, 2 Kings 19:4, Nehemiah 5:9, Isaiah 51:7, Daniel 11:18).[197]

The term "*yuḥarrifūn*" used by the Qur'an could also mean that some Jews are bending the words by having a crooked (*munḥarif*) interpretation of the words or turning away (*inḥirāf*) from the words, not necessarily changing the words themselves. The term "*taḥarraf*" can mean to turn aside.[198] Hence, if there is corruption in scriptures, it means that the interpretation of the words might have been corrupted but the words of God remain intact. However, there is also a possibility that the term "*yuḥarrifūn*" does not even mean changing the interpretation, but simply going back to the root meaning of the word, which is to turn away or to be crooked (*inḥirāf*). Some Qur'anic commentators such as al-Ṭabarī have debated the circumstances of revelation in Qur'an 5:41: was it revealed on the penalty for murder or that it was revealed on the penalty for adultery?[199] If we take these issues for a moment and identify whether or not the Jews have changed the meaning or the words of the Torah, it would give us few insights. Al-Ṭabarī says that the circumstance of revelation is perhaps when a Jew wanted to ask Muḥammad about the penalty for murder. If Muḥammad concluded that it is capital punishment, then the Jews would not accept it.[200] However, the penalty for deliberate murder, according to the Torah (i.e., Exodus 21:12–14), is death. Hence, if the term "*yuḥarrifūn*" in Qur'an 5:41 was meant for this issue, then it is apparent that the text of the Torah is not changed, but that some Jews hoped for a different outcome from Muḥammad.

If the issue is on the penalty for adultery, then we also arrive at the same conclusion. Al-Ṭabarī states that another opinion of the circumstance of revelation is that some Jews went to Muḥammad to ask him about the penalty for adultery.[201] They decided that if Muḥammad says that the penalty is that the adulterers are lashed and carried on donkeys, they would accept it. However, if otherwise he issues the penalty of stoning, then they would not accept it. According to classical exegetes, such as al-Ṭabarī, they state that Muḥammad eventually asks what the penalty is according to the Torah, and at the end it was found to be stoning.[202] Perhaps Muḥammad was referred to Deuteronomy 22:23–27.

If we do accept the circumstance of revelation of Qurʾan 5:41, then we find that the Jews neither changed the texts of the Torah, nor even interpreted it differently. What they did was simpler than all that. They simply did not want to adhere to the rules outlined in the Torah. However, they neither changed the words in the texts nor attempt to change its meaning. Consequently, we conclude from this discussion, if we accept the stories on the circumstances of revelation, then "*taḥrīf*" in here means something different. It simply means that some of the Jews are not adhering to the Torah with neither changing the text nor meaning. We can always question the reliability of the circumstances of revelations as narrated by classical Qurʾanic commentators. However, if we do accept its reliability, then we find the term "*taḥrīf*" in the Qurʾan means something completely different than what is even assumed in *Lisān al-ʿarab* (i.e., the change in meaning). It means exactly what its root meaning is, which is crooked (*inḥirāf*). That instead of adhering to (*tuqīmū*) the Torah, as according to Qurʾan 5:66 and 5:68, they are moving away (*yuḥarrifūn*) from it, neither changing the text nor its meaning.

If we do not accept the reliability of the circumstances of revelation of Qurʾan 5:41, then we would need to look closely at the Qurʾan for clues to see what it could possibly mean by the term "*yuḥarrifūn*." The clue in the Qurʾanic usage between "*tuqīmū*" and "*yuḥarrifūn*" seems highly likely, as both are even used within the same chapter, and therefore, it provides the possible context for the vocabulary. Moreover, in the second verse coming after Qurʾan 5:41 it states: "And how is it that they come to thee for judgment, when they have the Torah, wherein is God's Judgment? Yet even after that, they turn their backs, and they are not believers."[203]

From the context, it seems likely that Qurʾan 5:43 refers to the same issue as Qurʾan 5:41. In other words, although Qurʾan 5:41 says that some Jews "*yuḥarrifūn*," Qurʾan 5:42 says that if they do come for a ruling, then they are to be judged justly. Qurʾan 5:43 states with a seemingly surprised tone that why would they (the Jews) come for a ruling, when they have the Torah with them with God's rules? If the term "*yuḥarrifūn*" means that the Jews changed either the text or the meaning, then why would the Qurʾan almost immediately later require them to use the Torah? Also, Qurʾan 5:43 states that although they have God's ruling in the Torah, they would still turn away. This may imply that the term "*yuḥarrifūn*" means that the Jews are turning away from the text, and not that they either changed the text or meaning. The phrase, "*yuḥarrifūn al-kalim min baʿd mawāḍiʿih*," might mean that they turn away from the words after they are placed. Others have suggested that they take them out of their context (*mawḍūʿ*).[204] Reynolds argues that the Qurʾan is very specific in that sense of "*taḥrīf*," in which words are taken out of context.[205] Due to the rhetoric, there is always a possibility that a plurality of meanings might be intended, especially when using polysemous terms, such as (*ḥ r f*).

Another keyword that one needs to take into consideration in attempting to understand the meaning of "*taḥrīf*" in the Qurʾan is the term "*yalwūn*." In Qurʾan 4:46, after it accuses that some Jews "*yuḥarrifūn*," it states that they twist (*layyan*) their tongues. In Qur'an 3:78, it states that some of the People of the Book twist (*yalwūn*) their tongues so that it would appear as if it were from scriptures, but that it is not from scriptures, and that they say it is from God, when it is not from God. If the term "*yuḥarrifūn*" is related to the term "*yalwūn*," then it means that the text is kept unchanged. The reason is because it does not associate changing the writings of scriptures with the term "*yuḥarrifūn*," but that tongues are twisted. If tongues are twisted, it means they say things not from scriptures and not that they changed the text of scriptures, a conclusion also arrived by Tarakci and Sayar.[206]

The Qur'an does show that there are some people who used to write books with their own hands and then claim that they are from God (i.e., Qur'an 2:79). However, there is no evidence that this verse is talking necessarily of the Bible. It could be talking about apocrypha or pseudepigrapha texts that were asserted to be divinely inspired. I am not stating that the Qur'an is accusing these texts of not being divinely inspired, but perhaps the Qur'an is referring to some of them or even perhaps others, but not the Bible.[207] In describing this verse, Reynolds suggests, "it [the Qur'an] argues against those who treat the words of humans as revelation, while neglecting the words of God."[208] As such, Qur'an 5:66–68 requires them to return to God's words in the Torah and Gospel instead. If the Bible had been changed or rewritten, then it would not at all request the People of the Book to turn back to their scriptures. Qur'an 5:68 shows that at least at the time of Muḥammad, Jews and Christians should adhere to their own books, implying that the original scriptures were still in their hands.[209] Fred Donner also suggests that Muḥammad and the Believers movement included Jews and Christians who were not asked to change their identities and were expected to adhere to their revealed books.[210]

A verse in the Qur'an suggests that the prophecy of the coming of a prophet (without revealing his name) is mentioned in the Torah and the Gospel (i.e., Qur'an 7:157). Not finding such an explicit mention in either the Torah or the Gospel has made some medieval Muslim scholars suggest that it was deleted from the Bible.[211] However, the Qur'an here may suggest that there were allusions to the coming of a prophet as in a prophet like Moses mentioned in Deuteronomy 18:14–22 and the Jews waiting for the Prophet as mentioned in the Gospel of John 1:19–24. If the Qur'an refers to these verses as references to a prophet to come, then it does not prove that there have been any corruptions.

There is a Qur'anic reference, in which Jesus told his disciples that a messenger named Aḥmad would come after him (i.e., Qur'an 61:6), that Imām al-Ḥaramayn al-Juwaynī (d. 478/1085) considers proof that the Gospel is corrupted.[212] I will not delve into the debate on whether Aḥmad is a proper name and a reference to Muḥammad or not. Nor will I delve into whether the term "*aḥmad*" is a reference to the Paraclete mentioned in the Gospel of John (i.e., John 14:16, 14:26).[213] The Qur'anic text does not state that this saying of Jesus is in the Gospels. Hence, whether or not it is in the New Testament is also in no way proof that the text is corrupted. The corruption of scriptures to mean changing the words of God has no indisputable evidence in the Qur'an. Some Muslim scholars, such as Ibn Taymiyyah, also believe that the Qur'an, as the final revelation from God, suspends the laws in the scriptures that have come before it and supersedes it, although Ibn Taymiyyah argues that a later revelation does not abrogate (*naskh*) its preceding one.[214] However, the Qur'an does not necessarily agree with that concept, as will be shown later in this section.

Qur'an 2:113 states that Jews and Christians argue against each other, each claiming that the other is wrong, even though they read the same scripture, which is the Hebrew Bible. Later Muslims also made a similar claim that both Jews and Christians are wrong.[215] Actually, the Qur'an specifically denounces such claims from anybody and calls those who make such claims people without knowledge: "The Jews say, 'The Christians stand on nothing,' and the Christians say, 'The Jews stand on nothing,' though they recite the Book. Likewise, did those who know not speak words like theirs. God will judge between them on the Day of Resurrection concerning that wherein they differed."[216]

Also, the Qur'an steadfastly states that Jews and Christians stand upon nothing unless they resurrect and uphold their scriptures, which proves that their scriptures are not corrupt in the sense that the words have changed. Interestingly, from a linguistics point of view the term "*taḥrīf*" means to bend, as in "*inḥirāf*,"[217] and for that reason the Qur'an requests the Jews and Christians to uphold their scriptures using the term "*tuqīmū*," which means to straighten, to uphold, and to resurrect, in contrast to bending. Hence, the Qur'an may seem to state that some would like to bend (*yuḥarrifūn*) the rules of God in scriptures, when they actually need to uphold (*tuqīmū*) them.

> 68 Say, "O People of the Book! You stand on naught till you observe (*tuqīmū*) the Torah and the Gospel, and that which has been sent down unto you from your Lord." Surely that which has been sent down unto thee from thy Lord will increase many of them in rebellion and disbelief. So grieve not for disbelieving people.
> 69 Truly those who believe, and those who are Jews, and the Sabeans, and the Christians—whosoever believes in God and the Last Day and works righteousness, no fear shall come upon them, nor shall they grieve.[218]

From the above verse, a relationship between the terms "*tuqīmū*" and "*yuḥarrifūn*" is established, as "*tuqīmū*" means to straighten as opposed to "*yuḥarrifūn*," which means to bend. This would be one of the creative associations that Muḥammad was capable of doing, given his state of mind. If anything, the Qur'an actually attempts to uphold the veracity of the Torah.

> 43 And how is it that they come to thee for judgment, when they have the Torah, wherein is God's Judgment? Yet even after that, they turn their backs, and they are
> not believers. 44 Truly We sent down the Torah, wherein is a guidance and a light, by which the prophets who submitted (*aslamū*) [unto God] judged those who are Jews, as did the sages and the rabbis, in accordance with such of God's Book as they were bidden to preserve and to which they were witnesses. So fear not mankind, but fear Me! And sell not My signs for a paltry price. Whosoever judges not by that which God has sent down—it is they who are disbelievers.[219]

These verses, at least at the time of Muḥammad, request the Jews to judge in accordance to the Torah (e.g., Qur'an 3:93, 5:43). In actuality, the same is also requested for the Christians to judge in accordance to the Gospel (i.e., Qur'an 5:47), where the Qur'an later states that it has been revealed to confirm the truth (*muṣaddiqan*) of the scriptures that have come before it (e.g., Qur'an 2:101, 3:3, 4:47, 5:48, 6:92, 10:37, 12:111, 46:12, 46:30), neither falsifying them nor abrogating them, but guarding them in safety.

> [47] Let the people of the Gospel judge by what God has sent down therein. Whosoever judges not by that which God has sent down—it is they who are iniquitous. [48] And We have sent down unto thee the Book in truth, confirming the Book that came before it, and as a protector over it. So judge between them in accordance with what God has sent down, and follow not their caprices away from the truth that has come unto thee. For each among you We have appointed a law and a way. And had God willed, He would have made you one community, but [He willed otherwise], that He might try you in that which He has given you. So vie with one another in good deeds. Unto God shall be your return all together, and He will inform you of that wherein you differ.[220]

Tarakci and Sayar also present the concept that the Bible may contain indecent stories, such as Lot lying with his daughters as a reason why some Muslims may find the Bible corrupt.[221] However, Tarakci and Sayar argue that not finding these stories in the Qur'an does not imply that they had not happened. Besides, the concept that prophets are infallible (*ʿiṣmah*) is not even found in the Qur'an.[222] If there exist any apparent contradictions between the Bible and the Qur'an, perhaps it opens a dimension for us to examine the intended meanings in both, and not necessarily that the Qur'an is attempting to undermine the validity of the Bible, especially since it explicitly states that it defends the veracity of the Bible. Perhaps we can use Averroës' principle of allegory in that if the apparent literal senses contradict, then we will need to reconcile them allegorically.[223] As such, if there are apparent literal contradictions between the Bible and the Qur'an, then it may be necessary to resort to allegorical meanings to reconcile them. Besides, with Muḥammad's state of mind giving double meanings in his sayings and precise use of words, allegorical meanings may be highly plausible.

In this section, in brief, the term "*yuḥarrifūn*" brings up three theories, and not one of them has the notion of altering the actual words in the Bible. The first is Mazuz's proposition that it might be referring to some homiletic interpretations by rabbis in the Talmud, when word vocalizations are changed or split to arrive to a different meaning. The second is the proposition that the term might be referring to changing words intentionally by rabbis while translating them in targums. The third is the possible reference of its root meaning, to bend (*inḥirāf*), as some Jews wish to bend the rules laid down by the Torah or turn away from them, when they are being asked to uphold (*tuqīmū*) them instead. As all may provide us with plausible explanations, I lean more toward the last theory given the contrast that the Qur'an makes between the terms "*yuḥarrifūn*" and "*tuqīmū*" within the same chapter. However, due to the polysemous nature of the term, perhaps multiple meanings were equally intended, especially given the state of mind of Muḥammad to convey double or more meanings.

Intertextuality between the Qur'an and the Bible

As seen in this chapter, I had to tackle two issues to prove that intertextuality between the Qur'an and the Bible is expected. The first issue is the exclusivity of Islam from a Qur'anic perspective. It has been shown that exclusivism has no Qur'anic basis. The second issue is the notion of the corruption (*taḥrīf*) of scriptures, which is perhaps found to mean turning away from scriptures. Hence, it does not mean that the text of scriptures has been changed. Since it does not mean the text has been changed and that the Qur'an accepts the veracity of the Bible, then it would seem natural to allow for intertextuality between the Qur'an and the Bible. In the medieval age, this conclusion is reached by Al-Biqāʿī in his *al-Aqwāl al-qawīmah fī ḥukm al-naql min al-kutub al-qadīmah*. A number of scholars in recent years have argued that the Qur'an is best read in conversation with the Bible and Biblical literature.[224] To adhere to a good epistemology, one needs to look at it from a Qur'anic perspective devoid of the opinions of post-Qur'anic literature. I hope I have shown in this chapter that the Qur'an accepts other scriptures and at times even requires that other scriptures are read (e.g., Qur'an 3:93). The Qur'an seems to expect its audience to have a good knowledge of the Bible, as will be shown in a few examples in the next three chapters.

5

In the Name of the Father and the Son and the Holy Spirit

In this and the next two chapters, a few examples will be given to show the role of intertextual polysemy between the Qur'an and the Bible. It is evident from the Qur'an that it is aware of the Bible, as it attempts to engage with it. This awareness might have been either oral or textual. Muḥammad might have been able to make clever associations in the Qur'an with terms used by Jews and Christians. This might further be attested by Muḥammad asking one of his scribes, Zayd ibn Thābit, to learn the books of the Jews.[1]

These three chapters attempt to show that there is more sophistication in the engagement between the Qur'an and the Bible than mere borrowings, as discussed in Chapter 2. There was a lot of discussion on borrowing by previous scholars, including the likes of Abraham Geiger, Charles Torrey, William St. Clair Tisdall, and Richard Bell.

The examples in this chapter show the engagement between Qur'anic terms and Christian terminology. The first example is about the concept of Son of God and the relationship between the terms "*ibn Allah*" and "ʿ*abd Allah*." The second example is about God the Father. The third example recalls the example from Chapter 3 about the clinging unto God and how it fits in the teaching of spiritual birth through intertextuality with the Gospel of John. In Chapter 6, the fourth example demonstrates how the Qur'an is not necessarily contradicting the New Testament on the issue that Jesus Christ is begotten of God, but is attempting to interpret John's Gospel. In Chapter 7, the fifth example illustrates Qur'anic engagement with the Incarnation of the Word in the Gospel of John. The sixth example is an extensive use of intertextuality between the Qur'an with the creation story of Genesis and the Gospel of John to give an overview of the extent of the use of intertextual polysemy in hermeneutics. These examples illustrate how the Qur'an may be seen as an interpreter of the Bible and Biblical literature and not as contradicting them. As such, the notions of exclusivism, corruption (*taḥrīf*) of earlier scriptures, and theology or Christology of later Muslims were perhaps not at all the intention of the Qur'an.

Since many of the examples are related to the Gospel of John, I must briefly introduce it for those who are not very familiar with it. Theologically and Christologically, the Gospel of John stands distinguished from the Synoptic Gospels.[2] For Muslims to understand its content, it may be wise to call it a Sufi Gospel. In that, I mean that it is very mystical and spiritual, which may be compared to the works of Ibn ʿArabī[3] or the esoteric works of the Ismāʿīlīs. This, however, is not my opinion alone, as Clement of

Alexandria (d. *c.*215 CE), one of the Church Fathers, stated the following about the Gospel: "But John, last of all, perceiving that what had reference to the body in the gospel of our Saviour, was sufficiently detailed, and being encouraged by his familiar friends, and urged by the Spirit, he wrote a spiritual gospel."[4]

Interfaith dialogue between Jews, Christians, and Muslims arrives at many things in common when it comes to ethics and morality.[5] Some may argue that irreligious individuals are even more likely to be law-abiding citizens than those who affiliate themselves with a religion,[6] which suggests that ethics and morality are not constrained within religion.[7] Acts of kindness and charity, for example, go beyond the borders of any religion.[8] Whether in common sayings about generosity within Jewish, Christian, and Muslim texts or the sayings of Buddha and Krishna, such ethics and morality are not typically confined to only one faith.[9] There exist commonalities between religious and even irreligious individuals when it comes down to ethics and morality.[10] When interfaith dialogue discusses human values that can be observed within the contexts of humanism, it is questionable whether we are having an interfaith dialogue or discussing humanism under the cloak of faith.

When interfaith or even intra-faith dialogue starts to discuss theological issues, however, we find ourselves behind roadblocks from understanding one another. In the history of Christianity, for example, there have been many debates on theological matters such as Christology, which is the study of the nature and person of Jesus Christ.[11] Such debates have created schisms within the Church and many accusations of heresy.[12] Similarly, Muslim history has had theological debates between various theological schools of thought.[13]

Today, we find that interfaith theological dialogue between Christians and Muslims has reached a stalemate.[14] Mahmoud Ayoub suggests that the most urgent goal of Christian–Muslim dialogue is for both parties to accept the legitimacy and authenticity of the other's traditions.[15] Neither faith is ready to compromise its understanding of its sacred texts on what God or Christ is. Some of these stumbling blocks between Christianity and Islam are the concepts from the Gospels of Jesus as the Son of God, God as the Father, Jesus as Begotten of God, and the Incarnation of the Word in Jesus Christ, as will be discussed in the examples in this and the next two chapters. I do hope that, with the examples in these three chapters, a closer relationship between the Qur'an and the Bible may be seen. These examples may shed light that the theology and Christology intended by the Qur'an or Muḥammad may seem to be distinct from how it later developed in the Muslim community.

Son (ibn) of God

If the Qur'an asks Christians to follow the Gospel[s], why does it seem to attack an understanding directly found in the Gospel[s], which is the notion that Jesus is the Son of God? As it is argued that Muḥammad seems to make creative associations while engaging with the Bible, we need to investigate this apparent contradiction. The term under investigation in this example is specifically "*ibn Allah*," which is only mentioned in Qur'an 9:30. It does not generally consider the definition of "*ibn*" in "*ibn Allah*," as a general definition of the term "*ibn*" in the Qur'an, which is mentioned many times, especially when discussing Jesus "*ibn Maryam*." The term "*ibn*" is a polysemous term and could be used differently by the Qur'an, where I argue that its definition in the context of Qur'an 9:30 does not necessarily mean "son."

The term Son (*huion*) of God must be distinguished from only-begotten (*monogenous*) of God. When the Qur'an often speaks against God begets or begotten, the term "*walad*" or "*yalid*" is used. The term Son of God is correctly rendered as "*ibn Allah*," which is only mentioned in a single verse in the whole Qur'an.

> 30 The Jews say that Ezra is "*ibn*" of God, and the Christians say that the Messiah is "*ibn*" of God. Those are words from their mouths. They resemble the words of those who disbelieved before. God curse them! How they are perverted (*yu'fakūn*)! 31 They have taken their rabbis and monks as lords apart from God, as well as the Messiah, son of Mary, though they were only commanded to worship one God. There is no god but He! Glory be to Him above the partners they ascribe. 32 They desire to extinguish the Light of God with their mouths. But God refuses (not desires / *ya'ba*) to do aught but complete His Light, though the disbelievers be averse.[16]

The figure of Ezra in the Qur'an is somewhat enigmatic, especially since it is associated with the term "*ibn Allah*," which is generally assumed to be Son of God. As such, Paul Casanova considered 'Uzair mentioned in the Qur'an not the Biblical Ezra, but Azael, who according to haggadic literature is one of the fallen angels.[17] The reasoning he provides is that he considers "*ibn Allah*" in Qur'an 9:30 as a reference to the sons of God mentioned in Genesis 6:2–4 about fallen angels and that Azael is also pronounced Uziel, which could have come into Arabic as 'Uzair.[18] There have been cults of angelic veneration in Judaism.[19] However, if we do take this argument as plausible, why would the Qur'an specifically mention Azael from among all other angels as whom the Jews call the Son of God? According to the midrash, Shemhazai and Azael (Azazel) are two angels who, after the creation of the human, argue with God the unworthiness of human creation, and request that they descend to earth.[20] However, when they do, they marry humans and beget children, who corrupt the earth as much as humans.[21] It is said that Shemhazai repents, but Azael does not, and continues to sin and incites humans to sin.[22] It is said that two he-goats are sacrificed on the Day of Atonement, one for God to pardon the sins of Israel, and one for Azael, such that he bears the sins of Israel (i.e., Leviticus 16:8–10).[23] Azael is mentioned several times in the Book of Enoch (e.g., Enoch 6:7) as one of the guards. It seems unlikely that the Jews would venerate a sinful angel as a son of God. If they were to give such divine status to any of the angels, then it would seem more appropriate to consider one of the archangels, such as Metatron, Michael, or Raphael, to name a few, who are more highly respected and venerated. However, why would the Qur'an specifically name Azael instead of the other angels that descended to earth, such as Shemhazai, who at least repented, according to Jewish tradition? Besides in Psalm 29:1, the term sons of deities (*bni alim*) is used, according to the Talmud, as a reference to the patriarchs.[24]

There seems little to doubt that the Jews venerate and elevate the status of Ezra above Azael, due to his role in building the Second Temple, writing the Torah, and reorganizing the Sanhedrin.[25] Hence, it seems counterintuitive to think the Qur'an specifically mentions Azael as being venerated as a Son of God in a way that Christians would venerate Christ. Actually, the verse that comes after the term "*ibn Allah*" mentions that the Jews and Christians take their priests (*aḥbārahum*) and monks (*ruhbānahum*) as lords (*arbāban*). This could further support that ʿUzair in the Qur'an is a reference to Ezra for his role in reorganizing the Sanhedrin as an authority for the interpretation and jurisprudence of Jewish law. Ezra 7:25–26 affirms Ezra's authority in appointing judges for the Israelites. In here, as a motif, this authority invested to Ezra by the King of Persia is akin to the authority invested to Moses by God. This makes Ezra like a second Moses, who not only wrote the Torah, but also played a role in the foundation of the Sanhedrin. Also, the midrash mentions Ezra and his companions, "*Ezra wa-ḥaburato*."[26] In the Great Assembly, Ezra and his companions (*aḥbār*) convene to discuss Jewish law. Ezra had such a great role in the Sanhedrin and its organization that the Qur'an in the verse after mentioning Ezra as "*ibn Allah*" (i.e., Qur'an 9:31) discusses the Jews and Christians taking their priests (*aḥbār*) and monks as lords (*arbāban*).[27] As Christ is mentioned in both verses of Qur'an 9:30–31, the relationship between Ezra and the "*aḥbār*" is evident, while there is no relationship between Azael or any angel with the rabbinic tradition or priesthood of ancient Judaism.

The Biblical Ezra, also known as Esdras in Greek, is considered by Casanova and Torrey to be referred by the name Idrīs in the Qur'an.[28] Although Richard Bell agrees with Paul Casanova and Charles Torrey,[29] William Montgomery Watt, in his revision of Richard Bell, does not confirm such a conclusion.[30] Finding the relationship between Esdras and Idrīs does not provide us with conclusive evidence that the two names are one and the same, according to James Bellamy.[31] Also, Yoram Erder is not convinced that Ezra is Idrīs, but considers Idrīs to be Enoch.[32] Arthur Jeffery considers ʿUzair a corruption of the name Ezra, in which Muḥammad either did not comprehend the name or that he deliberately made it in the diminutive form.[33]

Ezra is praised in Jewish tradition for restoring the Torah after it was forgotten. Muslim tradition is aware of this praise as it is referred to by *mufassirīn*,[34] such as al-Ṭabarī and others.[35] Traditional Muslim history books also make mention of it, such as Ibn Kathīr's *al-Bidāyah wal-nihāyah*.[36] Ibn ḥazm, in his book *al-Faṣl fil-milal wal-ahwā' wal-niḥal*, calls Ezra by the names ʿIzzar and ʿIzra al-Warrāq (Ezra the Scribe) instead of ʿUzair.[37] Interestingly, the only verse in the Qur'an mentioning the term Son of God (*ibn Allah*) claims that the Jews call Ezra, the Son of God. This claim does not spring from any historical evidence that any Jew has ever claimed that Ezra is the Son of God. John Walker puts it as, "no historical evidence can be adduced to prove that any Jewish sect, however heterodox, ever subscribed to such a tenet."[38]

James Bellamy suggests that the text of the Qur'an using the term Ezra as the Son of God to be a misreading of Jewish apocryphal texts (i.e., 2 Esdras 14:9 and 2 Esdras 2: 42–48).[39] The texts state, "For you shall be taken away from all, and from henceforth you shall remain with my Son, and with such as be like you, until the times be ended,"[40] and "So he answered and said unto me, It is the Son of God, whom they have confessed in the world. Then began I greatly to commend them that stood so stiffly for the name of the Lord."[41] Neither of these statements considers the Son of God a reference to Ezra, but as it is written in the apocryphal text named after Ezra, Muḥammad might have mistook them to be a reference to Ezra, according to Bellamy. Bellamy states, "It is clear that Muḥammad or his informant confused the name of the prophet Esdras, which is also the title of the book, with the Son of God seen by Esdras in the vision."[42] However, such an argument seems unlikely. There are other apocryphal books that also mention the Son of God (e.g., Wisdom of Solomon 2:18, 5:5, 18:13). Yet, that does not mean Muḥammad mistook the Jews calling Solomon the Son of God. Nonetheless, even if other apocryphal texts were not accessed by Muḥammad, it still seems highly unlikely that Muḥammad would make a claim against the Jews that is counterintuitive to what he already knows and understands of their religion and theology from the Jews of Madīnah, if they even existed, who are more likely precursors of rabbinic Judaism.[43]

Traditional Muslim commentators on the Qur'an realized that this claim in the Qur'an is not in accordance to the knowledge they had of the Jewish community around them. Al-Ṭabarī states that perhaps one Jew called Phinehas claimed that Ezra is the Son of God.[44] In an alternative account by the authority of Ibn ʿAbbās, al-Ṭabarī and Ibn Kathīr relate Ezra's story that God taught him the Torah after it was forgotten, and that people claimed that Ezra must be the Son of God for receiving the Torah.[45] Nonetheless, this account is not historically found in Jewish literature.[46] Al-Rāzī adds that there were possibly three Jews who came to Muḥammad claiming that they cannot believe in him since he does not state that Ezra is the Son of God.[47] Alternatively, al-Rāzī and al-Ṭabarsī suggest that there might have been a Jewish sect that made such a claim, but that this sect is currently extinct.[48] Ibn Ḥazm suggests that it is the extinct sect of Sadducees who made the claim that Ezra is the Son of God, and that they were from Yemen.[49] Al-Maqdisī (d. 355/966) narrates that when Christians claimed that the Messiah is the Son of God, in a challenge some Jews claimed that it is Ezra who holds that title.[50] He notes that Palestinian Jews made such a claim.[51] Ṣāliḥ al-Hāshimī even gives this mythical Jewish sect a name, calling them al-Muʾtamaniyyah, and goes on to say that Christianity was influenced by them.[52] Nonetheless, why would the Qur'an mention a statement like that about a small Jewish sect, if it ever even existed?

In actuality, the Jews in the time of Jesus found Jesus blasphemous for claiming to be the Son of God.[53] If the Qur'an asserts that Jews claim Ezra is the Son of God, then from the outlook, it seems to be an apparent misinformation or a misreading of apocryphal work, as some scholars have suggested.[54] Beyond Islamic scholarship and literature, there is no Jewish literature that agrees to the claim that Ezra is the Son of God.

There is yet a possibility that we might have misinterpreted and misunderstood the meaning of the term Son of God (*ibn Allah*) as mentioned in the Qur'anic verse. The Qur'anic verse is trying to explain the meaning of the term, but exegetes might have overlooked it. Using intertextual polysemy might provide us with an alternative interpretation of the term. The term for "son" (*ibn*), which is rooted in the term "*b n y*," and its various morphologies is found in the opening passages of the Book of Ezra in the Bible, but it is not understood in the sense of "son."

> [1] In the first year of Cyrus king of Persia, in order to fulfill the word of the LORD spoken by Jeremiah, the LORD moved the heart of Cyrus king of Persia to make a proclamation throughout his realm and to put it in writing:
>
> [2] "This is what Cyrus king of Persia says:
>
> "The LORD, the God of heaven, has given me all the kingdoms of the earth and He has appointed me to build (*li-bnut*) a temple for him at Jerusalem in Judah. [3] Anyone of his people among you—may his God be with him, and let him go up to Jerusalem in Judah and build (*w-ibn*) the temple of the LORD, the God of Israel, the God who is in Jerusalem."[55]

The Book of Ezra discusses the building of the Second Temple in Jerusalem. The word for "son" is "*ibn*" with its root word "*b n y*,"[56] which besides meaning son, also means building or the verb to build[57] and also means stone.[58] Therefore, the term Son of God (*ibn Allah*) may also mean Building of God, or more precisely, the Temple of God. The Talmud makes use of the wordplay with "*b n y*" by stating about children, "Read not 'your children (*banayikh*)' but 'your builders (*bonayikh*).'"[59] Matthew 3:9 and Luke 3:8 state Jesus saying, "God is able from these stones to raise up children for Abraham." Although the Peshitta uses the terms "*kypha*ʾ" for stones and "*bra*ʾ" for children, it only makes us wonder if it were meant to also make a wordplay between stones (*abanim*) and children (*banim*).

The root term for "*ibn*" is "*b n*" or "*b n y*," which is a polysemous term that can mean either son or building.[60] In Hebrew and Aramaic, "*bn*" is used to mean son and to build,[61] as the root Hebrew term "*b n h*" means to build.[62] Genesis 2:22 shows God taking the rib of man and building (*yiben*) a woman. Perhaps in that sense a son is also called a "*bn*," one who is built by his parents. From the same root, the term "*ibn*" in Akkadian, Ugaritic, Hebrew, Aramaic, and Ethiopic also means stone,[63] which has a similar meaning to its Arabic cognate.[64] In the Hebrew Bible, stones are sometimes used to serve as memorials (e.g., Genesis 28:18, 31:45–46, Joshua 4:6–7). In the Jacob's ladder narrative (i.e., Genesis 28:18), the place where the stone (*ibin*) is erected is called Bethel (the House of God). In Jacob's blessings to his sons, when he blesses Joseph, he calls him "*ibin yisrael*" (Stone of Israel) and prays by the God who will help (*ya*ʿ*zer*) him (i.e., Genesis 49:24–25). In the Book of Samuel, "*Ibin ha-*ʿ*Ezer*" even comes to light: "Then Samuel took a stone (*ibin*) and set it up between Mizpah and Shen. He named it Ebenezer (*Ibin ha-*ʿ*Ezer*), saying, 'Thus far the Lord has helped us (ʿ*azarnu*).'"[65]

Samuel traveled year by year to Bethel, where Jacob set a stone and built an altar to God; to Gilgal, where Joshua was before setting a stone (*ibin*) that will witness against Israel in Shechem (i.e., Joshua 24:26–27) in the same place that Jacob hid the people's foreign gods on his way to Bethel (Genesis 35:1–15); and to Mizpah, where he himself set a stone (*ibin*) nearby (i.e., 1 Samuel 7:17), and where Jacob also set a stone (*ibin*) as a mark of covenant with Laban (i.e., Genesis 31:44–53). Samuel then returns to his home in Ramah, where he also built (*yibin*) an altar to God (i.e., 1 Samuel 7:18). The existence of *Ibin ha-*ʿ*Ezer* in the Book of Samuel does bear an interesting homophone to "ʿ*uzayr ibn*." Its first occurrence in the Book of Samuel is where Samuel and the Israelites encamped before the battle against the Philistines (i.e., 1 Samuel 4:1). The name comes again when the Philistines capture the Ark of the Covenant from *Ibin* *ha-ʿEzer* and take it to Ashdod (i.e., 1 Samuel 5:1), although the place is only named "*Ibin ha-ʿEzer*" after the Israelite defeat the Philistines (i.e., 1 Samuel 7:12).

Isaiah 8:14 states that God will become a stone (*ibin*) and a stumbling block to both houses of Israel, which the New Testament cites as a reference to the Messiah (i.e., Romans 9:33, 1 Peter 2:8). Isaiah 28:16 also makes a reference of a stone (*ibin*) laid down by God that the New Testament also cites as a reference to the Messiah (i.e., Romans 9:33, 1 Peter 2:6). The Messiah referred to as a stone is also mentioned in Matthew 21:42 and Acts 4:11 citing Psalm 118:22, which is the stone (*ibin*) that the builders (*bonim*) rejected. The terms "*ibn*" (stone) and "*bny*" (build) might be etymologically related in that stones are used for building.

The Book of Ezra frequently uses the term "*bn*" and its morphological permutations in the context of building the Temple of God in Jerusalem. The Book of Ezra, as an example, includes the following passage: "Be it known unto the king that we went into the province of Judea to the house of the great God, which is built (*binaʾ*) with great stones (*ibin*), and timber is laid in the walls, and this work (*ʿabidah*) goes (*ʿabad*) fast on, and prospers in their hands."[66]

In the Book of Ezra, the term "*ibn*" is used in the context of an instruction to build God's Temple. If we intertextualize between the Qurʾan and the Book of Ezra and contextualize the Qurʾanic verse in accordance to the Biblical narration in the Book of Ezra to build the Temple of God in Jerusalem, then we may have an alternative meaning for the term "*ibn Allah*." For a moment, if we consider the term "*ibn Allah*" to mean the Building of God, or in its Biblical context, the Temple of God, then the Qurʾanic verse would be stating, "And the Jews say that the Temple of God is Ezra and the Christians say that the Temple of God is the Messiah."[67] If we accept this understanding, we do know that Ezra is not himself a Temple of God, but it could be a Qurʾanic allusion of the Jewish belief that the Temple of God is in Jerusalem, as stated in the Book of Ezra about building the Second Temple. Nonetheless, the term "*ʿa z r*," which is the root of the name Ezra or ʿUzair, is a polysemous term with various meanings. It means help in Hebrew, Aramaic, and Arabic.[68] In addition, "*ʿazarah*" is sometimes associated with the ledge surrounding Ezekiel's altar (i.e., Ezekiel 43:14, 43:17, 43:20, 45:19) or the temple court (2 Chronicles 4:9, 6:13).[69] As such, Qurʾan 9:30 may be translated as, "And the Jews say Ezra (or Temple Court)[70] is the Building (Temple) of God and the Christians say the Messiah is the Building (Temple) of God." More correctly so, the Christians do indeed state that the Messiah's body is itself the Temple of God.[71] Also, the Messiah "*ibn Allah*" might be a reference to God's stone (*ibin*) that is a stumbling block, as referred to in the New Testament. If we are to understand the term "*ibn Allah*" in the context of Temple of God, then what seems to be the Qurʾanic objection? Since the Qurʾan continues to state that this is a saying with their mouths (*bi-afwāhihim*), it may be intertextualized with other passages of the Qurʾan where this term is also used, such as,

> O you who believe! Take not intimates apart from yourselves; they will not stint you in corruption. They wish you to suffer. Hatred has appeared from their mouths (*afwāhihim*); yet what their breasts conceal is greater. We have indeed made clear the signs for you, were you to understand."[72]

> And that He may know the hypocrites. And it was said unto them, "Come, fight in the way of God or defend [yourselves]." They said, "Had we known there would be fighting, we would have followed you." That day they were closer to disbelief (*lil-kufr*) than to belief (*lil-īmān*), saying with their mouths (*bi-afwāhihim*) what was not in their hearts. And God knows best what they conceal.[73]

> O Messenger! Let them not grieve thee, those who hasten unto disbelief (*fil-kufr*), those who say, "We believe" (*āmannā*) with their mouths (*bi-afwāhihim*), while their hearts believe not, and those who are Jews, who listen to lies and to others who have not come to thee. They distort the meaning of the word, saying, "If you are given this, then take it, but if you are not given this, then beware!" For whomsoever God desires that he be tried, thou hast no power to avail him aught against God. They are those whose hearts God desired not to purify. Theirs is disgrace in this world, and in the Hereafter they shall have a great punishment.[74]

In these Qur'anic passages, it seems that when the Qur'an uses the term "with their mouths (*bi-afwāhihim*)" it is contrasted that what they say with their mouths is not the same as it is in their hearts. Also, Qur'an 9:30 mentions that when the Jews and Christians say things with their mouths, they imitate the unbelievers of before using the term "*kafarū*." This term is also found in Qur'an 3:167 and 5:41, as mentioned above. This could make use of a different understanding of the Qur'anic passage. If the Jews and Christians are making a claim about the Temple of God, it is nothing but a saying with their mouths, implying it is not in their hearts. Perhaps the Qur'an here is suggesting that the Jews and Christians should not only say where the Temple of God should be, either in Jerusalem as stated in the Book of Ezra or the Messiah himself as stated in the Gospel of John (i.e., John 2:21), but also they themselves should have their hearts as a Temple of God, in which I have argued in an article that the *Qiblah* passages of the Qur'an are in reality an allusion to the *Shema*ʿ emphasizing the role of the heart over the direction of prayer.[75] From the same Qur'anic chapter, the term "with their mouths (*bi-afwāhihim*)" is also used in the following verse, "How, since if they prevail over you, they will not observe any kinship or treaty with you? They please you with their mouths (*bi-afwāhihim*), while their hearts refuse. And most of them are iniquitous."[76]

The Qur'an here shows a contrast that what their mouths say is dissimilar to what is in their hearts. It appears that the Qur'an later states that those who claim the Temple of God to be that in Ezra or the Messiah attempt to extinguish God's light with their mouths and God desires not to allow it: "They desire to extinguish the Light of God with their mouths (*bi-afwāhihim*). But God refuses to do aught but complete His Light, though the disbelievers be averse."[77]

The above passage is also found in a different chapter, which also subtly uses a term rooted in "*b n y*."

> [1] Whatsoever is in the heavens and whatsoever is on the earth glorifies God, and He is the Mighty, the Wise. [2] O you who believe! Why do you say that which you do not do? [3] Grievously odious is it in the Sight of God that you say that which

you do not do. 4 Truly God loves those who fight in His way in ranks, as if they were a solid structure (*bunyān*). 5 And [remember] when Moses said unto his people, "O my people! Why do you hurt me, though you know well that I am the Messenger of God unto you?" So when they swerved, God caused their hearts to swerve; and God guides not iniquitous people. 6 And [remember] when Jesus son of Mary said, "O Children of Israel! Truly I am the Messenger of God unto you, confirming that which came before me in the Torah and bearing glad tidings of a Messenger to come after me whose name is Aḥmad." And when he came unto them with clear proofs, they said, "This is manifest sorcery." 7 Who does greater wrong than one who fabricates lies against God, while he is being called to submission (*islām*)? And God guides not wrongdoing people. 8 They desire to extinguish the Light of God with their mouths (*bi-afwāhihim*), but God completes His Light, though the disbelievers be averse.[78]

The phraseology of Qur'an 9:32 and 61:8 are the same. Also to note, both Qur'an 9 and 61 are assumed to be Madinan chapters. In Qur'an 61, what seems to be the objection is that some people attempt to extinguish God's light with their mouths by saying falsehoods. Earlier in the same chapter, it criticizes people who say what they do not do, which could mean that they say what is not truly in their hearts (i.e., Qur'an 61:2). Hence in Qur'an 9:30, one might consider that the Qur'anic objection is not what they are saying with their mouths about the Temple of God, but it is because their mouths say something different than their hearts. Perhaps their hearts should be where the Temple of God (*ibn Allah*) is or perhaps they should truly believe the Temple of God is in Jerusalem or is the Messiah, and not just say that with their mouths. The Gospel of John provides us with a distinction between the profession of faith by the lips and understanding spiritual mysteries. In the Gospel of John, Nicodemus appears to profess faith in Jesus as man of God, but nonetheless fails to understand the mysteries related in his teachings. Jouette Bassler states, "If, however, Nicodemus's [*sic*] profession of faith seems to be acceptable within the framework of this Gospel, Jesus' response to Nicodemus seems to indicate that on another level *inaccessible to the reader* it is *not* acceptable."[79] In discussing Nicodemus' encounter with Jesus, Arthur Canales also arrives at the same conclusion that the profession of faith needs to be internalized in the heart,[80] and he also states, "If religion is only externalized in ritual and not internalized in a person's heart; religion becomes ineffective."[81] However, though in John 3 Nicodemus seems to profess faith by the lips while not fully understanding the mysteries that Jesus is teaching, he nonetheless seems to have become a good disciple of Jesus in the later accounts in the Gospel of John (i.e., John 7:45–52 and John 19:38–42).[82]

While discussing Qur'an 9:30, Fazlur Rahman suggests the light intended in the passage is a reference to Islam,[83] agreeing with classical exegetes such as al-Ṭabarī and Ibn Kathīr.[84] He also recognizes the relationship between the passages in Qur'an 9:32 and 61:8.[85] If we do take into consideration intertextuality between the passages, Qur'an 61:7 talks about *islām*, which is the surrender of a person to God, and therefore, there is a possibility that the light referred to in Qur'an 61:8 might be the surrender to God. If we take this into consideration when understanding the light in Qur'an 9:32 as well, then perhaps having the Temple of God in a person's heart is also an allusion of this surrender to God.

As another interesting note, Qur'an 61:4 uses the term "*bunyān*" meaning structure or building sharing the same root as "*ibn*." The keywords of the passages in Qur'an 9 and 61 discussed might show that these passages allude to each other. Using intertextual polysemy, as seen, may provide us with a different understanding than that seen by classical exegetes. However, perhaps the Qur'an is not trying to emphasize that Jews and Christians should not point the temples of God, either in Jerusalem or the Messiah, but they themselves need to embody the Temple of God, and this concept moves in parallel to Paul's epistle to the Corinthians.[86] "[19] Do you not know that your bodies are temples of the Holy Spirit, who is in you, whom you have received from God? You are not your own; [20] you were bought at a price. Therefore honor God with your bodies."[87]

When Paul states "You are not your own," in this passage in 1 Corinthians, it would suggest that the person has surrendered him/herself to God, which is *islām*. Due to this surrender of the self to God, the bodies have indeed become temples of the Holy Spirit. Paul stating, "you were bought at a price," also resembles a reference within the same Qur'anic chapter:

> Truly God has purchased from the believers their souls and their wealth in exchange for the Garden being theirs. They fight in the way of God, slaying and being slain. [It is] a promise binding upon Him in the Torah, the Gospel, and the Quran. And who is truer to His pact than God? So rejoice in the bargain you have made. That indeed is the great triumph.[88]

There is a scholarly debate as to which "body" Paul is referring to, the individual body or the communal body (i.e., the church).[89] Jamieson et al. suggest that Paul here is using a metaphor describing the *Shekhinah*, which is typically identified as the Spirit of God, taking its place within the sanctuary of the body.[90] Commenting on Pauline understanding of the temple, Howard Marshall states the following:

> Just as the Shekinah [*sic*] was present when Jews read the Torah together,[91] so Jesus is present when his people meet in his name. Jesus himself is the 'temple' for his people (Jn. 2:21). It can be said, therefore, both that Jesus is the place where God is present and that his presence with his people constitutes them as the place of God's presence. Jesus both is the new temple in himself and constitutes his people as the new temple.[92]

The *Shekhinah* (*al-Sakīnah* in Arabic) is mentioned few verses before Qur'an 9:30 (i.e., Qur'an 9:26), where the passage states that *al-Sakīnah* had descended upon the messenger and the believers. On the body being a temple of the Holy Spirit as described by Paul, Richard Pratt states, "The Holy Spirit takes up residence in believers, making their bodies a holy place for the dwelling of God's special presence."[93] This is a general description of the *Shekhinah*.[94]

About 1 Corinthians 6:19–20, Richard Lenski states, "As the Spirit's sanctuary we belong wholly to him, and that certainly includes also our body, so that this body itself can be called his sanctuary."[95] Here Lenski is describing a full surrender to God. Commenting on Paul's passage, Charles Barrett suggests that a person is a slave to sin, and thus, "he could be freed only by becoming again what he had been created to be—the son and servant of God."[96] In other words, Barrett seems to equate being a son of God with surrendering to God by accepting being His servant. Since the context of this passage in Paul's epistle is about fornication, then it might appear that this metaphor is that of the marriage between the body and the Holy Spirit. Hence, the statement, "you were bought at a price," may serve two purposes as suggested by Charles Talbert that it is either similar to the purchase of slaves or the payment of a dowry.[97] Charles Hodge states that there are two characteristics of a temple. First, it is the dwelling place of God, and therefore, holy. Second, the proprietorship of a temple is God. In other words, the believer completely surrenders his self and body to God.[98]

Using intertextual polysemy between the Qur᾿an and itself, as well as between the Qur᾿an and the Bible, may provide us with different insightful conclusions in such hermeneutics. These intertextualities might further indicate the polysemous nature of understanding the term "*ibn Allah*," as a reference to the Temple of God. In Qur᾿an 9:30, the term "deluded from the truth (*yu᾿fakūn*)" is used. Here, the Qur᾿an asserts that the Jews and Christians who with their mouths make claims (of what is perhaps not in their hearts) are deluded from the truth (or lying) using the term "*yu᾿fakūn*." The root of the term is "*i f k*" meaning "lie" in Arabic,[99] and also meaning to pervert, to reverse, or to turn back in Aramaic.[100] This might support the concept that the Qur᾿anic objection is that Jews and Christians say with their mouths what is not in their hearts, or in other words, they are lying, in which their outer appearance is not the same as their inner realities. The same term is used against the sorcerers with Moses, in which their sorcery is described as "*ya᾿fikūn*," in which the outer appearance of their magic is different than its inner reality.

> **117** And We revealed unto Moses, "Cast thy staff!" And, behold, it devoured all their deceptions (*ya᾿fikūn*). **118** Thus the truth came to pass, and whatsoever they did was shown to be false. **119** Then and there they were vanquished and turned back (*inqalabū*), humbled. **120** And the sorcerers were cast down prostrate. **121** They said, "We believe in the Lord of the worlds . . ."[101]

This passage describes the sorcerers as soon as they realized that Moses' rod is eating up the magic that they tried to make; they believed in him using the term "*inqalabū*." Accordingly, if the sorcerers lied (*ifk*), they needed to "*inqalab*," which means to return, to put something upside down or inside out.[102] However, the root of the term is "*qalb*," which also means heart.[103] If the Jews and Christians are saying a lie by saying with their mouths what is not in their hearts, then the Qur᾿an might allude here that they need to internalize with their hearts (*qulūb*) what they say with their mouths.

The term "*ibn*" is polysemous. In the context of Qur᾿an 9:30, especially since the Qur᾿an talks of Ezra (or Temple Court) as "*ibn Allah*," it specifically is an allusion to the Building of God, or more specifically the Temple of God. Hence, this is not a general definition of the term "*ibn*" in the Qur᾿an, but specifically the Qur᾿anic usage of the term "*ibn Allah*," which is only mentioned in Qur᾿an 9:30.

Although the Qur'an uses the term "*ibn Allah*" in only one verse, throughout the Qur'an it points many times that God does not give birth, using the root term "*w l d*." Sometimes, this concept is given in general (e.g., Qur'an 18:4, 6:101–102, 10:68, 17:111, 19:88–93, 21:25–26, 23:91, 25:1–2, 37:149–162, 39:1–4, 43:81, 72:3, 112:3), as the ancient Arabs used to believe that some of their deities and angels are daughters of Allah.[104] However, some of this concept is used in the Qur'an specifically relating to Jesus Christ (e.g., Qur'an 4:171–172, 19:35–36). Noticeably, in many parts of the Qur'an, whenever it talks against God giving birth using the term "*wld*," it confirms that the subject is a servant (*ʿabd*) instead. Hence, the root of the word "*ʿabd*" is found nearby many of the verses in the Qur'an that explicitly speak against the concept of God giving birth (*w l d*) (e.g., Qur'an 6:101–102, 19:88–93, 21:25–26, 25:1–2, 37:149–162, 39:1–4, 43:81), and especially when the notion of God giving birth (*wld*) to Jesus Christ is rejected, it reaffirms that Jesus Christ is a "*ʿabd*" of God (i.e., Qur'an 4:171–172, 19:35–36).

> 171 O People of the Book! Do not exaggerate in your religion, nor utter anything concerning God save the truth. Verily the Messiah, Jesus son of Mary, was only a messenger of God, and His Word, which He committed to Mary, and a Spirit from Him. So believe in God and His messengers, and say not "Three." Refrain! It is better for you. God is only one God; Glory be to Him that He should have a child (*wld*). Unto Him belongs whatsoever is in the heavens and whatsoever is on the earth, and God suffices as a Guardian. 172 The Messiah would never disdain to be a "*ʿabd*" of God; nor would the angels brought nigh. Whosoever disdains His service (*ʿibadatih*), and is arrogant, He will gather them unto Himself all together.[105]

The usage of the word "*ʿabd*" by the Qur'an carries an interesting understanding of the term "*ibn Allah*," which is not necessarily born of God (*wld Allah*). The word "*ʿabd*" carries several meanings, in which the most common meaning is servant or slave.[106] However, "*taʿabbud*" also means to worship,[107] "*ʿabbada*" and "*taʿbīd*" also mean to make, to create, to form, or to produce, as in building a road (*taʿbīd al-Ṭarīq*).[108] In Hebrew and Aramaic, the term includes the meaning to make, to labor, to serve, to worship, to create, to perform, or to act.[109] Its usage in the meaning to make and to create is especially used in the Bible in the Books of Ezra, Jeremiah, and Daniel (e.g., Ezra 4:15, 19, 22, 5:8, 6:8, 11–13, 16, 7:18, 21, 23, 26, Jeremiah 10:11, Daniel 2:5, 3:1, 15, 29, 4:2, 35, 5:1, 6:10, 22, 27, 7:21). The root of the terms "*ibn*" and "*ʿabd*" are also used together in Ezra 5:8. It is perhaps because a servant or a slave (*ʿabd*) performs, labors, or makes (*yuʿabbid*) things that he is called a "*ʿabd*."[110]

Conclusion

The Qur'an rejects the term born of God (*wld Allah*) in favor of the word "*ʿabd*," especially whenever it distinctively speaks of Jesus Christ. However, it does not favor the word "*ʿabd*" when it uses the term "*ibn Allah*." There is perhaps a relationship between the meaning of the terms "*ʿabd*" and son "*ibn*" in Muḥammad's mind. As "*ibn*" means to build, and from "*ibn*" comes the form "*mabna*," which means building, so is from the word "ʿ*abd*" comes the form "*maʿbad*," which means temple. Hence, if the term "*ibn Allah*" can be an allusion to the Building of God (*mabna Allah*), so can the term "ʿ*abd Allah*" be an allusion to the Temple of God (*maʿbad Allah*). The Kaʿbah in Makkah, which is a Temple of God, is called "*al-baniyyah*."[111] Also, as "ʿ*abd Allah*" could mean made by God so is "*ibn Allah*" could mean built by God.[112] The Qur'an emphasizes the term "ʿ*abd*" instead of "*walad*," but it does not show this preference when it critiques the term "*ibn*." The reason may lie in the relationship between the polysemous meanings of the terms "ʿ*abd*" and "*ibn*." Also, the term "ʿ*abd Allah*" could mean the work of God, as His work comes through His servants, who work for Him. As such, if the Qur'an prefers the term "ʿ*abd*" for Jesus, it should not be seen as derogatory to Christian Christology, for even the Gospel of John shows the Son doing the work and the will of the Father (e.g., John 5:19–47).

There is also a likelihood that Qur'an 9:30 is alluding to the Jewish Temple in Jerusalem and the Christian concept of Jesus as the Temple of the Body. There is also a likelihood that when Qur'an 9:30 states, "That is a saying from their mouths," does not necessarily mean that what is said is not true. Rather, it might mean that they do not believe in what they are saying—saying something with their mouths, when their hearts are averse to it.

Fatherhood of God

How would Muḥammad reconcile the Gospel[s], which he asks the Christians to follow, and the notion of the Fatherhood of God? The answer may be investigated from a linguistic point of view using intertextual polysemy as well with Muḥammad's creative state of mind. The root of the word for father in Arabic, Hebrew, and Aramaic is "*ab*."[113] If the term is related to "*abah*" or "*aby*," it can mean desire or be willing in Hebrew and Aramaic,[114] or it can mean unwilling or undesired in Arabic and Ethiopic.[115] In Arabic, the root "*a b y*" usually means desiring not.[116] A more accurate word for the term God the Father is "*āb*," when compared to the term for father (*ab*), in which its root could be "*a w b*" or "*a y b*."[117] The term "*abah*" meaning desire, in Aramaic and in Hebrew, is utilized numerously within the Pentateuch (e.g., Genesis 24:5, 24:8, Exodus 10:27, Leviticus 26:21, Deuteronomy 1:26). However, the Bible mainly uses this word in a negative manner, usually to show that something is not desirable or not to follow. Rarely, however, has it been used in a positive context (e.g., Isaiah 1:19). In Hebrew, Aramaic, and Arabic, the term "*awb*" or "*ayb*" means to return to, as in "*iyāb*" meaning to return, as well as "*awwāb*" meaning one who returns.[118] The term "*twb*" also means to return,[119] and as such "*awwāb*" and "*tawwāb*" can be synonymous.[120] Although in Hebrew and Aramaic, the root "*ayb*" is typically used for enemy, as it is also used in Akkadian and Ugaritic to allude to enemy,[121] the term may actually be rooted in the meaning to return, as it is used in Arabic. The Arabic term for enemy, as used by the Qur'an, is "ʿ*adw*." Its relationship with "ʿ*awd*" is a possibility, as ambiguously used in Qur'an 17:8.[122]

The Qur'an states that the place of desire or return (*al-maʾāb*) is to God (i.e., Qur'an 3:14, 13:29, 13:36). The meaning of "*maʾāb*" as a place of return (*marjaʿ*) is also evident in classical Qur'anic commentaries, such as al-Ṭabarī, al-Rāzī, and Ibn Kathīr.[123] The Qur'an also uses the term "*awwābīn*" for those who desire God or return to God (i.e., Qur'an 17:25, 38:19, 50:32). The Qur'an also uses the words for servant or temple (*'abd*) several times within the same verse or proximity as the term for return or desire (*ma'āb*) (i.e., Qur'an 13:36, 78:39). The Qur'an even describes, within the same verse, David and Solomon as "*'abd*" and as those who desired or returned to God (*awwāb*) (i.e., Qur'an 38:17, 30). The linguistic style of the Qur'an describes Job (Ayyūb), whose root name also means return or desire,[124] as a "*'abd*" who desired or returned to God (*awwāb*) (i.e., Qur'an 38:44). Chapter Ṣād actually uses the terms "*awwāb*" and "*ma'āb*" many times (e.g., Qur'an 38:25, 38:40, 38:49). In a couple of verses, the Qur'an uses the term "*ma'āb*" negatively, as a place of bad desire or a bad place to return to (i.e., Qur'an 38:55, 78:22). The Qur'an has also used the term "*aby*" immediately after it talks about the concept of "*ibn Allah*." The term "*ya'ba*" from the root "*a b y*" is used to mean that God refuses or desires not His Light to be extinguished by people's mouths.

> 30 The Jews say that Ezra is "*ibn*" of God, and the Christians say that the Messiah is "*ibn*" of God. Those are words from their mouths. They resemble the words of those who disbelieved before. God curse them! How they are perverted (*yu'fakūn*)! 31 They have taken their rabbis and monks as lords apart from God, as well as the Messiah, son of Mary, though they were only commanded to worship one God. There is no god but He! Glory be to Him above the partners they ascribe. 32 They desire to extinguish the Light of God with their mouths. But God refuses (not desires / *ya'ba*) to do aught but complete His Light, though the disbelievers be averse.[125]

The Qur'an has also used the same root word (*a b y*) for Satan's sin. Satan's only sin, according to the Qur'an, was his pride and having an ego (e.g., Qur'an 2:34, 15:31, 20:116). Perhaps the Qur'an tries to portray a message that this is the type of desire that needs to be uprooted, while planting the desire of selflessness. Also, the Qur'an uses the same word for Pharaoh not desiring or refusing God's request through Moses, "And We verily did show him (Pharaoh) all Our Signs, but he denied them and refused (*aba*)."[126] It is also the same word stated in Exodus with Pharaoh's refusal: "But the LORD hardened Pharaoh's heart, and he would not (*abah*) let them go."[127]

Conclusion

Besides meaning God the Father (*al-āb*), Muḥammad perhaps imagined the term to also mean that God is the one desired or returned to. However, this does not mean that God the Father and the Son of God have completely different meanings than those known as some mystical filial relationship, which shall be shown in the next section. However, Muḥammad seems to have made creative associations from his understandings of the Gospel[s], while reciting the Qur'an. He capitalizes on polysemous Arabic terms in choosing specific words that provide double meanings in constructing his arguments.

Spiritual birth

In Chapter 3, the method of intertextual polysemy used to portray the clinging of the fetus in the mother's womb is used as a metaphor for those who cling unto God. Spiritually, it describes the creation of the human being as being born of God in a metaphorical sense. In the Gospel of John, Jesus describes the Divine Mystery of being born again. The significance of this mystery in the Gospel of John is that the Gospel speaks so expressively about the Son of God immediately after talking about the process of spiritual birth (i.e., John 3:1–21):

> 3 Jesus replied, "Very truly I tell you, no one can see the kingdom of God unless they are born again."
>
> 4 "How can someone be born when they are old?" Nicodemus asked. "Surely they cannot enter a second time into their mother's womb to be born!"
>
> 5 Jesus answered, "Very truly I tell you, no one can enter the kingdom of God
> unless they are born of water and the Spirit. 6 Flesh gives birth to flesh, but the
> Spirit gives birth to spirit. 7 You should not be surprised at my saying, 'You must be
> born again.' 8 The wind blows wherever it pleases. You hear its sound, but you cannot tell where it comes from or where it is going. So it is with everyone born of the Spirit."
>
> 9 "How can this be?" Nicodemus asked.
>
> 10 "You are Israel's teacher," said Jesus, "and do you not understand these things?
> 11 Very truly I tell you, we speak of what we know, and we testify to what we have
> seen, but still you people do not accept our testimony. 12 I have spoken to you of earthly things and you do not believe; how then will you believe if I speak of
> heavenly things? 13 No one has ever gone into heaven except the one who came
> from heaven—the Son of Man. 14 Just as Moses lifted up the snake in the wilderness,
> so the Son of Man must be lifted up, 15 that everyone who believes may have eternal life in him."
>
> 16 For God so loved the world that He gave His one and only Son, that whoever
> believes in him shall not perish but have eternal life. 17 For God did not send His
> Son into the world to condemn the world, but to save the world through him.
> 18 Whoever believes in him is not condemned, but whoever does not believe stands condemned already because they have not believed in the name of God's one and only Son.[128]

The Gospel of John makes great use of symbolism.[129] Mary Coloe says about this passage, "The literal meaning is nonsense forcing the hearer/reader to look for a 'surplus of meaning.' So Nicodemus is asked to go beyond the literal meaning of 'birth' to a deeper meaning."[130] This is a notion that would be agreeable to the Stoics, Philo, and Averroës, as discussed in Chapter 2. In the passage, the use of symbolism in the discourse between Jesus and Nicodemus concerning rebirth also shows that such symbolism remains enigmatic even to the highly learned in the community. As William Grese says, "The heavenly journey set before Nicodemus is not a trip through the heavens to God, but through the enigmas and riddles that surround the heavenly revelation made available in Jesus."[131] The statements that are made by Jesus in regard to the rebirth are meant to be allegorically interpreted. Hence, it is meant to be seen as a symbol. Grese continues to state, "Nicodemus is not only superficial; he is also unable to pass beyond a very physical interpretation of rebirth as a repetition of the first birth."[132] Jesus' teachings on the concept of rebirth go beyond the physical interpretation. As such, the understanding of Jesus as Begotten of God, which the passage continues to elaborate on, would only be understood allegorically as well. Grese suggests that Nicodemus represents people who do not have a full grasp of the allegorical nature of Jesus' discourse, where he states, "In speaking to Nicodemus, Jesus is speaking to a representative of the world (in the dark)."[133] The reason Grese suggests it is in the dark is due to symbols in the text. Nicodemus comes at night asking questions, which is a representative of darkness, a meaning that Bassler also concurs with.[134] This interpretation, which is both literal and symbolic, is also evident in the interpretation of the early church fathers. Origen takes into consideration that Nicodemus came at night to secretly meet Jesus, but it is also symbolic of the night of his own ignorance.[135] Augustine makes a similar reference that Nicodemus seeing Jesus at night is symbolic of those in darkness seeking the light.[136] John the Evangelist appears to be very precise in his contrast between light and darkness, and this is even seen from the very beginning of his Gospel, where he speaks of John the Baptist, who is not the light, but coming to witness for it (i.e., John 1:6–8). Due to this precise use of words by John, then the detail of Nicodemus coming by night would serve this precise Evangelist's contrast,[137] and perhaps the irony of coming in the night to the Light of the World, as identified in his prologue.[138]

The concept of rebirth from a spiritual understanding is not necessarily foreign to the Jews, and as such could be the reason why Jesus tells Nicodemus that he is a teacher of Israel and still does not understand this concept. According to the Talmud, a proselyte is like a newborn baby.[139] Hence, the rebirth in Jesus' discourse with Nicodemus may be viewed as a spiritual conversion, which as a concept should not be alien to a Jewish teacher. Such a concept is also similar to that in Islam for a new convert, who is considered like a newborn infant,[140] as it is also the same as those performing ḥajj, where their sins are wiped out like the day they were born, as stated in the prophetic tradition, "Who comes to this house (Kaʿbah) and avoids sexual relations and sins, returns like the day his mother bore him."[141]

The Qurʾan describes the spiritual birth of the human being when comparing and analyzing the verses in sūrah al-ʿAlaq and sūrah al-Raḥmān. The physical is used as a metaphor to describe the spiritual. Now that the term for being born again may be understood from a spiritual context, then those who are spiritually born of God, through the process of being born again, as described by the Gospel of John and alluded to by the Qurʾan, may be called spiritual sons of God. As such, the Gospel of John talks about Christ Begotten of God and alluding to him as a son immediately after the narrative of being born again (i.e., John 3:16–17). This may also be intertextualized within the Gospel, where Jesus describes that people who enter heaven must become like little children,[142] for even the wording used in the verses, below, about those who enter the Kingdom of God is very similar to the wordings used by Jesus for those who are born again/from above (e.g., Matthew 19:13–15), especially since the Kingdom of God is only mentioned in the Gospel of John in the Nicodemus narrative.

> [13] People were bringing little children to Jesus for him to place his hands on them, but the disciples rebuked them. [14] When Jesus saw this, he was indignant. He said to them, "Let the little children come to me, and do not hinder them, for the kingdom of God belongs to such as these. [15] Truly I tell you, anyone who will not receive the kingdom of God like a little child will never enter it." [16] And he took the children in his arms, placed his hands on them and blessed them.[143]

According to Islamic tradition, the first verses of Qur'anic revelation are Qur'an 96:1–5.[144] As these verses are found to be a possible allusion to spiritual birth, perhaps it is alluding to Muḥammad's own spiritual birth. Nicodemus goes to Jesus at night, as Muḥammad claimed that revelation came to him at night. Muḥammad called the night of his revelation the Night of Measure (*laylah al-qadr*). What is interesting is that the term "*qdr*" in Hebrew and Aramaic means darkness.[145] If we assume that this definition also existed in Arabic in the past, then perhaps *laylah al-qadr* would also mean the night of darkness. The Qur'an describes itself to have been revealed at night calling it *laylah al-qadr*. Perhaps the Qur'an attempts to state that it has been revealed in the darkness of the night to take people out of darkness into the light. "[1] Truly We sent it down in the Night of Power. [2] And what shall apprise thee of the Night of Power? [3] The Night of Power is better than a thousand months. [4] The angels and the Spirit descend therein, by the leave of their Lord, with every command. [5] Peace it is until the break of dawn."[146]

If Qur'an 96:1–5, which is described in Islamic tradition to have been revealed during *laylah al-qadr*, is an allusion to spiritual birth as described in the Gospel of John, then we need to search for further clues that connect *laylah al-qadr* with the Gospel of John.[147] The Qur'an describes *laylah al-qadr* as a night when the angels and the Spirit descend until dawn. The Gospel of John does talk about angels ascending and descending upon the Son of Man. "He then added, 'Very truly I tell you, you will see "heaven open, and the angels of God ascending and descending on" the Son of Man.' "[148]

This passage in the Gospel of John is, in itself, a possible allusion to Jacob's ladder.[149] Jacob sees a vision *at night* of a heavenly ladder, which angels ascend and descend on (i.e., Genesis 28:12). The term for the stone that Jacob uses as a pillow in Genesis 28:11, 28:18, and 28:22 is "*ibn*." John 1:51 may be referring to Jesus as the stone (*ibn*) pillar or ladder to heaven. This, in particular, may be John's intention since the stone pillar erected by Jacob in Genesis 28:22 is considered God's house, even calling the place Bethel, which means God's house (i.e., Genesis 28:19). In John 2:19–21, it becomes evident that Jesus' body is itself described as the Temple of God or God's house. Perhaps John suggests that the oil that Jacob pours on the stone pillar (i.e., Genesis 28:18) is symbolizing Jesus as the anointed one (Messiah), especially when Genesis 31:13 recounts the pouring of oil in Bethel and calls the ritual "*mashaḥta*" (same root as messiah) for anointing it.

The detail that this ladder is seen at night is perhaps used by the Qur'an in that the descent of the angels and the Spirit occur also at night during *laylah al-qadr*. The

Hebrew Bible calls Jacob's ladder "*sullam*." This term is only used once in the whole text of the Hebrew Bible and it is cognate to the Arabic term for ladder as well, which is also "*sullam*."[150] In the earliest texts of the Qur'an, the term "*salām*" and "*sullam*" is written in the same manner of "*s l m*," which may be seen in Qur'an 97:5. However, even though the intertextuality between the terms "*sullam*" and "*salām*" may be a point of coincidence, Muḥammad's perception of angels coming down on *laylah al-qadr* might still, in itself, be an allusion to Jacob's ladder. According to Qur'an 97:5, one may infer that the descent of angels and the Spirit cease at dawn, which may be likened to the detail in Genesis 28:18 that states Jacob taking the stone that was under his head and erects it as a pillar in the early morning.

As Qur'an 97:4 describes angels and the Spirit descending in *laylah al-qadr*, which is better than a thousand months, Qur'an 70:4 describes the angels and the Spirit ascending in a day (note that it opposes the night), which measures fifty thousand years. The term used for measure is "*miqdār*," which is also rooted in "*q d r*." Perhaps it is just a coincidence, but Qur'an 70:8 describes the heaven as oil, while Jacob put oil on the stone he slept on, after seeing the vision of the ladder to heaven (i.e., Genesis 28:18).

In another place, the Qur'an describes how nonbelievers ask for the angels to descend so that they may believe (i.e., Qur'an 15:7). The response is that angels do not descend except with "*ḥaqq*" (truth) (i.e., Qur'an 15:8). Then, it says that God sent down "*al-dhikr*" (Qur'an) (i.e., Qur'an 15:9), which is related to Qur'an 15:6 when the nonbelievers ask the person who "*al-dhikr*" descended upon. Then, the Qur'an describes how previous messengers were also not believed (i.e., Qur'an 15:10–13). Afterward, the Qur'an states that even if a gate of heaven opened and they ascend (i.e., Qur'an 15:14), they would claim that it is just an illusion (i.e., Qur'an 15:15). In Qur'an 15:7–15, the nonbelievers challenge Muḥammad to have angels descend so they may believe in him. Then, it says that the angels only descend in "*ḥaqq*" and that the Qur'an descended from God. Qur'an 15:8–9 is perhaps an allusion to the Qur'an descending in *laylah al-qadr* (i.e., Qur'an 97:1), when the angels do indeed descend (i.e., Qur'an 97:4). Qur'an 15:14–15 state that if a gate of heaven opens and they ascend, they would still not believe. Qur'an 15:21 states that anything that descends is with a known measure (*qadar*), which is also rooted in "*q d r*." If Qur'an 15:8–9 is an allusion to Qur'an 97:4, then there is a likelihood that both are allusions to Genesis 28:12 and John 1:51, since Qur'an 15:14 speaks of a gate of heaven opening, similar to Jacob describing the place as the gate of heaven in Genesis 28:17 and John 1:51 quotes Jesus that heaven opens.

In yet another place, Qur'an 32:5 states, "He arranges matter (*yudabbir al-amr*) from the heaven to the earth; then it will ascend to Him in a day measured (*miqdāruhu*) a thousand years of those which you count." Here, although this passage does not talk about angels, it might be a reference to the Spirit, using the term "*amr*," which Qur'an 17:85 associates with the Spirit. Also, as subsequently will be illustrated in the last example of Chapter 7, the term "*yudabbir al-amr*" might be an allusion to the Messiah. In addition, this passage also uses the term "*miqdār*," which is rooted in "*qdr*." If Qur'an 32:5 is an allusion to Qur'an 97:1–5, then perhaps both are allusions to Jacob's ladder in Genesis 28:17 and John 1:51.

These could be additional clues of allusions between traditionally the first passages of the Qur'an with the Gospel of John making further indication that the Qur'an might have alluded to Muḥammad's own spiritual birth from above, and therefore, he is trying to assume authority that he is receiving a heavenly message from the Spirit and the archangel Gabriel that descended on him in *laylah al-qadr*.

Conclusion

Here we see that comparing the intertextual polysemy within the Qur'an about those who spiritually cling unto God with the Gospel of John brings us to a good example of the method of intertextual polysemy. If a person clings unto God as a fetus clings into its mother's womb, then it could be an allusion of spiritual birth and the person spiritually becoming a child of God. Hence, the Qur'an may not necessarily speak against God having children, as long as it emphasizes that these are to be understood spiritually and not physically. However, on the Qur'anic understanding of "*walad*" and its use of Jesus, the next chapter, I hope, would provide further insights.

6

Begotten of God

Theological debates between mainstream Christianity and Islam usually arrive at stumbling blocks. One of these stumbling blocks is the understanding from the New Testament that Jesus Christ is Begotten of God. Although appreciating the plethora of distinctive Christian theologies and Christologies that have existed historically and those that still exist today, the various forms of Christian theologies on the matter are not dealt with here. Here, I will look at the Bible and the Qur'an from a textual perspective, without the theological implications of textual interpretations.

While the New Testament, and especially the Gospel of John, emphasizes that the Messiah is Begotten of God, the Qur'an candidly declares that God neither begets nor is begotten (e.g., Qur'an 112:3). If we take the understandings from a literal point of view, we find that these two scriptures are in plain contrast with one another, and accordingly create the gap of theological dogma between Christians and Muslims. I argue that even if we do take the term Begotten of God from a literal point of view, the Qur'an does not seem to be contradicting the New Testament, but it is interpreting it instead. Although Heikki Räisänen suggests that it is more important to interpret the Qur'an through the Qur'an and not through the Bible, it is evident that the Qur'an is actually invoking the use of the Bible and in direct engagement with it,[1] as it attempts to interpret it. Hence, it is important to make a textual analysis between the Qur'an and the Bible to identify the possible meanings. Unfortunately, some scholars attempt to make historical assumptions of possible Christian influences on the authorship of the Qur'an, while neglecting the literary analysis of the Qur'anic discourse in its attempt to interpret the Bible.[2]

This is not about the history of Muslim and Christian relations from an historical perspective. It is specifically a comparative study between Christian and Muslim scriptures. Accordingly, I will not be making any historical assumptions, and consequently, I will not be making any historical conclusions. I will be making an analysis that is mainly textual through a linguistic approach, by simply stating that the Qur'an is interpreting the Bible in the topic of Jesus as Begotten of God without rejecting the concept at all. The Qur'an simply interprets Begotten of God with the concept of "*takwīn*" instead of "*tawlīd*."[3] As I have been arguing, the theology and Christology of the Qur'an may be different than how it was later developed in the Muslim community. Muḥammad's intentions seem to have been marred by later Muslims who sought to differentiate themselves from the Judeo-Christian roots of the Qur'an.[4]

To be

The terms Begotten of God and Son of God are two distinct terminologies. Since they can be sometimes confused with each other, it is very important to note their distinction from a linguistic point of view, besides even their possible theological implications.[5] The Greek term in the New Testament for Son is "*huios*," which corresponds to the Arabic "*ibn*" in the Qur'an. Even though the Qur'an many times rejects that God has begotten (*walad*), the term "*ibn Allah*" is only mentioned in a single passage in Qur'an 9:30, which has already been discussed in Chapter 5. The Greek term for begotten is rooted in "*gennaō*" or "*ginomai*" meaning to generate and corresponding to the Arabic "*walad*" or "*kawwan*." For the purpose of an accurate textual analysis, it is necessary to keep in mind the two distinct terminologies for Begotten and Son and how the Qur'an specifically engages with each one of them.

The Qur'an always rejects that God has begotten using the root of the term "*walad*." In some instances where the Qur'an denies that God has begotten, it reaffirms instead that whatever God wills, He but says to it "be," and it is (*kun fa-yakūn*) (e.g., Qur'an 2:116–117, 19:35). This Qur'anic concept and distinction between "*tawlīd*" and "*takwīn*," in which both can be understood as generation, is important. As such, the Greek terminology of "begotten" in the New Testament needs to be carefully analyzed.

According to the Gospel of John, the Logos, which is typically understood as Jesus Christ, is the only-begotten (*monogenous*) of God (i.e., John 1:14). The term "*monogenēs*" is used in John 1:18, "*monogenē*" is used in John 3:16, and "*monogenous*" is repeated in John 3:18. There are two related theories on the etymology of "*monogenēs*." One theory suggests the roots are from the term "*monos*," meaning only, and the term "*genos*," meaning derived or a kind.[6] Hence, "*monogenēs*" could mean "one of a kind (unique)" and not necessarily "only-begotten."[7] The Septuagint uses the term "*monogenēs*" for the Hebrew "*yaḥīd*," which means only but understood as only child in Judges 11:34. However, the Septuagint also uses the term "*agapētos*" for "*yaḥīd*" (e.g., Genesis 22:2, 22:16, Jeremiah 6:26, Amos 8:10, Zechariah 12:10). The second theory on the etymological roots of "*monogenēs*" suggests the terms "*monos*" and "*ginomai*,"[8] but this is still related to the first theory. The possible etymological root of "*genos*" is "*gignomai*," which is to be born, to become, or to beget.[9] The term "*gignomai*" is related to "*ginomai*," which is the Ionic and Hellenistic form of the verb.[10] The verb "*ginomai*" means "to become." Hence, the root meaning of "*monogenēs*" is either "unique" or "only become." If the meaning is "unique," then it should not be considered as "begotten,"[11] and therefore, may not be an issue in the Qur'an. In Hebrews 11:17, the term "*monogenē*" is used as a reference to Abraham's son Isaac while being offered as a sacrifice. Isaac is not the "only" one whom Abraham begat, but he is "unique," as he was conceived by a barren woman at old age. If the author of Hebrews was thinking through Genesis 22:2 in making the statement, the Septuagint does not translate Abraham's only (*yaḥīd*) son in Genesis 22:2, 22:12, and 22:16 as "*monogenē*," but translates it as "*agapētos*," meaning beloved. Perhaps the translators writing the Septuagint understood the term "*yaḥīd*" as the only beloved of Abraham, knowing that generally speaking Isaac is not the only son of Abraham. Nonetheless, it might still be understood as "only" of Abraham and Sarah, as a couple. The Synoptic Gospels use the term "*agapētos*" to describe Jesus as the beloved son (i.e., Matthew 3:17, 17:5, Mark 1:11, 9:7, Luke 3:22). In a parable, Mark and Luke also relate Jesus talking of a beloved son using the term "*agapēton*" (i.e., Mark 12:6, Luke 20:13). If the meaning of "*monogenē*" is "only become," then it would be related to the Arabic term "*takawwan*" instead of "*tawallad*," which this chapter examines.

Beyond the Gospel of John, the New Testament uses the term begotten in some other instances as well. In Acts 13:33, the term "*gegennēka*" (have begotten) is used, while quoting Psalm 2:7, using the same Greek term as it is in the Septuagint and translating it from the Hebrew "*yelidti*," which is cognate to the Arabic "*yalid*" and "*walad*." The same Greek term "*gegennēka*" is used in Hebrews 1:5 and repeated in Hebrews 5:5, which also quotes Psalm 2:7. In 1 John 4:9, it reiterates the concept from John 3:16, where God loves the world and sends his "*monogenē*" to save the world through him. In 1 John 5:1, it uses the terms "*gegennētai*" and "*gegennēmenon*" to mean "has been born," as a reference to those who are born of God. It continues in 1 John 5:18 using the term "*gegennēmenos*" for "who has been born" and the term "*gennētheis*" for "who was born," also as references to those born of God. The various morphologies for the term "begotten" are rooted in the term "*gennaō*" or "*genna*."[12] The term "*genna*" is related to "*genos*" and "*gignomai*," and there is a debate on the origin of the geminate "*nn*."[13] One explanation is that the "*nn*" is a restoration of the root "*gen-*" after "*genos*."[14] Although there is a controversy on the best way to translate "*monogenēs*," I will use "only-begotten," because it is the most popular translation. Regardless of how it is translated, I am not looking at it from a Greek scholar point of view. Instead, I argue how the Qur'an understands it. I argue that the Qur'an understands it as "*takawwan*" in Arabic instead of "*tawallad*," or more precisely since the Greek term "*monogenēs*" is a noun, the Qur'an interprets it as "*mutakawwan*" instead of "*mutawallad*," for the reasons I will provide.

The difference between the Greek terms "*gennaō*" and "*gignomai*" can sometimes be ambiguous. The same is with the English terms, such as "born of" and "beget," in which the father begets, but the mother bears.[15] The term "to be" in Greek can either fall under the root "*ginomai*" or "*eimi*." The term "*ginomai*" is usually understood to mean "become," which would correspond to the Arabic "*kn*." The term "*eimi*" is the typical verb "to be," which can also correspond to "*kn*." In addition, considering the difference between the Arabic understandings of "*tawlīd*" and "*takwīn*," it could be ambiguous on which would correspond to the Greek "*gennaō*" or "*ginomai*." This concept is also similar to the Hebrew "*ehyeh*" and "*yalid*." I will further explicate how the terms between the Arabic/Hebrew and the Greek terminologies are not always consistent with the use of few examples.

Semitic languages do not always explicitly use the verb "to be," as it is usually understood from context. If the term is made explicit, then it corresponds to the Arabic "*kn*" or the Hebrew "*hyh*." For example, to say "I am who (that) I am" in Arabic could be done in two ways. If the term "to be" is to be understood from context, then it would be translated as, "*innī ana*" or "*innanī ana*," which the Qur'an describes how God identifies Himself to Moses in Qur'an 20:12–14. If the term "to be" is used explicitly, it may be translated as "*akun mn (alladhī) akun*."[16] In Exodus 3:14, the phraseology uses the term "to be" explicitly, in which it corresponds to the Hebrew "*ehyeh asher ehyeh*." The

Septuagint translates it as "*egō eimi o'Ōn kai eimen*," using the term "*eimi*" for "*ehyeh*." However, the Hebrew term "*ehyeh*" is not always translated to a term corresponding to the Greek "*eimi*." For example, in Genesis, when the Hebrew term "*yhy*" is understood as "let there be," the Septuagint uses "*genēthēto*," while when it is understood as "there was," the Septuagint uses "*egeneto*." Accordingly, the term "to be," whether in Hebrew (*hyh*) or Arabic (*kn*), can sometimes correspond to either the Greek roots "*ginomai*" or "*eimi*." However, the Arabic and Hebrew terms "*wld*" or "*yld*" would particularly be understood as corresponding to the Greek root "*gennaō*" and its various related morphologies.

Logos

In Qur'anic literary style, the distinction between the concepts of "*tawlīd*" and "*takwīn*" must be carefully noted and analyzed, especially on the issue of Jesus as Begotten of God. While the Qur'an seems adamant to deny the concept of "*tawlīd*," it is contrasted with a strong affirmation of "*takwīn*." However, how those concepts should be translated, let alone even understood, can be debated. Since the Arabic term "*kn*" corresponds to the Hebrew "*hyh*," which is subsequently translated sometimes through Greek roots of "*ginomai*" or "*eimi*," we are in an awkward position when doing a textual analysis between the Arabic Qur'an and the Greek Gospel. Which word corresponds to which becomes speculative. However, I argue that the Qur'anic discourse attempts to interpret the Greek Gospel with a particular understanding of the term by emphasizing "*takwīn*" and denying "*tawlīd*." The reason, I argue, that the Qur'an tries to make such an emphasis is due to the theological implication that the Qur'an apparently believes the Gospel is trying to portray. According to the Qur'an, Jesus Christ is not "*walad*" (begotten) of God. On the contrary, God says to Jesus "*kun fa-yakūn*" (be and he becomes). If God says to Jesus "be" (*kn*) and so he becomes (*fa-yakūn*), then Jesus is indeed become (*takawwan*) of God. As such, the Qur'an does not truly deny that Jesus is become of God, but distinguishes between begotten from "*tawlīd*" and become from "*takwīn*." Even though the Qur'an seems to firmly deny Jesus is "*tawallad*" of God, it at the same time firmly affirms that Jesus is "*takawwan*" of God, in which both terminologies are still compatible with the Greek root of "*ginomai*," as shown earlier. However, the reason the Qur'an is making such a distinction so fervently is perhaps in its attempt to interpret the Gospel of John. I argue that the Qur'an attempts to interpret and identify the Logos with the term "to be" (*kn*), and it is for that reason that the Qur'an emphasizes "*takwīn*," while denying "*tawlīd*." As the Qur'an is touching on the subject of Jesus Christ Begotten of God, then it is imperative to compare the language of the Gospel of John on this topic, as it is only one of the four canonical Gospels that rhetorically insists on Christ "*monogenē*" of God.[17] I argue that understanding the Logos is imperative to the understanding of the "*monogenous*" in John's prologue. I also argue that the Qur'an attempts to make such a relationship between the Logos and the "*monogenē*," while interpreting John's intentions. Even though Räisänen suggests that it is important to interpret the Logos from Muḥammad's point of view and not a Christian one,[18] I argue that the Qur'an is not bringing a new view of the Logos, but is actually trying to interpret John's definition thereof. It has been argued before by Robert Zaehner that the Qur'an, unlike later Muslim Christology, does not deny the divinity of Jesus or the Johannine Logos.[19]

As Roger Haight states, "No biblical [*sic*] text has had more influence on the development of christology [*sic*] than the Prologue to John's gospel."[20] The Qur'an may appear to have a different Christology than that presented in John's prologue. Since the Qur'an may present itself with a different Christology, but at the same time not denying the Gospel[s], then we must try to understand this apparent contradiction, if indeed it is. Such a contradiction seems unlikely to pass through an intelligent and creative Muḥammad, unless he did not see it as a contradiction himself. For that reason, I argue that the Qur'an is not refuting the Gospel of John, but is attempting to interpret it instead.

There have been attempts of reconciling the Christologies by understanding certain Shīʿī concepts,[21] such as a tradition attributed to ʿAlī ibn Abī Ṭālib describing himself and his progeny, as the Word and Spirit of God, who are light that dwelled in their bodies.[22] However, we must try to distinguish between what is considered Qur'anic and what is considered part of a post-Qur'anic tradition.

The prologue of the Gospel of John (i.e., John 1:1–18) is typically described as logically distinct from the main body of the Gospel, and by some regarded to adopt a pre-Christian hymn.[23] M. John Farrelly states: "This pre-Christian hymn is not gnostic; it is probably a fragment of an ancient myth of Wisdom adapted to 'Word' in a Judeo-Hellenistic milieu, reflecting the medium by which the transcendent God made contact with the created world."[24]

Farrelly suggests that the Word in the Gospel of John is different than that of Philo, as it becomes incarnate in the historical figure of Jesus.[25] John does not use the term Sophia (Wisdom), but keeps it as Logos (Word),[26] giving reason why some scholars do not accept it as a source for Johannine Logos.[27] Farrelly refers to John 1:14, in which John identifies the Word as the Son of God, which he then uses this title as a reference to Jesus in the rest of the Gospel.[28] Nonetheless, John 1:14 specifically uses the term "*monogenous*," which I would like to keep distinct from the term "son" (*huiou*) that John uses in John 3:16–18. We should acknowledge that John does not explicitly identify Jesus as either the Logos or the "*monogenē*" throughout his Gospel, but does identify Jesus as the Son (*huios*/*huiou*) of God (e.g., John 10:36, 20:31).

Rudolf Bultmann suggested similarities between John's Gospel and Gnostic writings.[29] Craig Evans portrayed similarities between John's Gospel and Gnostic writings, namely the Coptic *Trimorphic Protennoia*, the Syriac *Odes of Solomon*, and *Corpus Hermeticum*.[30] The parallels portrayed are striking, though Evans dismisses them.[31] Since the existence of pre-Christian Gnosticism is debatable, with some scholars debating against concrete evidence of their existence,[32] then perhaps they were influenced by John's Gospel, and not the other way round.

Charles H. Dodd argued the similarities between Philo's writings with that of John in using common symbolism, such as "*logos*" and "*shepherd*."[33] He argues that Johannine literature may best be viewed through its Jewish roots. Some scholars find parallelism between John's prologue and Jewish Wisdom writings.[34] James Dunn considers John 1:1–14 to contain nothing unusual for a Hellenistic Jew who is familiar with Philo's mystical hermeneutics or Wisdom literature.[35]

Philo frequently calls God's speech in the Hebrew Bible "*logos*," perhaps due to the Septuagint's rendition of God's word (*debar*) as "*logos*" (e.g., Exodus 20:1, Deuteronomy 1:1). Philo mentions the word that caused the whole world to be made as God's "logō," referring to Deuteronomy 34:5.[36] When describing the "*logos*," which made the world become (*ginomenō*), Philo suggests that God's word and action come automatically together,[37] which is echoed by a tradition attributed to ʿAlī ibn Abī Ṭālib.[38]

Ed L. Miller suggests that the origins of the Johannine Logos should not go beyond Johannine literature (i.e., not influenced by either Greek "Wisdom" literature or Philo's Logos).[39] He suggests that the term "*logos*" is often used in the body of the Gospel, and is sometimes used to signify the message and teachings of Jesus.[40] However, Miller sometimes uses the term "word" in John's Gospel very loosely, as he also accepts the term "*rhēma*."[41] However, there are truly other instances in which Jesus' "word(s)" are rooted in "*logos*" (e.g., John 4:41, 5:24, 7:40, 8:31).

At the beginning of the Gospel of John, the topic that the author addresses is that of the Logos.[42] "In the beginning was the Logos, and the Logos was with God, and the Logos was God (or God was the Logos)."[43] The theological implication at the beginning of the Gospel of John is that the Logos is identified as God.[44] John, starting with "in the beginning (*en archē*)," resembles Genesis.[45] It appears as if John attempts to interpret the prologue of Genesis,[46] perhaps because the Jewish midrash relates the beginning of Genesis with the Messiah.[47]

The Gospel continues to state about the Logos, "All things came into being (*egeneto*) through him, and without him not one thing came into being (*egeneto*) that has become (*gegonen*)."[48] According to John, the Logos is the source of all things that came to be (*egeneto*). Also, the Logos is the life that is the light (*phōs*) of all people (i.e., John 1:4). This light (*phōs*) shines in the darkness and the darkness cannot overcome it (i.e., John 1:5). The allusions of John continue to be related to Genesis. First, there is the phrase "in the beginning," which parallels with Genesis 1:1. John uses the terminology found in the Septuagint, "*en archē*." Second, John states that the Logos is the source of all that came to be, which parallels the Genesis account of generation on how God made things to be, by saying "let there be." John also employs the terminology used in the Septuagint of the things that came to be, "*egeneto*." Third, John describes this source as the Logos, which is the Word, giving it an impression that it is a form of speech or something articulated. This also has parallels in Genesis whenever it states "and God said, let there be (*genēthēto*)."[49] Fourth, John suggests that the Logos is light, which shines in darkness. This also parallels Genesis that the first thing that God said was for light to become, and It divided the light from the darkness.

If we are to read Genesis independent of the Gospel of John, then it might be appropriate to suggest that God is the source of all things that came to be, and the Word that God uses to bring things to be is "be," which is "*yhy*" in Hebrew translated as "*genēthēto*" in the Septuagint. The apparent difference that John seems to be taking is identifying the Word as God. However, that should not be surprising. In Exodus 3:14, when Moses asks God to identify Itself, the answer is, "*ehyeh asher ehyeh*," which means "I am who I am." As such, God identifies Itself to Moses with the word, "be."[50] In Exodus 6:3, God is explicitly identified as "*Yahweh*," which might be apparently also rooted in the term "*hyh*" meaning "be."[51] Therefore, the name of God, *Yahweh*, is more appropriately understood as *The Being*, the one who is present, or the one who brings forth things that become (a God who acts).[52] On the meaning of *Yahweh* in Exodus 6:2, the Talmud states, "The Holy One, blessed be He, said to Moses, 'I am He who spoke and the world came into being.' "[53]

Some scholars also suggest that John's prologue, especially John 1:14–18, has a relationship with Exodus 33–34.[54] It is suggested that John 1:17 compares the giving of the Law through Moses in Sinai, while grace and truth came through Jesus Christ.[55] It is also suggested that seeing the glory (*doxan*) in John 1:14 is contrasted with Moses asking to see God's glory (*doxan*/*doxa* in the Septuagint; rooted in "*k b d*" in Hebrew) in Exodus 33:18 and 33:20.[56] John 1:18 states, "No one has ever seen God; the only-begotten (*monogenēs*) God,[57] who is at the Father's side, he has made him known." This is contrasted when Moses asks to see God, and God tells him that he cannot see Its face, but only Its back (i.e., Exodus 33:20–23; Qur'an 7:143). If John 1:14 is a reference to the glory (*k b d*) in Exodus 33:18 and 33:20, then there might be an interesting reference of John 1:18 in Qur'an 90:3–4, "And the father (begetter/*wālid*) and that which was born (begotten/*walad*) (or that which was not begotten). We have created the human in *kabad*."[58] This is the only instance where the root "*k b d*" is used in the Qur'an.

These passages may shed light on Qur'an 112:1–4, "Say, He (*huwa*) is Allah the One (*aḥad*). Allah the indivisible (bound/yoke) (*ṣamad*).[59] Neither begets (*yalid*) nor begotten (*yūlad*). And nor is there one (*aḥad*) to subvert (*kufuwan*) Him." It has already been suggested that the first passage asserting the unity of God using the term "*aḥad*" echoes the Jewish *Shema*,[60] "Hear O Israel: The Lord our God the Lord is one (*Shema Yisrael, YHWH Elohaynu YHWH aḥad*)."[61] The Talmud Yerushalmi emphasizes the term "*aḥad*."[62] Since "*ṣamad*" may mean to join or to yoke,[63] then this further may suggest an intertextuality between these passages with the *Shema*, as the *Shema* is considered "the acceptance of the yoke of the kingdom of heaven."[64] According to classical exegetes, such as al-Ṭabarī, the circumstances of revelation (*asbāb al-nuzūl*) is due to Jews asking Muḥammad to speak of his God,[65] which might further support its probable reference to the *Shema* in that it might have been a response to the Jews. Although the current sources of the possible connection between this Qur'anic chapter with the *Shema* emphasize the term "*aḥad*," it may be noted that the first verse uses "*qul huwa Allah aḥad*," in which the pronoun "*huwa*" (He) may have its own Semitic etymology meaning to be,[66] which also resonates with God's name (Yahweh) in the *Shema*.[67] In addition to this, the term "*qul*" (say) may be understood that it is a speech, in which the listener is expected to hear, which may also be a reference to the *Shema* that means "hear." The chapter is called al-Ikhlāṣ, which is typically understood as sincerity or devotion, but it could also mean salvation or exclusiveness.[68] Also, it may mean loins, or to withdraw, to untie, to extract, or to show oneself strong (ready for fighting).[69] Usually, a Qur'anic chapter is named using a word that exists in its content, but there are few exceptions (e.g., Qur'an 1, 21). Qur'an 112 is one of those few exceptions. If Ikhlāṣ means sincerity or devotion, then this might echo the second verse of the *Shema*, "Love the Lord your God with all your heart, with all your soul, and with all your might"[70] and the subsequent verses, which may be understood that a person must have full devotion to God in whatever they do. The Talmud interprets "with all your heart" to mean with both your good and bad inclinations.[71] It interprets "with all your soul" to mean even if God takes your soul.[72] It interprets "with all your might" to mean with all your wealth.[73]

This now brings us to Qur'an 112:3–4, which states that this inseparable God neither begets (*yalid*) nor is begotten (*yūlad*). Although it has been suggested that these passages are directly denying the Nicene Creed,[74] they may be engaging with both the Nicene Creed and the principal Trinitarian foundation that might have evolved into the pseudo-Athanasian Creed.[75] First, it seems that the Qur'an is still trying to emphasize the concept of "*takwīn*" by denying "*tawlīd*," which as suggested earlier that the use of "*huwa*" might be denoting Yahweh in the *Shema* that is perhaps rooted in the term "be." Second, the pseudo-Athanasian Creed talks of three persons without dividing the essence, which could also be associated with the term "*ṣamad*" that may mean inseparable. Third, the term "*kufuwan*" may hold several meanings one of which is equal, and perhaps it is engaging with the pseudo-Athanasian Creed, which states that the three persons are coequal, but Jesus Christ is only equal to the Father pertaining to him being Son of God, but inferior to the Father pertaining to his manhood. If the root of this term is "*k f a'*," then this is the only passage in the Qur'an that uses it, very much like "*ṣamad*," making both of these terms *hapax legomena*. If, however, it is rooted in "*k f y*," then there indeed are many passages that use it.

I admit that how the Qur'an attempts to engage with the Nicene Creed and perhaps the foundations of what later came to be known as the pseudo-Athanasian Creed seems like a puzzle.[76] The pseudo-Athanasian Creed, for example, suggests that the Godhead's essence is indivisible and coequal, but the persons are separate. Is the Qur'an denouncing the pseudo-Athanasian Creed, which attempts to separate the persons of the Godhead, while agreeing to that God's essence is indivisible? Edwin Walhout suggests the following on the pseudo-Athanasian Creed: (i) it presupposes a docetic mentality, (ii) it defines the Trinity docetically, and (iii) its acceptance requires fideism, and is used to distinguish Christianity from other religions, such as Islam.[77] Qur'an 4:171–172 explicitly asks Christians not to say "three." Though the elements that make up the Trinity may have started in early Christianity, but as a doctrine, it was explicitly defined by Tertullian (d. 225 CE).[78] While the Nicene Creed is not explicit about the Trinity, in which the Godhead is in three persons, the pseudo-Athanasian Creed explicitly says they are three in one God. Perhaps the Qur'an is more adamant against the foundations of the Trinity as it evolved into the pseudo-Athanasian Creed than the Nicene Creed. When elaborating on the Nicene Creed, Ambrose (d. 397 CE) states: "So, then, he himself who calls the Son of God the maker of heavenly things, has also plainly said that all things were made in the Son, that in renewal of His works He might by no means separate the Son from the Father, but unite Him to the Father."[79]

The Qur'an seems to interpret the Gospel of John without denying it. According to Genesis, God is the source of all things that came to be, and the Word that God uses to bring forth everything to be is "be" (*yhy/genēthēto*). According to Exodus, God is identified to be Himself the Word "be" (*Ehyeh/Yahweh*).[80] John states that the Word is the source of all things that came to be (*egeneto*) and the Word was in Itself God. In a later discourse, John quotes Jesus saying, "Truly, truly, I say to you, before Abraham was (*genesthai*), I am (*egō eimi*)."[81] John, here, brings the Septuagint's translation of "I am" (*ehyeh*) in Exodus 3:14. Therefore, it seems likely that John considers the Logos as the

Word "be," which is the source of all things that came to be, and it in itself is identified with the name of God. Ambrose states:

> Therefore, let the soul which wishes to approach God raise herself from the body and cling always to that Highest Good which is divine, and lasts forever, and which was from the beginning and which was with God,[82] that is, the Word of God. This is the Divine Being "in which we live and are and move."[83] This was in the beginning, this is: "The Son of God, Jesus Christ in you," he says, "in whom there was not Yes and No, but only Yes was in him."[84] He Himself told Moses to say: "He who is hath sent me."[85]

Although I do not see in Ambrose's letter that he defines the Word with the name of God (*Ehyeh*/*Yahweh*), there is one source that suggests this relationship.[86] Nonetheless, at least this seems to be how the Qur'an interprets the Gospel of John when it insists on "*takwīn*" instead of "*tawlīd*."

> 116 And they say: "God has begotten (*waladā*)."[87] Glory be to Him! Rather, unto Him belongs whatsoever is in the heavens and on the earth. All are devoutly obedient to Him, 117 the Originator of the heavens and the earth. When He decrees a thing, He only says to it, "Be!" and it is (*kun fa-yakūn*).[88]

> 34 That is Jesus son of Mary—a statement of the truth, which they doubt. 35 It is not for God to take a child (*walad*). Glory be to Him! When He decrees a thing, He only says to it, "Be!" and it is (*kun fa-yakūn*).[89]

The Qur'an in these verses does not seem to outright deny that God generates. The Qur'an is simply denying that God generates through "*tawlīd*," and instead insists that God generates through "*takwīn*." According to the Qur'an, God makes things become through the word "*kn*," as can be seen in various Qur'anic passages (e.g., Qur'an 6:73, 16:40, 36:82, 40:68), and not through "*yld*," as can be seen in other various Qur'anic passages (e.g., Qur'an 6:101, 25:2). Therefore, even on the topic of Jesus, the Qur'an seems to be emphasizing how it interprets John's understanding of the Logos, using the Word "*kn*," which is the keyword, and not "*wld*." This shows that the Qur'an is adopting a Johannine interpretation of Christ as the Word of God, which is not necessarily created but an agent of creation.[90] Early Muslim theological schools, such as the Ash'arī and Mu'tazilī, emerged debating whether or not the words of God, the Qur'an, is created or uncreated.[91] "Truly the likeness of Jesus in the sight of God is that of Adam; He created him from dust, then said to him, 'Be!' and he is (*kun fa-yakūn*)."[92]

Although Muslim thought has associated the term for creation with "*kn*" (be), we realize from the above verse that it is not necessarily so. As stated earlier, the term "*khlq*" may also hold the meaning to divide and not only create, but regardless, the above Qur'anic passage states that God did the "*khalq*" and then (*thumma*) said "be." There are two types of the term "then" in Arabic, "*fa-*" and "*thumma*." The term "*fa-*" is usually understood to mean immediately after, while the term "*thumma*" is usually understood to mean after a while.[93] The above verse uses the term "*thumma*," which means that it is stating that God "*khlq*" Adam from dust, and *then* (after a while) said to him "be," and immediately after (*fa-*) saying "be," he becomes. Using the term "*thumma*" does not only imply that God saying "be" is an occurrence after a while, but also implies that God saying "be" is not necessarily a direct consequence of "*khlq*" from dust. However, the term "*fa-*" implies that the "becoming" (*yakūn*) is in direct consequence of saying "be" (*kn*). The Qur'an explicitly shows that God did not say "be" to create. The Qur'an is distinguishing between creation and being.[94] They are *not* the same. God created and then (after a while) said "be," and saying "be" is not even necessarily a consequence of God's creation. Notably, the above passage does not use the title "messiah" for Jesus. However, when the Qur'an uses the term "*kalimah*" (Word) for Jesus, it uses the title "messiah." "When the angels said, O Mary, truly God gives thee glad tidings (*yubashshiruki*) of a Word (*bi-kalimah*) from Him, whose name is the Messiah, Jesus son of Mary, high honored in this world and the Hereafter, and one of those brought nigh."[95]

If the Qur'an is interpreting John's Logos with the term "be," then perhaps it may be understood from the Qur'an that God created Jesus' physical body from dust through Mary, and this Jesus without the "messiah" title is simply the physical body. However, when the Word (*kalimah*), which is "be," dwells within this body of Jesus, he is given the title "messiah," and this "be" is in itself perhaps uncreated, because it is the source and agent of creation.[96] Prominently, the term used to mean glad tidings of this Word is "*yubashshiruki*" that is rooted in "*b s h r*," which is polysemous and one of its meanings is "flesh." The Incarnation of the Word will further be explored in the next chapter. Qur'an 5:17 and 5:72 seem to suggest that God is not the Messiah the son of Mary. Qur'an 5:17 asks who will be able to subvert God, if God wills to "*yuhlika*" the Messiah son of Mary and his mother and everyone on earth. The root "*h l k*" is polysemous with meanings ranging from death, destruction, and falling.[97] In Hebrew and Aramaic, the term is associated with walking, passing, or moving from one place to another.[98] Perhaps in Arabic it came to mean passing away, as a person goes from one place to another.[99] Also, the meaning of destruction in Arabic might also have come from the meaning making them go away (wipe out).

Possibly, when the Qur'an uses the term "son of Mary," it is distinguishing between the human Jesus who has the Word in him (giving him the title "messiah"), from the Word itself, which is perhaps uncreated. I have a strong inclination to assume that the Qur'an apparently is aware of the Christological differences between the Gospel of John and the rest. Take note that in the Gospel of John there is no reference of Jesus' human birth from Mary.[100] To further support the notion that, when the Qur'an speaks of Jesus without using the term "messiah," it is specifically talking of Jesus' physical body, is the following verse: "when He said, 'O Jesus, I shall take thee and raise thee unto Me, and purify thee of those who disbelieved, and place those who followed thee above those who disbelieved, until the Day of Resurrection. Then unto Me is your return, and I shall judge between you concerning that wherein you used to differ.' "[101]

This verse is suggesting that Jesus' physical body (not the "messiah") will die. Just few verses later, in Qur'an 3:59, it states that Jesus' physical body (not the "messiah") is created from dust, and the Word, "*kn*," comes later. As stated earlier, defining "*takwīn*" and "*tawlīd*" may both hold the meaning of generation, corresponding to the Greek roots "*ginomai*" and "*gennaō*." However, the Qur'an perhaps provides us with a clue of what it considers the difference between those two terms in a passage that precedes the one above. "She said, 'My Lord, how shall I have a child (*walad*) while no flesh [human] (*bashar*) being has touched me?' He said, 'Thus does God create whatsoever He will.' When He decrees a thing (*amran*), He only says to it, 'Be!' and it is (*kun fa-yakūn*)!"[102]

According to this passage, Mary asks how she can beget (*walad*), when no flesh (man) had touched her. The Qur'an does not deny that Jesus is begotten through "*tawlīd*," as long as it emphasizes that the "*tawlīd*" is something that had come from Mary, while "*takwīn*" is something that had come from God. Even though the above passage does not even answer whether or not Jesus is even begotten (*tawallad*) from Mary, the passages below confirm that Jesus was, in fact, somehow begotten through "*tawlīd*." However, it is not God that had begotten him through "*tawlīd*," for according to the Qur'an, God had begotten him through "*takwīn*" instead:

> 33 Peace be upon me the day I was born (*wulidtu*), the day I die, and the day I am raised alive!" 34 That is Jesus son of Mary—a statement of the truth, which they doubt. 35 It is not for God to take a child (*walad*). Glory be to Him! When He decrees a thing (*amran*), He only says to it, "Be!" and it is (*kun fa-yakūn*).[103]

The Qur'an appears to differentiate the concept of "*tawlīd*" from the concept of "*takwīn*" in that "*tawlīd*" is understood as physical birth, while "*takwīn*" is something more abstract. John attempts to differentiate between the concepts of physical birth and born of God when stating, "who were born (*gennaō*) not of blood, nor of the will of flesh (*sarkos*), nor of the will of man (*andros*), but of God."[104] According to the Qur'an, Mary questions how she can beget (*walad*) when no flesh (man) had touched her. Hence, in the Qur'an, to beget through "*tawlīd*," it is assumed that it is physical flesh. Since "*tawlīd*" and "*takwīn*" can share the same root in Greek, which is "*gennaō*" or "*ginomai*," John apparently had to make an explicit statement differentiating between that which is born physically and that which is born through God. Actually, John even furthermore explicates the difference between begotten of flesh and begotten of God, when describing the mystery of being born again in a conversation between Jesus and Nicodemus:

> 3 Jesus replied, "Truly, truly, I tell you, unless one is born (*gennēthē*) again, he cannot see the kingdom of God." 4 "How can a man be born (*gennēthēnai*) when he is old?" Nicodemus asked. "Can he enter a second time into his mother's womb and be born (*gennēthēnai*)?" 5 Jesus answered, "Truly, truly, I tell you, unless one is born (*gennēthē*) of water and the Spirit, he cannot enter the kingdom of God. 6 That which is born (*gegennēmenon*) of the flesh (*sarkos*) is flesh (*sarkos*), and that which is born (*gegennēmenon*) of the Spirit is spirit. 7 You should not be surprised at my saying, 'You must be born (*gennēthēnai*) again.' 8 The wind blows wherever it pleases. You hear its sound, but you cannot tell where it comes from or where it is going. So it is with everyone born (*gegennēmenos*) of the Spirit."[105]

The term used by John for being born is rooted in the Greek "*gennaō*." John differentiates between those born of flesh (*sarkos*) and those born of the Spirit. In the

Qur'an, Mary uses the term "*walad*" as an understanding of being born of flesh (*bashar*). Meanwhile, when the Qur'an rebukes that God begets through "*tawlīd*," it reaffirms that whatever God commands (*amr*), He says to it, "be" (*kn*), especially in the case of Jesus (i.e., Qur'an 3:47, 19:35). The Qur'anic usage of God's command (*amr*) in these passages may be significant in trying to understand the Qur'anic differentiation between the concepts of "*tawlīd*" and "*takwīn*." According to the Qur'an, the Spirit is identified with God's command (*amr*), "They ask thee about the Spirit. Say, 'The Spirit is from the Command (*amr*) of my Lord, and you have not been given knowledge, save a little.' "[106] Therefore, the concept of "*tawlīd*," according to the Qur'an, is understood as born of flesh (*bashar*), while the concept of "*takwīn*" may be understood as those born of God's command (*amr*) that is associated with the Spirit. While John seems to make an explicit differentiation between those born of flesh from those born of the Spirit by handling the Greek "*gennaō*," the Qur'an is simply making this differentiation by using two distinct words "*tawlīd*" and "*takwīn*."

Therefore, the Qur'an is not necessarily contradicting the New Testament when it outright denies that Jesus is begotten (*walad*) of God. Actually, the Qur'an is interpreting the Gospel of John using precise words by identifying the Logos with the word "be," which is in Itself God (*Ehyeh/Yahweh*), and the Qur'an precisely distinguishes between those born of flesh and those born of the Spirit. After John makes the distinction between those born of flesh and those born of the Spirit, he continues stating expressively that God sent His "*monogenē*" to save the world, but there are those who still do not believe in the name of the "*monogenous*" Son of God (i.e., John 3:16–19). The Qur'an seems to agree that Jesus is "*takawwan*" of God, as it is to be understood spiritually (*takawwan*) and not physically (*tawallad*). However, as stated earlier, the Qur'an is at the same time not denying that Jesus is also a physical person, as he was "*walad*" of flesh from Mary, and was also become (*takawwan*) of God. On a sermon about the nativity of Jesus Christ, Augustine states that there are two births; one, which is divine, and another, which is human.[107] On the portrayal of Mary, the mother of Jesus in the Gospel of John, Turid Seim concludes the following:

> But there is no female principle involved in the divine begetting and birth-giving. The mother does not matter because matter is what she provides. The only-begotten God/Son who is in the *κόλπον* of the Father (John 1.18) bears the children of God, in whom the σπέρμα, that is, the πνεῦμα of God, abides. They are begotten as born not of bloods, not of the will of flesh or of the will of man, but of God . . .[108]

Seim concludes that the role of the mother as childbearer is nonexistent in the Gospel of John as the author attempts to distinguish physical birth from a spiritual birth.

There have been suggestions of the Johannine Logos' relationship with the *Memra* of the Targum, which also keeps it within the context of Semitic Jewish instead of Hellenistic notions.[109] The *Memra* is the Aramaic rendition of the Word in the Targum, sometimes denoting the Word of God. The *Memra* might have been a clue to the "*yhy*" in Genesis 1. After all, the *Memra* is rooted in "*amar*," which means "said" that Genesis 1 frequently uses to describe whenever God "said" something, and the first thing that God "*amar*" (said) is "*yhy*." Some scholars, such as Martin McNamara have dismissed the *Memra* as a background to John's Logos. In discussing the weakness of the *Memra* theory, McNamara states: "To begin with, whereas in John Logos is not just another manner of expressing the divine Name but is a term rich in theological import, the Memra of the Targum seems to be a term devoid of special content; it appears to be merely another way of saying 'God' or 'the Lord.'"[110]

Given the analysis portrayed in the relationship between the Logos and "*yhy*," I must disagree with McNamara's analysis in that John's Logos is in fact a reference to the Name of God (*Ehyeh*/*Yhwh*). John appears to be cautious in using the Logos as a reference to avoid using and spelling out God's name of the Hebrew Bible. It is possible that rendering God's name (*Yhwh*) would be too great a feat for John, that he would rather refer to it indirectly in keeping with its traditional sanctity. Besides, the Aramaic *Memra* of the Targum could have been exactly that; being related to the "*amar*" of Genesis 1, which is "*yhy*," associated with the name of God. Daniel Boyarin states: "In the Targumim we can see, or at any rate, construct a picture of how the Memra has also come into being in the exegesis of Gen 1:3. Exod. 3:12–14 (the theophany of the burning bush) and its targumic expositions are key texts."[111]

Boyarin continues by stating about how God reveals His name to Moses in Exodus 3:12–14: "According to the Palestinian Targum, preserved in MS Neofiti 1, the Aramaic here reads: 'I, My *Memra*, will be with you.' The other targumim maintain this interpretation but add the element of the *Memra* as supporter, thus, 'And he said: Because my *Memra* will be for your support.'"[112]

The *Memra* of the Targum is clearly a reference to the "*amar*" of Genesis 1, which is "*yhy*," and the name of God in Exodus 3:14, which is "*Ehyeh*."[113] Accordingly, Boyarin does not suggest that the Logos being God is the juncture between John and Judaism, but it is specifically the Incarnation of the Logos that causes such difference.[114] However, by suggesting John's Logos is the term "be" (*hyh*), which the Targumim calls the *Memra*, it has also been suggested that it does not necessarily mean that it is completely distinct from the notion of Wisdom in the Bible and Jewish literature.[115] In any case, given the evidence, the Logos being a reference to "*hyh*," rooted in the very Hebrew name of God and its relationship with the *Memra* of Targum provides us with a good plausible origin and definition of John's concept.

Conclusion

Is the Qur'an right to interpret the Johannine Logos with the term "be?" There is a likelihood that the Johannine Logos is related to the word "be," which is from the term "*yhy*" (rooted in *h y h*) in Genesis 1 that is translated in the Septuagint as "*genēthēto*." John perhaps associates the Logos as God, because the Hebrew Bible identifies God as "*Ehyeh*," which might also have been permutated morphologically into *Yhwh*. Through the medium of this Logos, everything was created in Genesis 1, and even more specifically starting with the light, which John uses in his prologue. The first word that God utters in Genesis 1 is "*yhy*." If we answer the above question with "perhaps, yes," then the reason why the Qur'an is trying to associate the term "*monogenous*" with the notion of "*takwīn*" instead of "*tawlīd*" becomes evident.

The Qur'an would not contradict John's description, "And the Word became (*egeneto*) flesh (*sarx*)."[116] When the Qur'an suggests that the likeness of Jesus is that of Adam, he created him of dust, then said to him "be" and he becomes, it confirms that Jesus is flesh made of dust, as it might also suggest that Jesus is perhaps the word "be" becoming within that flesh.

As I deliberated, this section does not look into the Christological or theological implications of its observations. I am simply comparing the New Testament's text of Jesus as Begotten of God, and the Qur'anic interpretation of the same. The texts do not seem to contradict. Actually, the Qur'an is shown to be interpretive of the Bible, and does not necessarily deny it. However, the significance of this theologically is beyond the scope of this book or even the method of intertextual polysemy. As such, the Qur'an does not seem to contradict itself, when it asks Christians to adhere to the Gospel[s], while refuting its Christology. The Qur'an seems to be interpreting, in this case, the Gospel of John, and not denying it. It seems to associate the Logos with the term "be." Ibn Taymiyyah realizes the significance of the term "be" in Genesis as God's word of generation, but does not associate Jesus with this word.[117] It is apparent that Muḥammad's intention in the Qur'an is distinct from how Christology later developed in the Muslim community.

7

The Incarnation and the Water of Life

The Incarnation and the Temple of the Body

The Gospel of John seems to be direct about the Incarnation of the Word. If the Qur'an expects the Christians to follow the Gospel[s] (i.e., Qur'an 5:47, 5:66, 5:68), then what is in Muḥammad's mind that might reconcile the Incarnation of the Word? We need to search for possible clues in the Qur'an.

Ibn Taymiyyah wrote a response refuting the Christian faith and the Incarnation.[1] Within the mainstream Islamic context, the thought of God incarnating into human flesh is very foreign and to some extent sacrilegious.[2] This example textually compares the Qur'an concept of the creation of human flesh to the Gospel of John's understanding of the Incarnation. It brings to light that the Qur'an perhaps indeed emerged through the sectarian milieu of its time between the different churches as John Wansbrough suggests.[3]

Knowing Muḥammad's state of mind and his ability to link things together in an intertextual methodology using polysemy, we may search for subtle clues about incarnation within the Qur'an. This section illustrates that, textually, the Qur'an generally shows that the creation of human flesh is from clay, and then God establishes it (*sawwaytuhu*) using the same terminology as He establishes (*istawa*) on His Throne and then breathes into the clay from His Spirit. Perhaps this would be an inner-Qur'anic allusion that the flesh becomes as if it is the Throne of God or the Temple of God. The flesh is human, but the Spirit that resides within the flesh is God's. The Gospel of John portrays Jesus Christ as the Temple of the Body (i.e., John 2:21). If the Incarnation of the Logos is the union of the divine in human flesh, then perhaps we find Muḥammad speaking into the Christian milieu of his time. As Abdulaziz Sachedina argues, if Muslims continue solely to use their heritage from classical scholars as a basis of Christian–Muslim relations, then they will not be able to respond to today's notion of pluralism.[4] Perhaps a similar argument can be made about Churches and their inherited traditions. As such, if we are to place a mediator in any Christian–Muslim dialogue, it perhaps should not be based on tradition and its early sources. The scriptural text in each of those faiths would probably be the best mediator.

Creation of human flesh

According to the Qur'an, the creation of human flesh seems to be forthright from clay (e.g., Qur'an 6:2, 22:5, 30:20, 35:11, 40:67). The Qur'an states that when God wanted to create human flesh, He informed the angels about it and told them that as soon as He formed it (*sawwaytuhu*) and breathed into it from His Spirit, they were to bow down before it: "so when I have proportioned him (*sawwaytuhu*) and breathed into him of My Spirit, fall down before him prostrating."[5]

It is necessary to understand the meaning of the terms used in these Qur'anic verses, as perhaps Muḥammad is using inner-Qur'anic allusions. The term used for fashioning the human flesh is "*sawwaytuhu*." This term shares the same root as the term used by the Qur'an for God establishing (*istawa*) on His Throne (i.e., Qur'an 7:54, 10:3, 13:2, 20:5, 25:59, 32:4, 57:4). The term has a polysemous nature, in which "*sāwa*" is to be equal; "*sawwā*" means to form, and "*sawiyyā*" means upright.[6] The Qur'an uses those various meanings in different verses. It is used to mean that people are to be made one (or equal) with the earth, as a metaphor of dying as if placed in a grave (i.e., Qur'an 4:42, 91:14). It is used to mean to be made equal (*yastawī*/ *nusawwīkum*/ *yastawūn*) (i.e., Qur'an 4:95, 5:100, 6:50, 9:29 11:24, 13:16, 16:75–76, 26:98, 32:18, 35:12, 35:19, 35:22, 39:9, 39:29, 40:58, 41:34, 57:10, 59:20). It is used to mean a place of equality or equal chances (*suwā*) (i.e., Qur'an 20:58). It is used to refer to resting or sitting, even besides God sitting on the Throne. The term "*istawat*" is employed to mean Noah's ark resting on the mountain after the flood (i.e., Qur'an 11:44) and "*istawayt*" is used to mean the people resting on or mounting Noah's ark or on the back of animals (i.e., Qur'an 23:28, 43:13). The term here means to form or to be made upright (*sawwaytuhu*/ *sawwāk*/ *sawwāhu*/ *sawwā*) (i.e., Qur'an 15:29, 18:37, 32:9, 38:72, 75:4, 75:38, 79:28, 82:7, 87:2, 91:7). It functions to mean filling (*sāwa*), as when Dhul-Qarnayn filled between the two steep mountains (i.e., Qur'an 18:96). It is also used to mean upright (*sawiyyā*) (i.e., Qur'an 19:17, 19:43, 67:22). These are various morphologies of the term in the Qur'an.

In Hebrew, the term "*shwh*" also means to be equal, having the same meaning to its Aramaic cognate.[7] Its meaning also includes to be even or level.[8] This can also be seen in its Qur'anic usage using the terms "*istawa*" or "*istawat*," which in some ways hold the meaning to be even or level on whatever is being mounted, either the throne or an animal. This does suggest a similar Semitic etymology for the term, which is to be equal.[9] Being even means to be on equal level. A similar term to "*shwh*" is "*mshl*,"[10] which is cognate to the Arabic "*mthl*," meaning "to be like."[11] The question on how the term "*sawwā*" also came to mean "to form" might be understood from the term "*mthl*" and making something "like it." This is best understood from the term "*timthāl*," which typically means statue, and used in its plural form in Qur'an 21:52 and 34:13. A statue of a human or animal form is called "*timthāl*" because it is in the likeness (*mthl*) of what it is formed as. The term "*swy*," however, is not simply likeness, but also sameness, which is understood as equal or being on the same level. One might understand that the Qur'anic usage of "*sawwaytuhu*" does not only mean "formed," but perhaps more precisely, "made him equal and like Me." This might correspond with Genesis 1:26–27, where the human is made in the image and likeness of God.

Looking at the classical commentaries on the verses about forming human flesh (i.e., Qur'an 15:29, 38:72), al-Ṭabarī seems to have refrained from deeply analyzing its meaning.[12] This could either mean that he considered the meaning was self-evident requiring no interpretation, or that he considered the meaning so ambiguous that he could not define it, or that he did not want to inquire into the theological implications of interpreting this verse. Al-Rāzī gives "*sawwaytuhu*" two possible definitions.[13] He explains that it could mean "formed his image" or "made his body proportionate." Al-Rāzī also explains that the breathing of God's Spirit (*al-rūḥ*) into the flesh is like the wind (*al-rīḥ*) going through the cavities of a body, by which he does note the polysemous nature between the terms for spirit (*rūḥ*) and wind (*rīḥ*).[14] In al-Rāzī's commentary on the prostration of the angels, he states that some have suggested that Adam was like a *qiblah* (a focal point of prayer), and not the object of worship.[15] Al-Rāzī dismisses any suggestion that the created flesh is likened to simply a *qiblah*, because this does not embrace the honor intended for that flesh.[16] However, if the likening of the flesh to a *qiblah* is accepted, then the flesh can be considered similar to the Kaʿbah in Makkah. If that is the case, then the honor given to that flesh is that it has become the House of God. Al-Masʿūdī (d. 346/956) states that "God made Adam a place of prayer (*miḥrāba*), a Kaʿbah, a gateway, and a *qiblah* in which prostrated to it the righteous, the spirituals, and the lights."[17] The prostration of the angels unto Adam gives him the honor that he is a *qiblah*, and he would be the connecting relationship between the angels and God, since he was created in God's image.[18]

Although the Kaʿbah is a *qiblah*, it still has its place of honor, having a greater honor than other mosques or houses of worship, according to a tradition attributed to Muḥammad.[19] Hence, since the Kaʿbah is a *qiblah*, it also brings along with it the notion of honor. Though the Kaʿbah is honored, it still has lesser honor than human beings, according to Islamic tradition.[20] As such, there is a possibility to conclude, as al-Rāzī points out, that though people prostrate toward the *qiblah* that does not mean that the *qiblah* is more honored than them. Therefore, even if angels prostrate toward Adam, since Adam can be considered a *qiblah*, it does not necessarily mean he is more honored than the angels.[21] This is the concept that al-Rāzī objects to, since people's prostration toward the Kaʿbah does not necessarily mean that the Kaʿbah is more honored than they are, while the angels' prostration to Adam is honorific. He concludes, therefore, that Adam cannot have been simply a *qiblah*. Otherwise, Satan would have had no problem prostrating toward him. Al-Shaʿrāwī (d. 1419/1998) suggests that the prostration toward the Kaʿbah is not because it has any sort of divinity, but that it was made honorable by God's commandment.[22] Similarly, he states that the angels' prostration toward Adam does not prove that he is divine in himself, but that he was made honored by God's commandment. Al-Baghawī (d. 516/1122) suggests that Adam is considered a *qiblah* to the angels.[23] Al-Rāzī suggests that since the prostration of the angels was for Adam (*li-Adam*) and not toward Adam (*ila Adam*), it cannot be perceived that Adam was simply a *qiblah*.[24] The Muʿtazilah maintains that Adam was considered a *qiblah*, though still more honored than the Kaʿbah.[25] In Imām al-ʿAskarī's[26] (d. 260/874) commentary on the Qurʾan, he reports that the angels' prostration to Adam indicates his being a *qiblah* which, however, is still more honored than the angels.[27] Al-Majlisī (d. 1111/1698) also reports that the prostration of the angels to Adam is in such a way that he is considered a *qiblah*, but though just a *qiblah*, is still more honored than the angels.[28] Perhaps in this sense, Adam is not simply a Kaʿbah, because the Kaʿbah is a House of God built of stones by people's hands, while Adam is a House of God made by the hands of God. It could mean that Adam is indeed a *qiblah* but very unlike that of the

Ka'bah, according to the Qur'an. The Ka'bah remains made of stones, while Adam is the dwelling place of the Spirit of God Itself. As such, it is a *qiblah* and also more honored than the angels, since the spark of divinity, which is the Spirit of God, dwells in him. Perhaps here, we are reminded by how the Qur'an could be alluding to the heart instead of the Ka'bah.[29] We are also reminded of the term "*ibn Allah*" that was also discussed in Chapter 5, in which would mean that the human has become a Temple of God.

Al-Ṭabarsī interpretation of "*sawwaytuhu*" is also similar to that of al-Rāzī, in which the term refers to the formation of the human flesh.[30] Similarly, the breathing of God's Spirit into the flesh is also portrayed as wind going through the bodily cavities. He also suggests that the Spirit of God was joined with Adam, as an honor.

Let us attempt to use intertextuality to understand the meaning of "*sawwaytuhu*." First, it is imperative to analyze the possible definition of forming. The term "*istawa*" is used in the Qur'an for Moses having grown into adulthood (i.e., Qur'an 28:14). It is not used necessarily for Moses being formed. Hence, there could be different meanings for the term "*sawwaytuhu*" and it can be understood as not necessarily meaning to form an image. Al-Ṭabarī shows the variation of what people considered the age of "*istiwā'*," as some suggest thirty, others thirty-three, and some others forty.[31] Al-Rāzī suggests that "*al-istiwā'*" of Moses is the completion of his strength and bodily uprightness.[32] He argues that the human body is born in weakness and then grows to strength. He also suggests that after the human body has grown in strength for some time, it starts to wane again at old age. Hence, he assumes that "*istiwā'*" would be when the bodily strength is completed. However, the term "*sawwaytuhu*" can be understood from a different perspective, using the intertextual polysemy that Muḥammad might have been able to produce, given his psychological state. The terms for God establishing (*istawa*) on the Throne and the formation of human flesh are found within a close contextual proximity in the following verses:

> 4 God it is Who created the heavens and the earth and whatsoever is between them in six days. Then He mounted (*istawa*) the Throne. Apart from Him you have neither protector, nor intercessor. Will you not, then, remember? 5 He directs the affair from Heaven unto earth; then it ascends unto Him in a day whose measure is as a thousand years of that which you reckon. 6 Such is the Knower of the Unseen and the seen, the Mighty, the Merciful, 7 Who made beautiful all that He created, and Who began the creation of man from clay. 8 Then He made his seed from a draught of base fluid. 9 Then He fashioned him (*sawwāhu*), and breathed into him of His Spirit, and endowed you with hearing, sight, and hearts. Little do you give thanks![33]

In the above verses it is important to note that the Qur'an is first stating how God established (*istawa*)[34] on His Throne and then discusses the creation of the human flesh in a way similar to that in Qur'an 15:28–29 and Qur'an 38:71–72, in which the human flesh is created from mud (clay) and then is formed (*sawwaytuhu*) and breathed into from God's Spirit. Although the Qur'an does not usually have any special chronological order in its text, the above verses strikingly, and unusually, show that God first created the human from mud (clay), and then made his progeny from fluid (sperm), and only then he fashioned him and breathed into him from His Spirit. The

Qur'an uses the term "then" (*thumma*) in these verses, as if implying some sort of chronology. The creation from clay and perhaps the formation from clay is not "*istiwā'*." Being created from sperm also is not "*istiwā'*." It seems that only afterward the term "*sawwāhu*" and the breathing from God's Spirit occurs. This actually also resembles the following verse: "Indeed, We created you, then We formed you, then We said unto the angels, "Prostrate yourselves before Adam." And they all prostrated, save Iblīs; he was not among those who prostrated."[35]

The above verse also seems to contain a strange chronology, which is implied by the term "then" (*thumma*).[36] It appears as if the Qur'an shows that people were created and given shape, and only then were the angels commanded to bow down before Adam. Here again it shows the creation of the human and its progeny, and then the commandment was given to the angels to bow down before Adam. This is similar to the chronology seen in Qur'an 32:7–9, which also shows the creation of the human and its progeny, and then the "*istiwā'*" of human flesh and breathing of God's Spirit occurs, implying the time when the angels were commanded to bow down. It is not clear whether the human progeny had already been created when the angels bowed down before Adam.[37]

Using intertextuality to find any inner-Qur'anic allusions, especially since the terms "*istawa*" on the Throne and the fashioning of human flesh (*sawwāhu*) are located within a contextual proximity, it may be understood that God fashioned the human flesh (*sawwaytuhu*) in the same way that He established (*istawa*) on His Throne, since the terms share the same root meaning. The polysemous term "*sawwaytuhu*" may hold multiple valid definitions due to the rhetoric style of the Qur'an. However, if we keep in mind the suggestion that the bowing down to human flesh could be as if the human flesh is similar to a *qiblah*, and if we understand the notion that a *qiblah* is a House of God, then there could be a completely different understanding that we can obtain using intertextual polysemy.

Since the human flesh is formed (*sawwaytuhu*) in the same way that God established (*istawa*) on His Throne, then perhaps the human flesh may be understood as the Throne of God. In Muḥammad's use of symbolism, perhaps he is creating inner-Qur'anic allusions. When the Spirit of God is breathed into the human flesh, then It establishes (*istawa*) Itself inside the flesh, which becomes the Throne of God (*sawwaytuhu*). Because the Spirit of God resides within the flesh, the flesh becomes as if it is the House of God, where Its Throne is, and therefore, the *qiblah*. As such, the angels might have been commanded to bow down to the human flesh, not because the human flesh is to be worshiped, but because the human flesh has been honored to house the Spirit of God like a *qiblah* (House of God). Nonetheless, the human flesh is perhaps even more honored than the Ka'bah according to Muḥammad, as previously seen in the prophetic tradition; the reason might be because the Ka'bah is a House of God built with stones and made by human hands, whereas the human is a House of God built by the hands of God, and therefore, is even more honored.

Prostration to Adam or Jesus

Although the general commentators, including al-Rāzī, denote that the person in question in the verses about the creation of flesh and breathing into it from God's Spirit is Adam, some of the verses do not explicitly name him (i.e., Qur'an 15:29, 38:72). Actually, al-Rāzī, while discussing this verse, explicitly refers back to sūrah al-Baqarah (i.e., Qur'an 2:34), which mentions Adam. Exegetes extrapolated that the creation of flesh mentioned in Qur'an 15:29 and 38:72 are references to Adam. Nonetheless, it is still important to note that these two verses do not mention the name. This brings to attention two possibilities. The obvious inference is that it does indeed refer to Adam. However, the story shares similarities to one in the New Testament, which perhaps refers to Jesus Christ. "Perhaps" because these verses in the New Testament do not mention the name of Jesus Christ, denoting him only as the Son. "And again, when God brings His firstborn into the world, He says, 'Let all God's angels worship him.' "[38] This verse in the New Testament might be related to a verse in Deuteronomy, which is currently not found in the Masoretic text, but it is still found in the Septuagint and the Dead Seas Scrolls: "Rejoice, ye heavens, with him, and let all the angels of God worship him; rejoice, ye Gentiles, with his people, and let all the sons of God strengthen themselves in him."[39]

Whether the flesh in question in the Qur'an is a reference to Jesus Christ or Adam is important to note, as to the possible difference in the storyline between Christians and Muslims. However, the Qur'an states that the creation of Jesus is likened to that of Adam, as seen in the following verse: "Truly the likeness of Jesus in the sight of God is that of Adam; He divided [created] him from dust, then said to him, "Be!" and he is (*kun fa-yakūn*)."[40]

If Jesus is created in a similar way as Adam, then this perhaps brings into question whether or not the Qur'an may assume that the creation of Adam and asking the angels to prostrate to him also took place with Jesus. It is difficult to understand who Muḥammad had in mind. The Throne of God is described in Ezekiel's vision, where above the Throne he sees the likeness of a human (*adam*) (i.e., Ezekiel 1:26). It should be well noted that the Hebrew usage of Adam may not always mean the first human, since the term for human in Hebrew is usually also understood as "*adam*."[41] Therefore, when the Qur'an explicitly declares in some verses that God asked the angels to bow before Adam, is it to be understood the first Adam, or is it understood to be a human (*adam*)?[42] This is especially important, because in the verses that use the term "*bashar*," instead of Adam, this term means flesh, but it can also be understood generally as a human. Therefore, if we do adopt the definition of Adam to be synonymous with "*bashar*," which means a human, then understanding the Qur'anic usage of Adam can be somewhat vague. From a linguistic perspective, Adam may be understood either as the first human or as simply a human, "*adam*," and more precisely, flesh (skin).[43]

There is no evidence that the Akkadian usage of "*adam*" carries the meaning of man or human, but that it is used to mean dark, red, red soil, and red blood.[44] This meaning is also carried over in other Semitic languages.[45] Its relationship with blood (*dm*) is obvious in all Semitic languages.[46] There have been suggestions to its relation with "*dmh*/*dmy*,"[47] which is the term used in Genesis 1:26 stating that "*adam*" was created in the likeness (*demot*) of God. In Arabic, the term "*dm*" is rooted in "*d m y*,"[48] which also holds the meaning of likeness. This is attested in the usage of "*dumya*" for a statue or a doll, as in the sense that it is an image.[49] This brings further the relationship between Genesis 1:26, which states the creation of "*adam*" in the image and likeness (*demot*) of

God, and the Qur'anic usage of forming of flesh using the term "*sawwaytuhu*," which is made equal and like.

The term "*adam*" has various polysemous meanings:[50] "*adam*" can mean a mixture,[51] and as such the name Adam is given as he is created from mud, which is a mixture of clay and water.[52] Also, "*adam*" can mean meat or bread.[53] The term also means skin.[54] The term "*adamah*" means inner layer of the skin (dermis), while the surface layer (epidermis) is called "*bashrah*," which is rooted in "*bashar*."[55] Therefore, when the Qur'an discusses the prostration of the angels to "*adam*" (i.e., Qur'an 2:34, 7:11, 17:61, 18:50, 20:116) or to the "*bashar*" (i.e., Qur'an 15:28–29, 38:71–72) whom He is creating, is it referring specifically to the first Adam, or to a human whom God creates and breathes into from His Spirit (without specifying a name)? As discussed earlier, it is even possible to understand that if the Qur'an argues that the creation of Jesus is similar to that of Adam, then it might even be referring to Jesus and asking the angels to prostrate to him. Although the Septuagint translation of the Bible shows a verse speaking of a person whom the angels obey, it is important to note that the midrash relates that after the angels were told of the creation of Adam in God's image, some objected.[56] Nonetheless, after Adam's creation, the angels mistook him for a divine being and wanted to call him "Holy" (*kiddush*). As a result, God caused Adam to fall asleep, so that the angels would know that Adam is not divine.[57] In the Qur'an, the story is related that when the angels were told of the creation of Adam, they questioned this since they praised and called upon the name of God as "Holy," while the human was not righteous (i.e., Qur'an 2:30). There are various parallels in the story of Adam's creation between Jewish and Muslim literature, which are not within the scope of this example.[58]

Throne of God

As seen earlier, it may be inferred from the Qur'an that the flesh is created in the same way that God establishes on Its Throne. Therefore, perhaps the human flesh before which the angels were asked to prostrate has become the Throne of God, where Its Spirit resides. There is a possibility that this is an inner-Qur'anic allusion. If we consider the human flesh to be the Throne of God, then it can also mean that the human flesh is the Temple of God. According to the Gospel of John, Jesus seems to have referred to his own body as a temple.

> 19 Jesus answered them, "Destroy this temple, and I will raise it again in three days."
> 20 They replied, "It has taken forty-six years to build this temple, and you are going to raise it in three days?" 21 But the temple he had spoken of was his body. 22 After he was raised from the dead, his disciples recalled what he had said. Then they believed the scripture and the words that Jesus had spoken.[59]

If we consider the creation of human flesh as described by the Qur'an as a description of the Throne of God or His Bodily Temple, then the Qur'anic text may not necessarily contradict the Gospel on the concept of the Temple of the Body, and this is especially seen in the example given in Chapter 5 about the term "*ibn Allah*." Muḥammad may not have been speaking against the concept of the Incarnation of the

Word, according to the Christian sectarian milieu of his time. Also, in the Epistle to the Hebrews, the Son and the Throne of God are brought together within the context of the angels' prostration (i.e., Hebrews 1:6–8).

The Presence of God is known as the *Shekhinah* in Judaic thought.[60] The *Shekhinah* is cognate to *al-Sakīnah*, which is mentioned in the Qur'an (i.e., Qur'an 9:26, 9:40, 48:26). However, *al-Sakīnah* is not typically understood as the Spirit of God by classical Muslim commentators. It is understood as the calmness and comfort that God bestows upon the hearts of believers.[61] Classical commentators suggest that *al-Sakīnah* is linguistically related to "*sukūn*," which means calmness.[62] Al-Simnānī's (d. 736/1336) interpretations of *al-Sakīnah* are that it is divine emanation (*fayḍ*).[63] Yet, the term "*sakīnah*" is rooted in "*sakan*," which also means dwelling place.[64] Al-Ṭabāṭabā'ī (d. 1402/1981) states the possibility that *al-Sakīnah* is the Spirit.[65] It is possibly the Holy Spirit, or the Spirit of God dwelling (*sakan*) in the believer's heart. If the Spirit of God makes the heart inside the flesh Its dwelling place (*sakan*), then it may imply the heart becoming the House or Temple of God, and as such the place of the Throne of God. The inner-Qur'anic allusion of using the term "*sawwaytuhu*" and "*istawa*" may then bring this symbolic understanding in Muḥammad's state of mind. After all, the Hebrew term "*shwh*," cognate to the Arabic "*swy*," also holds the meaning of calmness (e.g., Psalm 131:2).

Incarnation of the Word

The Incarnation of the Word in the form of Jesus Christ is a mystery to the early Christian community. It was a subject of heated debates in the early Church and the cause of various theories (heresies) on the nature of Christ. Arius (d. 336 CE) considers the Son of God second in rank to God the Father. To Arius, the Son of God cannot be God, because the Son may change and swerve, while God in the Bible says, "I am, I am, and I change not."[66] Arius was denounced as a heretic in the First Council of Nicaea in 325. Athanasius (d. 373 CE) played a major role in denouncing Arius' views, and was credited with what has later been known as the pseudo-Athanasian Creed.[67] However, Christology or the nature of Christ is not an issue in this chapter.[68]

Since the creation of human flesh is analyzed textually, above, from the Qur'an, it is also important to compare textually the Incarnation from the Bible. The theological nature of Christ is not precisely evident from the Bible. However, what is evident from the Gospel of John is that the Word became flesh and dwelt among us (i.e., John 1:14). To keep it in simple terms, the Gospel of John seems to be talking about a Word, which is apparently divine in nature becoming flesh. The Qur'an seems to be talking about the Spirit of God also taking the form of flesh. "Seems" and "apparently" are used here because I am not comparing the theological schools of thought in their interpretation of these verses, but simply comparing the texts. Muḥammad would have had access to the text of the Gospels and would have made his creative allusions linguistically, but I cannot tell for sure.

As in the history of Christianity there have been various schools of thought on the nature of the Word and the relationship of the Son to the Father,[69] so within Muslim history there are also various theological schools of thought on the nature of the Spirit of God, as to whether it is a creature (created) or of the same essence as God. Al-Dārmī (d. 255/893), for example, differentiates between the Word of God and the Spirit of God.[70] According to him, the Word of God is uncreated, while the Spirit of God is a creature. Abu Bakr al-Kalābādhī (d. 380/990) relates that the spirits are created just as the bodies are created.[71] However, in my opinion, there might be some confusion among classical Muslim scholars on the nature of the spirit (*rūḥ*) and the soul (*nafs*). Abu Bakr al-Kalābādhī, for example, does not discuss the nature of the soul. It seems that in his cosmology, a creature is made of body and spirit. Similarly, ʿAlī ibn Ḥazm al-Andalusī (Ibn Ḥazm) also asserts that the spirit is a creature, by providing evidence that people's spirits are punished in Hell.[72] Here, again, it seems there might be some confusion between spirit (*rūḥ*) and soul (*nafs*). The Qur'an seems to imply the creation of souls (i.e., Qur'an 4:1), but does not imply the creation of the Spirit.[73] Actually, in the process of creation of human flesh, it seems that the Qur'an states that the flesh is created from clay, but the Spirit is breathed from God. It is not necessarily evident that the Spirit is equated with the soul according to the Qur'an, but that they are distinct entities. As such, it seems many classical Muslim scholars might have confused the spirit with the soul. Actually, Ibn Ḥazm explicitly claims that the terms "soul (*nafs*)," "spirit (*rūḥ*)," and "breath (*nasmah*)" are synonymous.[74]

Ibn Qayyim al-Jawziyyah affirms that the Spirit is a creature.[75] He states that Christians believe that the Spirit of God is from God's essence and that the same essence is inside the body of Christ.[76] As such, Christ is uncreated, because he is of the same essence as God. He even states that some Shīʿī schools of thought consider the Spirit of Adam in the same way as Christians consider Christ; he argues against this Shīʿī belief, and he even refers to Ibn Taymiyyah's argument on the Spirit being a creature.[77] Nonetheless, in Twelver Shīʿī thought, the Spirit of God, which is bestowed upon Adam, is also considered a creature.[78] It is also related by Imām al-Bāqir[79] (d. 144/733) and Imām al-ṣādiq[80] (d. 148/765) that the Spirit is a creature with vision, strength, and help that God bestows on the hearts of messengers and believers.[81] Al-Majlisī explicitly responds to Christian theology by suggesting that the Holy Spirit is a creature and not uncreated.[82] The Incarnation of the divinity is not completely alien in some Muslim thought, to which Ibn Qayyim al-Jawziyyah might have been responding. The Ismāʿīlīs, and more specifically the Druze doctrine, have the concept of God in man (*lāhūt wa nāsūt*).[83]

The Confession of Chalcedon asserts that Christ is acknowledged in two natures, which are united in one Persona and Subsistence.[84] Certain churches did not recognize this creed and have become known as non-Chalcedonian Churches or the Oriental Orthodox Churches.[85] The Coptic Church also retained Cyril of Alexandria's formula of the Incarnation, where Christ is to be acknowledged *from* two natures, instead of *in* two natures. The Coptic Church maintains that at the union of the divine and human nature, Christ only had a single nature synthesized from those two. This is in contrast to the Confession of Chalcedon where both natures of Christ are preserved even in the union. Thomas Aquinas (d. 1274 CE) wrote a full treatise dealing with the nature of the Incarnation in his *Summa Theologica*, stating:

> As Damascene says, the Divine Nature is said to be incarnate because It is united to flesh personally, and not that It is changed into flesh. So likewise, the flesh is said

> to be deified, as he also says, not by change, but by union with the Word, its natural properties still remaining, and hence it may be considered as deified, inasmuch as it becomes the flesh of the Word of God, but not that it becomes God.[86]

If we take Thomas Aquinas' interpretation of Christology, it seems evident that he asserts the Confession of Chalcedon of the two natures of Christ united into a single persona, yet distinct. He clearly states that the flesh is deified just because it is united with the Word, but the flesh is not God. It is the Word that is inside the flesh that makes the flesh deified, but the flesh remains distinct and would not in itself be considered God. If we take that interpretation into consideration and compare it with the Qur'anic text, that God created the flesh and hence the flesh is not God, because it is created and only after creation is the flesh breathed into from God's Spirit, then it is possible to imagine that the Qur'an perhaps adopts a Thomas Aquinas interpretation of the union between a divine entity and human flesh. R. C. Zaehner interprets the Qur'an as thus:

> The Incarnation of Christ, then, breathed from the Spirit of God, is thus regarded as an event as momentous as the original creation or the universal resurrection at the end of time. This would seem to indicate that Muḥammad must, again unconsciously, be reproducing the Christian idea of Christ as the new Adam and as the 'first fruits' of the resurrection.[87]

Zaehner interprets Qur'an 3:59 and Qur'an 19:34 as follows: "Christ, then, in the Qur'ān, would appear to be both the Word of God and therefore divine, and truly man, but He is not the 'son' of God for reasons that we have already explained (i.e., Christ is not the physical son of God)."[88]

This section deals with a textual comparison between the Gospel and the Qur'an. It appears that Christians and Muslims debate this issue, not because their scriptures necessarily contradict, but simply because of their interpretation of Christology. As shown in the earlier examples, Muḥammad might have had a different view of theology and Christology than that adopted by later Muslims. Later Muslims perhaps wanted to be distinct from their Jewish and Christian peers. As such, Muslim thought on the matter would not go far beyond the already existing debates between the early churches, where inherited tradition continues to have consequences to this day among the various denominations. However, what Muḥammad had in mind might have not necessarily been different to the already charged debates of the early Church.

The Qur'an does not explicitly show that the Spirit is created. As interpretations were attempted, various theological schools of thought, in both Christian and Islamic history, sprang up to attempt to understand the nature of the Spirit and the fusion of the Spirit into a human body. Those different theologies exist within each of those traditions. Just as Arianism and Nestorianism appear in the Christian tradition due to differing interpretations of, and not because they believed in a different, scripture, then perhaps seeming differences between the Qur'an and the Gospel[s] on the issue of the Incarnation of the Logos in the form of Jesus Christ are also dependent on the interpretation of the text. It does not necessarily show that scriptures themselves are in contradiction. This might mean that Muḥammad had some knowledge of the Christian milieu, and appeared to adopt certain theology and Christology into the Qur'an without attempting to contradict the Gospel[s]. As some would be aware that if the Qur'an seems to somehow portray human flesh with a divine Spirit united together, then it may contradict the Qur'anic verses stating, "They indeed have disbelieved who say, 'God is the Messiah, son of Mary.'"[89] However, it may be difficult to determine whether the Qur'an is stating that the Father is not equal to the Son, or as Günther Risse[90] suggests, that the Qur'an in these passages is denying a Monophysite Christology.[91]

Although this section does not deal with the theological implications of the Qur'anic interpretations on the Throne of God as a human being, it is interesting to note a dialogue between Abu Ra'ita and a Muslim on the theological implication of believing God sitting on the Throne and the Incarnation. A Muslim objection could be that God cannot be simultaneously in heaven and incarnated. However, Abu Ra'ita, a miaphysite Jacobite theologian in the early ninth century CE, attempted to find evidence from the Qur'an that agrees to such a Christian belief.[92] Abu Ra'ita focused on the Muslim belief of God establishing on His Throne as means for a theological dialogue with the Christian belief in Incarnation. The issue Abu Ra'ita was trying to convey is that if Muslims believe that God can be in heaven and on His Throne simultaneously without necessarily dividing God in parts, then theologically it would not be different to how a Christian believes that God is in heaven while incarnated simultaneously either.[93]

The Throne and the Temple

Apparently, the Qur'an considers Adam (or a human) to be created from clay. When he is "established" as God "establishes on His Throne," and God breathes into him from Its "Spirit," then the angels are to bow down before him. This could be perhaps an allusion that the said human has become a *qiblah*, the House or Temple of God, and the Throne of God. It is also apparent from the Qur'an that Jesus is made in the same way as Adam. Therefore, it might also be possible that God commanded the angels to bow before Jesus, according to the Qur'an. From the Qur'an, one might conclude that God created the human from clay, which is human in nature, but breathed into it from Its Spirit, which could be divine in nature. Therefore, this human whom God created and breathed into from Its Spirit might seem to have dual natures, a human nature and a divine. The Qur'an also explicitly portrays Jesus as a Spirit from God (i.e., Qur'an 4:171). The clay seemed to have been created, as the Qur'an explicitly suggests, but the Spirit is debatable, as the Qur'an is not explicit in its nature, and perhaps does not even want to discuss the matter deeply (e.g., Qur'an 17:85). If the Spirit was not a mystery and had a simple definition, perhaps the Qur'an would have defined it explicitly, as the interpreters have. Since the Qur'an does not explicitly define it, then this could be a cause of contemplation of the Spirit's nature.[94] Do we interpret scriptures in light of theology or do we interpret theology in light of scriptures? This is a theologian's chicken and egg question.

Conclusion

If we leave theology aside and simply compare scriptures between the Gospel[s] and the Qur'an, then scriptures do not seem to be in contradiction on the matter of the formation of Christ. Perhaps Jesus is flesh from clay, as even the Gospel[s] show that he had a body, although the Gnostics have argued against this in the past, but his spirit is God's Spirit.[95] Although the concept of the Incarnation is a mystery, if in simple terms it refers to some flesh from clay with God's Spirit or divine Logos inside it, then we can conclude something from that. The Qur'an also literally states that flesh is made from clay and breathed into from God's Spirit. Also, Qur'an 3:59 suggests that Jesus' body was from clay and then God says to it "be" (*kn*), which as described earlier is how the Qur'an interprets John's Logos. So this "*kn*" resided within that flesh. If that is what the Incarnation is all about, then scriptural texts do not contradict each other. Muslim theologians may have taken an Arian or a Nestorian Christology, but the texts alone do not necessarily contradict. This might mean that Muḥammad did not explicitly speak against the Gospel[s]' teachings, especially in light of the Qur'an asking the people of the Gospel[s] to follow the Gospel[s] (i.e., Qur'an 5:46, 5:66, 5:68).

By using intertextual polysemy for Qur'anic hermeneutics and identifying the possibility of using Qur'anic allusions that the flesh is perhaps the Throne of God, then it seems there is more to the Spirit than just mere creation and an invitation for further dialogue on the matter. The Christian–Muslim dialogue on the Incarnation does not seem to have arisen from contradictory scriptures, but from the interpretations thereof. Since the early churches had to undergo various ecumenical councils in an attempt to unite the churches, then we may not necessarily view Christian–Muslim debates to be anything but ecumenical councils, which are simply debating matters of Christology because of their interpretation of scriptures, and not because the text of their scriptures is necessarily in contradiction. As such, we must ask ourselves again whether we interpret theology in light of scriptures, or scriptures in light of theology.

The Water of Life, the Logos, and the Messiah

This example shows intertextualities between the Qur'an and the Bible, and perhaps more specifically of the Water of Life, its relationship with the Logos, and the Messiah, who as argued earlier the Qur'an interprets him being begotten through "*takwīn*" instead of "*tawlīd*." The intertextualities are somewhat intensive and would suggest that Muḥammad was in a state with low latent inhibition, making creative connections. The Qur'an states in the following passage that water makes every living thing. I postulate that this is perhaps a reference by the Qur'an for the Water of Life.

> [30] Have those who disbelieve not considered that the heavens and the earth were sewn together and We rent them asunder? And We made every living thing from water. Will they not, then, believe? [31] And We placed firm mountains in the earth, lest it shake beneath them, and We made wide tracts between them as paths, that haply they may be guided. [32] And We made the sky a canopy preserved; yet they turn away from its signs. [33] He it is Who created the night and the day, the sun and the moon, each gliding in an orbit. [34] We have not ordained perpetual life for any human being before thee. So if thou diest, will they abide forever? [35] Every soul shall taste death. We try you with evil and with good, as a test, and unto Us shall you be returned.[96]

Looking carefully at these verses, the Qur'an seems to be saying that everything lives via water (i.e., Qur'an 21:30). It continues to state that no physical flesh (*bashar*) had eternal life (i.e., Qur'an 21:34) and that every soul (*nafs*) tastes death (i.e., Qur'an 21:35). Since the Qur'an is talking about life and death in these passages, then there is a likelihood that the water mentioned in Qur'an 21:30 is a reference to the Water of Life, in which it is not the physical flesh (*bashar*) that receives it according to Qur'an 21:34, but the soul (*nafs*), which is dead according to Qur'an 21:35.

There is a resemblance between these Qur'anic passages and the story of creation in Genesis. The first point of intertextuality is that the heavens and the earth were one and they were split. In Genesis 1:1 the term used for God creating the heavens and the earth is "*bara*'." Among its various meanings, such as create, it specifically means to fashion by cutting or splitting.[97] *Lisān al-ʿarab* shows that "*bara*'" is synonymous with the term "*khlq*."[98] Besides meaning to portion, to measure, and to make smooth, the term "*khlq*" also means to split and to divide, as it would mean fashioning or creating via the process of division and the Hebrew Bible uses the term "*khlq*" specifically in the meaning to split and to divide.[99] The Hebrew term "*br*'" is also associated with the meaning to separate and to divide.[100] When Genesis 1:1 states that God "*bara*'" the heavens and the earth, it would mean God divided the heavens and the earth. This presumes that the heavens and the earth were a single entity and then divided or that the heavens and the earth were each a single entity and split, as the heavens split with rain and the earth split with plants.[101] Perhaps allegorically, the heavens and the earth were joined together and then split, just as Adam (made of earth) was in Paradise (in heaven) before the Fall, and then they were split apart from each other (i.e., Qur'an 2:35–39, 7:19–25, 20:117–123).

The second point of intertextuality between the above Qur'anic passages and Genesis is the term "*rtq*." In a tradition attributed to Ibn ʿAbbās, when he was asked what came first, day or night, he answered that the heavens and the earth were "*rtq*," defining "*rtq*" as darkness.[102] This would also resemble Genesis 1:1, where darkness was over the face of the deep, before God said let there be Light in Genesis 1:3. The third point of intertextuality is the water in Qur'an 21:30 and Genesis 1:2, which I will return to after discussing the rest of the points of intertextuality. The fourth point is the term "*fijāj*," which resembles the Qur'anic call to Ḥajj that people will come from deep valleys (*fajj ʿamīq*) (i.e., Qur'an 22:27).[103] So, there is the earth, and there are the depths of the earth (*fijāj*). This resembles that there was darkness in the deep, according to Genesis 1:2. The midrash interprets the deep as Hell or the dwelling place of the dead,[104] connecting it with Daniel 2:22 and with this verse in Proverbs:[105] "**18** But little do they know that the dead are there, that her guests are deep (*ʿimqi*) in the realm of the dead (*sheol*)."[106]

Since Qur'an 21:35 discusses death and if Genesis 1:2 alludes to the deep, which is the place of death, according to the midrash, then it might further connect the Qur'anic passages with Genesis making it the fifth point of intertextuality. The sixth point of intertextuality between the above Qur'anic passages and Genesis is the heavens and the signs of the heavens. Qur'an 21:32 discusses the heavens as a ceiling, which would resemble the expanse in Genesis 1:6–8. Also, Qur'an 21:32 states that there are signs (*āyāt*) in the heavens, which are elaborated in Qur'an 21:33 to be the division (*khlq*) of the night and day, and the sun and the moon. This would resemble the following verses in Genesis:

> 14 And God said, "Let there be lights in the vault of the sky to separate the day from the night, and let them serve as signs (*utut*) to mark sacred times, and days and years, 15 and let them be lights in the vault of the sky to give light on the earth." And it was so. 16 God made two great lights—the greater light to govern the day and the lesser light to govern the night. He also made the stars. 17 God set them in the vault of the sky to give light on the earth, 18 to govern the day and the night, and to separate light from darkness. And God saw that it was good.[107]

Genesis 1:14 talks about signs in the heavens using the Hebrew term "*utut*," which is cognate to the Arabic "*āyāt*" mentioned in Qur'an 21:32. Also, Genesis 1:14 states that these signs are used to count seasons (*moʿadim*), days, and years, which is the purpose of having night and day, and the sun and moon in Qur'an 21:33. Genesis 1:16 is explicit that God made two great lights in the heavens, the greater light to rule the day, which is the sun, and the lesser light to rule the night, which is the moon. Also, counting seasons uses the term "*moʿadim*," which means appointed times, and is sometimes used for the times of festivals in the Hebrew Bible (e.g., Leviticus 23:4), which brings us to the "*ahilla*" (new moons) in Qur'an 2:189 that are considered *mawāqīt* (appointed times) for Ḥajj. The midrash is specific that these signs for knowing the "*moʿadim*" in Genesis 1:14 are references to the three pilgrimages mentioned in the Torah.[108] The midrash connects Genesis 1:14 with this verse in the Psalms:[109] "19 He made the moon to mark the seasons, and the sun knows when to go down."[110] Textually, Qur'an 21:30–35 show significant intertextuality with Genesis 1. This brings us back to the water, which is found in Qur'an 21:30 and Genesis 1:2. Similar to Genesis 1, which talks about the creation of the heavens and the earth in six days, the following Qur'anic verse also states the creation of the heavens and the earth in six days and that the Throne of God was on water, which may be similar to the Spirit of God hovering on the surface of the water in Genesis 1:2. "He it is Who created the heavens and the earth in six days, while His Throne was upon the water, that He may try you as to which of you is most virtuous in deed. Yet if thou sayest, 'Truly you shall be resurrected after death,' the disbelievers will surely say, 'This is naught but manifest sorcery!'"[111]

The midrash states that the Spirit of God that hovered over the face of the waters in Genesis 1:2 is a reference to the Messiah.[112] According to Rashi's (d. 1105 CE) commentary on Genesis 1:2, he interprets the Spirit of God as the Throne of Glory that was suspended in the air and hovered over the waters,[113] making further intertextuality between Genesis 1 and Qur'an 11:7. However, since Rashi is a medieval Jewish scholar, he may or may not have been impacted by the Qur'an. If there is intertextuality between the above verse and Genesis 1, then we can also see further intertextuality between the that verse and Qur'an 21:30–35, in which both of these passages talk about death and life. There is a possibility, therefore, that the water that makes every living thing alive in Qur'an 21:30 is a reference to the Water of Life. When interpreting Genesis, the midrash states that the Throne of Glory was among the first things made, connecting it with

Psalm 93:2, and emphasizing the relationship between Qur'an 21:30–35, Qur'an 11:7, and Genesis 1.[114] However, there is further intertextuality that may be perceived: all the Qur'anic passages that discuss the creation of the heavens and the earth in six days are allusions to Genesis. For example, consider the following passage:

> Truly your Lord is God, Who created the heavens and the earth in six days, then mounted the Throne. He causes the night to cover the day, which pursues it swiftly; and the sun, the moon, and the stars are made subservient by His Command (*bi-amrih*). Do not creation and command (*al-amr*) belong to Him? Blessed is God, Lord of the worlds (*al-ʿālamīn*)![115]

As in the previous passages, the establishment on the Throne may be perceived as the Throne of Glory, which might be the interpretation of the Spirit of God hovering over the waters in Genesis 1:2. The creation of the sun, moon, and stars in the above passage is in connection with Genesis 1:14. Also, another keyword in this passage is the term "*amrih*" and "*amr*." This might also be an allusion to the Spirit of God corresponding to the Qur'anic definition of the Spirit, which is from the "*amr*" of God (i.e., Qur'an 17:85). Also, in Genesis, when it states that "God said," it also uses the Hebrew term "*amr*" (e.g., Genesis 1:3, 1:6, 1:9, 1:11, 1:14, 1:20, 1:24, 1:26, 1:28, 1:29).

There is also a possible connection between the above passage and Qur'an 21:34 in the discussion of eternal life. Although the term "*al-ʿālamīn*" is used many times in the Qur'an and is assumed to denote the worlds,[116] the word may also suggest eternity and everlastingness.[117] The following Qur'anic passages that also mention the creation of the heavens and the earth in six days may also be an allusion to Genesis.

> 3 Truly your Lord is God, Who created the heavens and the earth in six days, then mounted the Throne, directing the affair (*yudabbir al-amr*). There is no intercessor, save by His Leave. That is God, your Lord; so worship Him! Will you not remember? 4 Unto Him is your return all together; God's Promise is true. Verily He originates creation, then He brings it back, that He may recompense with justice those who believe and perform righteous deeds. As for the disbelievers, theirs shall be a drink of boiling liquid and a painful punishment for having disbelieved. 5 He it is Who made the sun a radiance, and the moon a light, and determined for it stations, that you might know the number of years and the reckoning [of time]. God did not create these, save in truth. He expounds the signs for a people who know. 6 Surely in the variation of the night and the day and whatsoever God has created in the heavens and on the earth are signs for a people who are reverent.[118]

These passages also have much intertextuality between them and Genesis. Qur'an 10:3 discusses the creation of the heavens and the earth in six days, which is in relation to Genesis 1, as the first point of intertextuality. The establishment on the Throne is likened to the establishment on the Throne of Glory, which is the allusion of the Spirit of God hovering over the waters in Genesis 1:2, as a second point of intertextuality. Similar to the previous example, the use of the keyword "*amr*" is also an allusion to the Spirit of God, as a third point of intertextuality.

Another keyword used in Qur'an 10:3 is the term "*yudabbir*," which would be the fourth point of intertextuality. The term "*dabar*" is polysemous with various meanings. According to *Lisān al-'arab*, it means behind, back, or that which comes afterward, and much of the Arabic meanings sprout from this definition.[119] It also means death or the plague,[120] as physical death typically comes afterward. The term "*tadabbur*" means "*tafakkur*" as it comes after obtaining knowledge and then discerning and contemplating it.[121] The term "*yudabbir*" also means to talk and to speak.[122] It also means to write.[123] In Hebrew and Aramaic, it also means speech or word, as speech is to say words,[124] or pasture and wilderness.[125] A "*dibr*" or "*dabbūr*" is a bee or a wasp,[126] and is possibly called that due to the stinger located on its back. In Hebrew, besides the above definitions of the root "*dabar*," the term also means rafts or floats.[127]

The term "*yudabbir al-amr*" in Qur'an 10:3 has a multidimensional significance in its intertextuality with Genesis and the Gospel of John.[128] Since the term "*yudabbir*" means to speak and the term "*amr*" means to speak and to command,[129] as Genesis 1 shows plenteous times that God says commands using the term "*amr*," then the term "*yudabbir al-amr*" may be an allusion to Genesis 1. Since the Qur'an defines the Spirit with the term "*amr*" (i.e., Qur'an 17:85) and the midrash defines the Spirit of God in Genesis as the Messiah,[130] then the term "*yudabbir al-amr*" in Qur'an 10:3 might also be an allusion to the Messiah, especially since the Qur'an also defines the Messiah as a Spirit from God (i.e., Qur'an 4:171). Both the Qur'an and the Gospel of John define the Messiah as the Logos or the Word of God (e.g., Qur'an 4:171, John 1:1). Another term for the Word is "*dabar*." Andreas Köstenberger relates John's Logos with the Hebrew Bible's "*dbr*."[131] John Ronning suggests that the Johannine Logos might be related to the Aramaic term for word (*ma'mara*), which shares the same root as "*amr*," that are found in Jewish targums.[132] The term "*amr*" is sometimes rendered as "*logos*" in the Septuagint (e.g., Proverbs 1:2, Isaiah 41:26). In the Hebrew Bible, the term "*dbr*" is also sometimes used in the sense of commandments or regulations from God,[133] and is sometimes conjoined with the term "*amr*" (e.g., Psalm 147:15), which can also hold the same sense.[134] The Qur'an typically uses "*amr*" in the sense of command. Exodus 20:1 uses both terms "*dbr*" and "*amr*," when God reveals Itself and provides the Ten Commandments.

The Hebrew Bible sometimes uses the term "*dabar*" as a Word of God or a message from God (e.g., Judges 3:20, 1 Samuel 9:27, 1 Chronicles 17:3),[135] and the term in the Septuagint is sometimes also rendered as "*logos*" (e.g., Judges 3:20, 1 Chronicles 17:3). The term "*amr*" is also used as a vehicle for a message given by messenger(s) (e.g., Genesis 32:3–4, Judges 11:12–15).[136] As such, if the Qur'an considers the Messiah as a Word of God, then perhaps the word (*dbr* or *amr*) is a message and therefore, the Messiah might be the message (word) from God calling Jesus a "*rasūl Allah*" (messenger of God) (i.e., Qur'an 4:171). It might be understood that as the Word (*dbr* or *amr*) of God, the Messiah is both the message and the messenger. As such, textually, the Qur'an calling the Messiah a messenger of God (*rasūl Allah*) should not be seen as a derogatory term opposing any Christian Christology.

Etymologically, the term "*amr*" might mean to be bright, to make visible, to see, or to inform.[137] In Ugaritic, it means to see or to make visible, which has similar meanings in Akkadian and Ethiopic.[138] This suggests that this etymology is perhaps ancient, as it crosses over different Semitic languages geographically. The Arabic term "*amārah*," meaning sign,[139] would possibly descend from such an etymology. Genesis 1 shows the use of "*amr*" many times to bring into existence many things, as discussed earlier, and then calls some of these things, "*utut*" (signs), which is cognate to "*āyāt*" that the Qur'an uses. Perhaps the "*amr*" of God is understood as a sign (*āyah*). Perhaps, it is God making things visible or known. The *TDOT* discusses scholars considering speaking (*amr*) to be etymologically connected to making thoughts visible.[140]

There are many forms of intertextual parallelism that can be obtained between the first chapter of Genesis and the first chapter of the Gospel of John, as discussed earlier.[141] The first one is how John starts his Gospel by adopting the same phraseology as Genesis with, "In the beginning," which is "*en archē*," the same used in the Septuagint translation of Genesis. However, to add into this intertextuality, the Gospel of John states that everything was made through the Word (i.e., John 1:3). According to Genesis 1, every time God made something, it uses the term "*amr*." If the Word is "*dabar*" and the Qur'an uses the term "*yudabbir al-amr*," then the Qur'an might be alluding to the Messiah as the "*dabar*" (Word), which is the "*amr*" stated in Genesis 1. As such, everything was made through the word in Genesis attesting to John 1:3. Also, in the midrashic interpretation of Genesis 1:3, it states that the heavens were made through a word (*dabar*), citing this verse from the Psalms:[142] "[6] By the word (*debar*) of the Lord the heavens were made, and by the breath (*ruaḥ*) of His mouth their entire host."[143]

As the midrash cites this verse in its interpretation to Genesis 1:3, it is worth noting the intertextuality between the term for breath and Spirit (*ruaḥ*) in Genesis 1:2. The entire host of the heavens in Psalm 33:6 would be their luminaries, such as the sun, moon, and stars in Genesis 1:14. Therefore, since Psalm 33:6 equates the word (*dabar*) with the Spirit (*ruaḥ*), and since the midrash equates the Spirit of God with the Messiah,[144] then the Messiah is the Word (*dabar*), and that word is the "*amr*" in Genesis 1, in which everything was made through. According to Genesis 1:3, the word that is uttered is "*yhy*," which means "be." According to Exodus 3:14, God identifies Itself with the term "be" in the following passage. "[14] God said (*yo'mer*) to Moses, 'I am who I am (*ehyeh asher ehyeh*).' And He said (*yo'mer*), 'Say (*to'mar*) this to the people of Israel: "I am (*ehyeh*) has sent me to you." ' "[145]

The name of God is further explicated in Exodus as Yahweh in the following passage: "[2] God spoke (*yedabbir*) to Moses and said (*yo'mer*) to him, 'I am (*yhwh*). [3] I appeared to Abraham, to Isaac, and to Jacob, as God Almighty, but by my name (*yhwh*) I did not make myself known to them.' "[146]

Genesis 1:3 states that God "said" using the term "*amr*." The first thing said is the word "*yhy*." God identifies Itself as the term "*ehyeh*" in Exodus 3:14 and as Yahweh in Exodus 6:2–3. Hence, God identifies Itself with the first word It says (*amr*) in Genesis. Therefore, linking Psalm 33:6 with Genesis 1:3, the first word (*debar*) that comes out of God's breath (or Spirit) (*ruaḥ*) is "*yhy*," which is in itself identified as God, according to Exodus. As such, John identifies the Word (*dabar*) that God says (*amr*) as "*yhy*," which in itself is the name of God, "*ehyeh*" or Yahweh, and that according to Genesis, God made everything through it. Perhaps with such interpretation and logical thinking by John, he states the following:

> [1] In the beginning was the Word, and the Word was with God, and the Word was God.[2] He was in the beginning with God. [3] All things were made through him, and without him was not any thing made that was made. [4] In him was life, and the life was the light of men. [5] The light shines in the darkness, and the darkness has not overcome it.[147]

John starts his Gospel introducing the Messiah by interpreting Genesis. Genesis 1:2 states that darkness was over the face of the deep, which the midrash interprets as Hell or the realm of the dead, as discussed earlier. According to Genesis 1:3, the darkness was overcome when God said, "Let there be light." The midrash suggests that the light in Genesis 1:3 is a reference to the Messianic age.[148] As such, John 1:5 speaks of the light from Genesis 1:3 to overcome the darkness from Genesis 1:2. The darkness is also death, according to the midrash. Hence, as John contrasts the light with the darkness (i.e., John 1:5), so he is identifying the light specifically as life (i.e., John 1:4) to contrast it with death-like darkness. This brings us back to the Qur'anic passage that started all this. The water in Qur'an 21:30 has been argued earlier to be the Water of Life. As such, it confirms its own intertextuality not only with Genesis, but also with the Gospel of John, who is explicit in defining the light with life.[149]

We have seen the extent of intertextuality between "*yudabbir al-amr*" in Qur'an 10:3 with other passages of the Qur'an that discuss the creation of the heavens and the earth in six days, as well as between it and the Hebrew Bible and the Gospel of John. In this analysis, it has been identified that "*dabar*" is the Word in John. There are other passages in the Qur'an that would support this argument. It has been argued that the Word in John is the Hebrew term "*yhy*," which is from its root "*h y h*." The Qur'an says the following about the term to "be," and its process in God's command (*amr*): "[116] And they say, 'God has taken a child (*waladā*).' Glory be to Him! Rather, unto Him belongs whatsoever is in the heavens and on the earth. All are devoutly obedient to Him, [117] the Originator of the heavens and the earth. When He decrees a thing, He only says to it, 'Be!' and it is (*kun fa-yakūn*)".[150]

The above passages refer to the Messiah in that he is not begotten (*walad*) of God. To contrast it, Qur'an 2:117 talks about the primal origin of the heavens and the earth, making its allusion to the creation story in Genesis. It continues stating that the process of such origin is God's command (*amr*), which as described earlier is related to the Spirit (i.e., Qur'an 17:85) and to the creation story in Genesis, where the midrash defines the Spirit of God as the Messiah. Qur'an 2:117 continues to identify this "*amr*" with the term to "be" (*kn*). This makes the Qur'an identification of the commanding word of creation (*yudabbir al-amr*) with "*kn*," which is similar to John's interpretation that the Word is "*yhy*," as argued earlier. Here the Qur'an is attempting to distinguish between begotten from "*takwīn*" and begotten from "*tawlīd*." It denies that the Messiah "*tawallad*," but instead confirms that he is "*takawwan*," which could still mean begotten:

> She said, "My Lord, how shall I have a child (*walad*) while no flesh [human] (*bashar*) being has touched me?" He said, "Thus does God create whatsoever He will." When He decrees a thing (*amran*), He only says to it, "Be!" and it is (*kun fa-yakūn*)![151]

> [59] Truly the likeness of Jesus in the sight of God is that of Adam; He created him from dust, then said to him, "Be!" and he is[152] (*kun fa-yakūn*). [60] The truth (*al-ḥaqq*) is from thy Lord; so be not among the doubters.[153]

The above passages are in the same chapter and in an apparently similar context of introducing Jesus Christ. Similar to Qurʾan 2:116–117, the above passages identify Jesus with the word "*kn*." Another interesting keyword in Qurʾan 3:60 is the use of the term "*al-ḥaqq*." "He it is Who created the heavens and the earth in truth (*bil-ḥaqq*); and on the day He says 'Be!' and it is (*kun fa-yakūn*), His Word is the Truth (*al-ḥaqq*). And sovereignty is His on the Day when the trumpet is blown (*yunfakhu*), Knower of the Unseen and the seen; and He is the Wise, the Aware."[154]

The above passage is also related to Genesis, as it discusses the creation of the heavens and the earth through the word "*kn*." Similar to Qurʾan 3:60, it identifies this word or speech as the truth (*al-ḥaqq*). This may be seen to go in parallel with John 1:17, which states that the Law was given through Moses; grace and truth came through Jesus Christ.[155] It relates the Messiah with truth. John 14:6 further identifies Jesus as the truth and the life. The *Mishnah* links "In the beginning God created" in Genesis 1:1 with this verse in the Psalms:[156] "The sum of Your word (*dabar*) is truth, and every one of your righteous rules endures forever."[157]

Here, the Psalm defines the Word (*dabar*) of God as truth. Another term to note in Qurʾan 6:73 is "*yunfakh*," which is also used for the Spirit of God (e.g., Qurʾan 15:29, 21:91, 32:9, 38:72, 66:12). This might be an allusion to the Spirit of God in Genesis 1:2 and the Messiah. A different passage in the Qurʾan also brings these keywords together: "[34] That is Jesus son of Mary—a statement of the truth (*al-ḥaqq*), which they doubt. [35] It is not for God to take a child (*walad*). Glory be to Him! When He decrees a thing, He only says to it, 'Be!' and it is (*kun fa-yakūn*)."[158]

The above passages identify Jesus with the word of truth. Classical exegetes (*mufassirūn*) provide two opinions on what the truth refers to, as some suggest that Jesus is himself the truth, while others opine that the statement made about Jesus is the truth.[159] If the Qurʾan portrays that Jesus is the word of truth, it would be similar to John's declaration that Jesus is truth and life (i.e., John 14:6). The Qurʾan continues by denying that God begets using the term "*walad*" and instead affirms that God says the commanding (*amr*) word "*kn*" to generate, moving in parallel with the previous Qurʾanic passages.

The Qurʾanic passages discussed that state "*kun fa-yakūn*" are related to Jesus and the Messiah support the argument that the Qurʾan interprets John's definition of the Word as "be" (*kn*) (i.e., Qurʾan 2:116–117, 3:47, 3:59–60, 19:34–35) with an indirect reference to the Messiah in Qurʾan 6:73. The other Qurʾanic references to the term "*kun fa-yakūn*" are references to resurrection, or in other words on the occasion of life and death. As discussed earlier, this may also be an allusion to John's reference of the Messiah (i.e., John 1:4–5), while interpreting Genesis 1:2–3. For example, the following Qurʾanic references may also be of the Word:

> [38] And they swear by God their most solemn oaths [that] God will not resurrect those who die. Nay, but it is a promise binding (*ḥaqqan*) upon Him, though most

> of humankind[160] know not. [39] [This is so] that He might make clear unto them that wherein they differed, and that those who disbelieved might know that truly they were liars. [40] And Our Word unto a thing, when We desire it, is only to say to it, "Be!" and it is (*kun fa-yakūn*).[161]

This passage uses the keyword "*ḥaqq*," which, as discussed earlier, may be a reference to the Messiah or to the word "*kn*" (be) complementing its use in Qur'an 3:59–60, 6:73 and 19:34–35. However, since the above passages discuss resurrection, then it would also complement Qur'an 21:34–35, as well as the interpretation of darkness in Genesis 1:2 by the midrash and the interpretation of Genesis 1:2–3 by John in his Gospel (i.e., John 1:4–5). The other passage in the Qur'an that uses the term "*kun fa-yakūn*" is the following. "He it is Who gives life and causes death. So when He decrees a thing (*amran*), He only says to it, 'Be!' and it is (*kun fa-yakūn*)."[162]

Like the one before, this passage also discusses life and death, while implying that God can give life and death through the keywords "*amr*," which is related to the Spirit, and the commanding word "*kn*." As such, this might suggest that the water in Qur'an 21:30 is an actual reference to the Water of Life that resurrects a dead soul (and not necessarily flesh). Hereby, the intertextuality between the Qur'an, the Hebrew Bible, and the Gospel of John gives much of the interpretation of Genesis 1 and John 1 done by the Qur'an.

8

Allegorical Interpretation

This chapter extensively uses the methodology of intertextual polysemy to identify inner-Qurʾanic allusions. It is a working example of the extent of allegory that can be found in the Qurʾan. Allegory, here, is defined as a narrative with parallels using figurative and symbolic language as in metaphors to convey a teaching. In the context of the example in the chapter, allegory is a device to convey a moral and spiritual teaching.

Given Muḥammad's state of mind and his capacity to create metaphors and double meanings, while mastering the art of symbolism, we must seek further to understand inner-Qurʾanic allusions along with the double meanings that Muḥammad might have intended. An allegory can be considered as an extended metaphor,[1] and as such, those capable of creating metaphor may also be able to create allegory. It is through the meanings of the root terms, their polysemy and morphologies, and by intertextualizing these terms within the Qurʾan, that an allegorical interpretation may be found.

Forbidding usury (*ribā*)[2]

In the current age of globalization, world economies have intermingled. The downturn of an economy in any part of the world results in a domino effect, affecting many sectors and societies worldwide. Within the context of this global economy emerge two main branches of banking systems, conventional banking and Islamic banking.[3] Conventional banking is based on the adoption of an ancient method of lending and handling money with interest. This ancient method was transformed into a systematic method, shaping modern banking.[4]

Islamic banking is based on the notion of forbidding the use of usury (*ribā*). Instead, Islamic banking seeks methodologies that would coincide with conventional banking as long as it continues to be based within the framework of Sharīʿah principles. Nonetheless, as those methods of banking find themselves sometimes at odds with each other and competing to do business in a global economy, many researchers, bankers, and theologians have attempted to find ways for those two systems of banking to work coherently together within the global economy and to be as competitive with each other.[5]

However, as theologians, bankers, and researchers have delved into finding methods to make the two banking systems work together in the modern age, they have immersed themselves in the methods of Islamic banking and answering the question "how." In reality, one must try to answer the question "why" are such rulings part of Islamic Sharīʿah beyond the context of morality? In other words, what was Muḥammad's intent in making such laws presented in the Qur'an, knowing his creative capacity in using Arabic words, as seen from the previous examples? Many theologians and researchers, when asked the reasons behind the Islamic method of banking, try to answer the question on the basis of ethics and philosophy.[6] They imply that the conventional method is unethical, which is a controversial statement to generalize all conventional financial institutions.[7]

Many jurists find the prohibition of usury (*ribā*) is mainly due to its exploitive nature.[8] However, when faced with questions of opportunity loss and inflation, their answer goes into morality and ethics of finance. Traditional scholars reason that the purpose for the prohibition is that it seeks the greater good of the community.[9] Siddiqi considers the purpose of the Sharīʿah (*maqāṣid al-Sharīʿah*) on the issue of usury (*ribā*) as Ibn al-Qayyim explains it: preserving people's rights, saving them from harm, and ensuring the welfare of society.[10]

However, the end-user, whether they opt to use a conventional method of banking for their finances or the Islamic method, faces similar frustrations. It does not matter what people call it, with different names, the actual financial obligations and implications experienced by the end-user do not differ much between the systems. The majority of Islamic banking customers choose this method solely for the purpose of consciousness toward religious obligations, but they are otherwise ignorant of Islamic financing methods.[11] Although Islamic banking allows defaulting due to poverty, the financial institution in such cases may retain the control of assets except in certain extreme circumstances of distress (i.e., Qur'an 2:280). Nonetheless, conventional banking also allows the same through a legal procedure of bankruptcy or bankruptcy protection. Although the methodology may seem dissimilar, the end result usually requires foreclosure of the asset.[12] Although the end-user may not feel the difference between the services provided by Islamic banking and conventional banking, the main differences between the two lay in the investment opportunities taken. Islamic banking does not allow the banks to participate in risk trading activities. Hence, the difference is found in the investment operations of the banks, while the end-user may not feel any difference in the services provided.[13]

Today, and due to the ignorance of the majority of customers and bankers, Islamic banking has become more of a brand name and less of what the essence of Islamic banking is supposed to be. This chapter attempts to dive deep into Muḥammad's psyche through the method of intertextual polysemy to understand the inner-Qur'anic allusions that Muḥammad might have intended.

Definitions of *ribā* and *ḥarām*

The root of the word (*ribā*) means to increase, to grow in size, and to raise (especially children as in *tarbiyah*).[14] It also means interest or a usurer.[15] Also, it means magnanimity, greatness,[16] or a hill (raised ground).[17] The terms "*rby*" and "*rbb*" may have more than just wordplay in their meanings.[18] As "*rby*" means to increase or to be great, "*rbb*" also means abundance, multitude, someone who is of a high (great) status, or rabbi, which is a teacher who raises (*yurabbi*) students.[19] Also, it means a master, a lord (or the Lord).[20] Since the roots "*r b y*" and "*r b b*" both hold meanings of increase, abundance, or greatness, then there is perhaps a relationship between them through their meaning. From a different root, but with transposed letters, the word "*ryb*" means to doubt or to bring a case against someone.[21] Nonetheless, as discussed under methodology, this relationship between words with transposed letters would not be found very often in the allusions.

In the Islamic context, the usage of the word "*ḥalāl*" has become to mean permitted, while the usage of the word "*ḥarām*" has become to mean forbidden. It is very important to understand the meanings of these words from a linguistic point of view. Linguistically, "*ḥarām*" means sacred,[22] just like the Sacred Mosque (*al-Masjid al-ḥarām*). Also, as pilgrims wear the "*iḥrām*," they enter into a sacred state. However, "*ḥalāl*" means profane, or simply something that is not sacred.[23] An occupation is called "*iḥtilāl*" from the same root, as it is considered a desecration. The Qur'an forbids "*ribā*," and specifically, eating (*akl*) "*ribā*." The Qur'an in another verse uses the root of the word "*ribā*" (as a hill), when discussing money matters alongside with a root for eating, and increase: "And the parable of those who spend (*yunfiqūn*) their wealth (*amwālahum*) seeking God's Good Pleasure, and out of a confirmation in their souls, is that of a garden upon a hill (*rabwa*): a downpour strikes it, and brings forth its fruit twofold. And if a downpour strikes it not, then a soft rain. And God sees whatsoever you do."[24]

This verse is compared with the verses that forbid "*ribā*," specifically through the keywords of the roots "*n f q*," "*a k l*," and "*r b y*":

> 274 Those who spend (*yunfiqūn*) their wealth by night and by day, secretly and openly, shall have their reward with their Lord (*rabbihim*). No fear shall come upon them, nor shall they grieve. 275 Those who devour (*ya'kulūn*) usury (*al-ribā*) shall not rise except as one rises who is felled by the touch of Satan. That is because they say, "Sale (*al-bay'*)[25] are simply like usury (*al-ribā*)," though God has permitted (*aḥall*) sale (*al-bay'*) and forbidden (*ḥarram*) usury (*al-ribā*). One who, after receiving counsel from his Lord (*rabbih*), desists shall have what is past and his affair goes to God. And as for those who go back, they are the inhabitants of the Fire, abiding therein. 276 God blights (*yamḥaq*) usury (*al-ribā*) and causes acts of charity to grow (*yurbī*). And God loves not any sinful ingrate. 277 Truly those who believe, perform righteous deeds, maintain the prayer, and give the alms shall have their reward with their Lord (*rabbihim*). No fear shall come upon them, nor shall they grieve. 278 O you who believe! Reverence God, and leave (*dharū*) what remains (*baqiya*) of usury (*al-ribā*), if you are believers. 279 And if you do not, then take notice of a war from God and His Messenger. If you repent, you shall have the principal of your wealth, and you shall neither wrong nor be wronged.[26]

The usage in the verses above for people not fearing and not grieving (*lā khawfun 'alayhim wa-lā hum yaḥzanūn*) is a statement that is found several times in other verses in the Qur'an, including many times about people who spend (*yunfiqūn*) their money for the sake of God (e.g., Qur'an 2:112, 2:262).

Other verses also forbid eating (*akl*) "*ribā*" (i.e., Qur'an 3:130, 4:161). In Qur'an 3:130, "*ribā*" is forbidden to be doubled doubled (*aḍʿāfan muḍāʿafa*). Interestingly the root of the word "*ḍaʿīf*" not only means to double, but also means weakness (e.g., Qur'an 2:161, 9:91, 14:21, 30:54, 40:47).[27] In another verse, the Qur'an shows that the real doubling are those who spend for the cause of God and give alms; they are the ones whose rewards are truly doubled (i.e., Qur'an 30:39): "That which you give in usury, that it might increase (*ribā liyarbuwa*) through other people's wealth, does not increase (*yarbū*) with God. But that which you give in alms, desiring the Face of God—it is they who receive a manifold increase (*al-muḍʿifūn*)."[28]

This verse emphasizes that it is not even lending money without interest that gets multiplied (or rewarded) with God, but specifically giving alms and charity, since in giving alms and charity, the money is not lent, but is given freely without expecting even the capital to be repaid. The same reasoning also exists in Christianity against usury (*ribā*) or lending for repayment in general:[29]

> 34 And if you lend to those from whom you expect repayment, what credit is that to you? Even sinners lend to sinners, expecting to be repaid in full. 35 But love your enemies, do good to them, and lend to them without expecting to get anything back. Then your reward will be great, and you will be children of the Most High, because He is kind to the ungrateful and wicked.[30]

Analyzing verses Qur'an 2:274–279 shows that there is a difference between "*ribā*" and sale (*bayʿ*). To understand what is "*ribā*," sale (*bayʿ*) must also be understood. "*Bayʿ*" does not really mean trade. Trade is "*tijārah*," and the Qur'an uses both words together in one verse implying that they are not necessarily synonymous (i.e., Qur'an 24:37). Also interestingly as the Qur'an asks to give up (*dharū*) what remains of "*ribā*" (i.e., Qur'an 2:278) in the same manner it asks to give up (*dharū*) sale (*bayʿ*), when prayer on Friday is called (i.e., Qur'an 62:9).

"*Bayʿ*" also means to attest, to delay, and to rejoice.[31] The root of the word also means to give allegiance (*bayʿah*), as those who gave allegiance to the Prophet and to God (i.e., Qur'an 48:10, 48:18). "*Bayʿ*" is not trade, but more specifically sale, although it may sometimes mean buying; they are generally taken as opposites.[32] Buying is "*shirāʾ*," while "*bayʿ*" is sale and the action of both is called "*tijārah*" (trade), which is an action of both buying and selling.[33] It is noteworthy that the Qur'an specifically permits sale with "*bayʿ*" and does not use the term for trade (*tijārah*) when forbidding usury (*ribā*).

God's business deal

The Qur'an does not allow "*ribā*," but allows specifically sale (*bayʿ*). The Qur'an uses the word for sale (*bayʿ*) and not trade as "*ḥalāl*," because sale is not sacred or divine. In Muḥammad's allegorical usage of words, God does not sell. It is people who sell themselves to God. God is the buyer, Who buys the souls of the believers who sell their souls to God, as according to the following Qur'anic passage:

> Truly God has purchased (*ishtara*) from the believers their souls and their wealth in exchange for the Garden being theirs. They fight in the way of God, slaying and being slain. [It is] a promise binding upon Him in the Torah, the Gospel, and the Quran. And who is truer to His pact than God? So rejoice in the sale (*bi-bayʿikum*)[34] you have sold (*bāyaʿtum*). That indeed is the great triumph.[35]

Since God is the buyer, the Qur'an uses the word "*ḥalāl*" specifically for sale (*bayʿ*) and neither for trade nor purchase. Since God never sells, but lends and buys, then it is only sale that is "*ḥalāl*," meaning not sacred.

Hence, in Muḥammad's perhaps linguistic creativity, the Qur'an portrays that those who give allegiance (*bayʿah*) to God have sold themselves to God (i.e., Qur'an 9:111, 48:10, 48:18). Since they sell themselves to God, He provides them with doubles of doubles of what they have bargained for (i.e., Qur'an 2:276). For that reason, when God fulfills the duty of the souls of the people whom He purchased, they are given their right in full (i.e., Qur'an 2:281).

To understand it from the Qur'anic context according to Muḥammad's assumed psyche, people are not the owners of their souls, but God owns them. When is "*ribā*" in the picture? It occurs when people take loans for a period of time. Hence, immediately after the Qur'an steadfastly talks about "*ribā*" being sacred that only God is allowed to do, it discusses loans (*dayn*) in a verse known to be the longest verse in the Qur'an (i.e., Qur'an 2:282). Being the longest verse in the Qur'an may also provide it with some significance. Since loans are given for a period of time and then are repaid, perhaps Muḥammad had in mind to keep it a very long verse, because the period of time needs to be long giving extensions to the borrower.

In this verse, the Qur'an uses the words if you loan a loan (or judged a judgment) (*tadāyantum bidayn*) for a period of time (*ila ajalin musammā*), then it needs to be written in a book (or contract). The phrase "*ila ajalin musammā*" is found in the Qur'an plenty of times. Each person's soul is given also for a period of time (*ajalin musammā*) (i.e., Qur'an 30:8, 35:45, 39:42, 40:67–68, 42:14–15, 71:4): "that He may forgive you some of your sins and grant you reprieve until a term appointed (*ila ajalin musammā*). Truly when the term (*ajal*) of God comes, it will not be delayed, if you but knew."[36]

Therefore, people take a loan (*dayn*) from God by taking their souls for a period of time (*ila ajalin musammā*). Consequently, souls are loaned from God, as people are not the owners. People need to sell (*bayʿ*) it back to God before the period of time comes, so that people gain the necessary interest (*ribā*) on the loan (*dayn*) (i.e., Qur'an 2:276). Perhaps in Muḥammad's symbolic usage of polysemous terms, the day the loan (*dayn*) is given back to God (*al-Dayyān*) is *Yawm al-Dīn* (Judgment Day), because the word for "*dayn*" and "*dīn*" share the same root word. It could mean religion, but it truly means judgment, similar to "*qaḍa*."[37] Hence, when the soul is taken for a period of time (*ila ajalin musammā*), the word "*qaḍa*" sometimes is found nearby in the Qur'an (e.g., Qur'an 39:42, 40:67–68, 42:14). When the Qur'an discusses the Day of Judgment (*Yawm al-Dīn*) and the explanation of what *Yawm al-Dīn* is, it specifies that souls are not owned by the selves, but it is God Who is the owner, and therefore it is to be understood that it is the day this debt (the soul) is repaid.

> "[17] And what will apprise thee of the Day of Judgment (*Yawm al-Dīn*)? [18] Then what will apprise thee of the Day of Judgment (*Yawm al-Dīn*)? [19] A day when no soul will avail another soul in any way, and the Command that Day is God's."[38]

The Day of Judgment (*Yawm al-Dīn*) is also called by the Qur'an the Day of Reckoning (*Yawm al-ḥisāb*). The word "*ḥisāb*" means accounting, as it is the day the soul is accounted for. It is when the soul's final account and debt is settled (i.e., Qur'an 21:48). Deconstructing Muḥammad's mind needs to be further investigated to understand the verse of the loan (*dayn*):

> O you who believe! When you contract a debt (*tadāyantum bidayn*) with one another for a term appointed (*ila ajalin musammā*), write it down (*fa-ktubūh*). And let a scribe (*kātib*) write (*liyaktub*) between you justly (*bil-ʿadl*), and let not any scribe (*kātib*) refuse to write (*yaktub*) as God taught him (*ʿallamahu*). So let him write (*fa-liyaktub*), and let the debtor dictate, and let him reverence God his Lord (*rabbah*), and diminish nothing from it. And if the debtor is feeble-minded or is weak, or is unable to dictate himself, then let his guardian dictate justly (*bil-ʿadl*). And call to witness two witnesses from among your men, and if there are not two men, then a man and two women from among those whom you approve as witnesses, so that if one of the two errs, the other can remind her. Let not the witnesses refuse when they are called, and be not averse to write it down (*taktubūhu*), small or great, with its term (*ila ajalih*). That is more equitable with God, more sure for the testimony, and more likely to keep you from doubt (*tartābū*). Unless it is trade (*tijārah*) of present goods that you transact between yourselves: then there is no blame upon you not to write it (*taktubūhā*). And take witnesses when you sell between yourselves (*tabāyaʿtum*).[39] And let neither scribe (*kātib*) nor witness be harmed. Were you to do that, it would be iniquitous of you. And reverence God. God teaches you, and God is Knower of all things.[40]

The keywords (i.e., *dyn*, *ajl*, *musammā*, *ktb*, *rbb*, *ʿadl*, and *ryb*) in this verse need to be compared with the following verses. The verse above appears to discuss commercial transactions and contracts that need to be written down in a book. The verses below use the same keywords, in which the Qur'an is being described as the Book. Hence, Muḥammad might be alluding to the fact that the Qur'an is the commercial transaction between God and souls.

> [13] He has prescribed for you as religion (debt) (*al-dīn*) that which He enjoined upon Noah, and that which We revealed unto thee, and that which We enjoined upon Abraham, Moses, and Jesus, that you uphold religion (debt) (*al-dīn*) and not become divided therein. Grievous for the idolaters is that to which thou callest them. God chooses for Himself whomsoever He will and guides unto Himself whosoever turns in repentance. [14] They did not become divided till after knowledge had come unto

> them, out of envy (*baghyan*) among themselves. And were it not for a Word that had preceded from thy Lord (*rabbika*) unto a term appointed (*ila ajalin musammā*), judgment (*laquḍiya*) would have been made between them. Yet truly those who were bequeathed the Book (*al-kitāb*) after them are indeed confounded by doubt (*murīb*) regarding it. [15] Therefore, summon (*fadʿū*), and stand firm as thou hast been commanded. Follow not their caprices, and say, "I believe in that which God has sent down as a Book (*kitāb*), and I have been commanded to establish justice (*li-aʿdila*) among you. God is our Lord and your Lord (*rabbuna wa rabbukum*). Unto us our deeds, and unto you your deeds; there is no argument between us and you. God will gather us together (*yajmaʿu*) and unto Him is the journey's end."[41]

These verses are then also compared with the following using the keywords (i.e., *bghy*, *rbb*, and *qḍy*): "And We gave them clear proofs from the Command. And they differed not till after knowledge had come unto them, out of envy (*baghyan*) among themselves. Thy Lord (*rabbaka*) will surely judge (*yaqḍī*) between them on the Day of Resurrection regarding that wherein they used to differ."[42]

In the verse of *dayn*, the Qurʾan emphasizes that any loan taken for a period of time (*ila ajalin musammā*) has to be written in a book (or contract) by someone faithful (*bil-ʿadl*). In Qurʾan 42:14–15, the verses specify that a Word from God is brought down for a period of time (*ila ajalin musammā*) to judge (*qaḍa*) matters between them and that the Book brought by God is believed by someone commanded to be faithful and just (*li-aʿdila*). The similarities are interesting. In Qurʾan 42:15, it says that God will bring people together (*yajmaʿu*), which shares its root word with Friday (*al-Jumuʿa*). The Qurʾan forbids selling when the call for prayer on Friday (*al-Jumuʿa*) is made, until it is fulfilled (or judged) (*quḍiyat*) as in "*qaḍa*" (i.e., Qurʾan 62:9–11).

In the verse of *dayn*, the Qurʾan seems to be talking about commercial contracts as a metaphor (*tashbīh*) and a similitude to the transaction that God makes with the souls. If we look at the usage of precise terminologies, the verses seem to allude to each other. As the Qurʾan commands that a book is written in such transactions, God has made covenants with people by revealing to them a book (*kitāb*), according to the Qurʾan. Also, the reason that the verse of *dayn* emphasizes having a book is that people may forget or have doubts (*tartābū*). In Qurʾan 42:14, it states that those who inherited the Book (*al-kitāb*) have become suspicious with doubts (*murīb*); which the Qurʾan many times reject that there is any doubt in the Book (i.e., Qurʾan 2:2, 10:37, 32:2).

According to the Qurʾan, people can make commercial transactions at any time except during the call of prayer for Friday (*al-Jumuʿa*). Hence, allegorically, when it is time for God to judge the people on that which they are in dispute, there is no selling (*bayʿ*), for that is the Day of Judgment (*Yawm al-Dīn*), the day that the loan (*dayn*) is returned back to God. It is that Day, according to the Qurʾan, that is called the Day of the Gathering (*Yawma al-Jamʿ*), which there is no doubt about (*la rayb*) (i.e., Qurʾan 3:9, 3:25, 4:87, 6:12, 18:21, 22:7, 40:59, 42:7, 45:26, 45:32): "Our Lord (*rabbanā*), Thou art the Gatherer (*jāmiʿ*) of humankind[43] unto a Day about which there is no doubt (*la rayb*). Truly God will not fail the tryst."[44]

Also, in the verse of *dayn*, it talks about the scribe to write as God taught him to write, and that God is the teacher. This is similar to the description of the Qurʾan, which once Muḥammad recited according to traditional accounts, which stated that God teaches by the Pen, teaching the human that which he knew not. Perhaps Muḥammad is trying to remind people that the Qur'an is a book without a doubt (*la rayb*) and that the Qur'an is the commercial transaction between God and souls, for it is God who teaches writing as stated in the verse of *dayn*.

> "1 Recite (*Iqra'*) in the Name of thy Lord Who divided (created),[45] 2 divided (created) man from a clinging (*'alaq*).[46] 3 Recite! (*Iqra'*) Thy Lord is most noble, 4 Who taught (*'allam*) by the Pen, 5 taught (*'allam*) the human[47] that which he knew not."[48]

Paying the debt

In Muḥammad's creative mind, using symbolism and the art of allegory, it may be understood that the commercial transaction between people is a mirror of how God deals with souls. It is important to understand how people repay their debt to God, according to the Qur'an. People do not own their souls, for the soul has been loaned to them by God for a period of time (*ila ajalin musammā*). To repay the debt is to surrender (*islām*) the debt back to God. Since the words "*dīn*" and "*dayn*" are from the same root, the Qur'an states that the debt (*dīn*) to God is "*islām*" (surrender) (i.e., Qur'an 3:85). Hence, for people to repay their debts back to God, they need to surrender their souls to God, and God is quick to do the accounting (*ḥisāb*) of that soul and settle its debt: "Truly the religion (debt) (*dīn*) in the sight of God is *islām* (submission). Those who were given the Book differed not until after knowledge had come to them, out of envy (*baghyan*) among themselves. And whosoever disbelieves in God's signs, truly God is swift in reckoning (*al-ḥisāb*)."[49]

Most jurists claim that there are two types of verses "*muḥkam*" and "*mutashābih*" (i.e., Qur'an 3:7).[50] It may be understood that, in Muḥammad's mind, the verses of *muḥkamāt*, as in the verses against *ribā*, have a *ḥikmah* (wisdom), and the end of it is *mutashābih* (*wa ukhar mutashābihāt*). Muḥammad seems to allude to allegorical interpretations of the Qur'an, in which he was mastering the art of symbology using linguistic means in his recitation.

We need to understand the allegory in Muḥammad's mind while having verses allude to each other. Are the commercial transactions between people, as portrayed in the Qur'an, the metaphor for the commercial transaction between God and souls, or is the commercial transaction between God and souls the metaphor for the commercial transactions between people? It seems likely that the Qur'an is portraying the commercial transaction between people as the metaphor (*mutashābih*) for Muḥammad's reality, which is the commercial transaction between God and souls.

The verse, which discusses rulings and metaphors using the root of the word "*ibtighā'*," suggests that some people seek discord and schisms. This is the same root word used when describing that some people have selfish envy (*baghyan*) with the Qur'an as the Book (commercial contract) in the verses previously discussed (i.e.,

Qur'an 3:19, 3:85, 42:14, 45:17). Compare the following passage's keywords with aforementioned passages (i.e., *bghy*, *rbb*, *ryb*, *jm'*).

> 7 He it is Who has sent down the Book upon thee; therein are signs determined (*muḥkamāt*); they are the Mother of the Book, and others symbolic (*ukhar mutashābihāt*). As for those whose hearts are given to swerving, they follow that of it which is symbolic (*tashābah*), seeking (*ibtighā'*) temptation and seeking (*ibtighā'*) its interpretation. And none know its interpretation save God and those firmly rooted in knowledge. They say, "We believe in it; all is from our Lord." And none remember, save those who possess intellect. 8 "Our Lord (*rabbanā*), make not our hearts swerve after having guided us, and bestow upon us a mercy from Thy Presence. Truly Thou art the Bestower. 9 Our Lord (*rabbanā*), Thou art the Gatherer (*jāmi'*) of humankind[51] unto a Day about which there is no doubt (*la rayb*)." Truly God will not fail the tryst.[52]

Forgiveness of debts

The commercial contracts between people, according to the Qur'an, seem to allude to the commercial contract that God has with souls. The Qur'an perhaps portrays that God has given people their souls as a loan for a period of time, and He wrote a commercial transaction, the Qur'an, to remind the people such that they may not fall into suspicion, similar to how the verse of *dayn* describes the commercial transaction of loans (i.e., Qur'an 2:282). Souls need to be sold (*bay'*) back to God to gain the necessary profit in complete surrender of that debt to God's will (i.e., Qur'an 3:19). If Muḥammad wants his audience to see the connection on how dealing between people is mirroring how God deals with souls, then it should be understood that if souls seek to be forgiven by God for their own debts, the souls should also forgive the debts of each other.

9

Conclusion

When there are many patterns that emerge that seem meaningful, then it seems less likely to have been coincidental. Randomness is the distinction between the discourse of a schizophrenic and a creative genius, who is able to build meaningful patterns, instead. Indeed, when looking into the natural world, there are many patterns that can emerge, seemingly coincidental through the chaos of things. However, identifying patterns in human speech or writing seems less likely to be coincidental. As such, if the Qur'anic text is showing some kind of pattern, which is not very different than an intelligent person with psychosis-like symptoms, which do fit the symptoms of Muḥammad, then these Qur'anic examples seem to support the suggestion of the neuropsychological basis in its construct. If there was only a single example, or two, or three, then we may be skeptical of any kind of pattern emerging. However, when many more examples of this hermeneutical method provide meaningful insight, then there is a possibility that it is not random.

There have been many attempts to interpret the Qur'an throughout history. However, as modern scholars are questioning the accuracy of the interpretation by classical commentators (*mufassirīn*), there is a need to find interpretations that are not solely dependent on classical exegesis. Muslim early and medieval post-Qur'anic literature seems to have been trying to fill in the gaps without fully understanding the Biblical context or subtext that the passages are trying to engage with. This book looks into Muḥammad's state of mind and tries to unlock these creative associations in the Qur'an that an intelligent Muḥammad would have been able to construct. If that were not the case, then perhaps it looks into the literary creative intertextuality the Qur'an has within itself and with the Bible, regardless of the reason.

As stated, I find the most compelling reason with the least assumptions is that Muḥammad seems to have delved into a psychosis-like state, but due to his high intelligence, it protected him from diving into mental illness and allowed him to be highly creative, making ingenious associations and wordplay between terms within the Qur'an and Biblical literature. It does not at all assume that Muḥammad borrowed excerpts from Judeo-Christian literature, but made more intelligent engagement with the Biblical literature, in perhaps his attempt to interpret the Bible. As Wasserstrom puts it, "The model of 'influence and borrowing,' by means of its over-emphasis on genetic origination, may in fact obscure insight into a mature interreligious sharing."[1] Zayd ibn Thābit, who traditionally is considered one of the Prophet's scribes and who wrote down the Qur'an, studied, according to one tradition cited by Ibn Sa'd, Hebrew and/or Syriac, as well the Jewish texts,[2] thereby making this kind of interwoven textual allusion to Jewish and Christian literature in the Qur'an a possibility.[3]

The method of intertextual polysemy, as shown, is simple, in which terms are brought back to their roots and an understanding of their various semantic definitions. They are then intertextualized with various places in the Qur'an and the Bible where these terms occur to find possible connections between them. As a piece of literature, the Qur'an must be seen through the eyes of pre-Qur'anic literature. The sources of the Qur'an cannot have been based on post-Qur'anic literature and what their authors assume the Qur'an means. Academically, the source of the Qur'an can best be seen in the lens of pre-Qur'anic literature. As such, introducing intertextuality between the Qur'an and the Bible may seem to be a more probable approach academically, without necessarily going through post-Qur'anic authors who have attempted to distinguish the Qur'an from the Bible.

There is a possibility that Muḥammad had a very positive view of Biblical literature. However, when his community grew after his death, they wanted to be independent from their rivals, such as the Jews and the Christians. The community that became independent wanted to show that they had something better than the Jews and the Christians, and as such suppressed anything that suggested otherwise.

This may further be illustrated by Abraham's sacrificial son and why al-Ṭabarī, one of the earliest commentators, suggests that it is Isaac,[4] while later commentators, such as al-Rāzī and Ibn Kathīr, narrate that there were differences of opinion among Muslims on whether it was Isaac or Ishmael, and later conclude that it was Ishmael.[5] Reuven Firestone shows how there were two groups of Muslims, those who supported the notion that the sacrificial son is Isaac, and those who supported the notion that it was Ishmael, and while the former group were from the earliest accounts, later generations adopted the latter group's opinion. Firestone states:

> It becomes clear from our reading of the sources that Isaac was originally understood to have been the intended victim, but that this view was eclipsed by a new perspective, which held Ishmael to have been intended. Ṭabarī was the first to record the various arguments supporting each son. While he tried to demonstrate that Isaac was the proper reading, the arguments supporting Ishmael were already quite imposing by his generation. After Ṭabarī, the exegetes citing arguments and giving their own opinions were unanimous in considering Ishmael to be the intended victim, though most cited arguments supporting both views. Even the Shīʿite Ṭabarsī, who quoted Shīʿite versions considering Isaac to have been the intended sacrifice, held that it was Ishmael. And Thaʿlabī, who often followed Ṭabarī, seemed to consider Ishmael the intended Sacrifice [*sic*] as well. Like the other exegetes after Ṭabarī, Ibn Kathīr believed that the intended sacrifice was Ishmael and did not hesitate to give his own views of the matter. His major argument was based on the weakness of those sources claiming that it was Isaac.[6]

Perhaps the lack of evidence from Muslim literature that the Qur'an is engaging with the Bible is due to Muslims wanting to distinguish their religion from Judaism and Christianity. Some Muslim scholars were trying as much as possible to make conclusions that differentiated and alienated them from the Jews and Christians and for that reason attempted to suppress any knowledge that would show similarities, when Muḥammad was more accepting of the notions in the Bible, but perhaps had his own interpretation thereof, in which the Qur'an perhaps hints at when stating, "Verily, this Quran recounts unto the Children of Israel most of that wherein they differ."[7]

There needs to be further research on the method of intertextuality as it may provide us with creative connections and insights to possible inner meanings of the Qur'an, and especially to understand the apparent contradictions that may exist between the Qur'an and the Bible. It is argued that Muḥammad is an intelligent person and, therefore, he is unlikely to have these apparent contradictions, even if we apply rhetoric. Muḥammad is capable of making symbolic and allegorical meanings from the image he is trying to create constructed by the use of precise words and terminologies in the Qur'an.

Words of a language are symbols and signs of what they represent. They are not themselves reality. Determining the meaning of words through the study of semantics and semiotics is a process whereby we try to define those symbols and understand what they represent in reality. Hence, we can only understand words symbolically. Therefore, I find the literal understanding of words to be somewhat of an oxymoron. Only a real apple is a precise apple, whereas the word "apple" is only a symbol representing it. As such, we must understand what the symbol of the word "apple" represents, and that is done symbolically. Since all language is symbolic in its representation of reality, then deciphering the meaning of those symbols becomes a difficult task.

The use of intertextual polysemy, as demonstrated through examples in this book, provides us with a different perspective of how scriptures, both the Bible and the Qur'an, may be interpreted. It does not necessarily provide a single authoritative interpretation of scriptures, but it looks at them with a completely different understanding, and perhaps one that is deeply spiritual in its nature. This is something that Muḥammad would have been able to do creatively, given his psychological state. He tried to represent what he perceived as spiritual truths into reality and he used words as symbols to fulfill his representation.

There are various types of maps of the earth with different projections. Only the real earth is earth, while our mapping of the earth is nothing but a representation of what the earth looks like. Because the earth is three-dimensional, while our maps are usually two-dimensional, when projecting the earth onto these maps, it loses several of its attributes. As such, there are many different types of projections that are used for different purposes. Some projections provide us with correct scale of distance, while distorting shape and area. Others provide us with correct shapes, while distorting distances and area. Still others provide us with correct areas, while distorting shapes and distances. We should not ask ourselves which, if any, specific projection is more correct than the others. However, we can ask ourselves which projection more correctly suits our purpose. Scriptural interpretations and their various methods could be considered as something very similar to projections.

Different methods of scriptural hermeneutics are different projections of scriptures. It does not mean that any specific method of interpretation is more correct than another, but that each may suit different purposes. Scriptures may not only be three-dimensional, but multidimensional. This makes interpretation of scriptures even more challenging than our mapping of the earth. Different methods provide us with different perspectives.

Several controversial Sufis, such as Ibn ʿArabī and al-ḥallāj, might have been misunderstood because they projected a multidimensional object from a different perspective to that which most people were used to. A popular projection called the Mercator projection shows the island of Greenland larger than South America. If people do not know the reality of the earth, in that South America is immensely much more enormous than Greenland, then someone representing the map with a different projection that shows a more accurate size may be considered a heretic. The earth remains the earth in its reality, and our projections of it are the only things that change. If we know how to use those projections and how to make them fit reality, then we will better understand reality. Since none of the projections is without distortion, then we must also accept that any interpretation of scriptures is not perfect.

The reason I have emphasized a linguistic approach through intertextual polysemy is to understand the meanings of scriptures instead of using the traditional approaches. The Qur'an never identified a specific methodology for its interpretation, except for (i) clinging unto God to teach the Qur'an, and (ii) the supremacy of its language. Muḥammad seems to have been using selective Arabic words that are polysemous, having plentiful meanings. As such, the Qur'an may be providing us with a master key to unlock itself. Lexical semantics, intertextual polysemy, and etymology are fundamental aspects of trying to understand the meanings of the Qur'an by trying to go deep into Muḥammad's psyche to understand his intentions. This seems to be the only tangible method for interpretation that the Qur'an expects its audience to use. As such, I find projecting scriptures using this method, though still not without distortions, is a projection the Qur'an itself seems to require people to use to understand it better. The traditional methods of interpretation, which heavily rely on the interpretation by precedent (*tafsīr bil-ma'thūr*) or circumstances of revelation (*asbāb al-nuzūl*), do not use a method of projection sanctioned by the text of the Qur'an itself. Although I do not essentially consider them incorrect methods, they are projections that may not necessarily have been expected by Muḥammad. Muḥammad seems to have focused himself on a linguistic approach that is capable of providing inner-Qur'anic allusions.

If the story of Muḥammad meditating in a cave is inaccurate, then this means that the psychological diagnosis, as presented here, is equally inaccurate. If Muḥammad was a passive receiver of revelation, then perhaps the findings in here do not demonstrate the intentions of Muḥammad, but at least what the Qur'an expects from its audience in creating inner-Qur'anic allusions and Qur'anic-Biblical allusions. Perhaps when the Qur'an describes itself as a veiled book (*kitābin maknūn*) (i.e., Qur'an 56:78) or when it describes that some people have veils (*akinnah*) placed in their hearts so that they would not understand it (e.g., Qur'an 6:25, 17:45–46, 18:57, 41:5), it might be suggestive that what we today call "latent inhibition" is this veil. Perhaps the Sufi concept of "*kashf*" (unveiling) is reached when the mind reaches levels of decreased latent inhibition coupled with high intelligence,[8] and thus, previous stimuli that were associated with certain meaning, get different meanings during the state of "*kashf*."

If, however, Muḥammad's state of mind is inaccurate due to our having an inaccurate historical account and if Muḥammad did not receive revelation passively, this brings us to yet a different conclusion. It might suggest that the Qur'an is a literary style that combines inner-Qur'anic allusions, while also actively engaging with Biblical literature. As such, understanding these Qur'anic and Biblical allusions are very important in an attempt to interpret the Qur'an. How this came to be very creatively would suggest that the scribes and redactors of the Qur'an were very proficient linguistically in their Biblical knowledge. However, since this knowledge was not inherited by later Muslim scholars it might suggest a lacuna. The reason behind this lacuna may vary with different assumptions. That the knowledge of the scribes and redactors of these types of allusions disappeared from later Muslim literature may be possible. Nonetheless, how they disappeared will cause us to make many assumptions. It is more likely, however, that Muḥammad was in an altered state of consciousness, as these allusions and intertextualities would appear natural to him and he would simply be frustrated when his audience do not see what he sees. Otherwise, if he received revelation passively, then perhaps Muḥammad was even somewhat removed from these intertextualities, which caused such knowledge to have never been inherited down to later Muslims. Although the latter is a possibility, we will need to make many theological and philosophical assumptions to arrive at it. As such, from among the range of possibilities, the one with the least assumptions is that Muḥammad was in an altered state of consciousness.

One thing that we may be able to distinguish from this study is that the Qur'an does not attempt to contradict itself when it asks Jews and Christians to follow their scriptures, while still seeming to have a theology or Christology that is different from that the later Muslim community evolved to have.

The purpose of this study is to provide a framework for Qur'anic hermeneutics using a method called intertextual polysemy. Perhaps it allows us to understand Muḥammad's intention given his psychological state. I am only providing observations. Ultimately, you will need to decide yourself what to conclude from it. We are in search of the truth. I simply happened to stumble upon observations that may provide us with some insights, but it definitely does not mean that such an insight is exclusive. This was a simple, humble attempt to unravel some meanings to an otherwise mysterious piece of literature that some call scriptures.

Further research

Psychological Qur'anic criticism might be a new field to further explore and not only to include the author's psychology, but also the psychological states of Qur'anic characters in some of their detailed narratives. Insights from such findings may open some doors, especially when comparing the portrayal of Biblical characters in the Qur'an, for example.

Nonetheless, what is more important is to further develop the role of polysemy in the Qur'an and how terminologies are used as wordplay or tools for allusions, whether or not allegorical, and regardless of the psychology of the author. As seen in the examples of this book, intertextual polysemy appears to exist, whether within the Qur'an or between the Qur'an and the Bible. Whether this is caused by author(s) or by redactors is not as important as the purpose behind this tool. Perhaps once we know the purpose behind it, we could better identify who used it.

In addition, as post-Qur'anic literature appears to be heavily scrutinized for its ability to interpret the Qur'an, especially writings by classical commentators, then further research needs to be made in the exegetical methods of the Qur'an and the role of these commentaries. There is much relationship between the Qur'an and the Bible and many studies already exist on these relationships. However, much literature interprets the Qur'an based on post-Qur'anic literature when comparing it with the Bible, whereas caution is needed when doing so.

Understanding the "*nāsikh*" and "*mansūkh*" (the concept of abrogation) in the Qur'an was a tool that many early Muslims scholars have used to solve inconsistencies within the Qur'an. For example, in some instances the Qur'an shows that Jews, Christians, and Sabians are accepted, while at other times the Qur'an states that the "*dīn*" (understood as religion, but possibly debt from "*dayn*") accepted is "*islām*" (understood as Muḥammad's religion, but might be generally meaning "submission" or "surrendering the debt"). Classically, Muslim scholars resorted to the concept of abrogation in these instances. However, it is possible that Muslim scholars were only attempting to keep their doctrines consistent with the Qur'anic text, and not truly keeping the Qur'an consistent with itself. It is very much possible that the Qur'an is consistent with itself, if these passages are further scrutinized. As such, more research on the concept of abrogation is necessary.

Historically, the concept of "*muḥkam*" and "*mutashābih*" verses were defined as clear commandments and allegorical, respectively. However, as shown in the example of Chapter 8, it might not be so. Perhaps the laws of Sharī'ah are not the essence and are only metaphoric, while the spirit of these laws are the "*muḥkam*." As such, further research on the purpose of these laws and their meanings is essential.

Much more research can be done from the observations made. However, I wish to give a word of caution. One should not adhere to a single presupposition or to further work on a single agenda when trying to unravel meanings of any text. One should try as much as possible to be objective. I admit that the presupposition made in this book is that the Qur'an is authored by Muḥammad who had an altered state of consciousness. However, if you remove this presupposition, as in he did not have an altered state, or redactors having written it, or God has authored it, etc., it would not change the insights provided by such method. As such, I must repeat that we are in search of truth, whatever it may be, and not a defense of dogma. Therefore, our further research needs to keep that as our goal—the truth.

Notes

Chapter 1: The Science Behind Revelation

1 Macdonald, Duncan B., *Aspects of Islam* (New York: Macmillan, 1911), 63–64.
2 Rodinson, Maxime, *Muhammad: Prophet of Islam* (London: Tauris Parke Paperbacks, 2002), 54–60.
3 To assess methods for understanding personality traits and psychological assessments from psychobiography, see Runyan, William M., ed. *Life Histories and Psychobiography: Explorations in Theory and Method* (Oxford: Oxford University Press, 1982); Alexander, Irving A., "Personality, Psychological Assessment, and Psychobiography," *Journal of Personality* 56, no.1 (1988): 265–294.
4 These are the same reasons why Bas van Os also considers limitations to perform a sound psychobiography of Jesus. See van Os, Bas, "The Problem of Writing a Psychobiography of Jesus," in *Psychological Hermeneutics for Biblical Themes and Texts: A Festschrift in Honor of Wayne G. Rollins*, ed. J. Harold Ellens (London: T&T Clark, 2012), 84–96.
5 Examples include Sina, Ali, *Understanding Muhammad: A Psychobiography of Allah's Prophet* (n.p.: FaithFreedom Publishing, 2008); and Das, Sujit, *Islam Dismantled: The Mental Illness of Prophet Muhammad* (n.p.: Felibri Publications, 2012).
6 See also Szaluta, Jacques, *Psychohistory: Theory and Practice* (New York, NY: Peter Lang, 1999).
7 See Rollins, Wayne G., *Soul and Psyche: The Bible in Psychological Perspective* (Minneapolis, MN: Fortress, Press, 1999); Kille, D. Andrew, *Psychological Biblical Criticism* (Minneapolis, MN: Fortress Press, 2000); Ellens, J. Harold, and Rollins, Wayne G. *Psychology and the Bible: A New Way to Read the Scriptures* (Santa Barbara, CA: Greenwood, 2004); Rollins, Wayne G., and Kille, D. Andrew, *Psychological Insight into the Bible* (Grand Rapids, MI: Wm. B. Eerdmans, 2007); Daschke, Derek, and Kille, D. Andrew, eds., *A Cry Instead of Justice: The Bible and Cultures of Violence in Psychological Perspective* (London: Bloomsbury Academic, 2010); Ellens, J. Harold ed., *Psychological Hermeneutics for Biblical Themes and Texts* (London: Bloomsbury Academic, 2012). For more on Psychological Biblical Criticism and hermeneutics, see Edinger, Edward F. *The Bible and the Psyche: Individuation Symbolism in the Old Testament* (Toronto: Inner City Books, 1986); Halperin, David J. *Seeking Ezekiel: Text and Psychology* (University Park, PA: Penn State University Press, 1993); Drewermann, Eugen, *Discovering the God Child Within: A Spiritual Psychology of the Infancy of Jesus*, trans. Peter Heinegg (New York, NY: Crossroad, 1994); Miller, John W. *Jesus at Thirty: A Psychological and Historical Portrait* (Minneapolis, MN: Fortress Press, 1997); Meissner, William W. *The Cultic Origins of Christianity: The Dynamic of Religious Development* (Collegeville, MN: Liturgical Press, 2000); Berger, Klaus, *Identity and Experience in the New Testament* (Minneapolis, MN: Fortress Press, 2003); Efthimiadis-Keith, Helen, *The Enemy Is Within: A Jungian Psychoanalytic Approach to the Book of Judith* (Leiden: Brill, 2004); Kamp, Albert H. *Inner Worlds: A Cognitive*

Linguistic Approach to the Book of Jonah (Leiden: Brill, 2004); Newheart, Michael W. *My Name Is Legion: The Story and Soul of the Gerasene Demoniac* (Collegeville, MN: Liturgical Press, 2004); Capps, Donald, *Jesus the Village Psychiatrist* (Louisville, KY: Westminster John Knox, 2008); Capps, Donald *Jesus: A Psychological Biography* (Eugene, OR: Wipf and Stock, 2010); van Os, Bas, *Psychological Analyses and the Historical Jesus: New Ways to Explore Christian Origins* (London: Bloomsbury Academic, 2010).

8 El-Badawi, Emran, *The Qurʾan and the Aramaic Gospel Traditions* (Abingdon: Routledge, 2013).

9 Kille, *Psychological Biblical Criticism*, 28.

10 Galadari, Abdulla, "The *Qibla*: An Allusion to the Shemaʿ," *Comparative Islamic Studies* 9, no. 2 (2013): 165–193.

11 Qurʾan 43:23.

12 Ibid., 4:82.

13 Qurʾan 47:24.

14 This is not only a modern view of interpretation, but it also started with classical exegetes who tried to take into consideration the circumstances of revelations (*asbāb al-nuzūl*) in Qurʾanic exegesis.

15 Gibbs Jr. Raymond W., "Authorial Intentions in Text Understanding," *Discourse Processes* 32, no. 1 (2001): 73–80.

16 Gibbs Jr., Raymond W., Kushner, Julia M., and Mills III, W. Rob, "Authorial Intentions and Metaphor Comprehension," *Journal of Psycholinguistic Research* 20, no. 1 (1991): 11–30.

17 Katz, Albert N. and Lee, Christopher J., "The Role of Authorial Intent in Determining Verbal Irony and Metaphor," *Metaphor and Symbolic Activity* 8, no. 4 (1993): 257–279.

18 Understanding authorial intent can be filled with bias. For further details, see VanSledright, Bruce A., "What Does It Mean to Think Historically . . . and How Do You Teach It?" *Social Education* 68, no. 3 (2004): 230–233.

19 See Wansbrough, John, E., *Qurʾanic Studies: Sources and Methods of Scriptural Interpretation* (Oxford: Oxford University Press, 1977); Crone, Patricia and Cook, Michael, *Hagarism: The Making of the Islamic World* (Cambridge: Cambridge University Press, 1977); Wansbrough, John, E., *The Sectarian Milieu: Content and Composition of Islamic Salvation History* (Oxford: Oxford University Press, 1978); Crone, Patricia, *Slaves on Horses: The Evolution of the Islamic Polity* (Cambridge: Cambridge University Press, 1980). See also Rippin, Andrew, ed., *Approaches to the History of the Interpretation of the Qurʾān* (Oxford: Clarendon Press, 1988); Reynolds, Gabriel S., *The Qurʾān and Its Biblical Subtext* (Abingdon: Routledge, 2010).

20 Donner, Fred, *Muhammad and the Believers: At the Origins of Islam* (Cambridge, MA: Harvard University Press, 2010).

21 Donner, *Muhammad and the Believers*, 204.

22 For neuropsychology of creative individuals, see Camfield, David, "Neurobiology of Creativity," in *Neurobiology of Exceptionality*, ed. Con Stough (New York, NY: Kluwer Academic/Plenum, 2005), 53–72; Richards, Ruth, "A Creative Alchemy," in *The Ethics of Creativity*, eds. Seana Moran, David Cropley, and James C. Kaufman (Basingstoke: Palgrave Macmillan, 2014), 119–136.

23 Räisänen, Heikki, "The Portrait of Jesus in the Qurʾān: Reflections of a Biblical Scholar," *The Muslim World* 70, no. 2 (1980): 122–133.

24 Ibid., 124.

25 For an overview, you may refer to Almond, Philip C., *Mystical Experience and Religious Doctrine: An Investigation of the Study of Mysticism in World Religions* (Berlin: De Gruyter, 1982).

26 One of the earliest studies in modern psychology about religious experiences is James, William, *The Varieties of Religious Experience: A Study in Human Nature* (New York, NY: Longmans, Green & Co, 1902); Freud, Sigmund, "A Religious Experience," *The Psychoanalytic Review*, 20 (1933): 352; Proudfoot, Wayne, *Religious Experience* (Berkeley, CA: University of California Press, 1985). Carl Jung has devoted his life and work to understanding the psychology of mystical experiences; examples of his works include *Modern Man in Search of a Soul* (London: Kegan Paul, Trench, Trubner and Co., 1933) and *Psychology and Religion* (New Haven, CT: Yale University Press, 1938).

27 For an overview of the relationship between psychology, cognition, and neuroscience in religious experiences, see Paloutzian, Raymond F. and Park, Crystal L. eds., *Handbook of the Psychology of Religion and Spirituality* (New York, NY: The Guilford Press, 2013); Beit-Hallahmi, Benjamin and Argyle, Michael, *The Psychology of Religious Behaviour, Belief and Experience* (London: Routledge, 1997).

28 For an overview of neurotheology, see Newberg, Andrew B., *Principles of Neurotheology* (Farnham: Ashgate, 2010).

29 Brandt, P.Y., Clément, F., and Manning, R. R., "Neurotheology: Challenges and Opportunities," *Schweizer Archiv fur Neurologie und Psychiatrie* 161, no. 8 (2010): 305–309.

30 Ashbrook, James B., "Neurotheology: The Working Brain and the Work of Theology," *Zygon* 19, no. 3 (1984): 331–350.

31 Joseph, Rhawn, "The Limbic System and the Soul: Evolution and the Neuroanatomy of Religious Experience," *Zygon* 36, no. 1 (2001): 105–136.

32 Ibid., 105–106.

33 Ibid., 107.

34 For examples, see Schwarcz, H. P., Grün, R., Vandermeersch, B., Bar-Yosef, O., Valladas, H., and Tchernov, E., "ESR Dates for the Hominid Burial Site of Qafzeh in Israel," *Journal of Human Evolution* 17, no. 8 (1988): 733–737; Stringer, C. B., Grün, R., Schwarcz, H. P., and Goldberg, P., "ESR Dates for the Hominid Burial Site of Es Skhul in Israel," *Nature* 338 (1989): 756–758.

35 Zilhão, João, "Lower and Middle Palaeolithic Mortuary Behaviours and the Origins of Ritual Burial," in *Death Rituals, Social Order and the Archaeology of Immortality in the Ancient World: Death Shall Have No Dominion*, eds. Colin Renfrew, Michael J. Boyd, and Iain Morley (Cambridge: Cambridge University Press, 2015), 27–44.

36 This is suggested by Zilhão, "Lower and Middle Palaeolithic," 43.

37 Examples may be seen in Belfer-Cohen, Anna and Hovers, Erella, "In the Eye of the Beholder: Mousterian and Natufian Burials in the Levant," *Current Anthropology* 33, no. 4 (1992): 463–471.

38 Robert Gargett provides two possible theories in that Neanderthals either believed an afterlife or had an emotional capacity like ours. See Gargett, Robert H., "Grave Shortcomings: The Evidence for Neanderthal Burial," *Current Anthropology* 30, no. 2 (1989): 157–190.

39 Piel, Alexander K. and Stewart, Fiona A., "Non-Human Animal Responses Towards the Dead and Death: A Comparative Approach to Understanding the Evolution of Human Mortuary Practice," in *Death Rituals, Social Order and the Arcaheology of Immortality in the Ancient World: Death Shall Have No Dominion*, eds. Colin Renfrew, Michael J. Boyd, and Iain Morley (Cambridge: Cambridge University Press, 2015), 15–26.

40 Ibid., 23.

41 For more on the association between dreaming and religious experience see Kahn, David, "From Chaos to Self-Organization: The Brain, Dreaming, and Religious Experience," in *Soul, Psyche, Brain: New Directions in the Study of Religion and Brain-Mind Science*, ed. Kelly Bulkeley (New York, NY: Palgrave Macmillan, 2005), 138–158.

42 Between 1913 and 1916, Jung developed a meditation technique called "active imagination" for inducing visions. During hypnagogic states, he introduced visualization techniques to induce autonomous waking imaginations that were not consciously directed. For details of this technique, see Jung, Carl G. *Active Imagination* (Princeton, NJ: Princeton University Press, 1997). For more on the mystical visions across religions refer to Merkur, Dan, *Gnosis: An Esoteric Tradition of Mystical Visions and Unions* (Albany, NY: State University of New York Press, 1993).

43 You may refer to Yu, Calvin K. C., "Toward 100% Dream Retrieval by Rapid-Eye-Movement Sleep Awakening: A High-Density Electroencephalographic Study," *Dreaming* 24, no. 1 (2014): 1–17.

44 Louie, Kenway and Wilson, Matthew A., "Temporally Structured Replay of Awake Hippocampal Ensemble Activity during Rapid Eye Movement Sleep," *Neuron*, 29, no. 1 (2001): 1454–156.

45 See Hurovitz, Craig S., Dunn, Sarah, Domhoff, G. William, and Fiss, Harry, "The Dreams of Blind Men and Women: A Replication and Extension of Previous Findings," *Dreaming* 9, no. 2/3 (1999): 183–193; Kerr, Nancy H. and Domhoff, G. William, "Do the Blind Literally 'See' in Their Dreams? A Critique of a Recent Claim that They Do," *Dreaming*, 14, no. 4 (2004): 230–233. The difference between perception and visual imagery has to be noted. Congenitally blind individuals can construct visual forms and perceive spatial relationships having spatial mental imagery, but do not visually see; see Kaski, Diego, "Revision: Is Visual Perception a Requisite for Visual Imagery?" *Perception* 31, no. 6 (2002): 717–731; Aleman, Andre, van Lee, Laura, Mantione, Mariska H. M., and de Haan, Edward, "Visual Imagery Without Visual Experience: Evidence from Congenitally Totally Blind People," *Neuroreport* 12, no. 11 (2001): 2601–2604; D'Agostino, Armando, Castelnovo, Anna, and Scarone, Silvio, "Non-pathological Associations: Sleep and Dreams, Deprivation and Bereavement," in *The Neuroscience of Visual Hallucinations*, eds. Daniel Collerton, Urs P. Mosimann, and Elaine Perry (Chichester: Wiley, 2015), 59–89.

46 Krill, A., Alpert, H. J., and Ostfeld, A. M., "Effects of a Hallucinogenic Agent in Totally Blind Subjects," *Archives of Ophthalmology* 62, no. 2 (1963): 180–185.

47 Aleman et al., "Visual Imagery Without Visual Experience," 2601–2604.

48 Voss, Ursula, Tuin, Inka, Schermelleh-Engel, Karin, and Hobson, Allan, "Waking and Dreaming: Related but Structurally Independent—Dream Reports of Congenitally Parapelgic and Deaf-Mute Persons," *Consciousness and Cognition* 20, no. 3 (2011): 673–687.

49 Ibid.

50 McCreery, Charles, *Dreams and Psychosis: A New Look at an Old Hypothesis* (n.p.: Oxford Forum, 2008).

51 Nielsen, Tore A., and Stenstrom, Philippe, "What Are the Memory Sources of Dreaming?" *Nature* 437 (2005): 1286–1289.

52 Fingelkurts, Alexander A. and Fingelkurts, Andrew A., "Is Our Brain Hardwired to Produce God, or is Our Brain Hardwired to Perceive God? A Systematic Review on the Role of the Brain in Mediating Religious Experience," *Cognitive Processing* 10, no. 4 (2009): 293–326. The last statement refers to Newberg, Andrew B. and Lee, B. Y., "The Neuroscientific Study of Religious and Spiritual Phenomena: Or Why God Doesn't Use Biostatistics," *Zygon* 40, no. 2 (2005): 469–489.

53 Joseph, "The Limbic System."
54 See Catani, Marco, Dell'Acqua, Flavio, Thiebaut de Schotten, Michel, "A Revised Limbic System Model for Memory, Emotion, and Behaviour," *Neuroscience & Biobehavioral Reviews* 37, no. 8 (2013): 1724–1737. Also, for recent studies on the limbic systems (not just a single one), see Rolls, Edmund T., "Limbic Systems for Emotion and for Memory, but No Single Limbic System," *Cortex* 62 (2015): 119–157.
55 Joseph, "The Limbic System," 132; Saver, Jeffrey L. and Rabin, John, "The Neural Substrates of Religious Experience," in *The Neuropsychiatry of Limbic and Subcortical Disorders*, eds. Stephen Salloway, Paul Malloy, and Jeffrey L. Cummings (Washington, DC: American Psychiatric Press, 1997), 195–215.
56 Joseph, "The Limbic System," 132–133.
57 See Kéri, Szabolcs, "Genes for Psychosis and Creativity: A Promoter Polymorphism of the Neuregulin 1 Gene Is Related to Creativity in People with High Intellectual Achievement," *Psychological Science* 20, no. 9 (2009): 1070–1073; O'Reilly, Thomas, Dunbar, Robin, and Bentall, Richard, "Schizotypy and Creativity: An Evolutionary Connection?" *Personality and Individual Differences*, 31, no. 7 (2001): 1067–1078.
58 Lodge, Daniel J. and Grace, Anthony A., "Developmental Pathology, Dopamine, Stress, and Schizophrenia," *International Journal of Developmental Neuroscience* 29, no. 3 (2011): 207–213.
59 Kozbelt, Aaron, Kaufman, Scott Barry, Walder, Deborah J., Ospina, Luz H., and Kim, Joseph U., "The Evolutionary Genetics of the Creativity–Psychosis Connection," in *Creativity and Mental Illness*, ed. James C. Kaufman (Cambridge: Cambridge University Press, 2014), 102–132.
60 Lecture by Andani, Khalil {2017) "The Speaking Qur'an: Revelation in Sunni & Shia Islam," Austin, TX: University of Texas, 7 April 2017
61 Qur'an 26:193–194.
62 Al-Zarkashī (d. 794/1392), *al-Burhān fī 'ulūm al-Qur'ān* (Beirut: Dār Ihyā' al-Kutub al-'Arabiyyah, 1957), 1: 229–230.
63 Abu Zayd, Nasr Hamid, *Mafhūm al-naṣṣ: Dirāsah fī 'ulūm al-Qur'ān* (Ribat: al-Markaz al-Thaqāfī al-'Arabī, orig. 1998/2014), 42–52, 55–57.
64 Ibid.
65 Soroush, Abdulkarim, *The Expansion of Prophetic Experience: Essays on Historicity, Contingency and Plurality in Religion*, trans. Nilou Mobasser (Leiden: Brill, 2009), 209–211, 272.
66 Ibid., 336.
67 Ibid., 332–333.
68 Al-Zarkashī, *al-Burhān fī 'ulūm al-Qur'ān*.
69 Sayadmansour, Alireza, "Neurotheology: The Relationship Between Brain and Religion," *Iranian Journal of Neurology* 13, no. 1 (2014): 52–55.
70 See Ibn Isḥāq (d. 151/768), *Sīrah* (Beirut: Dār al-Fikr, 1978), 120–121; Ibn Hishām (d. 213/833) *Sīrah* (Cairo: Maktabat wa Maṭba'at Muṣṭafa al-Bābī al-Ḥalabī wa Awlādih, 1955), 1: 239–240.
71 We do not have conclusive evidence of Muḥammad eating less in the cave, but his seclusion might make it likely. This is also the opinion of Ibn 'Āshūr (d. 1973). See Ibn 'Āshūr, *al-Taḥrīr wal-tanwīr* (Tunis: al-Dār al-Tūnisiyyah lil-Nashr, 1984), 2: 172 on Qur'an 2:185.
72 Yung, Alison R. and McGorry, Patrick D., "The Prodromal Phase of First-Episode Psychosis: Past and Current Conceptualizations," *Schizophrenia Bulletin* 22, no. 2 (1996): 353–370.

73 Al-Ṭabarī (d. 310/923), *Jāmiʿ al-bayān fī taʾwīl al-Qurʾān*, ed. Aḥmad Shākir (Damascus: Muʾassassat al-Risālah, 2000), Q 74:1, 23:7–9.

74 Yung, and McGorry, "The Prodromal Phase of First-Episode Psychosis."

75 Ibn Isḥāq, *Sīrah*, 121.

76 Ibid., 121.

77 Auditory and visual hallucinations are also found in the writings of Ezekiel (a prophet from the Hebrew Bible). As Muḥammad also shows that God commands him to do things according to the Qurʾan, so is Ezekiel commanded to do things. The modern diagnosis of Ezekiel's state of mind is a case of schizophrenia. See Stein, George, "The Voices that Ezekiel Hears: Psychiatry in the Old Testament," *The British Journal of Psychiatry* 196, no. 2 (2010): 101.

78 Similarly, Ezekiel also interprets his hallucinations with grandiose delusions as stated by Edwin Broome, Jr. See Broome Jr., Edwin C., "Ezekiel's Abnormal Personality," *Journal of Biblical Literature* 65, no. 3 (1946): 277–292.

79 The Diagnostic and Statistical Manual of Mental Disorders version 4 (DSM-IV) published by the American Psychiatric Association (APA) states that for a schizophrenia diagnosis two or more of the following symptoms must exist, each present for a significant portion of time during a one-month period, (a) delusions, (b) hallucinations, (c) disorganized speech, (d) grossly disorganized or catatonic behavior, (e) negative symptoms. Muḥammad apparently had delusions and hallucinations. However, Muḥammad did not experience other symptoms such as social/occupational dysfunction or negative symptoms. Hence, he might not have been considered schizophrenic but what is considered not-otherwise-specified (NOS) psychotic disorder, since his symptoms are not specific to any type, according to DSM-IV. Frank Freemon also excludes a schizophrenia diagnosis due to Muḥammad's leadership ability. See Freemon, Frank R., "A Differential Diagnosis of the Inspirational Spells of Muḥammad the Prophet of Islam," *Epilepsia*, 17 (1976): 423–427. Although Freemon considers epileptic seizures as the likely diagnosis of Muḥammad, I find low latent inhibition coupled with high intelligence as the most likely diagnosis, where Muḥammad entered a psychotic state. But his intelligence protected him from delving into psychosis or mental illness, and instead made him very creative. Similarly, in the case of Ezekiel, Eric Altschuler also suggested that since schizophrenia causes diminished social functioning, then he also excludes schizophrenia as a possible diagnosis for Ezekiel, and considers temporal lobe epilepsy as a possible alternative. See Altschuler, Eric, "Did Ezekiel Have Temporal Lobe Epilepsy?" *Archives of General Psychiatry* 59, no. 6 (2002): 561–562. However, I consider Ezekiel also to have been a case of low latent inhibition coupled with high intelligence, who might have suffered from a psychotic state of mind without truly delving into psychosis or mental illness.

80 Joseph, "The Limbic System," 129; d'Aquili, Eugene and Newberg, Andrew, "Religious and Mystical States: A Neuropsychological Model," *Zygon* 28, no. 2 (1993): 177–200; de Ropp, R. S., "Psychedelic Drugs and Religious Experience," in *Magic, Witchcraft, and Religion*, eds. A. C. Lehmann and J. E. Myers (Mountain View, CA: Mayfield, 1993); Frazier, J. G. *The Golden Bough* (New York, NY: Macmillan, 1950); James, *The Varieties of Religious Experience*; Lehmann, A. C. and Myers, J. E. eds., *Magic, Witchcraft, and Religion* (Mountain View, CA: Mayfield, 1993); Malinowski, Bronislaw, *Magic, Science and Religion* (New York, NY: Doubleday, 1954); Neihardt, J. G. and Black Elk, *Black Elk Speaks* (Lincoln, NE: University of Nebraska Press, 1979); Smart, N. *The Religious Experience of Mankind* (New York, NY: Macmillan, 1969). For the last statement,

see Joseph, Rhawn, "Traumatic Amnesia, Repression, and Hippocampus Injury Due to Emotional Stress, Corticosteroids and Enkephalins," *Child Psychiatry and Human Development* 29, no. 2 (1998): 169–185; Joseph, Rhawn "Early Environmental Influences on Neural Plasticity, the Limbic System, and Social Emotional Development and Attachment," *Child Psychiatry and Human Development* 29, no. 3 (1999): 189–208; Joseph, Rhawn, "The Neurology of Traumatic 'Dissociative' Amnesia: Commentary and Literature Review," *Child Abuse and Neglect* 23, no. 8 (1999): 715–727; Joseph, Rhawn, *The Transmitter to God: The Limbic System, the Soul, and Spirituality* (San Jose, CA: University Press California, 2000).

81 Consider Michel Cuypers' works on the rhetoric style of the Qur᾽an. See Cuypers, Michel, *The Composition of the Qur᾽an: Rhetorical Analysis* (London: Bloomsbury Academic, 2015).

82 Krippner, Stanley, Richards, Ruth, and Abraham, Frederick D., "Creativity and Chaos While Waking and Dreaming," *Lumina* 21, no. 2 (2010): 7.

83 Muḥammad's mental state may be comparable to that of Abraham, Moses, Ezekiel, Jesus, and Paul who some modern psychiatrists studied and suspect to have had psychotic disorders. See Murray, Evan D., Cunningham, Miles G. and Price, Bruce, "The Role of Psychotic Disorders in Religious History Considered," *The Journal of Neuropsychiatry and Clinical Neurosciences* 24, no. 4 (2012): 410–426; van Nuys, Kelvin, "Evaluating the Pathological in Prophetic Experience (Particularly in Ezekiel)," *Journal of Bible and Religion* 21, no. 4 (1953): 244–251.

84 Barrantes-Vidal, Neus, "Creativity & Madness Revisited from Current Psychological Perspectives," *Journal of Consciousness Studies* 1, no. 3/4 (2004): 58–78.

85 See Eysenck, Hans J., "Creativity as a Product of Intelligence and Personality," in *International Handbook of Personality and Intelligence* eds. Donald H. Saklofske and Moshe Zeidner (Berlin: Springer, 1995), 231–247; Prentky, R. A., "Mental Illness and Roots of Genius," *Creativity Research Journal* 13, no. 1 (2010): 95–104; Fink, Andreas, Slamar-Halbedl, Mirjam, Unterrainer, Human F., and Weiss, Elisabeth M., "Creativity: Genius, Madness, or a Combination of Both?" *Psychology of Aesthetics, Creativity, and the Arts* 6, no. 1 (2012): 11–18.

86 Thalbourne, Michael A. and Delin, Peter S., "A Common Thread Underlying Belief in the Paranormal, Creative Personality, Mystical Experience and Psychopathology," *The Journal of Parapsychology* 58 (1994): 3–38.

87 It is inconclusive to state if Muḥammad had high working memory. He had scribes writing the Qur᾽an. This could mean that he may not necessarily have had high working memory, although it is more likely that he did, since scribes were perhaps used for preservation of the Qur᾽an for the community after Muḥammad's demise.

88 See Benedek, Mathias, Franz, Fabiola, Heene, Moritz, and Neubauer, Aljoscha C., "Differential Effects of Cognitive Inhibition and Intelligence on Creativity," *Personality and Individual Differences* 53, no. 4 (2012): 480–485; Carson, Shelley H., Petersen, Jordan B., and Higgins, Daniel M., "Decreased Latent Inhibition Is Associated with Increased Creative Achievement in High-Functioning Individuals," *Journal of Personality and Social Psychology* 85 (2003): 499–506; Drus, Marina, Kozbelt, Aaron, and Hughes, Robert R., "Creativity, Psychopathology, and Emotion Processing: A Liberal Response Bias for Remembering Negative Information Is Associated with Higher Creativity," *Creativity Research Journal* 26, no. 3 (2014): 251–262.

89 Braff, David L., "Information Processing and Attention Dysfunctions in Schizophrenia," *Schizophrenia Bulletin* 19 (1993): 233–259.

90 For a salutogenic sense of coherence concept on how people may establish a support system both internally and externally, see Antonovsky, Aaron, *Unraveling the Mystery of Health: How People Manage Stress and Stay Well* (San Francisco, CA: Jossey-Bass, 1987).

91 See Benedek et al., "Differential Effects." Also see Carson et al., "Decreased Latent Inhibition." Also see Carson, Shelley H., "Creativity and Psychopathology: A Shared Vulnerability Model," *Canadian Journal of Psychiatry*, 56 (2011): 144–153; Maçkali, Zeynep, Gülöksüz, Sinan, and Oral, Timuçin, "Creativity and Bipolar Disorder," *Turkish Journal of Psychiatry* 25, no. 1 (2014): 50–59.

92 Flaherty, Alice W., "Frontotemporal and Dopaminergic Control of Idea Generation and Creative Drive," *Journal of Comparative Neurology* 493, no. 1 (2005): 147–153.

93 Chiappe, Dan L. and Chiappe, Penny, "The Role of Working Memory in Metaphor Production and Comprehension," *Journal of Memory and Language* 56 (2007): 172–188.

94 Flaherty, "Frontotemporal and Dopaminergic Control."

95 Carson et al., "Decreased Latent Inhibition."

96 As attested in the traditional account from some Qur'anic passages (e.g., Qur'an 15:6, 34:46, 37:36).

97 Schuldberg, David, "Six Subclinical Spectrum Traits in Normal Creativity," *Creativity Research Journal* 13, no. 1 (2000): 5–16.

98 See Nunn, J. and Peters, E., "Schizotypy and Patterns of Lateral Asymmetry on Hemisphere-Specific Language Tasks," *Psychiatry Research* 103 (2001): 179–192; Langdon, R. and Coltheart, M., "Recognition of Metaphor and Irony in Young Adults: The Impact of Schizotypal Personality Traits," *Psychiatry Research* 125 (2004): 9–20.

99 Mitchell, R. L. C. and Crow, T. J., "Right Hemisphere Language Functions and Schizophrenia: The Forgotten Hemisphere?" *Brain: A Journal of Neurology* 128 (2005): 963–978.

100 See Mohr, C., Graves, R. E., Gianotti, L. R. R., Pizzagalli, D., and Brugger, P., "Loose but Normal: A Semantic Association Study," *Journal of Psycholinguistic Research*, 30 (2001): 475–483; Pizzagalli, D., Lehmann, D., and Brugger, P., "Lateralized Direct and Indirect Semantic Priming Effects in Subjects with Paranormal Experiences and Beliefs," *Psychopathology* 34 (2001): 75–80; Kiang, M. and Kutas, M., "Abnormal Typicality of Responses on a Category Fluency Task in Schizotypy," *Psychiatry Research* 145 (2006): 119–126; Grimshaw, G. M., Bryson, F. M., Atchley, R. A., and Humphrey, M., "Semantic Ambiguity Resolution in Positive Schizotypy: A Right Hemisphere Interpretation," *Neuropsychology* 24 (2010): 130–138.

101 Mohr et al., "Loose but Normal."

102 Gianotti, L. R. R., Mohr, C., Pizzagalli, D., Lehmann, D., and Brugger, P., "Associative Processing and Paranormal Belief," *Psychiatry and Clinical Neurosciences* 55 (2001): 595–603.

103 Grimshaw et al., "Semantic Ambiguity Resolution."

104 For an overview of related research, see Hinzen, Wolfram and Rosselló, Joana, "The Linguistics of Schizophrenia: Thought Disturbance as Language Pathology Across Positive Symptoms," *Frontiers in Psychology* 6 (2015): art. 971. http://dro.dur.ac.uk/15916/.

105 Andreasen, N. C. and Glick, I. D., "Creativity and Mental Illness: Prevalence Rates in Writers and Their First-degree Relatives," *American Journal of Psychology* 144 (1987): 1288–1292.

106 Kaufman, James C., "Dissecting the Golden Goose: Components of Studying Creative Writers," *Creativity Research Journal* 14, no. 1 (2002): 27–40.

107 The term "normal" individuals is as found in psychiatric and psychological literature. Personally, I think "normal" is not well defined. Every person is unique, and so it is common and normal to be unique, whichever, whatever, and however such uniqueness may exhibit.

108 See Baruch, Ilan, Hemsley, David R., and Gray, Jeffrey A., "Latent Inhibition and 'Psychotic Proneness' in Normal Subjects," *Personality and Individual Differences*, 9, no. 4 (1988): 777–783; Lubow, R. E., Ingberg-Sachs, Y., Zalstein-Orda, N., and Gewirtz, J. C., "Latent Inhibition in Low and High 'Psychotic-Prone' Normal Subjects," *Personality and Individual Differences* 13, no. 5 (1992): 563–572; Lubow, R. E. and Gewirtz, J. C., "Latent Inhibition in Humans: Data, Theory, and Implications for Schizophrenia," *Psychological Bulletin* 117, no. 1 (1995): 87–103.

109 See Leonhard, Dirk M. A., and Brugger, Peter, "Creative, Paranormal, and Delusional Thought: A Consequence of Right Hemisphere Semantic Activation?" *Neuropsychiatry, Neuropsychology, & Behavioral Neurology* 11, no. 4 (1998): 177–183; Rominger, Christian, Weiss, Elisabeth M., Fink, Andreas, Schulter, Günter, and Papousek, Ilona, "Allusive Thinking (Cognitive Looseness) and the Propensity to Perceive 'Meaningful' Coincidences," *Personality and Individual Differences* 51, no. 8 (2011): 1002–1006; Benedek, Mathias, Könen, Tanja, and Neubauer, Aljoscha C., "Associative Abilities Underlying Creativity," *Psychology of Aesthetics, Creativity, and the Arts* 6, no. 3 (2012): 273–281; Kenett, Yoed, N., Anaki, David, and Faust, Miriam, "Investigating the Structure of Semantic Networks in Low and High Creative Persons," *Frontiers in Human Neuroscience* 8 (2014): art. 407; Radel, Rémi, Davranche, Karen, Fournier, Marion, and Dietrich, Arne, "The Role of (Dis)inhibition in Creativity: Decreased Inhibition Improves Idea Generation," *Cognition* 134 (2015): 110–120.

110 Rominger et al., "Allusive Thinking."

111 Goss, James, "Poetics in Schizophrenic Language: Speech, Gesture and Biosemiotics," *Biosemiotics* 4, no. 3 (2011): 291–307.

112 Chaika, E., *Understanding Psychotic Speech: Beyond Freud and Chomsky* (Springfield, IL: Charles C. Thomas, 1990).

113 Forrest, D. V., "Poiesis and the Language of Schizophrenia," *Psychiatry* 28 (1965): 1–18.

114 Goss, James, "The Poetics of Bipolar Disorder," *Pragmatics & Cognition* 14, no. 1 (2006): 83–110; Goss, "Poetics in Schizophrenic Language."

115 Goss, "Poetics in Schizophrenic Language."

116 Chaika, E., "A Linguist Looks at 'Schizophrenic' Language," *Brain and Language* 1 (1974): 257–276, 270.

117 Goss, "Poetics in Schizophrenic Language," 293.

118 Lorenz, M., "Problems Posed by Schizophrenic Language," *Archives of General Psychiatry* 4 (1961): 603–610, 604.

119 Goss, "Poetics in Schizophrenic Language," 293.

120 Wrobel, J., *Language and Schizophrenia* (Amsterdam: John Benjamins, 1989), 106.

121 Goss, "Poetics in Schizophrenic Language," 293–294.

122 Kischka, U. Kammer, T. H., Maier, S., Weisbrod, M. Thimm, M., and Spitzer, M., "Dopaminergic Modulation of Semantic Network Activation," *Neuropsychologia* 34, no. 11 (1996): 1107–1113.

123 See Isen, A. Johnson, M., Mertz, E., and Robinson, G., "The Influence of Positive Affect on the Unusualness of Word Associations," *Journal of Personality and Social*

Psychology 48, no. 6 (1985): 1413–1426; Docherty, N. M. Hall, M. J., and Gordinier, S. W., "Affective Reactivity of Speech in Schizophrenia Patients and Their Nonschizophrenic Relatives," *Journal of Abnormal Psychology* 107 (1998): 461–467; Goss, "The Poetics of Bipolar Disorder."

124 For a comparison on the linguistic nature between individuals with bipolar disorder and schizophrenia, see Sanfilippo, L. C., and Hoffman, R. E., "Language Disorders in the Psychoses," in *Concise Encyclopedia of Language Pathology*, ed. F. Fabbro (Oxford: Elsevier Science, 1999), 400–407.

125 Goss, "The Poetics of Bipolar Disorder."

126 Hoffman, R. E., "Computer Simulations of Neural Information Processing and the Schizophrenia-Mania Dichotomy," *Archives of General Psychology* 44 (1987): 178–188, 187.

127 Qurʾan 56:77–80.

128 Al-Ṭabarī, *Jāmiʿ* (Q. 56:78), 23: 149–150.

129 Qurʾan 6:25.

130 Ibid., 17:45–46.

131 Ibid., 18:57.

132 Ibid., 41:5.

133 Bergen, Robert D., "Text as a Guide to Authorial Intention: An Introduction to Discourse Criticism," *Journal of the Evangelical Theological Society* 30, no. 3 (1987): 327–336, 335.

134 For an overview of the various schools of Qurʾanic exegesis, see Abdul-Raof, Hussein, *Schools of Qurʾanic Exegesis: Genesis and Development* (Abingdon: Routledge, 2010).

135 See Reynolds, *The Qurʾān and Its Biblical Subtext*, 3–22.

136 Nanji, A., "Ismaʿilism," in *Islamic Spirituality: Foundations*, ed. Seyyed Hossein Nasr (London: Routledge & Keegan Paul, 1987), 179–198.

137 For more information on Ismāʿīlī exegesis, refer to Steigerwald, Diana, "Ismaʿīlī Taʾwīl," in *The Blackwell Companion to the Qurʾan*, ed. Andrew Rippin (Malden, MA: Blackwell Publishing, 2006), 386–400.

138 Al-Ghazālī (d. 505/1111), *Iḥyāʾ ʿulūm al-dīn* (Beirut: Dār al-Maʿrifah), 2004.

139 Druze call themselves unitarians (*muwaḥḥidīn*), not to be confused with Unitarianism.

140 Firro, K. M., "The Druze Faith: Origin, Development and Interpretation," *Arabica*, 58, nos. 1/2 (2011): 76–99.

141 Al-Bukhārī (d. 256/870), *Ṣaḥīḥ al-Bukhārī*, ed. M. Z. N. Al-Nāṣir (Beirut: Dār Ṭawq al-Najāh, 2002), 4: 188 (#3244), 6: 115 (#4779), 6: 116 (#4780), 9: 144 (#7498).

142 Qurʾan 2:256.

143 ʿAlī ibn Ibrāhīm al-Qummī (d. 329/942), *Tafsīr al-qummī* (Beirut: Muʾassassat al-Aʿlamī lil-Maṭbūʿāt, 1991) on Q. 2:256.

144 Al-Ṭabarsī (d. 548/1153), *Majmaʿ al-bayān fī tafsīr, al-Qurʾān* (Beirut: al-Aʿlamī, 1995), on Q. 2:256.

145 See Ebstein, Michael, *Mysticism and Philosophy in al-Andalus: Ibn Masarra, Ibn al-ʿArabī and the Ismāʿīlī Tradition* (Leiden: Brill, 2014); Corbin, Henry, *History of Islamic Philosophy*, trans. Phillip Sherrad (London: Kegan Paul International in association with Islamic Publications, 1993), 97–98.

146 Such as the Apology of al-Kindī. See Muir, William, trans., *The Apology of al-Kindy: Written at the Court of al-Mâmûn (Circa A.H. 215; A.D. 830), in Defence of Christianity Against Islam* (London: Society for Promoting Christian Knowledge, 1887).

147 *Ijtihād* is the endeavor of a Muslim scholar to derive rules, theology, exegesis, etc.

148 In Biblical hermeneutics, there is a concept of double authorship of scriptures: the divine author and the human author. See Virkler, H. A. and Ayayo, K. G., *Hermeneutics: Principles and Processes of Biblical Interpretation* (Grand Rapids, MI: Baker Academic, 2007), 24–25. The divine author inspires and works with the human author in writing scriptures. Hence, even in Biblical hermeneutics, understanding the historical and social contexts of scriptures is usually important, but because of the double authorship of scriptures, it may not necessarily be enough. It is argued that the human author might have had a specific intention in certain scriptural passages, but the divine author might have had a greater intention that the human author might have not been aware of or had been incapable of fully perceiving. This theory in Biblical hermeneutics has become known as *sensus plenior* (fuller sense), which suggests that since the divine author of scriptures is one and the same, the divine author might have had a fuller sense of scriptures that go beyond the historicity and social contexts that the human author was bound by. For more on *sensus plenior* refer to Brown, Raymond E. "*Sensus Plenior* of Sacred Scripture" (Ph.D. dissertation, St. Mary's University, 1955). If we suggest that the divine author of scriptures, both the Bible and the Qur'an, could also be one and the same, then just as using the Bible to interpret itself or the Qur'an to interpret itself, perhaps each can also interpret the other. This does suggest that the divine author is the same.

If the divine author of scriptures, both the Bible and the Qur'an, is the same, then I will explore in my third argument whether intertextuality between the Bible and the Qur'an can hold some ground. The assumption is that if the divine author of the Bible and the Qur'an could be the same, then it would still seem to be the words of God interpreting themselves without contradicting the Qur'anic notion that God teaches the Qur'an. Even if we do not accept the notion of a divine author in either the Bible or the Qur'an, then it is best to understand the Qur'anic discourse in the context of pre-Qur'anic literature, such as the Bible, as a probable source of information. To the very least, it is apparent that the Qur'an is an active reader and fully engaging with the Bible. As such, it may be necessary to understand the Bible to further relate Qur'anic interpretations thereof.

149 Mutahhari, M., "Understanding the Uniqueness of the Qur'an," *al-Tawḥīd* 1 (1987): 9–23.

150 Heath, P., "Creative Hermeneutics: A Comparative Analysis of Three Islamic Approaches," *Arabica* 36, no. 2 (1989): 173–210.

151 See Rippin, Andrew, "The Function of Asbāb al-Nuzūl in Qur'ānic Exegesis," *Bulletin of the School of Oriental and African Studies, University of London* 51, no. 1 (1988): 1–20; Jaffer, A. and Jaffer, M., *Quranic Sciences* (London: ICAS Press, 2009), 67–71.

152 Calder, N., "*Tafsīr* from Ṭabarī to Ibn Kathīr: Problems in the Description of a Genre, Illustrated with Reference to the Story of Abraham," in *Approaches to the Qur'an*, ed. G. R. Hawting and Abdul-Kader A. Shareef (London: Routledge, 1993), 101–140, 105.

153 Abu Zayd, N., "The 'Others' in the Qur'an: A Hermeneutical Approach," *Philosophy Social Criticism* 36, nos. 3/4 (2010): 281–294.

154 For more on the fine line between creativity and madness, see Koh, Caroline, "Reviewing the Link Between Creativity and Madness: A Postmodern Perspective," *Educational Research Reviews* 1, no. 7 (2006): 213–221.

155 Qur'an 41:5.

156 Abrams, Meyer H., *Natural Supernaturalism: Tradition and Revolution in Romantic Literature* (New York, NY: W. W. Norton, 1973), 68.

157 Timmerman, John H., *Do We Still Need the Ten Commandments? A Fresh Look at God's Laws of Love* (Minneapolis, MN: Augsburg Fortress, 1997), 53.
158 See Forrest, Peter, *God Without the Supernatural: A Defense of Scientific Theism* (Ithaca, NY: Cornell University Press, 1996).
159 Abu Zayd, *Mafhūm al-naṣṣ*, 222–223.
160 Reynolds, *The Qur'ān and Its Biblical Subtext.*
161 Fishbane, Michael, *Biblical Interpretation in Ancient Israel* (Oxford: Oxford University Press, 1988).
162 Eslinger, Lyle, "Inner-Biblical Exegesis and Inner-Biblical Allusion: The Question of Category," *Vetus Testamentum* 42, no. 1 (1992): 47–58.
163 Beale, G. K., "Questions of Authorial Intent, Epistemology, and Presuppositions and Their Bearing on the Study of the Old Testament in the New: A Rejoinder to Steve Moyise," *Irish Biblical Studies*, 21 (1999): 152–180.
164 Moyise, Steve, "Authorial Intention and the Book of Revelation," *Andreas University Seminary Studies* 39, no. 1 (2001): 35–40.
165 Plummer, Robert L., "Righteousness and Peace Kiss: The Reconciliation of Authorial Intent and Biblical Typology," *The Southern Baptist Journal of Theology* 14, no. 2 (2010): 54–61.

Chapter 2: Interpretation According to the Qur'an

1 For more information on various schools of Qur'anic exegesis, see Abdul-Raof, *Schools of Qur'anic Exegesis*; Abdul-Raof, Hussein, *Theological Approaches to Qur'anic Exegesis* (Abingdon: Routledge, 2012).
2 From Derrida, J., "Linguistics and Grammatology," trans. G. C. Spivak, *SubStance* 4, no. 10 (1974): 127–181, 130.
3 Aristotle (d. 322 BCE), *De Interpretatione*, trans. E. M. Edghill (Adelaide: University of Adelaide, 2015).
4 Weber, Samuel, "Saussure and the Apparition of Language: The Critical Perspective," *Modern Language Notes* 91, no. 5 (1976): 913–938, 919.
5 Stubbs, M., *Words and Phrases: Corpus Studies of Lexical Semantics* (Oxford: Blackwell, 2001), 10.
6 Al-'Uthaymīn, Muḥammad Ṣ., *al-Uṣūl min 'ilm al-uṣūl* (Cairo: al-Maktabah al-Islāmiyyah, 2001), 97–104.
7 Galadari, Abdulla, "The *Taqlīd al-Ijtihād* Paradox: Challenges to Qur'anic Hermeneutics," *Al-Bayān: Journal of Qur'ānic and Ḥadīth Studies* 13, no. 2 (2015): 145–167.
8 Qur'an 12:2. This verse and the meaning of "*ta'qilūn*" will be critically studied later to show the meaning, "connect." It is an adaptation from Galadari, Abdulla, "The Role of Intertextual Polysemy in Qur'anic Exegesis," *International Journal on Quranic Research* 3, no. 4 (2013): 35–56.
9 Examples include al-Ṭabarī, al-Rāzī (d. 606/1210), Ibn Kathīr (d. 774/1373), and others.
10 See al-Wāḥidī (d. 468/1075), *Asbāb Nuzūl al-Qur'ān*, ed. 'Iṣām al-ḥumaydān (Dammam: Dār al-Iṣlāḥ, 1992).
11 Abu Zahrah (d. 1394/1974), *Zahrat al-tafāsīr* (Cairo: Dār al-Fikr al-'Arabī, n.d.), 8: 4105–4106, 9: 4491, 9: 4877; al-ḥijāzī, M. M., *al-Tafsīr al-wāḍiḥ* (Beirut: Dār al-Jīl al-Jadīd, 1993), 2: 168, 355, 814.

12 Al-Sha'rāwī, M. M. (d. 1419/1998), *al-Khawāṭir: tafsīr al-Sha'rāwī* (Cairo: Maṭābi' Akhbār al-Yawm, 1997) 12: 7688; Al-Khālidī, Ṣalāḥ. A., *al-Qur'ān wa naqḍ maṭā'in al-ruhbān* (Damascus: Dār al-Qalam, 2007), 166; al-Rūmī, F., *Ittijāhāt al-tafsīr fil-qarn al-rābi' 'ashr* (Riyadh: Idārāt al-Buḥūth al-'Ilmiyyah wal-Iftā' wal-Da'wah wal-Irshād, 3, 1986): 971.

13 Wansbrough, *Qur'anic Studies.*

14 See Andrew Rippin's article on John Wansbrough's *Qur'anic Studies: Sources and Methods of Scriptural Interpretation*: Rippin, "The Function of Asbāb."

15 See Ibn Sulaymān, Muqātil (d. 150/767), *Tafsīr Muqātil ibn Sulaymān*, ed. A. M. Shaḥāteh (Beirut: Dār Iḥyā' al-Turāth, 2003).

16 See al-Wāḥidī, *Asbāb Nuzūl.*

17 See al-Suyūṭī (d. 911/1505), *al-Itqān fī 'ulūm al-Qur'an*, ed. M. A. Ibrahīm (Cairo: Al-Hay'ah al-Miṣriyyeh al-'Āmmah lil-Kitāb, 1974).

18 Rippin, Andrew, "The Qur'an as Literature: Perils, Pitfalls and Prospects," *British Society for Middle Eastern Studies Bulletin* 10, no. 1 (1983): 38–47, 44.

19 Abdul-Raof, *Theological Approaches*, 10–27.

20 To argue against a traditional audience, further notes must be stated: Although the Ash'arī and Mu'tazilī theological schools of thought argued whether the Qur'an is created or eternal, they both agree that the Qur'an, in its entirety, existed in heaven in the Preserved Tablet (*al-Lawḥ al-Maḥfūẓ*) before its revelation piecemeal to Muḥammad. Refer to al-Shahrastānī (d. 548/1153), *al-Milal wal-niḥal* (Beirut: Mu'assassat al-ḥalabī, n.d.), 1: 70, 1: 107. Also refer to the footnotes of Al-Shāfi'ī, Yaḥya ibn Abī al-Khayr (d. 558/1163), *al-Intiṣār fil-radd 'ala al-mu'tazilah al-qadariyyah al-ashrār*, ed. S. Al-Khalaf (Riyadh: Aḍwā' al-Salaf, 1999), 1: 160, 2: 544, and 2: 571. Also refer to a citation from Muqātil ibn Sulaymān in Al-Nawawī (d. 676/1277), *Juz' fīh dhikr i'tiqād al-salaf fil-ḥurūf wal-aṣwāt*, ed. A. Al-Dimyāṭī (Cairo: Maktabat al-Anṣār, n.d.), 36. Also refer to Shams al-Dīn Al-Safārīnī al-ḥanbalī (d. 1188/1774), *Lawāmi' al-anwār al-bahiyyah wa-sawāṭi' al-asrār al-athariyyah li-sharḥ al-durrah al-muḍiyyah fī 'aqd al-firqah al-maraḍiyyah* (Damascus: Mu'assassat al-Khāfiqīn wa Maktabat-ha, 1982), 1: 136, 1: 164, 1:167–168, and 2: 288. If that is the case, it brings into question whether the circumstances of revelation (*asbāb al-nuzūl*) are even an integral part of the Qur'an. However, it can always be argued by Muslim theologians that God in Its omniscient knowledge of the future already knew the circumstances of which the Qur'an would be revealed and integrated them as part of the Qur'an. However, it is equally possible that the circumstances of revelation are not an integral part of the Qur'an and therefore not absolutely necessary for its interpretation. From an academic point of view, the reliability of the sources that narrate the circumstances of revelation (*asbāb al-nuzūl*) can always be brought into question, whether or not it should be taken into account.

One of the tenets of Muslim belief regarding the Qur'an is that it is for all times and places (*likulli zamān wa makān*) Al-Saḥīm, M. *al-Islām: Uṣūluhu wa-mabādi'uhu* (Riyadh: Ministry of Islamic Affairs, 2001) 136, even though such a tenet has no Qur'anic basis. If it is for all times, then it cannot be confined within a specific temporal context, and if it is for all places, then it cannot be confined within a specific social context.

21 The Qur'an many times uses the terms "*ta'qilūn*," "*yafqahūn*," "*yatadabbarūn*," etc. as a way to ask people to use reason and contemplate in an attempt to understand the meanings of Godly signs and/or the Qur'an.

22 Al-Bāqillānī (d. 403/1013), *Tamhīd al-awā'il fī takhlīṣ al-dalā'il* (Beirut: Mu'assassat al-Kutub al-Thaqāfiyyah, 1987), 515–516.

23 The infallibility doctrine appears to have developed in the eighth century by both Shīʿī and Sunnī scholars. The Shīʿī doctrine encompasses the infallibility of prophets and imams, while the Sunnī doctrine only attributes the infallibility of prophets. See Muḥammad Zakī-al-Dīn Ibrāhīm, *ʿIṣmat al-anbiyāʾ* (Cairo: Dār al-Naṣr, 1989).

24 The Qurʾan shows various example of sins and mistakes made by prophets, including disobedience to God's commandments, such as the story of Jonah (i.e., Qurʾan 21:87). Other examples include the killing of a man by Moses (i.e., Qurʾan 28:15), Abraham declaring lords besides God (though some exegetes consider this to be part of Abraham teaching his people) (i.e., Qurʾan 6:76–78), Abraham lying about not breaking the idols (though some exegetes consider this also for the purpose of teaching his people) (i.e., Qurʾan 21:62–67), and in a prophetic tradition, Abraham lying about Sarah calling her his sister instead of wife, similar to the story in the Torah (though Shīʿī tradition would consider this as evidence for "*taqiyya*" or lying for the purpose of avoiding harm). Nonetheless, even the Qurʾan shows examples of mistakes made by the prophet, such as ignoring a blind man (i.e., Qurʾan 80:1) or attempting to trick his wives (i.e., Qurʾan 66:1). In my opinion, if the doctrine of infallibility has any legal standing, then perhaps it needs to be redefined—possibly, prophets do err and commit sin, but that they are forgiven. In that sense, they could be considered "infallible," not that they never sin or make mistakes. There were debates among Muslim Sunnī scholars that addressed when the infallibility starts, whether at birth or after the call to prophethood. The debate also consisted on whether the infallibility encompasses all kinds of sin or particular ones, such as major sins (*kabāʾir*), minor sins (*ṣaghāʾir*), inadvertent error (*sahw*), forgetfulness (*nisyān*), and lapses (*zallāt*). The common denominator is usually the infallibility of prophets in their transmission of divine revelation. See Ahmed, Shahab, "Ibn Taymiyyah and the Satanic Verses," *Studia Islamica* 87 (1998): 67–124.

25 See Burton, J., "Notes Towards a Fresh Perspective on the Islamic Sunna," *Bulletin of the British Society for Middle Eastern Studies* 11, no. 1 (1984): 3–17.

26 Robson, James, "Tradition: Investigation and Classification," *The Muslim World* 41, no. 2 (1951): 98–112.

27 Robson, James, "Tradition, the Second Foundation of Islam," *The Muslim World* 41, no. 1 (1951): 22–33.

28 Robson, James, "The Material of Tradition I," *The Muslim World* 41, no. 3 (1951): 166–180.

29 Abdul-Raof, *Theological Approaches*, 28–29.

30 Ceccarelli, Leah, "Polysemy: Multiple Meanings in Rhetorical Criticism," *Quarterly Journal of Speech* 84, no. 4 (1998): 395–415.

31 Refer to Kaye, A. S., "Arabic Morphology," in *Morphologies of Asia and Africa*, ed. A. S. Kaye (Warsaw, IN: Eisenbrauns, 2007), 211–247. Also refer to Prunet, J.-F. "External Evidence and the Semitic Root," *Morphology* 16, no. 1 (2006): 41–67.

32 Kaye, "Arabic Morphology," 239. Also refer to a citation in Al-Khirāṭ, A. M., *ʿInāyat al-muslimīn bil-lughah al-ʿarabiyyah khidmah lil-Qurʾān al-karīm* (Riyadh: Mujammaʿ al-Malik Fahad li-Ṭibāʿat al-Muṣḥaf al-Sharīf, n.d.), 8.

33 On the definition of "*k t b*," refer to Al-Zabīdī (d. 1205/1790), *Tāj al-ʿarūs* (Alexandria: Dār al-Hidāyah, n.d), 4: 100–107.

34 Makram, ʿAbdulʿāl Sālim, *al-Mushtarak al-lafẓī fī al-ḥaql al-Qurʾānī* (Beirut: Muʾassassat al-Risālah, 1997), 44.

35 Al-ʿIzz ibn ʿAbdulsalām (d. 660/1262), *Al-Imām fī bayān adillat al-aḥkām* ed. Riḍwān Mukhtār ibn Gharbiyyah (Beirut: Dār al-Bashāʾir al-Islāmiyyah, 1987), 159.

36 Al-Suyūṭī, *al-Itqān*, 2: 144–165.

37 Ibid., 2: 144. *Faqīh* means a scholar or a jurist. This tradition is also quoted by Ibn ʿAsākir (d. 571/1175).
38 Ibid.
39 Ibid., 2: 145.
40 The *khawārij* is the group who opposed ʿAlī ibn Abī Ṭālib for accepting the mediation with Muʿāwiyah.
41 Ibid.
42 For a survey of classical books on Qurʾanic polysemy, refer to Makram, *al-Mushtarak al-lafẓī*.
43 Ricoeur, P., *Hermeneutics and the Human Sciences*, trans. J. Thompson (Cambridge: Cambridge University Press, 1998), 108.
44 Al-Maʿtūq, Aḥmad M., "Al-Alfāẓ al-Mushtarakah al-Maʿānī fil-Lughah al-ʿArabiyyah: Ṭabīʿatuhā, Ahammiyatuhā, Maṣādiruhā," *Majallah jāmiʿah umm al-qurā li-ʿulūm al-sharīʿah wal-dirāsāt al-islāmiyyah* 7 (21): 81–138.
45 Ceccarelli, "Polysemy."
46 Fraade, S. D., "Rabbinic Polysemy and Pluralism Revisited: Between Praxis and Thematization," *Association for Jewish Studies Review* 3, no. 11 (2007): 1–40.
47 For more on the role of polysemy in the midrash see Stern, D., *Midrash and Theory: Ancient Jewish Exegesis and Contemporary Literary Studies* (Evanston, IL: Northwestern University Press, 1996).
48 Stern, D., "Midrash and Indeterminacy," *Critical Inquiry* 15, no. 1 (1988): 132–161.
49 Ibid., 155–156.
50 Ibid., 161.
51 Ibid., 143–144.
52 Caplan, H., "The Four Senses of Scriptural Interpretation and the Mediaeval Theory of Preaching," *Speculum* 4, no. 3 (1929): 282–290.
53 Bloomfield, M. W., "Symbolism in Medieval Literature," *Modern Philology* 56, no. 2 (1958): 73–81.
54 Coulter, J. A., *The Literary Microcosm: Theories of Interpretation of the Later Neoplatonists* (Leiden: Brill, 1976), 87–89.
55 Ricoeur, P., *The Rule of Metaphor: The Creation of Meaning in Language* (London: Routledge, 2004), 143.
56 Ricoeur, *Hermeneutics and the Human Sciences*, 44.
57 Condit, C. M., Bates, B. R., Galloway, R., Givens, S. B., Haynie, C. K., Jordan, J. W., Stables, G., and West, H. M., "Recipes or Blueprints for Our Genes? How Contexts Selectively Activate the Multiple Meanings of Metaphors," *Quarterly Journal of Speech* 88, no. 3 (2002): 303–325.
58 Ibid.
59 Qurʾan 12:2.
60 Ibid., 43:3.
61 Refer to Al-Zabīdī, *Tāj al-ʿarūs*, on the definition of "*ʿa q l*," 30: 18–40.
62 Refer to Brown, F., Driver, S. R., and Briggs, C., *Enhanced Brown-Driver-Briggs Hebrew and English Lexicon of the Old Testament* (Bellingham, WA: Logos Research Systems, 2000), 786, henceforth *BDB*; Koehler, L. and Baumgartner, W., *The Hebrew and Aramaic Lexicon of the Old Testament* (Leiden: Brill, 2000), 878–879.
63 Qurʾan 12:2.
64 Ibid., 43:3.
65 Abu Zayd, Nasr H., "The Dilemma of the Literary Approach to the Qurʾan," *Alif: Journal of Comparative Poetics* 23 (2003): 8–47.

66 Ibid., 36–37.
67 For an overview of different understandings of God's speech in Islamic history, see Tritton, A. S., "The Speech of God," *Studia Islamica* 36 (1972): 5–22.
68 For more on the Muʿtazilī understanding of the Qurʾan, refer to Peters, J. R. T. M., *God's Created Speech: A Study in the Speculative Theology of the Muʿtazili Qāḍī l-Quḍāt Abu l-Ḥasan ʿAbd al-Jabbār ibn Aḥmad al-Ḥamadānī* (Leiden: Brill, 1976).
69 Abu Zayd, "The Dilemma of the Literary Approach to the Qurʾan."
70 For more on the Muʿtazilah and Ashʿarī view of language, refer to Abu Zayd, Nasr Hamid, *al-Ittijāh al-ʿaqlī fil-tafsīr: Dirāsah fī qaḍiyyat al-majāz fil-Qurʾān ʿind al-muʿtazilah* (Casablanca: Al-Markaz al-Thaqāfī al-ʿArabī, 1996), 70–82.
71 Abu Zayd, "The Dilemma of the Literary Approach to the Qurʾan."
72 Genesis 2:19–20.
73 Allen, William Sidney, "Ancient Ideas on the Origin and Development of Language," *Transactions of the Philological Society* 47, no. 1 (1948): 35–60.
74 Ibid., 45.
75 Ibid., 41.
76 Kieffer, B., "Herder's Treatment of Süssmilch's Theory of the Origin of Language in the *Abhandlung über den Ursprung der Sprache*: A Re-evaluation," *The Germanic Review: Literature, Culture, Theory* 53, no. 3 (1978): 96–105.
77 Allen, W. S., "Ancient Ideas on the Origin and Development of Language," 44.
78 For a survey of literacy in the classical world see Harris, W. V., *Ancient Literacy* (Cambridge, MA: Harvard University Press, 1991). Also refer to Bowman, A. K. and Woolf, G., *Literacy and Power in the Ancient World* (Cambridge: Cambridge University Press, 1994).
79 See Avis, P., *God and the Creative Imagination: Metaphor, Symbol and Myth in Religion and Theology* (Abingdon: Routledge, 1999).
80 For few examples of Joseph Campbell's books on religious symbology, see *Myths to Live By* (New York, NY: Viking Press, 1972); and *The Inner Reaches of Outer Space: Metaphor as Myth: Metaphor as Myth and as Religion* (New York, NY: Harper & Row, 1986). For Mircea Eliade, see *The Sacred and the Profane: The Nature of Religion* (Orlando, FL: Harcourt Books, 1959).
81 Eliade, *The Sacred and the Profane*, 183.
82 Al-Bukhārī, *Ṣaḥīḥ al-Bukhārī*, 2: 149 (#1597).
83 Campbell, J., *Thou Art That: Transforming Religious Metaphor* (Novato, CA: New World Library, 1996), 48.
84 Ibid.
85 See Campbell, *Thou Art That*, and Eliade, *The Sacred and the Profane*.
86 Dupré, L., *Symbols of the Sacred* (Grand Rapid, MI: Wm. B. Eerdmans Company, 2000).
87 Ricoeur, P., *The Rule of Metaphor*, 200.
88 Saussure, F., *Course in General Linguistics*, trans. W. Baskin, eds. P. Meisel and H. Saussy (New York, NY: Columbia University Press, 2011), 16.
89 Ibid., 113.
90 Bergen, "Text as a Guide."
91 Al-Bukhārī, *Ṣaḥīḥ al-Bukhārī*, 6: 182 (#4984).
92 See Ibn Taymiyyah (d. 728/1328), *Al-Īman* ed. M. al-Albānī (Amman: Al-Maktab al-Islāmī, 1996), 74; Al-Suyūṭī (d. 911/1505), *al-Wasāʾil fī musāmarat al-awāʾil* (Baghdad: Maṭbaʿat al-Najāḥ, 1950), 127.
93 Abū ʿUbaydah Muʿammar ibn al-Muthannā (d. 209/824), *Majāz al-Qurʾān* (Cairo: Maktabat al-Khānjī, 1961).

94 For an overview comparison between the approaches of Abū ʿUbaydah and al-Jurjānī (d. 471/1078), see Wansbrough, John E., "Majāz al-Qurʾān: Periphrastic Exegesis," *Bulletin of the School of Oriental and African Studies* 33, no. 2 (1970): 246–266.
95 Almagor, E., "The Early Meaning of Majāz and the Nature of Abū ʿUbayda's Exegesis," in *Studia Orientalia Memoriae D. H. Baneth Dedicata* (Jerusalem: Magnes, 1979). For more overview on Abū ʿUbaydah's usage of the term, also see Madelung, W., "Abū ʿUbayda Maʿmar b. Almuthannā as a Historian," *Journal of Islamic Studies* 3, no. 1 (1992): 47–56.
96 Almagor, "The Early Meaning of Majāz."
97 For further overview of Abū ʿUbaydah's use of "*majāz*" and its relation to the *majāz–ḥaqīqah* dichotomy, see Heinrichs, W., "On the Genesis of the *ḥaqīqa–majāz* Dichotomy," *Studia Islamica* 59 (1984): 111–140.
98 Ibid.
99 Narrator.
100 Abu-Deeb, K., "Studies in the Majāz and Metaphorical Language of the Qurʾān: Abū ʿUbayda and al-Sharīf al-Raḍī," in *Literary Structures of Religious Meaning in the Qurʾān*, ed. I. J. Boullata (Abingdon: Curzon, 2009), 310–353, 316.
101 Ibid., 310–353.
102 Ibn Taymiyyah, *Al-Īman*, 74.
103 Al-Jurjānī, Abdul-Qāhir (d. 471/1078), *Asrār al-balāghah* (Cairo: Maṭbaʿat al-Madanī, n.d.), 386.
104 Cited in Whittingham, Martin, *Al-Ghazālī and the Qurʾān: One Book, Many Meanings* (Abingdon: Routledge, 2007), 34.
105 Ibn Jinnī (d. 392/1002), *al-Khaṣāʾiṣ* (Cairo: al-Hayʾah al-Miṣriyyah al-ʿĀmmah lil-Kitāb, n.d.).
106 Al-Thaʿālbī (d. 429/1038), *Fiqh al-lughah wa sirr al-ʿarabiyyah*, ed. ʿA. al-Mahdī (Beirut: Dār Iḥyāʾ al-Turāth al-ʿArabī, 2002).
107 Al-Zamakhsharī (d. 538/1143), *al-Mufaṣṣal fī ʿilm al-lughah* (Beirut: Dār Iḥyāʾ al-ʿUlūm, 1990).
108 Al-Yāzijī (d. 1324/1906), *Najʿat al-rāʾid wa shirʿat al-wārid fil-mutarādif wal-mutawārid* (Cairo: Maṭbaʿat al-Maʿārif 1905). Al-Yāzijī was a Christian scholar of the Arabic language.
109 Baljon, J. M. S., "Qurʾanic Anthropomorphism," *Islamic Studies* 27, no. 2 (1988): 119–127.
110 This is based on the ḥanbalī stance of "without how" questioning.
111 See Al-Maḥmūd, ʿA., *Mawqif Ibn Taymiyyah min al-ashāʿirah* (Riyadh: Maktabat al-Rushd, 1995), 3: 1170–1176; al-Qāsimī, M. J. (d. 1332/1914), *Maḥāsin al-taʾwīl*, ed. M. B. ʿUyūn al-Sūd (Beirut: Dār al-Kutub al-ʿIlmiyyah, 1998), 5: 80–84.
112 Abu Naṣr al-Sijzī (d. 444/1052), *Risālat al-Sijzī ila Ahl Zubayd fil-radd ʿala man ankar al-ḥarf wal-ṣawt*, ed. M. ba-ʿAbdullah (Medinah: ʿImādat al-Baḥth al-ʿIlmī bil-Jāmʿah al-Islāmiyyah), 178–179.
113 Keddie, N. R., "Symbol and Sincerity in Islam," *Studia Islamica* 19 (1963): 27–63.
114 For more on Avicenna's use of allegory in Qurʾanic interpretation refer to Heath, P., *Allegory and Philosophy in Avicenna (Ibn Sînâ): With a Translation of the Book of the Prophet Muhammad's Ascent to Heaven* (Philadelphia, PA: University of Pennsylvania Press, 1992).
115 Cited in Wohlman, A., *Al-Ghazālī, Averroës and the Interpretation of the Qurʾan: Common Sense and Philosophy in Islam* trans. D. Burrell (Abingdon: Routledge, 2010), 42.

116 Keddie, "Symbol and Sincerity in Islam," 45.
117 Burckhardt, T., *Introduction to Sufi Doctrine* (Bloomington, IN: World Wisdom, 2008), 3; Arberry, A. J., *Revelation and Reason in Islam* (Abingdon: Routledge, 2008), 16; Amir-Moezzi, M. A., *The Divine Guide in Early Shiʿism: The Sources of Esotericism in Islam*, trans. D. Streight (Albany, NY: State University of New York Press, 1994).
118 Averroës (d. 595/1198), *The Decisive Treatise*, trans. C. E. Butterworth (Provo, UT: Brigham Young University Press, 2001), 10, 11.
119 The other imams of the Sunni tradition, Abū ḥanīfah (d. 150/767), Mālik ibn Anas (d. 179/795), and al-Shāfiʿī (d. 204/820) did not discuss the literal and allegorical senses of the Qurʾan. Ibn Taymiyyah, *Al-Īman*, 74–75.
120 Qurʾan 26:15.
121 Ibn ḥanbal (d. 241/855), *al-Radd ʿala al-jahmiyyah wal-zanādiqah*, ed. Ṣ. Shahīn (Riyadh: al-Thabāt, 2002), 92.
122 Ibid. The Jahmiyya is named after Jahm ibn Ṣafwān (d. 128746) who considered the Qurʾan created. Anti-Muʿtazilah polemics sometimes called the Muʿtazilah "Jahmiyya," since Jahm ibn Ṣafwān was the first known theologian who argues that the Qurʾan is created.
123 Ibid., 74.
124 If it is a message from God to Muḥammad, then it assumes that Muḥammad knew their meanings, but for some reason kept them secret from the general public. Otherwise, if Muḥammad indeed passively received his revelation, then there is also a possibility that Muḥammad might have not even understood the full meaning, which again brings into question the meaning of language and the role of the audience in making such meanings.
125 If this is the case, then one cannot consider the Qurʾanic audience to be for all times and places, which has no Qurʾanic basis anyway. However, there is also a possibility that it is God's message to humanity, but even Muḥammad was unaware of the meanings of the disjoined letters, making the language of the Qurʾan not necessarily hold any specific meaning to the community it was presented to. Instead, the meaning is univocal and set independent of the community receiving it. Hence, there is always a possibility of *sensus plenior* in Qurʾanic text, in which the human author is not always aware of the message intended by the divine author.
126 Asad, M., "Symbolism and Allegory in the Qurʾan," in *The Message of the Qurʾan* (appendix), Gibraltar: Dār al-Andalus, dist. (London: E. J. Brill, 1980).
127 There have been theories that the disjoined letters may be related to the Hebrew/Aramaic alphabets, which have meaning on its own. Other theories are that since Arabic letters have numerical values, that it is possibly part of some numerical code, as promulgated by Rashad Khalifa. For more on the traditional Muslim stance of the disjoined letters, see Kenawy, Salah, "A Linguistic Reading in the Disjointed Letters," *Islamic Quarterly* 42, no. 4 (1998): 243–255.
128 Al-Saqqāf, ʿAlawī ʿA., *Mawsūʿah al-firaq al-muntasabah lil-islām* (dorar.net, n.d.), 2: 405.
129 Ḥaqqī, Ismāʿīl (d. 1127/1715), *Rūḥ al-bayān fī tafsīr al-Qurʾān* (Beirut: Dār al-Fikr, 1994), 6: 238.
130 Abu al-ʿAbbās (d. 1224/1809), *al-Baḥr al-madīd fī tafsīr al-Qurʾān al-majīd*, ed. A. Raslān (Cairo: Dr. Ḥassan ʿAbbās Zakī, 1999), 2: 195.
131 This brings us to the crossroads of the Muʿtazilī and Ashʿarī schools of theology. If we take the Muʿtazilī perspective that the Qurʾan is created, because language is a human

invention, but that the Qur'an contains allegorical meanings on the anthropomorphic descriptions of God, then we can conclude there is symbology in the Qur'an that may only be interpreted allegorically. If we take the Ash'ari perspective that the Qur'an is uncreated, then it would mean that the language of the Qur'an was done independently of the receiving community, and therefore, we can still conclude that the language of the Qur'an may be understood beyond the social and historical context of Quraysh. Either perspective leads us to the conclusion that the social and historical contexts of the Qur'an may not be the only method or even the correct method in Qur'anic interpretation.

132 Mohammed, K., "Assessing English Translations of the Qur'an," *Middle East Quarterly* 12, no. 2 (2005): 58–71.

133 Al-Tha'labī (d. 427/1035), *al-Ashbāh wal-naẓā'ir*, ed. Muḥammad al-Maṣrī (Damascus: Sa'd al-Dīn Press, 1984).

134 Ibn al-'Imād, *Kashf al-sarā'ir fī ma'na al-wujūh wal-ashbāh wal-naẓā'ir*, ed. Fu'ād Abdulmon'im (Alexandria: al-Maktabah al-Miṣriyyeh, 2004).

135 Al-Suyūṭī, *al-Itqān*, 2: 144–145.

136 Shameli, N. A., "Mulla Sadr and Interpreting the Quranic Keywords in a Polysemous Method," *Tahqiqat-e Ulum-e Quran wa Hadith* 3, no. 1 (2007): 5–32.

137 Using http://www.altafsir.org/ as a comprehensive reference of the most prominent books of *tafsīr* of various Islamic schools, including Sunni, Shī'a, Ibadi, Sufi, etc.

138 Wafi, 'Alī 'Abdulwāḥid, *'Ilm al-lughah* (Cairo: Nahḍat Miṣr lil-Ṭibā'ah wal-Nashr, n.d.), 314–315. For examples of evolution of polysemous meanings, see Makram, *al-Mushtarak al-lafẓī*, 9–11.

139 Allen, W. S., "Ancient Ideas," 35–36.

140 Ibid.

141 Ibid.

142 Ibid., 41.

143 However, Plato did suggest that some names were given by a superhuman power. Allen, W. S. "Ancient Ideas," 38. If we adopt a Platonic definition of language, then this may suggest that even if the Qur'an may mostly contain conventional form of language, some words, such as the disjoined letters, could have a divine origin.

144 Allen, W. S., "Ancient Ideas," 53.

145 Ibid., 54.

146 O'Leary, De Lacey, *Comparative Grammar of the Semitic Languages* (Abingdon: Routledge, 2000), 175–176.

147 Allen, W. S., "Ancient Ideas," 56.

148 Amsler, M., *Etymology and Grammatical Discourse in Late Antiquity and the Early Middle Ages* (Amsterdam: John Benjamins, 1989), 31.

149 Al-Suyūṭī (d. 911/1505), *al-Mizhir fī 'ulūm al-lughah wa anwā'ihā*, ed. Fu'ād 'Alī Manṣūr (Beirut: Dār al-Kutub al-'Ilmiyyah, 1998), 1: 303–304.

150 Ibid.

151 Makram, *al-Mushtarak al-lafẓī*, 15–16.

152 Cited in al-Ṣāliḥ, Ṣ. I. (d. 1407/1987), *Dirāsāt fī fiqh al-lughah* (Beirut: Dār al-'Ilm lil-Malāyīn, 1960), 303–304.

153 Al-Suyūṭī, *al-Mizhir*, 292–304.

154 Ibid., 293.

155 Ibid.

156 Barr, James, *The Semantics of Biblical Language* (London: Oxford University Press, 1961).

157 Zaborski, Andrzej, "Etymology, Etymological Fallacy and the Pitfalls of Literal Translation of Some Arabic and Islamic Terms," in *Words, Texts and Concepts Cruising the Mediterranean Sea: Studies on the Sources, Contents and Influences of Islamic Civilization and Arabic Philosophy and Science*, eds. R. Arnzen and J. Thielmann (Leuven: Peeters, 2004), 143–148.
158 Saleh, Walid A., "The Etymological Fallacy and Qurʾanic Studies: Muhammad, Paradise, and Late Antiquity," in *The Qurʾān in Context: Historical and Literary Investigations into the Qurʾānic Milieu*, eds. A. Neuwirth, N. Sinai, and M. Marx (Leiden: Brill, 2010), 649–698.
159 Ibid., 659–660.
160 Rippin, Andrew, "RḤMNN and the ḤANĪFS," in *Islamic Studies Presented to Charles J. Adams*, eds. W. B. Hallaq and P. D. Little (Leiden: Brill, 1991), 153–168.
161 Beeston, A. F. L., "Himyarite Monotheism," in *Studies in the History of Arabia II: Pre-Islamic Arabia*, executive eds. Abdelgadir M. Abdalla, Sami Al-Sakkar, and Richard Mortel (Riyadh: King Saud University, 1984), 149–154.
162 Refer to Al-Zabīdī, *Tāj al-ʿarūs*, on the definition of "*ḥ n f*," 23: 168–173.
163 On the meaning of "*ḥ n f*," refer to Ibn Manẓūr (d. 711/1311), *Lisān al-ʿarab* (Beirut: Ṣāḍir, 1994), 9: 56–58.
164 Muslim (d. 261/875), *Ṣaḥīḥ Muslim*, ed. M. F. Abdul-Bāqī (Beirut: Iḥyāʾ al-Turāth al-ʿArabī, n.d.), 1: 130–131 (1.65, #232).
165 Zaborski, "Etymology, Etymological Fallacy."
166 Saleh, "The Etymological Fallacy and Qurʾanic Studies."
167 Barr, *The Semantics of Biblical Language*, 35.
168 Ibid., 39–43.
169 Ibid., 100–106.
170 Ibid., 102.
171 The Syriac term "*loḥem*" means to unite. Refer to *BDB*, 535–536; Koehler and Baumgartner, *The Hebrew and Aramaic Lexicon of the Old Testament*, 526. The Hebrew term "*milḥama*" is also used to mean "joined," as that the battle was joined in 1 Kings 20:29. On the root meaning of "*l ḥ m*" as join, refer to the Comprehensive Aramaic Lexicon Project of the Jewish Institute of Religion at the Hebrew Union College (http://cal1.cn.huc.edu/); on "*l ḥ m*," see Botterweck, G. J. and Ringgren, H., eds., J. T. Willis trans., *Theological Dictionary of the Old Testament*, revised edn (Grand Rapids, MI: William B. Eerdmans, 1977), 7: 521 (henceforth *TDOT*).
172 Refer to Al-Zabīdī, *Tāj al-ʿarūs* on the definition of "*l ḥ m*," 33: 403–411.
173 Ibid.
174 It is also suggested that "*l ḥ m*" means the core of something and when referring to plants "*alḥim*" means it has wheat (see Ibn Manẓūr, *Lisān al-ʿarab*, 12: 535 on "*l ḥ m*"). If that is the case, the bread would take its meaning from that.
175 I do not want to delve into all the examples provided by Barr, but I need to respond to some to show that his argument and those he is refuting are all dependent on interpretation. He cannot assert that such methods are often misused, although I must admit that they sometimes are. In one example, he shows that the term for "man" in the Hebrew Bible is sometimes used as "*geber*," which is rooted in strength, but that it does not always denote man as strong (Barr, *The Semantics of Biblical Language*, 144–147). He brings forth few examples from scriptures showing that the term is being used to show the weakness of "man" and not his strength (e.g., Psalms 88:4–5, 89:48–49). He assumes that these examples prove that we cannot understand the etymological root meaning to have any significance to the word's semantics.

However, that is not necessarily the case. For example, Psalm 88:4 states, "I am as a man (*geber*) who has no strength (*ayil*)." It is possible that the rhetoric style of this statement is an intentional oxymoron, using the term "*geber*" to starkly contrast "strength" with "no strength." Psalm 89:48 asks, "What man (*geber*) shall live and not see death?" Again, in here it could easily be interpreted that every mighty one (*geber*) will still see death. This would be an example of the rich rhetorical style of scriptures. Hence, Barr's claim that these methods are dangerous and absurd is not always valid. It is dependent on the interpretation. Barr is aware that using such methods would open doors to interpretations, in which the exegete would be subjective in his interpretation making anything at all to mean anything. However, this statement can be said to any sort of interpretation and not only due to etymology. It does not, however, suffice as evidence that an etymological approach would necessarily lead us astray. Perhaps the etymological approach would simply provide us with a different perspective.

176 Barr, *The Semantics of Biblical Language*, 107–160.

177 Qur'an 41:2–5.

178 A theologian might argue that if scriptures are believed to have a divine author, then could we also fairly assume that a divine author is not aware of or cares less about the etymological meanings of words?

179 Fishbane, *Biblical Interpretation*.

180 If scriptures, both the Bible and the Qur'an, are assumed to be divine and infallible in their nature, then one must assume that the divine author is fully aware of the meanings of the words, their polysemous nature, its morphological permutations, and its root-based etymology. Barr actually states that; "Words can only be intelligibly interpreted by what they meant at the time of their use, within the language system used by the speaker or writer" (*The Semantics of Biblical Language*, 139–140). He uses this statement as a way to refute certain linguistic methods of Biblical theology. However, he seems to have been unaware that such a statement creates a self-defeating theological loop that Biblical theologians would find sufficient to use his own words against him. If the speaker or author of scriptures is believed to be God, then what is the "time" or "place" in which the Biblical language would need to be understood as? Is God confined to a specific time frame in history or a specific social context, on which Its words would depend for their definition? If the author of scriptures is believed to be beyond time and space, then why would we need to assume that Its words can only be understood to be a meaning restricted to a specific time and space? If scriptures are the Word of God, which can therefore be inferred as the Logos, in which Jesus Christ has become the embodiment and the Incarnation of scriptures, then according to the Gospel of John, the Word of God is eternal and is God Itself. According to the Ash'ari school of thought, the Qur'an is also eternal. See al-Maḥmūd, *Mawqif Ibn Taymiyyah*, 448. Henceforth, if it is in God's attributes to be beyond space and time, then so would be Its words in scriptures. It would have to be assumed that the divine author has selectively used certain terms for specific reasons, and these reasons could also be beyond time and place, and not completely arbitrary. This does bring into question whether language itself is an arbitrary symbol or sign as Saussure understood it.

181 Isma'īl, M. B., *Dirāsāt fī 'ulūm al-Qur'ān* (Cairo: Dār al-Manār, 1999), 238–241.

182 Ibn Manẓūr, *Lisān al-'arab*, 1: 586–588, on "*'arb*."

183 *BDB*, 787; Koehler and Baumgartner, *The Hebrew and Aramaic Lexicon of the Old Testament*, 878, on "*'arb*."

184 Ibn Manẓūr, *Lisān al-ʿarab*, 1: 588, on "ʿ*arb*."

185 ʿUthmān is quoted to say to Qurʾanic copyists, "If you disagree you and Zayb ibn Thābit in anything in the Qurʾan, write it in the language of Quraysh, as it was revealed in their language." See al-Bukhārī, *Ṣaḥīḥ al-Bukhārī*, 4: 180 (#3506), 6: 183 (#4987). In another narration of the same saying of ʿUthmān, it is reported that he told the copyists, "If you disagree you and Zayd ibn Thābit in an Arabic of the Arabic Qurʾan, write it in the language of Quraysh, as the Qurʾan was revealed in their language." See al-Bukhārī, *Ṣaḥīḥ al-Bukhārī*, 6: 182 (#4984).

186 Further reading on Crone's argument that Islam did not rise in Makkah, see Crone, Patricia, *Meccan Trade and the Rise of Islam* (Princeton, NJ: Princeton University Press, 1987).

187 That prophetic saying states, "Gabriel recited on a *ḥarf* so I returned to him and I continued to add him and he adds me until he ended to seven *aḥruf*." In al-Bukhārī, *Ṣaḥīḥ al-Bukhārī*, 6: 184 (#4991). I hesitate to translate the term "*ḥarf*" in this prophetic tradition, as it may have various meanings. Another tradition also states that various companions have heard the Qurʾan from Muḥammad in different ways and that all were acceptable to Muḥammad adding, "This is how it was revealed. This Qurʾan was revealed on seven *aḥruf*, so read what is simple from it." See al-Bukhārī, *Ṣaḥīḥ al-Bukhārī*, 6: 184 (#4992).

188 Jepsen, A., "ʾ*arb*," in Botterweck and Ringgren, *Theological Dictionary of the Old Testament*, 11: 331.

189 Ibn Manẓūr, *Lisān al-ʿarab*, 1: 592 on "ʿ*arb*."

190 Ibid.

191 *BDB*, 786; Koehler and Baumgartner, *The Hebrew and Aramaic Lexicon of the Old Testament*, 876–877 on "ʿ*arb*."

192 *TDOT*, "ʿ*arb*," 11: 327.

193 Ibid., "ʿ*arb*," 11: 331–334.

194 Koehler and Baumgartner, *The Hebrew and Aramaic Lexicon of the Old Testament*, 878–879, on "ʿ*arb*."

195 Compare with Q. 16:103 and 41:44. See Ibn Manẓūr, *Lisān al-ʿarab*, 12: 385–386.

196 *BDB*, 785.

197 Ibn Manẓūr, *Lisān al-ʿarab*, 12: 386–387 on "ʿ*a j m*."

198 Ibid., 12: 386 on "ʿ*a j m*."

199 *BDB*, 786; Koehler and Baumgartner, *The Hebrew and Aramaic Lexicon of the Old Testament*, 878–879 on "ʿ*arb*." Also see *TDOT*, "ʿ*arb*," 11: 331.

200 *TDOT*, "ʿ*arb*," 11: 333.

201 Al-Azharī, Abu Manṣūr (d. 370/981), *Tahdhīb al-lughah*, ed. M. ʿU. Marʿib (Beirut: Dār Iḥyāʾ al-Turāth al-ʿArabī, 2001), 2: 221.

202 Rofé, A., *The Book of Balaam: A Study in Method of Criticism and the History of Biblical Literature and Religion* (Warsaw, IN: Eisenbrauns, 1979).

203 Crone and Cook, *Hagarism*.

204 Beyer, K., *The Aramaic Language: Its Distribution and Subdivisions*, trans. J. F. Healey (Göttingen: Vandenhoeck & Ruprecht, 1986), 27.

205 Healey, J. F., "Lexical Loans in Early Syriac: A Comparison with Nabataean Aramaic," *Studi Epigrafici Linguistici* 12 (1995): 75–84.

206 Ibid., 76.

207 Ibid., 78.

208 O'Connor, M., "The Arabic Loanwords in Nabatean Aramaic," *Journal of Near Eastern Studies* 45, no. 3 (1986): 213–229.

209 On Thamudic being a dialect of Arabic, see Milik, J. T., "Inscriptions grecques et nabatéennes de Rawwafah," *Bulletin of the Institute of Archaeology* 10 (1971): 54–59.
210 Graf, D. F. and Zwettler, M. J., "The North Arabian 'Thamudic E' Inscription from Uraynibah West," *Bulletin of the American Schools of Oriental Research* 335 (2004): 53–89.
211 For more on the Arabic influence onto the Nabataean Aramaic, especially in the area of Madāʾin Ṣāliḥ, see Healey, J. F., ed., *The Nabataean Tomb Inscriptions of Madaʾin Salih, Journal of Semitic Studies, Supplement 1* trans. S. Al-Theeb (Arabic section) (Oxford: Oxford University Press, 1994).
212 Healey, "Lexical Loans in Early Syriac," 79.
213 Watson, J., "South Arabian and Yemeni Dialects," *Salford Working Papers in Linguistics and Applied Linguistics* 1 (2011): 27–40.
214 Potts, Daniel P., "Trans-Arabian Routes of the Pre-Islamic Period," *Travaux de la Maison de l'Orient* 16, no. 1 (1988): 127–162.
215 For more on the topic, see Versteegh, C. H. M., *Arabic Grammar and Qurʾānic Exegesis in Early Islam* (Leiden: Brill, 1993).
216 Cited in Kopf, L., "Religious Influences on Medieval Arabic Philology," *Studia Islamica* 5 (1956): 33–59, 40–41.
217 Ibid., 47.
218 This might also be a possible reason why according to tradition, Muḥammad might have allowed various recitations of the Qurʾan.
219 Allen, Roger, *Arabic Literary Heritage: The Development of Its Genres and Criticism* (Cambridge: Cambridge University Press, 1998).
220 Al-Shaʿrāwī, *Tafsīr*, 15: 9166.
221 Luxenberg, Christoph, *Die syro-aramäische Lesart des Koran: Ein Beitrag zur Entschlusselung der Koransprache* (Berlin: Verlag Hans Schiller, 2000).
222 Lüling, Günter, *Über den Ur-Qurʾan: Ansätze zur Rekonstruktion vorislamischer christlicher Strophenlieder im Qurʾan* (Erlangen: Verlagsbuchhdlg, 1974).
223 Wansbrough, *Qurʾanic Studies*; Wansbrough, *The Sectarian Milieu.*
224 Galadari, "The *Qibla*."
225 Reynolds, *The Qurʾān and Its Biblical Subtext.*
226 Hawting, Gerald, "Review of Lüling," *Journal of Semitic Studies* 27 (1982): 111.
227 Fishbane, *Biblical Interpretation.*
228 Galadari, "The *Qibla*."

Chapter 3: Examples of Intertextual Polysemy from Qurʾanic and Arabic Perspectives

1 Al-Ṭabarī, *Jāmiʿ*, 24: 519–522 on Q. 96:1.
2 I translate "*khalaq*" as divided, based on my discussion in Galadari, Abdulla, "*Creatio ex Nihilo* and the Literal Qurʾan," *Intellectual Discourse* 25 (2017): 381–408.
3 I translate "*ʿalaq*" as clinging, instead of "blood clot" used by *TSQ*, as it appears to be perhaps more loyal to the original Arabic root meaning.
4 Unlike the *TSQ*, which translates "*al-insān*" as "man," I translate it as "the human."
5 Qurʾan 96:1–5.
6 The root of the term "*khlq*" means division, and it is mainly used in that definition by the Hebrew Bible.

7 For example, al-Ṭabarī, *Jāmiʿ*, 24: 519–522 on Q. 96:2; al-Ṭabāṭabāʾī (d. 1402/1981) *al-Mīzān fī tafsīr al-Qurʾān* (Beirut: Muʾassassat al-Aʿlami lil-Maṭbūʿāt, 1997), 20: 181 on Q. 96:2.
8 The method of intertextual polysemy is described in Galadari, "The Role of Intertextual Polysemy."
9 Qurʾan 55:1–4. There is a likelihood that "*bayān*" is not specifically speech, but clarity, which is the root meaning of the term.
10 It is also noteworthy to state that in Qurʾan 1:1, and traditionally, the recitation of the Qurʾan starts with the name of God, the Most Compassionate (*al-Raḥmān*), the Most Merciful (*al-Raḥīm*).
11 Fishbane, *Biblical Interpretation*.
12 The prophetic tradition (*ḥadīth*) states, "Everything has a bride, and the bride of the Qurʾan is al-Raḥmān." This tradition is narrated by ʿAlī ibn Abī Ṭālib as found in al-Bayhaqī (d. 458/1066), *Shuʿab al-īmān* (Riyadh: Maktabat al-Rushd, 2003) 4: 116 (#2265). Exegetes such as al-Biqāʿī (885/1480) narrates it in his interpretation of the surah. See al-Biqāʿī (d. 855/1480) *Niẓam al-durar fī tanāsub al-āyat wal-suwar* (Cairo: Dār al-Kitāb al-Islāmī), 19: 139.
13 Muslim, *Ṣaḥīḥ Muslim*, 4: 2169 (#2816), with a variant in 4: 2170 (#2816).
14 Ibn Manẓūr, *Lisān al-ʿarab* on "*srr*."
15 Ibid., on "*bṭn*."
16 John 3:3–12.
17 Al-Ṭabarī, *Jāmiʿ*, on Q. 18:65.
18 Ibn Manẓūr, *Lisān al-ʿarab*, 10: 227–231.
19 Ibid., 10: 225–226.
20 Al-Ṭabarī, *Jāmiʿ*, 4:538–600 on Q. 2:229–230.
21 This section is based on an example found in Galadari, "*Creatio ex Nihilo*."
22 Qurʾan 19:2.

Chapter 4: The Relationship Between the Qurʾan and the Bible

1 The Qurʾan usually talks of the Gospel in singular form, "*al-injīl*." As such, I am trying to show that the Qurʾan is speaking of the Gospels most probably, but is calling the collection in its singular form as Gospel. Perhaps there needs to be more study as to what Arab Christians used to call the Gospels in the time of Muḥammad. There might be a possibility they called them "*injīl*" as the collective works of the Gospels. This is perhaps coming from the Syriac Tatian's *Diatessaron*.
2 The concept of abrogation is a heated topic of debate between Muslim scholars. Many classical Muslim scholars, such as Abu ʿUbayd (d. 224/839), Abu Jaʿfar al-Naḥḥās (d. 377/949), Ḥibbat Allāh ibn Salamah (d. 410/1019), Makkī ibn Abu Ṭālib (d. 437/1045), Abu Bakr Ibn al-ʿArabī (d. 543/1148) (not to be confused with the Sufi mystic Muḥammad ibn ʿArabī), Ibn al-Jawzī (d. 597/1201), al-Zarkashī, and al-Suyūṭī have argued that some Qurʾanic verses have been abrogated. For a brief overview on the concept of abrogation from the point of view of classical Muslim scholars see Ushama, Thameem, "The Phenomenon of al-Naskh: A Brief Overview of the Key Issues," *Jurnal Fiqh* 3 (2006): 101–132.
3 Ali, Moch. "Rethinking the Semitic Texts: A Study of Intertextuality," *Studia Philosophica et Theologica* 8, no. 1 (2008): 72–89.

4 Reynolds, *The Qur'ān and Its Biblical Subtext.*
5 Firestone, Reuven, "The Qur'ān and the Bible: Some Modern Studies of Their Relationship," in *Bible and Qur'an: Essays in Scriptural Intertextuality*, ed. J. C. Reeves (Leiden: Brill, 2003), 2–3.
6 Wansbrough, *Qur'anic Studies.*
7 Wansbrough, *The Sectarian Milieu.*
8 Ibid. and also Reynolds, *The Qur'ān and Its Biblical Subtext.*
9 Qur'an 4:157.
10 As an example, consider the narrations mostly based on Wahb ibn Munabbih in al-Ṭabarī's *tafsīr* that perhaps one or more of Jesus' disciples was made in the likeness of Jesus. See Al-Ṭabarī, *Jāmi'*, 9: 367–377 on Q. 4:157.
11 Medieval Christianity has viewed Islam with hostility, possibly due to Muslim political and military threats against Christian territories. Islam had threatened Europe in both the west, in Spain and France, as well in the east, by the Ottomans. As such, many polemical works against Islam in medieval times have portrayed Muḥammad as a charlatan and an imposter, whose aim was to deceive the people. Medieval Judaism, on the other hand, did not feel especially threatened, since they did not have political autonomy anyway under Christian rule. The Jewish predisposition toward Islam might have influenced Abraham Geiger (d. 1874). Geiger did not view Muḥammad as an imposter like many of his predecessors and contemporaries, but viewed him as a sincere and a devout religious enthusiast, whose aims are characteristically noble. Geiger, Abraham, *Was hat Mohammed aus dem Judenthume aufgenommen?* (Bonn: F. Baaden, 1833).
12 Pregill, M., "The Hebrew Bible and the Quran: The Problem of the Jewish 'Influence' on Islam," *Religion Compass* 1, no. 6 (2007): 643–659.
13 Sasson, J. M., "Circumcision in the Ancient Near East," *Journal of Biblical Literature* 85, no. 4 (1966): 473–476.
14 Hecker, H. M., "A Zooarchaeological Inquiry into Pork Consumption in Egypt from Prehistoric to New Kingdom Times," *Journal of the American Research Center in Egypt* 19 (1982): 59–71; Lobban, R. A., "Pigs and Their Prohibition," *International Journal of Middle East Studies* 26, no. 1 (1994): 57–75.
15 Wasserstrom, Steven M., *Between Muslim and Jew: The Problem of Symbiosis Under Early Islam* (Princeton, NJ: Princeton University Press, 2014).
16 Ibid., 103.
17 Ibn Sa'd (d. 230/845), *al-Ṭabaqāt al-kubra* (Beirut: Dār al-Kutub al-'Ilmiyyah, 1990), 2: 273–274; al-Bukhārī, *Ṣaḥīḥ al-Bukhārī*, 6: 182 (#4984).
18 I am indebted to Ulrika Mårtensson who pointed this out to me.
19 Torrey, Charles C. *The Jewish Foundation of Islam* (New York, NY: Jewish Institute of Religion Press, 1933).
20 Jeffery, Arthur, *The Foreign Vocabulary of the Qur'ān* (Baroda: Oriental Institute, 1938).
21 Pennacchio, Catherine "Lexical Borrowing in the Qur'an: The Problematic Aspects of Arthur Jeffery's List," *Bulletin du Centre de recherché français à Jérusalem* 22 (2011), https://bcrfj.revues.org/6643.
22 Newby, Gordon "Observations About an Early Judaeo-Arabic," *The Jewish Quarterly Review* 61, no. 3 (1971): 212–221.
23 Bell, Richard, *The Origin of Islam in Its Christian Environment* (London: Frank Cass, 1968).
24 Pregill, M., "The Hebrew Bible and the Quran," 648.

25 See, for example, King, Leonard W., *Legends of Babylon and Egypt in Relation to Hebrew Tradition* (Oxford: Oxford University Press, 1916); Melvin, David, "The Gilgamesh Traditions and the Pre-history of Genesis 6:1–4," *Perspectives in Religious Studies* 8, no. 1 (2011): 23–32.
26 Barr, James, "The Question of Religious Influence: The Case of Zoroastrianism, Judaism, and Christianity," *Journal of the American Academy of Religion* 53, no. 2 (1985): 201–235.
27 Halliday, W. R., *The Pagan Background of Early Christianity* (Whitefish, MT: Kessinger, 2010).
28 Refer to *Tafsīr Muqātil ibn Sulaymān*.
29 Refer to Al-Thaʿlabī (d. 427/1035), *al-Kashf wal-bayān ʿan tafsīr al-Qurʾān*, eds. Abī Muḥammad ibn ʿĀshūr and Naẓīr al-Sāʿidī (Beirut: Dār Iḥyāʾ al-Turāth al-ʿArabī, 2002).
30 Albayrak, I., "Isrāʾīliyyāt and Classical Exegetes' Comments on the Calf with a Hollow Sound Q.20: 83–98 / 7: 147–155 with Special Reference to Ibn ʿAṭiyya," *Journal of Semitic Studies* 47, no. 1 (2002): 39–65. Also refer to Al-Madinah International University, *al-Dakhīl fil-tafsīr* (n.d.), 23. For an historical summary of the notion of "*isrāʾīliyyāt*" refer to Albayrak, I., "Re-Evaluating the Notion of Israʾiliyyat," *D. E. Ü. Ilahiyyat Fakültesi Dergisi* 14 (2001): 69–88.
31 Not only are there critics of "*isrāʾīliyyāt*" among Sunnī, but also among Shīʿī scholars. Refer to al-Muḥammadī, F. A., *Salāmat al-Qurʾān min al-taḥrīf* (Markaz al-Abḥāth al-ʿAqāʾidiyyah, n.d.), 449–451.
32 For more on Biblical scholarship in early Islam, refer to Adang, Camilla, *Muslim Writers on Judaism and the Hebrew Bible from Ibn Rabban to Ibn Hazm* (Leiden: Brill, 1996).
33 For more information on the Israelite tradition (*isrāʾīliyyāt*) see Muḥammad Ḥussain al-Dhahabī, *al-Isrāʾīliyyāt fil-tafsīr wal-ḥadīth* (Cairo: Maktabat Wahbah, 1990).
34 Albayrak, "Isrāʾīliyyāt and Classical Exegetes' Comments."
35 See Abu Shuhbah, Muḥammad, *al-Isrāʾīliyyāt wal-mawḍūʿāt fī kutub al-tafsīr* (Cairo: Maktabat al-Sunnah, 1983), 95; al-Rūmī, *Ittijāhāt*, 2: 757–758.
36 Al-Rūmī, *Ittijāhāt*, 2: 757–758.
37 As an example, see Abu Shuhbah, *al-Isrāʾīliyyāt*, 128.
38 Naʿnāʿah, R., *al-isrāʾīliyyāt wa atharuhā fī kutub al-tafsīr* (Damascus: Dār al-Qalam, 1970).
39 Al-Dhahabī, *al-Isrāʾīliyyāt*.
40 Al-Bukhārī, *Ṣaḥīḥ al-Bukhārī*, 4: 170 (#3461).
41 Kister, Meir J., "Ḥaddithū ʿan Banī Israʾīla wa la Ḥarajā: A Study of an Early Tradition," *Israel Oriental Studies* 2 (1972): 215–239.
42 Ibid.
43 Al-Qāsimī criticizes the use of stories that do not even correspond to Jewish scriptures and have very ambiguous sources. See al-Qāsimī, *Maḥāsin*, 35.
44 Twakkal, Abd Alfatah, "Kaʿb al-Aḥbār and the Isrāʾīliyyāt in the Tafsīr Literature" (M.A. diss., Institute of Islamic Studies, McGill University, 2007), 20.
45 See al-Qāsimī, *Maḥāsin*, 30–35.
46 Twakkal, "Kaʿb al-Aḥbār," 29.
47 His main logical argument is the prophetic tradition where Muḥammad states, "I am the child of the two sacrificed ones (*ana ibn al-dhabīḥayn*)," where this is assumed to be a reference of Ishmael, as one of the sacrificed ones. See Ibn Kathīr (d. 774/1373), *Tafsīr al-Qurʾān al-ʿaẓīm*, ed. Sāmī Salāmeh (Riyadh: Dār Ṭaybah, n.d.), 7: 28–31 on Q. 37:99–113.

48 Al-Ṭabarī, *Jāmiʿ*, 21: 72–90 on Q. 37:101–111.

49 E.g., Ibn Kathīr, *Tafsīr*, 7: 28–31 on Q. 37:99–113; al-Samarqandī (d. 373/983), *Baḥr al-ʿulūm* (unknown publisher, n.d.), 3: 146–150 on Q. 37:99–113; al-Rāzī (d. 606/1210), *Mafātīḥ al-ghayb* (Beirut: Iḥyāʾ al-Turāth al-ʿArabī, 2000), 26: 345–351 on Q. 37:102–113; al-Qurṭubī (d. 671/1273), *al-Jāmiʿ li-aḥkām al-Qurʾān*, ed. A. Aṭfīsh (Cairo: Dār al-Kutub al-Miṣriyyah, 1964), 15:98–114 on Q. 37:102–113.

50 al-Samarqandī, *Baḥr*, 3: 147 on Q. 37:99–113.

51 al-Rāzī, *Mafātīḥ*, 26: 346 on Q. 37:102–113.

52 Al-Qurṭubī, *al-Jāmiʿ*, 15:100 on Q. 37:102–113.

53 Al-Ṭabarānī (d. 360/970), *al-Tafsīr al-kabīr* (Amman: Dār al-Kitāb al-Thaqāfī, 2008), on Q. 37:101–113.

54 Firestone, Rueven, "Abraham's Son as the Intended Sacrifice (*Al-Dhabīḥ*, Qurʾan 37:99–113): Issues in Qurʾānic Exegesis," *Journal of Semitic Studies* 34, no. 1 (1989): 95–131.

55 Twakkal, "Kaʿb al-Aḥbār," 32.

56 Ibid., 35–37, 88.

57 Although the Book of Enoch is not canonical to the majority of Jewish traditions and Christian Churches, it is canonical to the Ethiopian and Eritrean Orthodox Churches. The New Testament, however, does cite and quote from the Book of Enoch (i.e., Jude 1:14–15), which might support the authenticity of the Book of Enoch as a Jewish religious work. Augustine did consider 1 Enoch as having something of divine inspiration in it, and as such repeated and cited in Jude's Epistle. See Williams, A., "Milton and the Book of Enoch: An Alternative Hypothesis," *The Harvard Theological Review* 33, no. 4 (1940): 291–299. Andreas Rivetus (d. 1651), a Calvinist theologian, considered the citation in Jude not as a proof of the authenticity of the Book of Enoch or even its existence. To him, Jude states that Enoch prophesied something, but that Jude says nothing of the Book of Enoch. Also see Williams, "Milton and the Book of Enoch." To him, Jude received inspiration on Enoch's prophecy. However, one might also argue that the Holy Spirit may cite other books that contain truths even if it does not consider the whole other text as truth. The Qurʾan also directly quotes (or alludes to) Biblical scriptures (e.g., Qurʾan 5:32, 45, 21:105). Muslim scholars may adopt a similar viewpoint where the Qurʾan might cite parts of the Bible confirming that the text contains truth, but not necessarily confirming the full text as true, although this is highly debatable, in which I will need to discuss the issue of corruption of scriptures known as "*taḥrīf*," according to the Qurʾan.

58 As examples from medieval polemics against Jews and Christians; see Ibn Ḥazm (d. 456/1064), *al-Faṣl fil-milal wal-ahwāʾ wal-niḥal* (Cairo: al-Khānjī, n.d.); Shihāb al-Dīn al-Qarāfī (d. 684/1285), *al-Ajwiba al-fākhirah ʿan al-asʾilah al-fājirah fil-radd ʿala al-millah al-kāfirah*, ed. Bikr Zakī ʿAwaḍ (Cairo: Saʿīd Raʾfat, 1987); Ibn Qayyim (d. 751/1350), *Hidāyah al-ḥayāra fī ajwibah al-yahūd wal-naṣāra*, ed. M. Al-Ḥāj (Jeddah: Dār al-Qalam, 1996); Ibn Taymiyyah (d. 728/1328), *al-Jawāb al-ṣaḥīḥ liman baddal dīn al-masīḥ*, ed. ʿAlī ibn Ḥasan, ʿAbdul-Azīz ibn Ibrahīm, and Ḥamdān ibn Muḥammad (Riyadh: Dār al-ʿĀsimah, 1984).

59 See Ibn Qayyim (d. 751/1350), *Ighāthat al-lahfān min maṣāʾid al-shayṭān*, ed. M. al-Faqī (Riyadh: al-Maʿārif, n.d.), 2: 351–354; Ibn Qayyim, *Hidāyah al-ḥayāra*, 312; al-Salmān, ʿAbdul ʿAzīz, *Mukhtaṣar al-asʾilah wal-ajwibah al-uṣūliyyah ʿala al-ʿaqīdah al-wāsiṭiyyah* (unknown publisher, 1997), 23–24; al-Qaḥṭānī, S. *Kayfiyyat daʿwat ahl al-kitāb ila Allah taʿāla fī ḍawʾ al-kitāb wal-sunnah* (Riyadh: Muʾassassat al-Juraisi lil-Tawzīʿ wal-Iʿlān, n.d.), 23.

60 Āl-Mu'ammar, 'Abdul 'Azīz (d. 1244/1828) *Minḥat al-qarīb al-mujīb fil-radd 'ala 'ibād al-ṣalīb* (unknown publisher, n.d.), 1: 250.
61 Al-Bukhārī, *Ṣaḥīḥ al-Bukhārī*, 9: 160.
62 Ibn Qayyim, *Ighāthat*, 2: 353.
63 Ibid.
64 Both the Qur'anic and Talmudic contexts are referring to Cain slaying Abel, which highly suggest the Qur'anic engagement with the Talmud. This is found in both the Bavli and Yerushalmi Talmuds. Refer to Neusner, Jacob, trans., *The Babylonian Talmud: A Translation and Commentary* (Peabody, MA: Hendrickson, 2011), Sanhedrin 37a, 4:5; also refer to Neusner, Jacob, trans. *The Jerusalem Talmud: A Translation and Commentary* (Peabody, MA: Hendrickson, 2008), Sanhedrin 4:5.
65 Although there is no scholarly consensus on the Jews referred to by the Qur'an (we do not even know if the Qur'an is referring to Jews in Medina), but there is a highly likelihood they have been precursors of Rabbinic Judaism due to the Qur'an's engagement specifically with the Talmud, as is also seen in Galadari, "The *Qibla*." Refer to Mazuz, Haggai, *The Religious and Spiritual Life of the Jews of Medina* (Leiden: Brill, 2014). Also refer to Newby, Gordon, *A History of the Jews of Arabia: From Ancient Times to Their Eclipse under Islam* (Columbia, SC: University of South Carolina, 1988), 57–59. Also refer to Lapin, Hayim, *Rabbis as Romans: The Rabbinic Movement in Palestine, 100–400 CE* (Oxford: Oxford University Press, 2012), 158. Also refer to Berkey, Jonathan, P. *The Formation of Islam: Religion and Society in the Near East, 600–1800* (Cambridge: Cambridge University Press, 2003), 46.
66 Al-Bukhārī, *Ṣaḥīḥ al-Bukhārī*, 4: 170 (#3461).
67 Qur'an 16:43, 21:7.
68 See Abu al-Muẓaffar (d. 471/1079), *al-Tabṣīr fil-dīn wa-tamyīz al-firqah al-nājiyah 'an al-firaq al-hālikīn*, ed. K. Y. al-Ḥūt (Beirut: 'Ālam al-Kutub, 1983), 181–182; Ibn Qudāmah al-Maqdisī (d. 620/1223), *Taḥrīm al-naẓar fī kutub al-kalām*, ed. A. M. S. Dimashqiyyah (Riyadh: 'Ālam al-Kutub, 1990), 49.
69 Al-Ṭabarī, *Jāmi'*, 17: 208 on Q. 16:43.
70 Ibn Kathīr, *Tafsīr*, 4: 573 on Q. 16:43.
71 Al-Qurṭubī, *al-Jāmi'*, 10: 108 on Q. 16:43.
72 Al-Rāzī, *Mafātīḥ*, 20: 211 on Q. 16:43.
73 Al-Ṭabarsī, *Majma'*, 6: 159 on Q. 16:43.
74 See Al-Biqā'ī (d. 885/1480), *al-Aqwāl al-qawīmah fī ḥukm al-naql min al-kutub al-qadīmah* (Cairo: Maktabat Jazīrat al-Ward, 2010). Al-Qāsimī mentions him as someone who has extensively used the Bible in his Qur'anic exegesis. See al-Qāsimī, *Maḥāsin*, 30–38.
75 Saleh, Walid A., "A Fifteenth-Century Muslim Hebraist: Al-Biqā'ī and His Defense of Using the Bible to Interpret the Qur'ān," *Speculum* 83 (2008): 629–654.
76 Ibid., 630–631.
77 Ibid., 633–634.
78 Ibid.
79 Al-Biqā'ī at times quotes from the Bible verbatim, and states, for example, this is "*naṣṣ al-tawrāh*" (the passage of the Torah) or "*qawluhu fil-tawrāh*" (His [God's] saying in the Torah). As an example, on the age of Adam, he quotes directly from Genesis 5:5; see al-Biqā'ī, *Niẓam*, 1: 271 on Q. 1:31–35. On the creation of Adam in God's image, he also quotes directly from Genesis 1:27 or 5:1–2; see al-Biqā'ī, *Niẓam*, 1: 280 on Q. 1:31–35. As an example, while quoting from the Gospel of Matthew, he states

"Matthew says" when quoting Matthew 9:35. He continues by quoting Matthew 11:2–3; see al-Biqāʿī, *Niẓam*, 6: 343 on Q. 5:109–111.

80 A mufti is a religious authority who is an expert in Islamic legal matters.

81 Saleh, "A Fifteenth-Century Muslim Hebraist," 634.

82 Ibid., 636–637.

83 Al-Qāsimī, *Maḥāsin*, 35. Al-Qāsimī brings up the prophetic tradition (*ḥadīth*) that states:

> The People of the Book used to read the Torah in Hebrew and used to interpret it to Muslims in Arabic, and so the prophet said, "Neither believe nor falsify the People of the Book, and say, 'We believe what has been revealed to us and what has been revealed to you.'"
>
> (My translation from al-Bukhārī, *Ṣaḥīḥ al-Bukhārī*, 6: 20 (#4485), 9: 111 (#7362), and 9: 157 (#7542), which is narrated in the *Ṣaḥīḥ* as a reference to Qurʾan 3:93)

This prophetic tradition also provides evidence in using scriptures, where Muḥammad is asserting to the believers the need to believe earlier scriptures. The context to which this tradition is being related by Abū Hurayra provides some insight that perhaps the reason why Muḥammad cautioned the Muslims is not because of doubting the Torah, but because the Muslims are not reading it as a primary source in its original language (Hebrew), but as a secondary source from Arabic commentaries thereof that are being told to them by the Jews. Thus Muslims did not have the opportunity to read it directly and as such were cautioned about how the Jews would interpret it for them. Therefore, this prophetic tradition cannot be used as evidence that Muḥammad had cautioned the usage of earlier scriptures, but cautioned on how they are being interpreted. On the other hand, it is not Muḥammad, but Ibn ʿAbbās who had cautioned the Muslims from asking the People of the Book, when the Qurʾan is a newer revelation. Al-Bukhārī, *Ṣaḥīḥ al-Bukhārī*, 9: 111 (#7363). Nonetheless, Ibn Kathīr had argued that some narrations of Ibn ʿAbbās could be from "*isrāʾīliyyāt*," as reported in al-Suyūṭī, *al-Itqān*, 4: 299. Such a statement, however, would contradict the Qurʾan, which requires Muslims to ask the People of the Book (i.e., Qurʾan 16:43, 21:7).

84 Although the *TSQ*, and generally the term "*ṭaʿām*" in this passage is understood as food, I argue that its meaning is closer to "commandments" or "judgments," which shares the same root and is used in this sense in Akkadian, Hebrew, and Aramaic languages, based on its root meaning "wise" see Oppenheim, A. Leo, Reiner, Erica, and Roth, Martha T., eds., *The Assyrian Dictionary of the Oriental Institute of the University of Chicago* (Chicago, IL: The Oriental Institute, 1956–2011), 19:46, 19:84–97; *TDOT*, 5:345–347; *BDB*, 380–381, similar to the Arabic "*ḥukm*" for commandment from the root meaning of wisdom, as well. The Qurʾanic context both before and after this verse has no mention of food, and therefore, the closest possible meaning given the context of this passage is "commandments."

85 Qurʾan 3:93.

86 Saleh, "A Fifteenth-Century Muslim Hebraist," 638. This argument is weak in that polemics usually quote the Bible to refute Jews and Christians, while al-Biqāʿī uses it to interpret the Qurʾan. There is a philosophical argument as to whether it is logical to quote a text, in which the polemic does not believe, to refute it. Polemic arguments that use texts believed to be false cannot be used to conclude truths, philosophically. As such, there is reason to consider al-Biqāʿī's quotes a more rational approach than that of polemics.

87 Saleh "A Fifteenth-Century Muslim Hebraist," 639–640. In part of his defense, he states that the majority of other scholars who oppose his method are of the Shāfiʿī school of thought, the same school to which he belongs. He argues that it is perhaps jealousy on their part, since scholars and jurists from other schools did not oppose him. As such, he concludes that he has the support of the Shāfiʿī *muftī* in Makkah, who praises his work and was eager to obtain a copy of his Qurʾanic commentary. Saleh, "A Fifteenth-Century Muslim Hebraist," 641.
88 Ibid., 643.
89 Al-Ṭabarī, *Jāmiʿ*, 10: 336–337 on Q. 5:43.
90 Qurʾan 5:43.
91 Saleh, "A Fifteenth-Century Muslim Hebraist," 644–645.
92 Ibid., 646.
93 Ibid., 649.
94 Ibid.
95 Ibid.
96 Ibid.
97 Ibid.
98 Ibid., 650.
99 Ibid.
100 Ibid., 651.
101 Ibid., 652.
102 Ibid., 635.
103 Guo, L., "Al-Biqāʿī's Chronicle: A Fifteenth Century Learned Man's Reflection on His Time and World," in *The Historiography of Islamic Egypt, c. 950–1800*, ed. Hugh Kennedy (Leiden: Brill NV, 2000), 121–148.
104 Chodkiewicz, M., *An Ocean Without Shore: Ibn Arabi, the Book, and the Law* (Albany, NY: State University of New York Press, 1993), 19.
105 For more details on the Qurʾanic passages that appear to be exclusivist in nature and how they are being interpreted in modern contexts, see Sirry, Munʾim, *Scriptural Polemics: The Qurʾan and Other Religions* (New York, NY: Oxford University Press, 2014).
106 Qurʾan 3:83–85.
107 For a comprehensive review of the term "*islām*" in the Qurʾan, see Smith, Jane I. *An Historical and Semantic Study of the Term "Islām" as Seen in a Sequence of Qurʾan Commentaries* (Missoula, MT: Scholars Press, 1975).
108 Ibn Ḥazm, *al-Faṣl*, 3: 109.
109 Ibid.
110 There is a long debate on the difference between the term "*islām*" and "*īmān*" among classical scholars, which is beyond the scope of this book.
111 Ibn Ḥazm, *al-Faṣl*, 3: 109.
112 Robson, James, " 'Islām' as a Term," *The Muslim World* 44, no. 2 (1954): 101–109.
113 Izutsu, T. *Ethico-Religious Concepts in the Qurʾan* (Montreal: McGill-Queen's University Press, 2002), 189–193.
114 Ibn ʿAbdulwahhāb (d. 1206/1792), *al-Rasāʾil al-shakhṣiyyah*, eds. S. Al-Fawzān and M. al-ʿAilaqi (Riyadh: Al-Imam Muhammad ibn Saud Islamic University), 170.
115 Ibn ʿAbdulwahhāb (d. 1206/1792), *Kashf al-shubuhāt* (Riyadh: Ministry of Islamic Affairs, 1998), 24.
116 Sirriyeh, E., "Wahhabis, Unbelievers and the Problems of Exclusivism," *Bulletin of the British Society for Middle Eastern Studies* 16 (1989): 123–132, 125.

117 For the Semitic etymology of the root "*s l m*," see *TDOT*, 15: 14–20, on "*s h l m*."
118 Ibn Manẓūr, *Lisān al-ʿarab*, 12: 289–301 on "*s l m*."
119 Ibid.
120 Ibn Taymiyyah, *al-Īmān*, 204–205.
121 Ibid., 205.
122 Ibid.
123 Ibid., 282–283, 296–297, 320–321.
124 Ibn Abī al-ʿIzz (d. 792/1390), *Sharḥ al-ʿaqīdah al-ṭaḥāwiyyah* (Riyadh: Ministry of Islamic Affairs, 1998), 534.
125 Ibid. Ibn Abī al-ʿIzz states that this *ḥadīth* is in the *Ṣaḥīḥ* and narrated by Abū Hurayra. The text of *Ṣaḥīḥ al-Bukhārī* is as follows, "Prophets are brothers in faith; their mothers are different and their religion is one." See al-Bukhārī, *Ṣaḥīḥ al-Bukhārī*, 4: 167 (#3443).
126 Ibid.
127 Ibid.
128 Shams al-Dīn al-Safārīnī, *Lawāmiʿ*, 2: 383.
129 Donner, *Muhammad and the Believers*, 71–73.
130 Ibn Abī al-ʿIzz, *Sharḥ*, 534.
131 Donner, *Muhammad and the Believers*, 71–73.
132 I translate "*al-nās*" as humankind as it seems more loyal to the Arabic, than the *TSQ*'s translation of "mankind."
133 I translate "*khalaq*" as divided, based on my discussion in Galadari, "*Creatio ex Nihilo*."
134 Qurʾan 49:13.
135 Asani, Ali S., "So That You May Know One Another: A Muslim American Reflects on Pluralism in Islam," *The Annals of the American Academy of Political and Social Science* 588 (2003): 40–51, 43.
136 Al-Ṭabarī, *Jāmiʿ*, 22: 309–312 on Q. 49:13.
137 I would call it a discussion instead of a debate.
138 Qurʾan 29:46.
139 As before, I translate "*al-nās*" as humankind as it seems more loyal to the Arabic, than the *TSQ*'s translation of "mankind."
140 Qurʾan 3:110.
141 Al-Ṭabarī, *Jāmiʿ*, 7: 107–108 on Q. 3:110.
142 Qurʾan 3:112–115.
143 Qurʾan 2:61–62.
144 Qurʾan 5:68–70.
145 There are other points of intertextuality, but I will stop it there, as it would go beyond the scope of this book.
146 Qurʾan 2:111–113.
147 In explaining this verse, al-Ṭabarī mentions that the term "*aslam*," which shares the same root as "*islām*" and "*muslim*," means to surrender. See al-Ṭabarī, *Jāmiʿ*, 2: 510–511 on Q. 2:112.
148 Qurʾan 2:121.
149 Qurʾan 5:66.
150 Ibn Manẓūr, *Lisān al-ʿarab*, 9: 43 on "*ḥ r f*."
151 Ibid., 12: 496 on "*q w m*." Also see *TDOT*, 12: 589–612, on "*q w m*."
152 Tarakci, M. and Sayar, S., "The Qurʾanic View of the Corruption of the Torah and the Gospels," *The Islamic Quarterly* 49, no. 3 (2005): 227–245.

153 Al-Hāshimī (d. 668/1269) *Takhjīl man ḥarraf al-tawrāt wal-injīl*, ed. M. A. Qadḥ (Riyadh: Maktabat al-ʿObaikān, 1998).
154 Mingana, A., "The Apology of Timothy the Patriarch Before the Caliph Mahdi," *Bulletin of the John Rylands Library* 12, no. 1 (1928): 137–298, 171, 191.
155 Al-Bukhārī, *Ṣaḥīḥ al-Bukhārī*, 3: 181 (#2685).
156 It sometimes bewilders me why some Muslims would sometimes take a *ḥadīth*, and in this case not even attributed to Muḥammad, as a rule, even when it contradicts the Qurʾan.
157 Al-Ṭabarī, *Jāmiʿ*, 17: 207–208 on Q. 16:43.
158 Tarakci and Sayar, "The Qurʾanic View," 228.
159 Ibid., 230.
160 Whether it is al-Ghazālī's work is highly debatable.
161 Whittingham, Martin, "The Value of *taḥrīf maʿnawī* (corrupt interpretation) as a Category for Analysing Muslim Views of the Bible: Evidence from *al-radd al-jamīl* and Ibn Khaldūn," *Islam and Christian–Muslim Relations* 22, no. 2 (2011): 209–222.
162 See Bowman, J., "The Debt of Islam to Monophysite Syrian Christianity," in *Essays in Honor of Griffithes Wheeler Thatcher*, ed. E. C. B. Maclaurin (Sydney: Sydney University Press, 1967), 200; Resnick, I., "The Falsification of Scripture and Medieval Christian and Jewish Polemics," *Medieval Encounters* 2, no. 3 (1996): 344–380.
163 Reynolds, Gabriel S., "On the Qurʾanic Accusation of Scriptural Falsification (*taḥrīf*) and Christian Anti-Jewish Polemic," *Journal of the American Oriental Society* 130, no. 2 (2010): 189–202, 197. See also Reynolds' reference on Syriac Fathers using a spiritual interpretation of the Hebrew Bible for typological purposes in Brock, Sebastian P., *The Bible in Syriac Tradition* (Piscataway, NJ: Gorgias Press, 2006), 59.
164 Reynolds, "On the Qurʾanic Accusation," 197–200.
165 Al-Ṭabarī, *Jāmiʿ*, 2: 248–249 on Q. 2:75.
166 Ibn Manẓūr, *Lisān al-ʿarab*, 9: 43 on "*ḥ r f*."
167 The term "*inḥirāf*" meaning crooked perhaps goes back to the time of the Qurʾan. There is a saying by Abū Hurayra stating, "*Āmantu bi-muḥarrif al-qulūb*," (I believe in the bender of the hearts). See Ibn Baṭṭah (d. 387/997), *al-Ibānah al-kubra* (Riyadh: Dār al-Rāyah wal-Tawzīʿ, 1995), 4: 171 (#1658).
168 Al-Ṭabarī, *Jāmiʿ*, 2: 248–249 on Q. 2:75.
169 See ibid., 15: 40–41 on Q. 10:15, and 17: 296–297 on Q. 16:101.
170 Ibid., 17: 68 on Q. 15:9.
171 Medieval Muslim polemics, such as Najm al-Dīn al-Ṭūfī (d. 716/1316), argue against the understanding of "*al-dhikr*" to mean the Torah and the Gospel using consensus of Qurʾanic commentators as evidence. However, as argued here, classical Qurʾanic commentaries may be plagued with opinions and assumptions based on presuppositions rather than facts. Hence, such evidence would have no Qurʾanic basis. See Najm al-Dīn al-Ṭūfī (d. 716/1316), *al-Intiṣārāt al-islāmiyyah fī kashf shubah al-naṣrāniyah*, ed. S. M. al-Qarnī (Riyadh: Maktabat al-ʿObaikān, 1999), 1: 289–300.
172 Qurʾan 6:34.
173 Ibid., 6:115.
174 Ibid., 10:64.
175 Ibid., 18:27.
176 Ibid., 48:15.
177 Ibid., 2:75.
178 Ibid., 4:46.
179 Ibid., 5:13.

180 Ibid., 5:41.
181 Mazuz, *The Religious and Spiritual Life*, 19–21.
182 Ibid., 19–20. Mazuz gives the following examples from the Babylonian Talmud: Ro'sh ha-Shana, 3a, 11a, 13b; Yōmā, 39a, 75b; Sukka, 31a, 52a, 55 a–b, 114a, 118b, 119b; Shabbat, 30b, 32b, 33a, 88b, 89a; Ḥaggīga, 27a; Mō'ed Qaṭan, 5a, 9b; Pesaḥīm, 49b, 117a; Meggīla, 13a, 14a, 15b, 25b, 28a–b; Ta'anīt, 4a, 7b, 9a; Berakhōt, 5a, 7b, 10a–b, 14a, 15b, 20a, 30b, 31b, 48b, 64a; Sōṭa, 5a–b, 9a, 11b, 12a, 13a, 35a, 37a; Nīdda, 13a, 73a; Ketūbōt, 5a, 67a, 111a–b; Qīddūshīn, 30a–b; Ḥūlīn, 27a, 60a; Qōdashīm, 29b; Zevaḥīm, 116b; Kerītōt, 28a; 'Avōda Zara, 3b, 4a, 11a; Sanhedrīn, 63b, 99b, 110b; Bavā Qammā, 10b, 81b; Bavā Meṣī'ā, 84a; Bavā Batrā, 74b, 75b, 118b; 'Eirūvīn, 21b, 54a–b.
183 Ibid., 19–20. Referring to the Babylonian Talmud, Shabbat 33a.
184 Ibid., 20. Referring to the Babylonian Talmud, Shabbat 89a.
185 Ibid., 20. Referring to the Babylonian Talmud, Shabbat 88b.
186 Ibid., 20–21.
187 Ibn Manẓūr, *Lisān al-'arab*, 9: 41–42 on "*ḥ r f*."
188 Al-Bukhārī, *Ṣaḥīḥ al-Bukhārī*, 4: 113 (#3219). Also variants in *Ṣaḥīḥ al-Bukhārī*, 6: 184 (#4991), 3: 122 (#2419), 6: 184 (#4992); Muslim, *Ṣaḥīḥ Muslim*, 1: 560 (#270/818), 1: 561 (#272/819), 1: 561 (#273/820), 1: 562 (#274/562).
189 Perhaps the term "*yuḥarrifūn*" is an Arabic equivalent to "*yutarjimūn*" at the time of the Qur'an. The term "*t r g m*" appears to be Aramaic. Rarely are Semitic roots quadrilateral, and this term appears to be one of them. We will need to find out when the term "*t r j m*" was adopted by the Arabs, as there is evidence perhaps it did exist in the time of the Qur'an. This might be of interest as literal translation is called in Arabic "*tarjamah ḥarfiyyah*," in which the root of the term "*ḥ r f*" is used to mean literal. The term "*tarjumān*" from the root "*t r j m*" appears in a prophetic tradition (*ḥadīth*), which states, "then one of you will stand up between God's hands without between him and Him a veil nor a translator (*tarjumān*) to translate (*yutarjim*) for him;" al-Bukhārī, *Ṣaḥīḥ al-Bukhārī*, 2: 108 (#1413). Also variants in *Ṣaḥīḥ al-Bukhārī*, 4: 197 (#3595), 8: 112 (#6539), 9: 132 (#7443), 9: 148 (#7512). Also in Muslim, *Ṣaḥīḥ Muslim*, 2: 703 (#1016). The term "*t r j m*" also appears in a tradition when Muḥammad asked Zayd ibn Thābit to learn the book of the Jews and that Ibn 'Abbās had a translator as well; *Ṣaḥīḥ al-Bukhārī*, 9: 76 (#7195); *Ṣaḥīḥ al-Bukhārī*, 9: 76 (#7196).
190 For more on Jewish targums and its role in interpretation of the Hebrew Bible, see Bowker, J. W. *The Targums and Rabbinic Literature: An Introduction to Jewish Interpretation of Scripture* (Cambridge: Cambridge University Press, 1969); McNamara, Martin, *Targum and New Testament: Collected Essays* (Tübingen: Mohr Siebeck, 2011); McNamara, Martin, *Targum and Testament Revisited: Aramaic Paraphrases of the Hebrew Bible: A Light on the New Testament* (Grand Rapids, MI: Wm. B. Eerdmans, 2010).
191 McNamara, *Targum and Testament Revisited*, 131; McNamara, *Targum and New Testament*, 239.
192 There is no consensus on the dating of the targums. Some scholars suggest that some targums were written during the Islamic period, while others suggest that at least some targums were perhaps written as early as the first century CE. See Flesher, Paul V. M. and Chilton, Bruce D. *The Targums: A Critical Introduction* (Leiden: Brill, 2011); Hayward, C. T. Robert *Targums and the Transmission of Scripture into Judaism and Christianity* (Leiden: Brill, 2010); Houtman, Alberdina and Sysling, Harry, *Alternative Targum Traditions: The Use of Variant Readings for the Study in Origin and History of*

Targum Jonathan (Leiden: Brill, 2009); McNamara, *Targum and Testament Revisited.* Nonetheless, this does not dismiss the existence of perhaps oral targum during the time of the Qur'an, which the Qur'an may be rejecting.

193 McNamara, *Targum and Testament Revisited*, 60.
194 Ibn Manẓūr, *Lisān al-ʿarab*, 9: 42–43 on "*ḥ r f.*"
195 See Ibn Manẓūr, *Lisān al-ʿarab*, 9: 43–44 on "*ḥ r f.*" Also see *TDOT*, 5: 209–211, on "*ḥ r p.*" Though there might seem to be a relationship between "*ḥirfah*" and "craft," the English term could trace its root to "*kraf*" in Proto-Germanic meaning strength.
196 Ibn Manẓūr, *Lisān al-ʿarab*, 9: 43–44 on "*ḥ r f.*"
197 *TDOT*, 5: 209–215, on "*ḥ r p.*"
198 Ibn Manẓūr, *Lisān al-ʿarab*, 9: 43 on "*ḥrf.*"
199 Al-Ṭabarī, *Jāmiʿ*, 10: 301–318 on Q. 5:41.
200 Ibid., 10: 301–302 on Q. 5:41.
201 Ibid., 10: 303–306 on Q. 5:41.
202 Ibid., 10: 303–306 on Q. 5:41.
203 Qur'an 5:43.
204 Tarakci and Sayar, "The Qur'anic View."
205 Reynolds, "On the Qur'anic Accusation."
206 Tarakci and Sayar, "The Qur'anic View."
207 In the view of the Church of Jesus Christ of Latter-Day Saints and as stated by Joseph Smith in the Doctrine and Covenants 91:1–2, "Verily, thus saith the Lord unto you concerning the Apocrypha. There are many things contained therein that are true, and it is mostly translated correctly. There are many things contained therein that are not true, which are interpolations by the hands of men."
208 Reynolds, "On the Qur'anic Accusation," 193.
209 Also compare with Q. 5:48.
210 Donner, *Muhammad and the Believers*, 87.
211 Ibn Qayyim, *Hidāyah al-ḥayāra*, 312–315, 416, 432; Ibn Taymiyyah, *al-Jawāb*, 2: 367.
212 Al-Juwaynī (d. 478/1085), *Shifāʾ al-ghalīl fī bayān mā waqaʿa fil-tawrāt wal-injīl min al-tabdīl*, ed. A. H. al-Saqqa (Cairo: Maktabat al-Azhariyyah lil-Turāth, 1978), 29.
213 For more on Aḥmad or Muḥammad see Jones, L. B., "The Paraclete or Mohammed: The Verdict of an Ancient Manuscript," *The Muslim World* 10, no. 2 (1920): 112–125; Smith, P., "Did Jesus Foretell Ahmed? Origin of the so-called Prophecy of Jesus concerning the Coming of Mohammed," *The Muslim World* 12, no. 1 (1922): 71–74; Guthrie, A. and Bishop, E. F. F., "The Paraclete, Almunhamanna and Aḥmad," *The Muslim World* 41, no. 4 (1951): 251–256; Watt, William Montgomery, "His Name is Ahmad," *The Muslim World* 43, no. 2 (1953): 110–117.
214 Ibn Taymiyyah, *al-Jawāb*, 3: 142–144.
215 Examples of medieval polemics against Jews and Christians; see Ibn Ḥazm, *al-Faṣl*; al-Qarāfī, *al-Ajwiba al-fākhirah*; Ibn Qayyim, *Hidāyah al-ḥayāra.*
216 Qur'an 2:113.
217 Classical Qur'anic commentators, such as al-Ṭabarī, make a note of this definition for the term "*yuḥarrifūn.*" See al-Ṭabarī, *Jāmiʿ*, 2: 248–249 on Q. 2:75.
218 Qur'an 5:68–69.
219 Qur'an 5:43–44.
220 Qur'an 5:47–48.
221 Tarakci and Sayar, "The Qur'anic View."
222 I will not delve in arguing the debate of infallibility of prophets in Islam, as it is an argument on its own, and will restrict my argument in this book in that it is not

based on the Qur'an. The Qur'an actually shows that prophets are as fallible as anyone else, such as Abraham lying (i.e., Qur'an 21:63), Jacob's sons leaving their brother Joseph in a well and then lying about it to their father (e.g., Qur'an 12:9–18), David mishandling judgments (e.g., Qur'an 38:21–25), Moses killing (e.g., Qur'an 28:15), Jonah specifically disobeying a divine command (e.g., Qur'an 21:87), and perhaps Muḥammad trying to refuse what God has made lawful (e.g., Qur'an 66:1).

223 Averroës, *The Decisive Treatise*, 10.

224 See Reynolds, *The Qur'ān and Its Biblical Subtext*; El-Badawi, *The Qur'an and the Aramaic Gospel Traditions*.

Chapter 5: In the Name of the Father and the Son and the Holy Spirit

1 Ibn Sa'd, *Ṭabaqāt al-kubra*, 2: 273–274; al-Bukhārī, *Ṣaḥīḥ al-Bukhārī*, 6: 182 (#4984). I am indebted to Ulrika Mårtensson for pointing this out to me.

2 See Gardner-Smith, P., *Saint John and the Synoptic Gospels* (Cambridge: Cambridge University Press, 1938); Smith, Dwight Moody, *The Theology of the Gospel of John* (Cambridge: Cambridge University Press, 1995); Dvorak, James D., "The Relationship Between John and the Synoptic Gospels," *Journal of the Evangelical Theological Society* 41, no. 2 (1998): 201–213; Bauckham, Richard and Mosser, Carl, eds. *The Gospel of John and Christian Theology* (Grand Rapids, MI: Wm. B. Eerdmans, 2008).

3 Wolfe, Michael W. "The World Could not Contain the Pages: A Sufi Reading of the Gospel of John based on the Writings of Muḥyī al-Dīn Ibn al-'Arabī (1165–1240 CE)," PhD diss., Columbia University, 2016.

4 Eusebius (d. 340 CE), *Eccl. Hist.*, VI.14, as translated from Valesius, *Life of Eusebius Pamphilus*, in Parker S. E. trans. *An Ecclesiastical History to the 20th Year of the Reign of Constantine* (London: Samuel Bagster, 1847), 247–248.

5 For examples, refer to Quddus, Munir, Bailey III, Henri, and White, Larry R., "Business Ethics: Perspectives from Judaic, Christian, and Islamic Scriptures," *Journal of Management, Spirituality & Religion* 6, no. 4 (2009): 323–334; and also refer to Wilson, Rodney, *Economics, Ethics and Religion: Jewish, Christian and Muslim Economic Thought* (New York, NY: New York University Press, 1997).

6 Beit-Hallahmi, Benjamin, "Morality and Immorality Among the Irreligious," in *Atheism and Secularity*, ed. Phil Zuckerman (Santa Barbara, CA: ABC-CLIO, 2010), 113–141.

7 Sinnott-Armstrong, Walter, *Morality Without God?* (Oxford: Oxford University Press, 2009); Cirrone, Steve *Secular Morality: Rhetoric and Reader* (n.p.: SFC Publishing, 2015).

8 For examples, refer to Bremmer, Robert H., *Giving: Charity and Philanthropy in History* (New Brunswick, NJ: Transaction, 2000): for specifically an example of a humanist approach to charity, see pp. 28–29.

9 As examples, refer to Wilson, Andrew, ed. *World Scripture: A Comparative Anthology of Sacred Texts* (St. Paul, MN: Paragon House, 1998); also refer to Hooper, Richard, ed. *Jesus, Buddha, Krishna, Lao Tzu: The Parallel Sayings—The Common Teachings of Four Religions* (Sedona, AZ: Sanctuary Books, 2007).

10 Refer to Gyatso, Tenzin (Dalai Lama XIV), *Beyond Religion: Ethics for a Whole World* (New York, NY: Houghton Mifflin Harcourt, 2011). For a critique of secular ethics, see

Mitchell, Basil, *Morality: Religious and Secular—The Dilemma of the Traditional Conscience* (Oxford: Oxford University Press, 1980).

11 For an overview of the different Christological and theological debates in Christian history, see McGrath, Alister E., *Historical Theology: An Introduction to the History of Christian Thought* (Chichester: Wiley-Blackwell, 2013).

12 For an overview of Church history, see Cairns, Earle E. *Christianity through the Centuries: A History of the Christian Church* (Grand Rapids, MI: Zondervan, 1996).

13 For an overview of the history of the development of Muslim theology, see Wensinck, Arent J. *The Muslim Creed: Its Genesis and Historical Development* (Cambridge: Cambridge University Press, 1932).

14 Jane Smith states, "Some advocates of Muslim-Christian dialogue, therefore, are adamant that the most appropriate arena for discussion is not theology, but ethics," Smith, Jane I., *Muslims, Christians, and the Challenge of Interfaith Dialogue* (Oxford: Oxford University Press, 2007), 75.

15 Ayoub, Mahmoud, "Christian–Muslim Dialogue: Goals and Obstacles," *The Muslim World* 94, no. 3 (2004): 313–319.

16 Qur'an 9:30–32.

17 Casanova, Paul, "Idris et 'Ouzair," *Journal asiatique*, 205 (1924): 356–360. For reference to the haggadic literature mentioning 'Aza'el see Neusner, *Babylonian Talmud*, Yoma 6:4.

18 Ibid.

19 Stuckenbruck, L. T., *Angel Veneration and Christology: A Study in Early Judaism and the Christology of the Apocalypse of John* (Tübingen: Mohr Siebeck, 1995).

20 Ginzberg, Louis, *Legends of the Jews* (Philadelphia, PA: The Jewish Publication Society, 2003), 135–136.

21 Ibid., 136.

22 Ibid.

23 Ibid. It may be interesting to note that Azael taking the sins of Israel may be seen with similarity as Jesus' crucifixion for the forgiveness of sins, according to John and Paul (e.g., John 1:29, Romans 4:25, 1 Corinthians 15:3).

24 Neusner, *Babylonian Talmud*, Rosh Hashanah 4:5.

25 The Sanhedrin is the council of experts initially founded through the seventy elders appointed by Moses to assist in governing the Jewish people.

26 Leviticus Rabbah 2:11.

27 The term "*arbāban*" is cognate of the Hebrew "*rabbi*."

28 Casanova, "Idris et 'Ouzair," 356–360; Torrey, *The Jewish Foundation*, 72.

29 Bell, R., *Introduction to the Qur'an* (Edinburgh: Edinburgh University Press, 1953), 163.

30 Watt, William Montgomery, *Bell's Introduction to the Qur'an* (Edinburgh: T&T Clark, 1970), 28, 191.

31 Bellamy, James A., "Textual Criticism of the Koran," *Journal of the American Oriental Society* 121, no. 1 (2001): 1–6.

32 Erder, Yoram, "The Origin of the Name Idrīs in the Qur'an: A Study of the Influence of Qumran Literature on Early Islam," *Journal of Near Eastern Studies* 49, no. 4 (1990): 339–350.

33 Jeffery, *The Foreign Vocabulary*, 214–215.

34 For a summary on 'Uzair in the Muslim tradition, see Ayoub, Mahmoud, "'Uzayr in the Qur'an and Muslim Tradition," in *Studies in Islamic and Judaic Traditions*, eds. W. M. Brinner and S. D. Ricks (Atlanta, GA: Scholars Press, 1986), 3–18.

35 Al-Ṭabarī, *Jāmiʿ*, 14: 202–203 on Q. 9:30.
36 Ibn Kathīr, *al-Bidāyah wal-nihāyah* (Beirut: Dār Iḥyāʾ al-Turāth al-ʿArabī, 1988), 2: 53–54.
37 Ibn Ḥazm, *al-Faṣl*, 1: 147–148, 156.
38 Walker, John, "Who is ʿUzair?" *The Muslim World* 19, no. 3 (1929): 303–306, 303.
39 Bellamy, "Textual Criticism."
40 2 Esdras 14:9.
41 2 Esdras 2:47.
42 Bellamy, "Textual Criticism," 5.
43 Mazuz, *The Religious and Spiritual Life.*
44 Al-Ṭabarī, *Jāmiʿ*, 14: 201 on Q. 9:30.
45 Ibid., 14: 202–203 on Q. 9:30. Also, Ibn Kathīr, *Tafsīr*, 4:118 on Q. 9:30.
46 Walker, "Who is ʿUzair?"
47 Al-Rāzī, *Mafātīḥ*, 16: 28 on Q. 9:30.
48 Ibid.; al-Ṭabarsī, *Majmaʿ*, 5: 42–43 on Q. 9:30.
49 Ibn Hazm, *al-Faṣl*, 1: 82.
50 Al-Maqdisī (d. 355/966) *al-Badʾ wal-tarīkh* (Port Saʿīd: Maktabat al-Thaqāfah al-Dīniyyah, n.d.), 3: 116.
51 Ibid., 4: 35.
52 Al-Hāshimī, *Takhjīl*, 2: 527–528.
53 Matthew 26:64–66, Mark 14:62–64, John 10:33–36.
54 Bellamy, "Textual Criticism."
55 Ezra 1:1–3.
56 Ibn Manẓūr, *Lisān al-ʿarab*, 14: 89 on "*b n y*." Also see *TDOT*, 2: 145–159, on "*bn*."
57 Ibid., 14: 89 on "*b n y*." *BDB*, 119–120. The *TDOT* states that some Hebrew scholars contend that the Hebrew term "*bn*" is rooted in "*b n h*," which is to build, and that the Aramaic term for son, "*br*," comes from "*baraʾ*," meaning to create. See *TDOT*, 2: 149, on "*bn*." Also see *TDOT*, 2: 167, on "*b n h*." It is important to note that "*b n y*" or "*b n h*" also means to create in Akkadian and Ugaritic. See *TDOT*, 2: 166–167, on "*b n h*."
58 Ibn Manẓūr, *Lisān al-ʿarab*, 14: 93 on "*b n y*." *BDB*, 6.
59 Neusner, *Babylonian Talmud*, Berakhot 9:1, 64a.
60 Ibn Manẓūr, *Lisān al-ʿarab*, 14: 89 on "*b n y*."
61 *BDB*, 119–120.
62 Ibid., 124. The *TDOT* states that some Hebrew scholars contend that the Hebrew term "*bn*" is rooted in "*b n h*," which is to build, and that the Aramaic term for son, "*br*," comes from "*baraʾ*," meaning to create. See *TDOT*, 2: 149, on "*bn*." Also see *TDOT*, 2: 167, on "*b n h*." It is important to note that "*bny*" or "*bnh*" also means to create in Akkadian and Ugaritic. See *TDOT*, 2: 166–167, on "*b n h*."
63 *BDB*, 6; *TDOT*, 1: 48–49, on "*a b n*."
64 Although not typically used in the form of "*abn*," the Arabic language uses the term "*lbn*" to also mean stone. Nonetheless, *Lisān al-ʿarab* gives an example of a man saying "*banāt masājid Allah*" to mean stones of mosques, which is from the root "*bny*." See Ibn Manẓūr, *Lisān al-ʿarab*, 14: 93 on "*bny*."
65 1 Samuel 7:12.
66 Ezra 5:8.
67 Qurʾan 9:30.
68 Ibn Manẓūr, *Lisān al-ʿarab*, 4: 562 on "*ʿa z r*." *BDB*, 740–741; *TDOT*, 11: 12–18, on "*ʿa z r*."
69 *BDB*, 741.

70 Temple court as a reference to the Temple in Jerusalem (*beit ha-miqdash*).
71 John 2:19–22. Utley states, "Christianity replaces the physical temple of the Jews with the spiritual temple of Christ's physical body as His corporate body, the church" in Utley, B. *Paul's Letters to a Troubled Church: I and II Corinthians* (Marshall, TX: Bible Lessons International, 2002), 76.
72 Qurʾan 3:118.
73 Qurʾan 3:167.
74 Qurʾan 5:41.
75 Galadari, "The *Qibla*."
76 Qurʾan 9:8.
77 Qurʾan 9:32.
78 Qurʾan 61:1–8.
79 Bassler, Jouette M., "Mixed Signals: Nicodemus in the Fourth Gospel," *Journal of Biblical Literature* 108, no. 4 (1989): 635–646, 637, original emphasis.
80 Canales, Arthur D., "A Rebirth of Being 'Born Again': Theological, Sacramental and Pastoral Reflections from a Roman Catholic Perspective," *Journal of Pentecostal Theology* 11, no. 1 (2002): 98–119.
81 Ibid., 101.
82 The history of Christianity also recounts Nicodemus the Christian such as in the Apocrypha, Gospel of Nicodemus. See Schneemelcher, W. ed. *New Testament Apocrypha* (Cambridge: James Clarke, 1991), 1: 502–536.
83 Fazlur Rahman, "Some Key Ethical Concepts of the Qurʾān," *The Journal of Religious Ethics* 11, no. 2 (1983): 170–185.
84 Al-Ṭabarī, *Jāmiʿ*, 14: 213–214 on Q. 9:32; Ibn Kathīr, *Tafsīr*, 4: 119–120 on Q. 9:32.
85 Ibid.
86 Commenting on this passage of Paul's epistle, Staton says, "Our body is just not 'our' body, but the temple of the Holy Spirit. The Holy Spirit lives inside us. Our bodies become the house of God's Spirit. God's temple is no longer a stationary building in one city in the Mideast, but a temple that walks around and lives in the community," in Staton, K., *Unlocking the Scriptures for You: First Corinthians* (Cincinnati, OH: Standard Publishing, 1987), 129.
87 1 Corinthians 6:19–20.
88 Qurʾan 9:111.
89 Gupta, Nijay K., "Which 'Body' Is a Temple (1 Corinthians 6:19)? Paul Beyond the Individual/Communal Divide," *The Catholic Biblical Quarterly* 72, no. 3 (2010): 518–536.
90 Jamieson, R., Fausset, A. R., and Brown, D., 1871, *Commentary Critical and Explanatory on the Whole Bible* (Hartford, CT: S. S. Scranton, 1997), on 1 Corinthians 6:19–20.
91 *Pirke Abot*, 3.2.
92 Marshall, Howard, "Church and Temple in the New Testament," *Tyndale Bulletin* 40, no. 2 (1989): 203–222, 218.
93 Pratt, Richard L. *Holman New Testament Commentary: I & II Corinthians*, ed. M. Anders (Nashville, TN: Broadman & Holman, 2000), 101.
94 Patai, R., "The Shekhina," *The Journal of Religion* 44, no. 4 (1964): 275–288. Also refer to *Baker Encyclopedia of the Bible* (Grand Rapids, MI: Baker Book House, 1988), 2: 1943; *The New Bible Dictionary* (Leicester: Inter-Varsity Press, 1996), 1090–1091; *Holman Illustrated Bible Dictionary* (Nashville, TN: Holman Bible Publishers, 2003), 1480.

95 Lenski, Richard C. H. *The Interpretation of St. Paul's First and Second Epistles to the Corinthians* (Minneapolis, MN: Augsburg, 1963), 269–270.
96 Barrett, Charles K. *Black's New Testament Commentary: The First Epistle to the Corinthians* (Peabody, MA: Hendrickson, 2000), 151–152.
97 Talbert, Charles H. *Reading Corinthians: A Literary and Theological Commentary on 1 & 2 Corinthians* (Macon, GA: Smyth & Helwys, 2002), 51.
98 Hodge, Charles, *An Exposition of the First Epistle to the Corinthians* (New York, NY: Robert Carter & Brothers, 1857), 106.
99 Ibn Manẓūr, *Lisān al-ʿarab*, 10: 390 on the meaning of "*a f k*."
100 *Comprehensive Aramaic Lexicon Project* at http://cal.huc.edu/, on the meaning of "*a p k*." In Christian Palestinian Aramaic and Syriac, the term "*p k h*" means foolish. However, its relationship with the Arabic "*i f k*" is unknown. See *Comprehensive Aramaic Lexicon Project*, on the meaning of "*p k h*."
101 Qurʾan 7:117–121.
102 Ibn Manẓūr, *Lisān al-ʿarab*, 1: 685 on the meaning of "*q l b*."
103 Ibid., 1: 687 on the meaning of "*q l b*."
104 Al-Kalbī (d. 204/819), *Kitāb al-aṣnām*, ed. A. Z. Pāsha (Cairo: Dār al-Kutub al-Miṣriyyah, 2000), 19. Also refer to al-Ṭabarī, *Jāmiʿ*, 22: 522 on Q. 53:19–22. Also refer to Ibn Ṭāhir al-Baghdādī (d. 429/1037), *al-Farq bayn al-firaq wa bayān al-firqah al-nājiyah* (Beirut: Dār al-Āfāq al-Jadīdah, 1977), 345.
105 Qurʾan 4:171–172.
106 Ibn Manẓūr, *Lisān al-ʿarab*, 3: 270–272 on the meaning of "*ʿabd*."
107 Ibid., 3: 273–274 on the meaning of "*ʿabd*."
108 Ibid., 3: 273 on the meaning of "*ʿabd*."
109 *BDB*, 712–713.
110 For more on the Semitic use of "*ʿabd*" and its use in the Hebrew Bible, see *TDOT*, 10:376–405, on "*ʿabd*."
111 Ibn Manẓūr, *Lisān al-ʿarab*, 14: 95 on the meaning of "*b n y*." Also in Abū al-Walīd al-Bājī (d. 474/1082) in his *al-Muntaqa* states that Ibn al-Sikīt (d. 244/858) defined *al-baniyyah* as the Kaʿbah, and that ʿUmar ibn al-Khaṭṭāb called it as such: Abū al-Walīd al-Bājī (d. 474/1082), *al-Munṭaqa sharḥ al-muwaṭṭaʾ* (Cairo: Dār al-Kitāb al-Islāmī, 1914), 4: 8. Ibn Sīdah (d. 458/1066) also mentions this definition of *al-baniyyah* from Ibn al-Sikīt: Ibn Sīdah (d. 458/1066), *al-Mukhaṣṣaṣ*, ed. Khalīl Ibrāhīm Jifāl (Beirut: Dār Iḥyāʾ al-Turāth al-ʿArabī, 1996), 1: 505.
112 The Kaʿbah is also called "*baniyyat Ibrahīm*," because it is built by Abraham. See Ibn Manẓūr, *Lisān al-ʿarab*, 14: 95 on the meaning of "*ʿabd*." As such, Jesus may be considered "*bani Allah*," meaning built or made by God, or more, so that he is the Temple of God.
113 *TDOT*, 1: 1–2, on "*ab*."
114 *BDB*, 2–3.
115 *TDOT*, 1: 24–25, on "*a b h*."
116 Ibn Manẓūr, *Lisān al-ʿarab*, 14: 3–5 on the meaning of "*a b y*."
117 *TDOT*, 1: 131, on "*a w b*."
118 Ibn Manẓūr, *Lisān al-ʿarab*, 1: 217–219 on the meaning of "*a w b*." Also see *BDB*, 15 and 33.
119 Ibid., 1: 233 on the meaning of "*t w b*."
120 Ibid., 1: 218–219 on the meaning of "*a w b*."
121 *TDOT*, 1: 212–213, on "*a y b*."

122 The Qurʾanic passage uses "ʿ*udttum ʿudnā*." This can either mean, if you return to us, we shall return, or if you come against us (enemy), we shall come against you (enemy). Which sense of the word is meant may be ambiguous, and possibly as part of the rhetoric, perhaps both meanings are intended.
123 Al-Ṭabarī, *Jāmiʿ*, 6: 258 on Q. 3:14; Ibn Kathīr, *Tafsīr*, 2: 22 on Q. 3:14; al-Rāzī, *Mafātīḥ*, 7: 163 on Q. 3:14.
124 Besides its meaning of the "persecuted one" as well. See *BDB*, 33.
125 Qurʾan 9:30–32.
126 Qurʾan 20:56.
127 Exodus 10:27; *BDB*, 2.
128 John 3:3–18.
129 Richard, E., "Expressions of Double Meaning and their Function in the Gospel of John," *New Testament Studies* 31, no. 1 (1985): 96–112.
130 Coloe, Mary L., *God Dwells With Us: Temple Symbolism in the Fourth Gospel* (Collegeville, MN: The Liturgical Press, 2001), 5.
131 Grese, William C., "'Unless One Is Born Again': The Use of a Heavenly Journey in John 3," *Journal of Biblical Literature* 107, no. 4 (1988): 377–693, 689.
132 Ibid., 691.
133 Ibid.
134 Bassler, "Mixed Signals," 638.
135 Wiles, Maurice F., *The Spiritual Gospel: The Interpretation of the Fourth Gospel in the Early Church* (Cambridge: Cambridge University Press, 1960), 24.
136 Augustine's Homilies on the Gospel of John, Tractate XI. See Schaff, Phillip, ed., *A Select Library of the Nicene and Post-Nicene Fathers of the Christian Church* (New York, NY: The Christian Literature, 1888), 75.
137 Koester, Craig R., *Symbolism in the Fourth Gospel: Meaning, Mystery, Community* (Minneapolis, MN: Fortress Press, 1995), 47; Renz, Gabi, "Nicodemus: An Ambiguous Disciple? A Narrative Sensitive Investigation," in *Challenging Perspective on the Gospel of John*, ed. John Lierman (Heidelberg: Mohr Siebeck, 2006), 261.
138 Ford, David F., "Meeting Nicodemus: A Case Study in Daring Theological Interpretation," *Scottish Journal of Theology* 66, no. 1 (2013): 1–17.
139 Neusner, *Babylonian Talmud*, Yebamot 6:6; also, Yebamot 11:2; also, Bekhorot 8:1.
140 Al-Rāzī, *Mafātīḥ*, on Q 8:38, 15: 482–483.
141 Al-Bukhārī, *Ṣaḥīḥ al-Bukhārī*, 2: 133 (#1521). Also Muslim, *Ṣaḥīḥ Muslim*, 2: 983 (#438.1350).
142 See Carroll, John T., "Children in the Bible," *Interpretation* 55, no. 2 (2001): 121–134, esp. n. 26.
143 Mark 10:13–16.
144 Al-Ṭabarī, *Jāmiʿ*, 24: 519–522 on Q. 96:1.
145 *BDB*, 871. Used in various passages of the Hebrew Bible, including Micah 3:6, which talks about prophets.
146 Qurʾan 97:1–5.
147 The connection between being reborn, *laylah al-qadr*, and the Gospel of John is further discussed in Galadari, Abdulla, "*Layla al-Qadr*: Muḥammad Assuming Authority by Alluding to the Gospel of John," in *New Trends in Qurʾanic Studies*, ed. Munʾim Sirry (London: Lockwood Press, forthcoming).
148 John 1:51.
149 Ambrose of Milan (d. 397 CE) suggested that John 1:51 is an allusion to Jacob's ladder. See Ambrose (d. 397 CE), *Seven Exegetical Works*, trans. Michael P. McHugh,

The Fathers of the Church: A New Translation, vol. 65 (Washington, DC: Catholic University of America Press, 1972), 155–156; Neyrey, Jerome H., "The Jacob Allusions in John 1:51," *Catholic Biblical Quarterly* 44, no. 4 (1982): 586–605; Clarke, Ernest. G., "Jacob's Dream at Bethel as Interpreted in the Targums and the New Testament," *Studies in Religion* 4 (1975): 367–377; Rowland, Christopher, "John 1.51, Jewish Apocalyptic and Targumic Tradition," *New Testament Studies* 30, no. 4 (1984): 498–507.

150 Ibn Manẓūr, *Lisān al-ʿarab* on "*s l m*."

Chapter 6: Begotten of God

1 Räisänen, "The Portrait of Jesus."

2 See Bell, *The Origin of Islam*; Claassens, G. H. M., "Jacob van Maerlant on Muhammad and Islam," in *Medieval Christian Perceptions of Islam*, ed. J. V. Tolan (New York, NY: Routledge, 1996), 211–232.

3 The term "*kn*" shares its possible proto-Semitic root in the meaning of establish. See Hecker, Bernice V. "The Biradical Origin of Semitic Roots," PhD diss., University of Texas at Austin, 2007, 107.

4 Donner, *Muhammad and the Believers*, 204; Firestone "Abraham's Son."

5 For a detailed textual analysis of the various terms for begotten and sonship in the Bible refer to Vellanickal, M., *The Divine Sonship of Christians in the Johannine Writings* (Rome: Typis Pontificiae Universitatis Gregorianae, 1976).

6 Bromiley, G. W., *Theological Dictionary of the New Testament*, eds. G. Kittel and G. Friedrich (Grand Rapids, MI: Wm. B. Eerdmans, 1964) 5: 738; Louw, J. P. and Nida, E., eds., *Greek–English Lexicon of the New Testament Based on Semantic Domains* (New York, NY: United Bible Societies, 1989), 1: 590; Bauer, W., *A Greek–English Lexicon of the New Testament and Other Early Christian Literature*, ed. F. W. Danker (Chicago, IL: The University of Chicago Press, 2000), 658.

7 Moulton, J. H. and Milligan, G., *Vocabulary of the Greek Testament* (Peabody, MA: Hendrickson, 1930), 416.

8 See the entry for "*monogenēs*" in Brannan, Rick, *The Lexham Analytical Lexicon to the Greek New Testament* (Bellingham, WA: Logos Research Systems, 2013).

9 Beekes, R., *Etymological Dictionary of Greek* (Leiden: Brill NV, 2010), 1: 266, 1: 272–273.

10 *TDOT*, 1: 681; Schwyzer, E., *Griechische Grammatik: auf der Grundlage von Karl Brugmanns Griechischer Grammatik. Bd. 2: Syntax und syntaktische Stilistik, vervollständigt und hrsg. Von Albert Debrunner. Handbuch der Altertumswissenschaft* (München: C. H. Beck, 1950), 215.

11 Moody, D., "God's Only Son: The Translation of John 3:16 in the Revised Standard Version," *Journal of Biblical Literature* 72, no. 4 (1953): 213–219.

12 Beekes, *Etymological Dictionary of Greek*, 1: 266.

13 Ibid.

14 Ibid.

15 Menken, Maarten J. J., "'Born of God' or 'Begotten by God'? A Translation Problem in the Johannine Writings," *Novum Testamentum* 51 (2009): 352–368.

16 Either "*akun*" or "*akūn*" may be used.

17 The reader is reminded the distinction made in the beginning between the terms of Begotten of God and Son of God, where the latter may be seen in other Gospels.

18 Räisänen, "The Portrait of Jesus," 124.
19 Zaehner, Robert C. "The Qur'ān and Christ," in *At Sundry Times: An Essay in the Comparison of Religions* (London: Faber & Faber, 1958), 209, 216.
20 Haight, Roger, *Jesus, Symbol of God* (Maryknoll, NY: Orbis Books, 1999), 173.
21 Mahmoud Ayoub has attempted to show similarities of the image of Jesus in Shī'ī thought as points of convergence with Christianity. See Ayoub, Mahmoud M., "Towards an Islamic Christology: An Image of Jesus in Early Shī'ī Muslim Literature," *The Muslim World* 66, no. 3 (1976): 163–188.
22 Al-Majlisī (d. 1111/1698), *Biḥār al-anwār, al-jāmi'ah li-durar akhbār al-a'immah al-aṭ-hār* (Beirut: Dār Iḥyā' al-Turāth al-'Arabī, 1983), 53: 46.
23 See Rochais, Gérard, "La formation du Prologue (Jn 1:1–18)," *Science et Esprit* 37, no. 1 (1985): 5–44, 161–187; Schnackenburg, Rudolf, *The Gospel According to St. John*, trans. Kevin Smith (New York, NY: Herder and Herder, 1968), 1: 221–281, 1: 481–505; Tobin, Thomas H., "Logos," in *The Anchor Yale Bible Dictionary*, ed. D. N. Freedman (New York, NY: Doubleday, 1992), 4: 348–356, 348; Dunn, James D. G., *Christology in the Making: A New Testament Inquiry into the Origins of the Doctrine of the Incarnation* (Grand Rapids, MI: Wm. B. Eerdmans, 1996) 239–250; Schnackenburg, Rudolf, *Jesus in the Gospels: A Biblical Christology* (Louisville, KY: Westminster John Knox, 1995), 283–394; Moloney, Francis, *Belief in the Word: Reading John 1–4* (Minneapolis, MN: Fortress Press, 1993).
24 Farrelly, M. John, *The Trinity: Rediscovering the Central Christian Mystery* (Lanham, MD: Rowman & Littlefield, 2005), 50–51.
25 Ibid., 52.
26 Ibid., 53.
27 See Ronning, John L. *The Jewish Targums and John's Logos Theology* (Peabody, MA: Hendrickson, 2010), 5; Tobin "Logos," 4: 354.
28 Farrelly, *The Trinity*, 51.
29 Bultmann, Rudolf, *Das Evangelium des Johannes* (Göttingen: Vandenhoeck & Ruprecht, 1941). There are several scholars who argue that John's prologue is Gnostic; the following references are from: Evans, Craig A. *Word and Glory: On the Exegetical and Theological Background of John's Prologue* (Sheffield: Sheffield Academic Press, 1993); see Deeks, David G., "The Prologue of St. John's Gospel," *Biblical Theology Bulletin* 6, no. 1 (1976): 62–78. For further analyses of John's prologue and perhaps its Gnostic or Hellenic Jewish tendencies, also see Schlier, Heinrich, "'Im Anfang war das Wort' im Prolog des Johannesevangeliums," *Wort und Wahrheit* 9 (1954): 169–180; Schnackenburg, Rudolf, "Logos-Hymnus und johanneischen Prolog," *Biblische Zeitschrift* 1 (1957): 69–109; Schnackenburg, Rudolf, "Und das Wort ist Fleisch geworden," *Internationale Katholische Zeitschrift* 8 (1979): 1–9; Eltester, Walther, "Der Logos und sein Prophet: Fragen zur heutigen Erklärung des johanneischen Prologs," in *Apophoreta: Festschrift fur Ernst Haenchen*, eds. Walter Eltester and Franz H. Kettler (Berlin: Verlag Alfred Töpelmann, 1964), 109–134; Langkammer, P. H., "Zur Herkunft des Logostitels im Johannesprolog," *Biblische Zeitschrift* 9 (1965): 91–94; Ridderbos, Herman N., "The Structure and Scope of the Prologue to the Gospel of John," *Novum Testamentum* 8, nos. 2/4 (1966): 180–201; Demke, Christoph, "Der sogenannte Logos-Hymnus im johanneischen Prolog," *Zeitschrift für die neutestamentliche Wissenschaft* 58, nos. 1/2 (1967): 45–68; Fascher, Erich, "Christologie und Gnosis im vierten Evangelium," *Theologische Literaturzeitung* 93, no. 10 (1968): 721–730; O'Neill, J. C., "The Prologue to St John's Gospel," *Journal of Theological Studies* 20, no. 1 (1969): 41–52; Wengst, Klaus, *Christologische Formeln und Lieder im Urchristentums* (SNT, 7,

Gütersloh: Gerd Mohn, 1972), 200–208; Zimmermann, Heinrich, "Christushymnus und johanneischer Prolog," in *Neues Testament und Kirche*, ed. Joachim Gnilka (Freiburg: Herder, 1974), 249–265; de la Potterie, Ignace, "Structure du Prologue de Saint Jean," *New Testament Studies* 30, no. 3 (1984): 354–381; Sevrin, Jean-Marie, "Le quatrième évangile et le gnosticisme: questions de méthode," in *Communauté johannique et son histoire: La trajectoire de l'Evangile de Jean aux deux premiers siècles* (Geneva: Labor et Fides, 1990), 249–268.

30 Evans, *Word and Glory*, 47–76.

31 Ibid., 75–76.

32 There is a scholarly debate between the origins of Gnosticism and its relationship with Jewish mysticism. Gershom G. Scholem suggests that Kabbalah might have emerged from Gnostic influences into Rabbinic Judaism. Possibly, pre-Christian Jewish Gnosticism might have existed and perhaps caused early Christian heresies, since Christian Gnosticism may bear a resemblance to Merkabah Mysticism as found in Hebrew and Aramaic texts, known as *Hekhaloth Books* during the early Talmudic period. He suggests that Gnosticism might have emerged from a rabbinic culture; see Scholem, Gershom G. *Jewish Gnosticism, Merkabah Mysticism and Talmudic Tradition* (New York, NY: The Jewish Theological Seminary of America, 1960). Moshe Idel challenged this notion suggesting that Kabbalah emerged from Rabbinic Judaism without any foreign influence; see Idel, Moshe *Kabbalah: New Perspectives* (New Haven, CT: Yale University Press, 1988). Mystical traditions, generally, share much in common, e.g., see Katz, Steven T., ed. *Comparative Mysticism: An Anthology of Original Sources* (Oxford: Oxford University Press, 2013). For looking into pre-Christian Gnosticism, the *Nag Hammadi Library* may shed some light to such an existence, which was then later Christianized. For debates for the existence of pre-Christian Gnosticism see Bultmann, Rudolf, "Die Bedeutung der neuerschlossenen mandäischen und manichäischen Quellen für das Verständnis des Johannesevangeliums," *Zeitschrift für die neutestamentliche Wissenschaft* 24 (1925): 100–145; Reicke, Bo, "Traces of Gnosticism in the Dead Sea Scrolls?" *New Testament Studies* 1, no. 2 (1954): 137–141; Yamauchi, Edwin M. *Pre-Christian Gnosticism: A Survey of the Proposed Evidences* (London: Tyndale Press, 1973); Yamauchi, Edwin M., "Pre-Christian Gnosticism in the Nag Hammadi Texts?" *Church History* 48, no. 2 (1979): 129–141. For debates against the existence of pre-Christian Gnosticism, see King, Karen L. *What Is Gnosticism?* (Cambridge, MA: Harvard University Press, 2003), 71–72, 83–84, 148, 181–190. Since Gnosticism and Kabbalah are both mystical traditions and may share similarities, this does not necessarily mean that one has influenced the other. Perhaps the neuroscience of the brain and the psychology of the mind, which humans share, provide similar insights for the simple reason that our genes are all related. If a person can distinguish the green color from the blue (assuming a person is neither blind nor color-blind and there is enough light for the eyes to perceive the different wavelengths) and another person can do the same, it does not at all mean that one has influenced the other. It is because our perception due to the common neural network is biologically the same. Those two persons may name the colors differently (like two different religious traditions with different semantics), but at least share the common concept that they are distinguished from one another. If mysticism is based on experiential insights that the mind may attempt to contextualize with its own understanding and presuppositions, then similarities between different mystical traditions should not be assumed as one necessarily influencing the other historically, but rather is best explained biologically; see d'Aquili, Eugene and Newberg, Andrew, *The Mystical Mind:*

Probing the Biology of Religious Experience (Minneapolis, MN: Fortress Press, 1999); d'Aquili, Eugene and Newberg, Andrew, *Why God Won't Go Away: Brain Science and the Biology of Belief* (New York, NY: Ballantine Books, 2001).

33 Dodd, Charles H., *Interpretation of the Fourth Gospel* (Cambridge: Cambridge University Press, 1953), 54–73.

34 Evans, *Word and Glory*, 83–94.

35 Dunn, *Christology in the Making*, 241.

36 Philo, *Philo* eds. F. H. Colson and G. H. Whitaker (Cambridge, MA: Harvard University Press, 1929–1962), "De Sacrficiis Abelis et Caini," 8; also a variant in "De Fuga et Inventione," 94–95.

37 Ibid., 65; also a variant in Philo, *Philo*, "De Vita Mosiis," 1.281.

38 A tradition attributed to ʿAlī ibn Abī Ṭālib portrays him stating, "*kn f-yakūn* is neither a sound that is rung nor a call that is listened to, but His words are an action that is made and performed. It was not before it existing, and if it were pre-existing, it would have been a second God," ʿAlī ibn Abī Ṭālib, *Nahj al-balāghah*, ed. Fāris al-Ḥassūn (Qom: Markaz al-Abḥāth al-ʿAqāʾidiyyah, 1999), Sermon 186, 427.

39 Miller, Ed L., "The Johannine Origins of the Johannine Logos," *Journal of Biblical Literature* 112, no. 3 (1993): 445–457.

40 Ibid.

41 Ibid.

42 It is not a concern here on Johannine origin of the Logos, whether it is to be understood as the "Word of God" (*dabar Yahweh*) from the Hebrew Bible or the late Jewish Sophia (Wisdom), as found in the wisdom literature and argued by Rudolf Bultmann or through any Hellenistic, Gnostic, or other definitions. Ed L. Miller suggests that it may not be necessary to identify the origins of Johannine Logos beyond the writings of John. See Miller, "The Johannine Origins." Here in this section, only how the Qurʾan interprets John's Logos is highlighted, without delving in its possible origins beyond the Bible.

43 John 1:1. This alternative rendition is from the Nestle-Aland (NA28) *Novum Testamentum Graece*, www.nestle-aland.com/en/read-na28-online/.

44 Moloney, *Belief in the Word*, 28.

45 Not only is it in the beginning of the sentence, but also in the beginning of the book. See León, D. Muñoz "El Pentateuco en San Juan," in *Entrar en lo Antiguo: Acerca de la relación entre Antiguo y Nuevo Testamento*, eds. I. Carbajosa and L. Sánchez Navarro, Presencia y diálogo 16 (Madrid: Facultad de Teología "San Dámaso," 2007), 107–166, esp. 153.

46 See Lenski, R. C. H., *The Interpretation of St. John's Gospel* (Minneapolis, MN: Augsburg, 1961), 27; Borgen, Peder J., "The Prologue of John—as Exposition of the Old Testament," in *Philo, John and Paul: New Perspectives on Judaism and Early Christianity*, Brown Judaic Studies, 131 (Atlanta, GA: Scholars Press, 1987), 75–102; Pagels, E. H., "Exegesis of Genesis 1 in the Gospels of Thomas and John," *Journal of Biblical Literature* 118, no. 3 (1999): 477–496; Painter, J., "Rereading Genesis in the Prologue of John?" in *Neotestamentica et Philonica*, eds. D. E. Aune, T. Seland, and J. H. Ulrichsen (Leiden: Brill, 2003), 179–201; Lioy, Dan, *The Search for Ultimate Reality: Intertextuality Between the Genesis and Johannine Prologues* (New York, NY: Peter Lang, 2005); Menken, Maarten J. J., "Genesis in John's Gospel," in *Studies in John's Gospel and Epistles: Collected Essays* (Leuven: Peeters, 2015), 131–145, esp. 137–139.

47 *Genesis Rabbah*, 2:4, 17. See Brown, Jeannine K., "Creation's Renewal in the Gospel of John," *The Catholic Biblical Quarterly* 72, no. 2 (2010): 275–290.

48 John 1:3.
49 The Logos described as speech is found in writings by Tertullian (d. 225 CE), Cyprian (d. 258 CE), and Ambrose (d. 397 CE). However, Tertullian in *Adversus Praxean 8* rejects the Gnostic notion that the Logos is simply God's spoken word and uttered speech, which is separate and ignorant of the Father. See Osborn, E. *Tertullian: First Theologian of the West* (Cambridge: Cambridge University Press, 2003), 123–124; Lapide, C. *The Great Commentary*, trans. T. W. Mossman (Edinburgh: John Grant, 1908), 20.
50 Commenting on "I am who I am," Philo suggests that there is no name for God, because it cannot be described; as such, it is only to be (*eimi*), Philo, *Philo*, "De Somniis," 1.230.
51 See Brownlee, W. H., "The Ineffable Name of God," *Bulletin of the American Schools of Oriental Research* 226 (1977): 39–46; Janzen, J. Gerald, "What's in a Name? 'Yahweh' in Exodus 3 and the Wider Biblical Context," *Interpretation* 33, no. 3 (1979): 227–239; Buber, Martin, *Moses: The Revelation and the Covenant* (New York, NY: Harper and Brothers, 1958), 53. Also compare with the following: Parke-Taylor, Geoffrey H. *Yahweh: The Divine Name in the Bible* (Waterloo, ON: Wilfrid Laurier University Press, 1975); de Moor, Johannes C. *The Rise of Yahwism: The Roots of Israelite Monotheism*, revised edn. (Leuven: Peeters, 1997), 108–136; Mettinger, Tryggve N. D., *Namnet och närvaron: Gudsnamn och gudsbild I Böckernas Bok* (Örebro: Bokforlaget Libris, 1987); Ahlstrom, Gosta W. *Who Were the Israelites?* (Winona Lake, IN: Eisenbrauns, 1986), 59–60; Reisel, Max, *The Mysterious Name of Y. H. W. H.: The Tetragrammaton in Connection with the Names of* EHYEH *ašer* EHYEH-*Hūhā-and Šem Hammephôrăs* (Assen: Van Gorcum, 1957); Murtonen, Aimo E., *A Philological and Literary Treatise on the Old Testament Divine Names ʾl, ʾlwh, ʾlhym, and Yhwh* (Helsinki: Societas Orientalis Fennica, 1952). There have been suggestions that the root of "*yhwh*" is possibly "*h w y*," which means to fall, Knauf, Ernst A., "Yahwe," *Vetus Testamentum* 34, no. 4 (1984): 467–472, and perhaps in context could mean "*tajallī*" (immanence) as it is used in Qurʾan 7:143 to denote when God reveals Itself to Moses.
52 See Abba, Raymond, "The Divine Name Yahweh," *Journal of Biblical Literature*, 80 no. 4 (1961): 320–328; Mowinckel, Sigmund, "The Name of the God of Moses," *Hebrew Union College Annual* 32 (1961): 121–133; Kosmala, Hans, "The Name of God (YHWH and HUʾ)," *Annual of the Swedish Theological Institute* 2 (1963): 103–120.
53 Nelson, W. D. trans., *Mekhilta De-Rabbi Shimon bar Yoḥai* (Philadelphia, PA: The Jewish Publication Society, 2006), Tractate Sanya, 2:2, 1B, p. 6.
54 Evans, *Word and Glory*, 79–83; Boismard, Marie-Émile, *St. John's Prologue* (Westminster: Newman, 1957), 135–145; Hooker, Morna D., "The Johannine Prologue and the Messianic Secret," *New Testament Studies* 21, no. 1 (1974): 40–58; Hanson, Anthony T., "John i. 14–18 and Exodus xxxiv," *New Testament Studies* 23, no. 1 (1976): 90–101; Hanson, Anthony T., *The New Testament Interpretation of Scripture* (London: SPCK, 1980), 97–109; Rissi, Mathias, "John 1:1–18 (The Eternal Word)," *Interpretation*, 31 no. 4 (1977): 395–401; Koester, Craig R., *The Dwelling of God: The Tabernacle in the Old Testament, Intertestamental Jewish Literature, and the New Testament* (Washington, DC: Catholic Biblical Association, 1989), 104.
55 Evans, *Word and Glory*, 80.
56 Ibid., 80–81.
57 "Or the only One, who is God." Some manuscripts: "the only Son."
58 In al-Ṭabarī's *tafsīr*, there is a debate on what "*wālid*" means, with some suggesting perhaps Adam, and what "*kbd*" means, with some suggesting perhaps uprightness, heaven, or hardship. See al-Ṭabarī, *Jāmiʿ*, 24: 431–435 on Q. 90:3–4. In Hebrew it

means heaviness, weighty, abundance, or riches, which might give the sense of someone's honor or glory. See *BDB*, 457–459. If it means abundance and wealth, then this may contextualize the term "*lbd*" in Qur'an 90:6, which also is used to mean abundance and wealth. The root "*k b d*" may be derived from the proto-Semitic "*kb*," which means weighty: see Hecker, "The Biradical Origin," 105. There is a Byzantine Greek translation of the Qur'an that translates "*kabad*" as "*se iskhu*" (in strength), which might suggest that it could have been understood as glory. Adel-Théodore Khoury and Christian Høgel report it, but do not understand the reason it is translated the opposite way of what Muslim exegetes later assumed: see Khoury, Adel-Théodore, *Les théologiens byzantins et l'islam: Textes et auteurs [VIIIe-XIIIe siècles]* (Leuven: Nauwelaerts, 1969), 120; and Høgel, Christian, "An Early Anonymous Greek Translation of the Qur'an: The Fragments from Niketas Byzantios' *Refutatio* and the Anonymous *Abjuratio*," *Collectanea Christiana Orientalia* 7 (2010): 65–119, 110.

59 Since the first verse affirms the unity of God, then the "*ṣamad*" in the second is more likely to mean indivisible, inseparable, bound, or yoke: *BDB*, 855. This would be cognate to "*ḍamad*," which means to join a wound or a pair of cattle: see Ibn Manẓūr, *Lisān al-ʿarab*, 3: 264–266 on "*ḍ m d*." In traditional *tafsīr*, such as al-Ṭabarī, there are various opinions for the meaning of "*ṣamad*." Among those conjectures are: (i) the one who is worshipped, (ii) the one who is not hollow, (iii) the one who neither eats nor drinks, and (iv) the one who nothing extracts: see al-Ṭabarī, *Jāmiʿ*, 24: 689–691 on Q. 112:2. Among its various meanings, it also means one's goal: Ibn Manẓūr, *Lisān al-ʿarab*, 3: 258–259 on "*ṣ m d*." A Byzantine Greek translation of the Qur'an by Theodore Abū Qurra (*c.*750–825 CE) translates "*ṣamad*" as "*sphyropēktos*," which means hammered together or closely united: van Ess, Josef, *The Youthful God: Anthropomorphism in Early Islam* (Tempe, AZ: Arizona State University, 1988), 5. Sometimes it is translated as beaten solid into a ball: Sahas, Daniel J., " 'Holosphyros'? A Byzantine Perception of 'the God of Muhammad,' " in *Christian–Muslim Encounters*, eds. Yvonne Y. Haddad and Wadi Z. Haddad (Gainesville, FL: University Press of Florida, 1995), 111; Griffith, Sidney H., "Byzantium and the Christians in the World of Islam: Constantinople and the Church in the Holy Land in the Ninth Century," *Medieval Encounters* 3, no. 3 (1997): 231–265, 262; or a hammered solid: Thāwdhūrus Abū Qurrah, *Schriften zum Islam*, eds. and trans. Reinhold Glei and Adel T. Khoury (Würzburg: Echter, 1995), 99. Nicetas of Byzantium (842–912 CE) later translates "*ṣamad*" as "*holosphyros*," meaning impenetrable: Förstel, Karl, ed. and trans. "Nicetas of Byzantium," *Schriften zum Islam* (Würzburg: Echter, 2000), 117; or entirely chased in metal: van Ess, *The Youthful God*, 5; or solid hammered metal: Meyendorff, John, "Byzantine Views of Islam," *Dumbarton Oaks Paper* 18 (1964): 113–132, 122; and Hanson, Craig L., "Manuel I Comnenus and the 'God of Muhammad': A Study in Byzantine Ecclesiastical Politics," in *Medieval Christian Perceptions of Islam: A Book of Essays*, ed. John V. Tolan (New York, NY: Garland, 1996), 61 and 75; or solid metal made into a sphere: Sahas " 'Holosphyros'?" 109. Most scholars believe that it is a mistranslation, or perhaps biased for polemical reasons. Sidney Griffith suggests that perhaps the Byzantines thought Muslims believe in a material, corporeal God: Griffith, "Byzantium and the Christians," 262. Christos Simelidis suggests that the Greek translations, which perhaps mean massive and solid, are accurate to the Arabic understanding of the term "*ṣamad*," during the ninth century CE: Simelidis, Christos "The Byzantine Understanding of the Qur'anic Term *al-Ṣamad* and the Greek Translation of the Qur'an," *Speculum* 86, no. 4 (2011): 887–913. If this were perhaps true, it might suggest why later Muslim exegetes had some kind of confusion of the

term "*ṣamad*." However, if we attempt to interpret Qur'an 112 as engaging with the *Shema* and perhaps the Athanasian and Nicene Creeds, as will be shown further, then it may more accurately be understood as God's covenant (the yoke of God) or perhaps more precisely, indivisible.

60 See Hirschfeld, Hartwig, *New Researches into the Composition and Exegesis of the Qoran* (London: Royal Asiatic Society, 1902), 35; Neuwirth, Angelika, "The Qur'an in the Field of Conflict Between the Interpretative Communities: An Attempt to Cope with the Crisis of Qur'anic Studies," in *Fundamentalism and Gender: Scripture-Body-Community*, eds. Ulrike Auga, Christina von Braun, Claudia Bruns, and Jana Husmann (Eugene, OR: Pickwick Publications, 2013), 123–124.

61 Deuteronomy 6:4.

62 Refer to Neusner, *Jerusalem Talmud*, Berakhot 2:1.

63 See the previous note on "*ṣamad*" and its possible connection to "*ḍamad*." *BDB*, 855. For few examples, compare its use in Numbers 25:3, 25:5, and Psalm 106:28. It has also been used to mean couple or pair (perhaps in the meaning of them being yoked together); for examples, compare in Judges 19:3, 19:10, and 1 Kings 19:19.

64 See Neusner, *Babylonian Talmud*, Berakhot 2:2. Also in Basri, Moshe, *Narratives of the Talmud: A Collection of Aggadot in the Babylonian and Jerusalem Talmuds and the Tosefta*, trans. Edward Levin (Jerusalem: Haktab Institute, 1994), 1: 24; Soloveitchik, Joseph B. *Worship of the Heart: Essays on Jewish Prayer*, ed. Shalom Carmy (New York, NY: Toras HoRav Foundation, 2003), 108. Also refer to Neusner, *Jerusalem Talmud*, Berakhot 2:1.

65 Al-Ṭabarī, *Jāmiʿ*, 24: 687–688 on Q. 112:1–4.

66 See Clark, Matityahu, *Etymological Dictionary of Biblical Hebrew: Based on the Commentaries of Samson Raphael Hirsch* (Jerusalem: Feldheim Publishers, 1999), 57. Compare with Klein, Ernst, *A Comprehensive Etymological Dictionary of the Hebrew Language for Readers of English* (Jerusalem: Carta, 1987), see entry on "*hwa*." Also see Fried, Isaac, *The Analytic and Synthetic Etymology of the Hebrew Language* (Boston, MA: The Hebrew Etymology Project, 2004), see entry on "*hwa*." In my opinion, the terms "*hwa*" (masculine) and "*hya*" (feminine) might be derived from "*ha*," which means to be or to exist. Because it is a third person pronoun, meaning the person is not necessarily present, it could be the reason why it uses the term to be or to exist to explicitly say, though not present, the person exists. Julian Morgenstern states:

> For, as is well known, in Hebrew—and in fact in all Semitic languages to a greater or less degree—the personal pronouns discharge a unique function: "*hwa*," for example, means not only "he," but also "he is," or perhaps somewhat more precisely, "the one who is" or "the one who exists."
>
> Morgenstern, Julian, "Deutero-Isaiah's Terminology for 'Universal God,'" *Journal of Biblical Literature* 62, no. 4 (1943): 273–274 (transliteration is mine)

67 The third person pronoun is sometimes substituted for or in conjunction with Yahweh in the Hebrew Bible (e.g., Deuteronomy 32:39, 2 Kings 2:14, Psalm 102:27, Isaiah 41:4, 43:10–13, 46:4, 48:12, Jeremiah 3:12). Bernhard Duhm suggests that Yahweh is an extension of "*hw*" (He), as God is called by some Arabs, as cited in Abba, "The Divine Name," 321–322. However, there are scholars that dismiss the connection between them: Abba, "The Divine Name," 320–328. Nonetheless, Isaiah 41:4 states, "I, *YHWH*, the first, and with the last ones; I am He (*hwa*)." Julian Morgenstern discusses this verse and states:

> But the question arises immediately, just what is the actual implication of "*hwa*." "He" is only a literal translation of the pronoun, but as such is almost meaningless. It is impossible to escape the conviction that the prophet had in mind something more specific than this, when he employed the pronoun here. Obviously in this distich "*hwa*" is in absolute parallelism with "*YHWH*"; and this parallelism suggests that "*hwa*" itself is a term which Deutero-Isaiah employs as a designation of the Universal God in precisely the same manner and with precisely the same implication as "*YHWH*."
>
> Morgenstern, "Deutero-Isaiah's Terminology," 271 (transliteration is mine)

Morgenstern continues giving examples from Isaiah and stating:

> Apparently "*hwa*" stands by itself, in syntactical isolation altogether out of keeping with its use as a pronoun. Seemingly "hwa" is here used as a noun, a name or designation of the Deity, as in fact a synonym of "*YHWH*" in the connotation, "the Universal God."
>
> Morgenstern, "Deutero-Isaiah's Terminology," 272 (transliteration is mine)

After giving many examples, Morgenstern concludes:

> All these passages lend added confirmation to our interpretation of the terms, 'YHWH' and 'hwa,' as used by Deutero-Isaiah as a designation for God, with the specific implication of 'the eternally existent One, the Eternal,' and show the strong influence which this great prophetic writer exerted upon the thought, theology, and literary style of the immediately ensuing age.
>
> Morgenstern, "Deutero-Isaiah's Terminology," 279 (transliteration is mine)

James Montgomery also suggests the connection between Yahweh and "Hū." However, he dismisses the relationship between Yahweh and the verb to be (*hyh*) in favor of "*hwa*." Montgomery, James A., "The Hebrew Divine Name and the Personal Pronoun Hū," *Journal of Biblical Literature* 63, no. 2 (1944): 161–163. As stated above in this note and the previous one, both Yahweh and "*hwa*" are probably related to the verb to be (*hyh*), and therefore dismissing Yahweh's relationship with "*hyh*" is perhaps misleading; Mowinckel, "The Name of the God of Moses," 121–133; Kosmala, "The Name of God," 103–120.

68 Ibn Manẓūr, *Lisān al-ʿarab*, 7: 26–29 on "*khlṣ*."

69 *BDB*, 322–323. Koehler and Baumgartner, *The Hebrew and Aramaic Lexicon of the Old Testament*, 321–322. Kaufmann, Stephen A., ed. *Targum Lexicon: Comprehensive Aramaic Lexicon Project* (Cincinnati, OH: Hebrew Union College, n.d.). From the meaning to withdraw may come the meanings to escape or to deliver, in which the meaning of salvation may be attributed to it. See *TDOT*, 4: 436–437, on "*ḥ l ṣ*."

70 Deuteronomy 6:5.

71 See Neusner, *Babylonian Talmud*, Berakhot 9:5; Neusner, *Jerusalem Talmud*, Berakhot 9:5.

72 Ibid.

73 Ibid.

74 Neuwirth, Angelika "The Two Faces of the Qurʾān: Qurʾān and Muṣḥaf," *Oral Tradition* 25, no. 1 (2010): 141–156, 153; Neuwirth, Angelika, *Der Koran als Text der Spatantike: Ein europaischer Zugang* (Frankfurt: Verlag der Weltreligionen im Insel Verlag, 2010).

75 The Nicene Creed, as adopted in 325 CE, did not originally explicitly give the Holy Spirit a status in the Godhead. The amendment to the Nicene Creed took place in the

First Council of Constantinople in 381 CE, which mentions the Holy Spirit as the Lord and Giver of life that proceeds from the Father. Just to note, the Holy Spirit in Judaism is not another person of the Godhead, but is an attribute of God's presence and power. Unlike the Nicene Creed, the pseudo-Athanasian Creed is not a product of an Ecumenical Council. It is attributed to Athanasius of Alexandria (d. 373 CE), but scholars believe it was written much after his death and that it is neither a creed nor written by Athanasius. Its origins are ambiguous. It appears to have originated in Europe in Latin. See Haring, Nicholas M., "Commentaries on the Pseudo-Athanasian Creed," *Medieval Studies* 34 (1972): 208–252; Krueger, Robert, "The Origin and Terminology of the Athanasian Creed," *Western Pastoral Conference of the Dakota-Montana District*, October 5–6 (1976). Philip Schaff states, "it appears first in its full form towards the close of the eighth or the beginning of the ninth century," Schaff, Philip, *Creeds of Christendom* (Grand Rapids, MI: Baker Book House, 1977), 36. This suggests that its relationship with the Qur'an is perhaps highly unlikely. However, the foundations that made this creed might have already existed and been debated among different Christian churches during the time of the Qur'an. For one of the early scholarly histories of the Athanasius Creed, see Waterland, Daniel, *A Critical History of the Athanasian Creed*, ed. John R. King (Oxford: James Parker, 1870).

76 Partly perhaps because the pseudo-Athanasian Creed may be seen as logically inconsistent allowing for contradictions to coexist. This does not mean that it is untrue, but that it allows for many ambiguities. See Cartwright, Richard, "On the Logical Problem of the Trinity," in *Philosophical Essays* (Cambridge, MA: MIT Press, 1990), 187–200.

77 Walhout, Edwin, *Christianity Down to Earth: Where We Are and Where We Should Be Going* (n.p.: Lulu Press, 2015), 179–180.

78 For more on Tertullian (d. 225 CE) refer to his treatise "Adversus Praxean." This was Tertullian's defense against Monarchianism, which emphasized God being one person. Tertullian, "Adversus Praxean," in *The Ante-Nicene Fathers*, eds. Alexander Roberts and James Donaldson (Buffalo, NY: The Christian Literature Company, 1885).

79 Ambrose, "On the Holy Spirit," #83, in Schaff, *A Select Library of the Nicene and Post-Nicene Fathers*, 10: 147.

80 On "Let there be" in Genesis 1:3 Sarna in his commentary states, "The directive *yehi*, found again in verses 6 and 14, is reserved for creation of celestial phenomena. Its usage here may be an allusion to the divine personal name YHVH." Found in Sarna, N. M., *The JPS Torah Commentary: Genesis* (Philadelphia, PA: The Jewish Publication Society, 1989), 7.

81 John 8:58.

82 1 Corinthians 7:31.

83 Acts 17:28.

84 2 Corinthians 1:19.

85 Exodus 3:14. Ambrose, "Letter 79," as translated in Beyenka, Mary M., trans., *Saint Ambrose Letters*, The Fathers of the Church: A New Translation, vol. 26 (Washington, DC: Catholic University of America, 1954), 437–447, 443.

86 The source extrapolates from Ambrose's "Letter 79" by stating, "The Word of God Is Yahweh, the One Who Is." In Elowsky, Joel C., ed., *Ancient Christian Commentary on Scripture: New Testament IVa, John 1–10* (Downers Grove, IL: InterVarsity Press, 2006), 1: 15.

87 The *TSQ* translates "*waladā*" as "taken a child." To conform with the thesis perpetuated in this chapter, I keep "has begotten" as the translation of this term.

88 Qur'an 2:116–117.
89 Qur'an 19:34–35.
90 Further discussion on the Incarnation of the Word and the creation of Jesus' physical body from the Qur'anic point of view appears in Chapter 7.
91 For more on the topic, see Martin, Richard C., "Createdness of the Qur'ān," *Encyclopedia of the Qur'ān*, ed. Jane D. McAuliffe (Leiden: Brill, 2005); Nawas, John A., "A Reexamination of Three Current Explanations for al-Ma'mun's Introduction of the Miḥna," *International Journal of Middle East Studies* 26, no. 4 (1994): 615–629. There is some ambiguity on the Shī'ī view. The Qur'an is usually considered created, but sometimes is referred to as "*muḥdath*," which may be interpreted as something with a temporal existence: al-Muḥaqqiq al-Ḥillī (d. 676/1277), *al-Maslak fī uṣūl al-dīn wa talīh al-risālah al-māti'iyyah*, ed. Riḍa al-Ustādī (Mashhad: Mujamma' al-Buḥūth al-Islāmiyyah, 1994). Ja'far al-Ṣādiq (d. 148/765) considered the Qur'an neither created nor coeternal, Ibn Bābawayh (d. 381/991), *al-Tawḥīd*, ed. Hāshim al-Ḥusaynī al-Ṭahrānī (Qom: Manshūrāt Jamā'ah al-Mudarrisīn fil-Ḥawzah al-'Ilmiyyah, 1978), 223–228; al-Shākrī, Ḥusayn, *al-Ṣādiq Ja'far 'alayh al-salām, Mawsū'ah al-muṣṭafa wal-'itrah (9)* (Qom: Nashr al-Hādī, 1997), 490–493. If a person speaks, their speech is neither created nor has it existed with the person since his existence. Nonetheless, some view that Ja'far al-Ṣādiq simply did not want to enter into a debate that appeared to have political motivations.
92 Qur'an 3:59. *TSQ* translates "*fa-yakūn*" in this instance as "was," as an exegetical inference of Adam's creation in the past. However, the Arabic term is in the present tense.
93 The term "*fa-*" used is grammatically known to have two meanings, conjoining (*'aṭf*) and following (*ittibā'*). This means that the conjoining also implies sequence (*tartīb*). See al-Mūṣalī, *al-Khaṣā'iṣ* (Cairo: Al-Hay'ah al-Miṣriyyah al-'Āmmah lil-Kitāb, n.d.), 2: 198. Looking at it from the grammatical understanding, if it says "*kun wa-yakūn*," it would mean "Be and (same time) it is." This would imply only conjunction without sequence. However, if it says "*kun thumma yakūn*," it would mean "Be, then (after a while) it is." This would imply sequence, but unlike "*fa-*," it does not assume necessarily an immediate consequence.
94 Aḥmad Ibn Ḥanbal states that the Qur'an differentiates creation (*khlq*) from command (*amr*) considering "Is it not His the division (creation) and the command (*alā lahu al-khalq wal-amr*)" (i.e., Qur'an 7:54) as a point showing that the terms are mutually exclusive. He states that the command (*amr*) is uncreated, since it is God's speech, Ibn Ḥanbal, *al-Radd*, 39–40, 106–107. Although he suggests that "*khlq*" requires "*amr*," basing it on Qur'an 16:40, Ibn Ḥanbal, *al-Radd*, 128, 164–165, the verse does not explicitly state that the "*amr*" is for creation and Qur'an 3:59, as discussed, shows, at least in that instance, creation (*khlq*) preceded being (*takwīn*). If, according to Ibn Ḥanbal, the "*amr*," which is "*kn*" is uncreated, then using the same logic the spirit (*al-rūḥ*) would also be uncreated, because it is from God's "*amr*" (i.e., Qur'an 17:85). However, this is not the stance of Ibn Ḥanbal, who states that the "*rūḥ*" is created and that Jesus is not the embodiment of the uncreated "*kn*," but is created by the uncreated "*kn*," Ibn Ḥanbal, *al-Radd*, 125–127. Ibn Qayyim states the different opinions on the spirit, according to Muslim thought, and concludes that it is created, although there is no explicit Qur'anic indication that it is. See Ibn Qayyim, *al-Rūḥ fil-kalām 'ala arwāḥ al-amwāt wal-aḥyā' bil-dalā'il min al-kitāb wal-sunnah* (Beirut: Dār al-Kutub al-'Ilmiyyah, n.d.), 144–155.
95 Qur'an 3:45.

96 One of the reasons that Ibn Ḥanbal states that the Word of God, "*kn*," and His command (*amr*) are uncreated, is because they are the agent of creation, Ibn Ḥanbal, *al-Radd*, 40–41. If they were created, then there needs to be another word, which also would be created, to create it, Ibn Ḥanbal, *al-Radd*, 164–165. Therefore, Ibn Ḥanbal sees this as an unending loop. Augustine also argues similarly:

> Now some unbelieving Arian may come forth and say that "the Word of God was made." How can it be that the Word of God was made, when God by the Word made all things? If the Word of God was itself also made, by what other Word was *it* made? But if thou sayest that there is a Word of the Word, I say, that by which *it* was made is itself the only Son of God. But if thou dost not say there is a Word of the Word, allow that that was not made by which all things were made. For that by which all things were made could not be made by itself. Believe the evangelist then. For he might have said, "In the beginning God made the Word:" even as Moses said, "In the beginning God made the heavens and the earth"; and enumerates all things thus: "God said, Let it be made, and it was made." If "said," who said? God. And what was made? Some creature. Between the speaking of God and the making of the creature, what was there by which it was made but the Word? For God said, "Let it be made, and it was made." This Word is unchangeable; although changeable things are made by it, the Word itself is unchangeable.
>
> (Augustine, *Tractates on John*, in Schaff, *A Select Library of the Nicene and Post-Nicene Fathers*, Tractate John 1.11, 7: 10)

For more on the Muslim debate regarding whether or not God's speech is created, refer to Tritton, "The Speech of God."

97 Ibn Manẓūr, *Lisān al-ʿarab*, 10: 503–508 on "*h l k*."

98 *BDB*, 229–237. Also for earlier Semitic usage of "*hlk*" to mean going, see *TDOT*, 3: 388–403.

99 This is not solidly defined if the pre-Islamic Arabs did not believe in an afterlife. Otherwise, this may suggest that they do, though not specifically resurrection of the dead. Yet, another theory is that the meaning of death was used by Semitic communities that believed in an afterlife and that pre-Islamic Arabs might have adopted it to mean death.

100 This will be further explained later in this section.

101 Qurʾan 3:55.

102 Qurʾan 3:47.

103 Qurʾan 19:33–35.

104 John 1:13.

105 John 3:3–8.

106 Qurʾan 17:85.

107 Augustine, Sermon 90.2, as taken from Augustine *Sermons on Selected Lessons of the New Testament*, in P. Schaff, ed., *Saint Augustine: Sermon on the Mount, Harmony of the Gospels, Homilies on the Gospels*, trans. R. G. MacMullen (New York, NY: Christian Literature, 1888) 6: 529.

108 Seim, Turid K., "Descent and Divine Paternity in the Gospel of John: Does the Mother Matter?" *New Testament Studies* 51, no. 3 (2005): 361–375, 375.

109 May, Eric, "The Logos in the Old Testament," *Catholic Bible Quarterly* 8, no. 4 (1946): 438–447; Hayward, C. T. Robert, "The Holy Name of the God of Moses and the Prologue of St John's Gospel," *New Testament Studies* 25, no. 1 (1978): 16–32;

Reed, D. A., "How Semitic Was John? Rethinking the Hellenistic Background to John 1:1," *Anglican Theological Review* 85, no. 4 (2003): 709–726.

110 McNamara, Martin, "*Logos* of the Fourth Gospel and *Memra* of the Palestinian Targum (Ex 12^{42})," *The Expository Times* 79, no. 4 (1968): 115–117.

111 Boyarin, Daniel, "The Gospel of the *Memra*: Jewish Binitarianism and the Prologue to John," *Harvard Theological Review* 94, no. 3 (2001): 243–284, 258.

112 Ibid.

113 Ibid., 259.

114 Ibid., 261.

115 Anderson, Gary, "The Interpretation of Genesis 1:1 in the Targums," *Catholic Biblical Quarterly* 52, no. 1 (1990): 21–29, 28.

116 John 1:14.

117 Ibn Taymiyyah, *al-Jawāb*, 3: 245.

Chapter 7: The Incarnation and the Water of Life

1 Ibn Taymiyyah, *al-Jawāb*, 3: 245.

2 For a more basic overview of early Christian–Muslim dialogues with a strictly traditional Islamic thought, see Beaumont, M. I. *Christology in Dialogue with Muslims: A Critical Analysis of Christian Presentations of Christ for Muslims from the Ninth and Twentieth Centuries* (Carlisle: Paternoster, 2005).

3 Wansbrough, *The Sectarian Milieu*.

4 Sachedina, Abdulaziz, "Islamic Theology of Christian–Muslim Relations," *Islam and Christian–Muslim Relations* 8, no. 1 (1997): 27–38.

5 Qur'an 15:29, 38:72.

6 Ibn Manẓūr, *Lisān al-ʿarab*, 14: 408–417 on "*s w y*."

7 *BDB*, 1000–1001.

8 Ibid.

9 *TDOT*, 14: 522–527, on "*shwh*."

10 Ibid., 14: 525, on "*shwh*." Also see Ibn Manẓūr, *Lisān al-ʿarab*, 11: 610 on "*mthl*." Also consider Isaiah 46:5, which uses these terms as if they were somewhat synonymous.

11 Also see Ibn Manẓūr, *Lisān al-ʿarab*, 11: 610 on "*mthl*."

12 Al-Ṭabarī, *Jāmiʿ* (Q. 15:29), 17: 100.

13 Al-Rāzī, *Mafātīḥ* (Q. 15:29) 19: 139.

14 Ibid.

15 Ibid.

16 Ibid. (Q. 2:34), 2: 427–428.

17 Al-Masʿūdī (d. 346/956), *Murūj al-dhahab wa maʿādin al-jawhar* (Beirut: Dār al-Fikr, 1966), 1: 33.

18 Ḥaqqī, *Rūḥ al-bayān*, 6: 28.

19 The honor of the Kaʿbah is related in prophetic traditions (*aḥādīth*). "Praying in my mosque is better than a thousand prayers in any other, except the Sacred Mosque," from al-Bukhārī, *Ṣaḥīḥ al-Bukhārī*, 2: 60 (#1190); also from Muslim, *Ṣaḥīḥ Muslim*, 2: 1012–1014 (#1394, #1395, #1396).

20 The prophet had said while circumambulating the Kaʿbah, "How good are you and good is your smell. How great are you and great is your sacredness. By the One whose Muḥammad's soul is in His hands, the sacredness of a believer is greater unto God than you, his money, his blood, and to think of him in goodness." Ibn Mājih

(d. 273/887), *Sunan Ibn Mājih*, ed. M. F. Abdul-Bāqī (Cairo: Dār Iḥyā᾽ al-Kutub al-ʿArabiyyah, n.d.) 2: 1297 (#3932).

21 Al-Saqqāf, ʿAlawī ʿA., ed., *al-Mawsūʿah Al-ʿaqdiyyah* (dorar.net 2013), 3: 266; Ibn Abī al-Ḥadīd (d. 656/1258) *Sharḥ nahj al-balāghah* (unknown publisher, n.d.), 13: 4.

22 Al-Shaʿrāwī, *Tafsīr*, 1: 510.

23 Al-Baghawī (d. 516/1122), *Maʿālim al-tanzīl fī tafsīr al-Qur᾽an* (Beirut: Dār Iḥyā᾽ al-Turāth al-ʿArabī, 2000), 1: 104.

24 Al-Rāzī, *Mafātīḥ* (Q. 2:34), 2: 427.

25 Ibn Abī al-Ḥadīd, *Sharḥ nahj al-balāghah*, 13: 4.

26 Imām Ḥassan al-ʿAskarī (d. 260/874) is the eleventh imam of the Twelver Shīʿa school of thought.

27 Al-ʿAskarī, *Tafsīr* (Qom: Madrasat al-Imām al-Mahdī, n.d.), 385. Also reported in Al-Shīrāzī, M., *Nafaḥāt al-Qur᾽an* (unknown publisher, n.d.), 3: 275.

28 Al-Majlisī (d. 1111/1698) *Biḥār al-anwār* (Beirut: Mu᾽assassat al-Wafā᾽, 1984), 11: 140, 16: 402.

29 Galadari, "The *Qibla*."

30 Al-Ṭabarsī, *Majmaʿ* (Q. 28:14), 7: 421.

31 Al-Ṭabarī, *Jāmiʿ*, refer to meaning of (Q. 28:14), 19: 535.

32 Al-Rāzī, *Mafātīḥ*, refer to meaning of (Q. 28:14), 24: 583.

33 Qur᾽an 32:4–9.

34 The term "*istawa ʿala al-ʿarsh*" is usually translated as "established on the throne." The term "*istawa*" is actually very ambiguous. It could mean sitting (*julūs*), but it is not quite sitting. Ibn Taymiyyah in his *Sharḥ* relates from Imām Mālik (d. 179/795) stating, "*Al-Istiwā᾽* (sitting) is known. The how is unknown. Believing in it is obligatory. Asking about it is an innovation" [suggesting that people should not ask about it]. Ibn Taymiyyah (d. 728/1328), *Sharḥ ḥadīth al-nuzūl* (Beirut: al-Maktab al-Islāmī, 1977), 32.

35 Qur᾽an 7:11.

36 For a further understanding of the term "*thumma*" see my discussion in Galadari, "*Creatio ex Nihilo*."

37 The concept of the creation of human progeny is known in some Muslim thought to have occurred already. This concept can be seen in the exegesis of Qur᾽an 22:27, where Abraham calls the people for Ḥajj, and those who believed have already accepted the call. Refer to the interpretation of Qur᾽an 22:27 from several exegetes, such as al-Ṭabarī, *Jāmiʿ*, 18: 605–616, al-Rāzī, *Mafātīḥ*, 23: 218–221, and Ibn Kathīr, *Tafsīr*, 5: 363–364.

38 Hebrews 1:6.

39 Deuteronomy 32:43—Septuagint; Brenton, Lancelot Charles Lee, ed., *The Septuagint Version of the Old Testament, with an English Translation: and with Various Readings and Critical Notes* (London: Samuel Bagster, 1884), 277. There is a Hebrew version of this text found in Qumran, known as *4QDeut32*; for more on this and its relation to Hebrews 1:6, see Cockerill, Gareth L., "Hebrews 1:6: Source and Significance," *Bulletin for Biblical Research* 9 (1999): 51–64.

40 Qur᾽an 3:59. *TSQ* translates "*fa-yakūn*" in this instance as "was," as an exegetical inference of Adam's creation in the past. However, the Arabic term is in the present tense.

41 *BDB*, 9–10.

42 This is further elaborated on in the Hebrew Bible; see Hess, Richard S., "Splitting the Adam: The Usage of ᾽Āadām in Genesis I–V1," *Studies in the Pentateuch* 41 (1990): 1–15. Also, this may be compared with the understanding of the "Son of Man (or Son

of Adam)" title for Jesus using for himself in the Gospels; see Cortés, Juan B. and Gatti, Florence M., "The Son of Man or the Son of Adam," *Biblica* 49, no. 4 (1968): 457–502.

43 *TDOT*, 1: 78, on "*a d m*."

44 Ibid., 1: 75–79, on "*a d m*."

45 Ibid.

46 Ibid., 3: 234–235, on "*dm*."

47 Ibid., 3: 236, on "*dm*." In Arabic, the root of "*dm*" is "*d m y*." See Ibn Manẓūr, *Lisān al-ʿarab*, 14: 267–271, on "*d m y*."

48 Ibn Manẓūr, *Lisān al-ʿarab*, 14: 267–271, on "*d m y*."

49 Ibid., 14: 271, on "*d m y*."

50 Refer to Ibn Manẓūr, *Lisān al-ʿarab* and Al-Zabīdī, *Tāj al-ʿarūs*; *BDB*, 9–10.

51 Ibn Manẓūr, *Lisān al-ʿarab*, 12: 8. Also in Al-Zabīdī, *Tāj al-ʿarūs*, 31: 190.

52 Ibn Manẓūr, *Lisān al-ʿarab*, 12: 12. *Lisān al-ʿarab* only refers due to Adam's creation from clay, which is also called "*adamah*." Also in Al-Zabīdī, *Tāj al-ʿarūs*, 13: 197.

53 Ibn Manẓūr, *Lisān al-ʿarab*, 12: 9.

54 Ibid., 12: 9–10. Also in Al-Zabīdī, *Tāj al-ʿarūs*, 13: 192.

55 Ibn Manẓūr, *Lisān al-ʿarab*, 12: 10. Also in Al-Zabīdī, *Tāj al-ʿarūs*, 13: 193. Both lexicons also portray the possibility of an opposite view, where the "*adamah*" is the epidermis and the "*bashrah*" is the dermis.

56 *Midrash Rabbah*, 1: 56–59.

57 Ibid, 1: 60–61.

58 Chipman, L. N. B., "Adam and the Angels: An Examination of Mythic Elements in Islamic Sources," *Arabica* 49, no. 4 (2002): 429–455.

59 John 2:19–22.

60 Patai, "The Shekhina."

61 Al-Ṭabarī, *Jāmiʿ*, refer to meaning of (Q. 9:26), 14: 189; Al-Rāzī, *Mafātīḥ*, refer to meaning of (Q. 9:26), 16: 19; Al-Ṭabarsī, *Majmaʿ* (Q. 9:26), 5: 32.

62 Ibid., Also see Zayd ibn ʿAlī (d. 122/740), *Tafsīr gharīb al-Qurʾān al-majīd*, ed. M. Y. Al-Dīn (Hyderabad: Taj Yusuf Foundation Trust, 2001), 107.

63 Al-Simnānī (d. 736/1336), *al-Taʾwīlāt al-najmiyyah fī al-tafsīr al-ishārī al-ṣūfī* (Beirut: Dār al-Kutub al-ʿIlmiyyah, 2009), Q. 9:26.

64 Ibn Manẓūr, *Lisān al-ʿarab*, 13: 213. Also in Al-Zabīdī, *Tāj al-ʿarūs*, 35: 198.

65 Al-Ṭabāṭabāʾī, *al-Mīzān*, 2: 294–295.

66 Malachi 3:6. This is based on Ambrose, where the verse is "I am the Lord," while Ambrose uses "I am, I am." This assumes that Ambrose perhaps calls the name of God, Yahweh, as I am, "Ehiyeh," as is also found in Exodus 3:14. This is compiled in Ambrose's (d. 397 CE) "Exposition of the Christian Faith," in *Nicene and Post-Nicene Fathers Second Series, Ambrose: Select Works and Letters*, trans. and ed. Phillip Schaff and Henry Wallace (New York, NY: Cosimo Inc., 2007), 10: 222.

67 See Athanasius (d. 373 CE), *Four Discourses Against the Arians* (n.p.: Fig Books, 2012).

68 The purpose of Chapters 5 to 7 is not to discuss Christology, but only to analyze the Qurʾanic description of creation of human flesh with the text of the Bible. In other words, I am not suggesting that the Qurʾan conveys a message of Incarnation of God in accordance to any creeds within Christianity. These chapters only suggest that there are various ways to interpret the Qurʾan. It could be interpreted in accordance to the Nicene Creed, Chalcedonian, non-Chalcedonian, Nestorian, Arian, etc. This means that one can argue a Chalcedonian creed through the Qurʾan or even a non-Chalcedonian creed. The text allows for multiple meanings. The only thing that the Qurʾan asserts is that Christ had a physical body and was human in every way, and,

hence, it argues against Docetism and some Gnostic beliefs that existed during early Christianity. However, the Qur'an can be interpreted in many other types of Christology that existed in the early Churches.

69 For more information on the early Christological controversies, see Norris Jr., Richard A. ed. *The Christological Controversy* (Philadelphia, PA: Fortress Press, 1980).

70 Al-Dārmī (d. 255/893), *Naqḍ al-Imām Abi Sa'īd 'Uthmān ibn Sa'īd 'Alī Al-Mrīsī al-Jahmī al-'anīd fima iftara 'ala Allāh 'azza wa jall mina al-tawḥīd*, ed. R. Ḥ. Al-Alma'ī (Riyadh: Maktabat al-Rushd, 1998), 2: 675.

71 Al-Kalābādhī, Abu Bakr (d. 380/990), *al-Ta'arruf li-madhhab ahl al-taṣawwuf* (Beirut: Dār al-Kutub al-'Ilmiyyah, n.d.), 68.

72 Ibn Ḥazm, *al-Faṣl*, 2: 130.

73 I use "Spirit" as God's own (perhaps the Holy Spirit). I use "spirit" as a general term of any kind of spirit, whether divine and holy or otherwise.

74 Ibn Ḥazm, 5: 58.

75 Ibn Qayyim, *al-Rūḥ fil-kalām*, 145.

76 Ibid.

77 Ibid.

78 Al-Shīrāzī, M., *al-Amthal fī tafsīr kitāb Allāh al-munzal* (unknown publisher, n.d.), 9: 111. In Al-Shīrāzī's *Tafsīr*, the use of the Spirit in the Qur'an has multiple meanings in different contexts. The Holy Spirit is the Spirit that helps prophets in their message, such as Jesus Christ. It is also used in the context of the angel of inspiration. It is also used in the context of the archangel. Also, it is used as the human spirit, which was used in Adam's creation; Al-Majlisī, *Biḥār al-anwār*, 4: 12, 58: 28, 58: 47, 71: 266; al-Māzandarānī (d. 1086/1699), *Sharḥ uṣūl al-kāfī*, eds. Abu al-Ḥasan al-Sha'rānī and 'Alī 'Āshūr (Beirut: Dār Iḥyā' al-Turāth al-'Arabī, 2000), 4: 122.

79 Imām Muḥammad al-Bāqir (d. 114/733) is the fifth Imām of the Shī'a, including among those who trace their schools to both the Twelver and Ismā'īlī. He is also considered a respected Islamic scholar among Sunni Muslims.

80 Imām Ja'far al-Ṣādiq is the sixth Imām of the Shī'a, also among those who trace their schools to both the Twelver and Ismā'īlī. He is a respected Islamic scholar even among Sunni Muslims. It is reported that the Sunni Imām Abu Ḥanīfah (d. 150/767), founder of the Ḥanafī school of jurisprudence, and Imām Mālik (d. 179/795), founder of the Mālikī school of jurisprudence, studied under Imām al-Ṣādiq. See Ibn al-Jizrī, *Manāqib al-asad al-ghālib mumazziq al-katā'ib wa muẓhir al-'ajā'ib Layth ibn Ghālib amīr al-mu'minīn Abī al-Ḥasan 'Alī ibn Abī Ṭālib*, ed. Ṭ. Al-Ṭanṭawi (Cairo: Maktabat al-Qur'ān, 1994), 83 (#95); Taymūr, Aḥmad (d. 1348/1930), *Naẓrah tārīkhiyya fī ḥudūth al-madhāhib al-fiqhiyya al-arba'ah: al-Ḥanafī, al-Mālikī, al-Shāfi'ī, al-Ḥanbalī, wa intishārihā 'ind jumhūr al-muslimīn* (Beirut: Dār al-Qādirī, 1990), 26.

81 Al-Ḥowayzī (d. 1112/1700), *Tafsīr nūr al-thaqalayn* (unknown publisher, n.d.), 3: 11–13, 3: 215–219.

82 Al-Majlisī (d. 1111/1698), *Mir'āt al-'uqūl fī sharḥ akhbār āl al-rasūl*, ed. Ja'far al-Ḥusaynī (Tehran: Dār al-Kutub al-Islāmiyyah, n.d.), 4: 274.

83 O'Connor, K. M., "The Islamic Jesus: Messiah-hood and Human Divinity in African American Muslim Exegesis," *Journal of the American Academy of Religion* 66, no. 3 (1998): 493–532. In some Muslim thought, including orthodoxy, the Holy Spirit is considered a creature and not divine, although there is no Qur'anic basis to suggest that.

84 For more on the orthodox systematic theology, see Crisp, Oliver D., *God Incarnate: Explorations in Christology* (London: Continuum, 2009).

85 For history of the churches' theology and Christology, see Hall, S. G. *Doctrine and Practice in the Early Church* (Grand Rapids, MI: Wm. B. Eerdmans, 2003).
86 Thomas Aquinas (d. 1274 CE) *Summa Theologica* (London: Burns Oates & Washbourne, n.d.), 3rd Part, Question II, 1st Article, Reply to Objection 3.
87 Zaehner, "The Qur'ān and Christ," 206–207.
88 Ibid., 209.
89 Qur'an 5:17, 5:72.
90 Risse, Günther, *Gott ist Christus, der Sohn der Maria: Eine Studie zum Christusbild im Koran* (Bonn: Borengässer, 1989).
91 A Monophysite Christology suggests that Jesus Christ is of a single nature that is either divine or a synthesis between the divine and human natures. This is based on the Churches that rejected the Council of Chalcedon in 451 CE. In contrast, the Chalcedonian formula maintains that Jesus Christ had two natures, divine and human during the Incarnation, that are distinct. In other words, the Chalcedonian churches maintain that Jesus Christ has two natures in one person.
92 Beaumont, M. I., "Early Christian Interpretation of the Qur'an," *Transformation* 22, no. 4 (2005): 295–203, 200.
93 Ibid.
94 According to orthodox Islam, the Spirit is distinct from God. However, I suggest that the Qur'an does not truly define it as either distinct or otherwise, giving it flexibility for it to be understood as either.
95 Some Gnostics believed that Jesus Christ was a pure spirit with a phantom body, a doctrine known as Docetism. For more information on Gnostic origins and beliefs see King, *What Is Gnosticism?*
96 Qur'an 21:30–35.
97 *BDB*, 135; Koehler and Baumgartner, *The Hebrew and Aramaic Lexicon of the Old Testament*, 53–154; Gesenius, William, *Gesenius' Hebrew-Chaldee Lexicon to the Old Testament* (Bellingham, WA: Logos Bible Software, n.d.), 138–139.
98 Ibn Manẓūr, *Lisān al-ʿarab*, 1: 31 on "*br'*."
99 Qur'an 23:14 uses the term "*khalaqnā*" to be more appropriate to its root meaning of "we divided" instead of its meaning to create in general. For the meanings to portion, to measure, and to smooth, see Ibn Manẓūr, *Lisān al-ʿarab*, 10: 85–92 on "*khlq*," "*akhlaq*," "*khilqah*," "*khalqā'*," and "*khalāq*." For these definitions and more specifically for the meaning of division and splitting, see *BDB*, 322–324.
100 *TDOT*, 2:245, on "*brʿ*."
101 Ibn Manẓūr, *Lisān al-ʿarab*, 10: 114 on "*r t q*." Also see Ibn Kathīr, *Tafsīr*, 5: 339 on Q. 21:30.
102 Ibid., 10: 114 on "*r t q*." Also see al-Ṭabarī (d. 310/923), *Tarīkh al-rusul wal-mulūk* (Beirut: Dār al-Turāth, 1967), 1: 61; Ibn Kathīr, *Tafsīr*, 5: 339 on Q. 21:30.
103 On the meanings of "*fajj*" as a path in a deep or distant valley, refer to Ibn Manẓūr, *Lisān al-ʿarab*, 2: 338–340 on "*f j j*." On the meaning of "*ʿamīq*" as deepness, depth, and distance, refer to Ibn Manẓūr, *Lisān al-ʿarab*, 10: 270–271 on "*ʿo m q*" and "*mutaʿammiq*." In Hebrew and Aramaic, the term "*ʿomq*" means deepness and valley (as a valley is a depth between mountains), and it is used as such in the Hebrew Bible. Refer to *BDB*, 770–771. In most Semitic languages, the meaning used for this term is in some way derived from depth. See *TDOT*, 11: 202–208, on "*ʿa m q*."
104 *Genesis Rabbah*.
105 Also compare with Job 10:19–22. In Job 10:22, the deep is darkness and without any order, which may be compared with Genesis 1:2.

106 Proverbs 9:18.
107 Genesis 1:14–18.
108 *Genesis Rabbah*, 6:1, 42.
109 Ibid., 6:1, 41.
110 Psalm 104:19.
111 Qur᾽an 11:7.
112 *Genesis Rabbah*, 2:4, 17.
113 Rashi (d. 1105 CE), *Torah with Rashi's Commentary* (Brooklyn, NY: Mesorah, 1998), Genesis 1:2.
114 *Genesis Rabbah*, 1:4, 6. The Qur᾽an typically states that God establishes on the Throne after the creation of the heavens and the earth (e.g., Qur᾽an 7:54, 10:3, 13:2, 25:59, 32:4, 57:4). Meanwhile, the midrash states that the Throne of Glory is among the first things created, although a chronology of when that occurred (before or after the creation of the heavens and the earth) is not shown.
115 Qur᾽an 7:54.
116 Some have suggested that "*al-ʿālamīn*" may refer to all creation and creatures. According to Ibn ʿAbbās, it is specifically to people and *jinn*. See al-Ṭabarī, *Jāmiʿ*, 1: 143–146 on Q. 1:2.
117 This would be the Hebrew and Aramaic definition of the word's cognate "*ʿolam*." See *BDB*, 761. The root "*ʿi l m*" means secret, hidden, or concealed. Thus, the age to come, which is presumed to be eternal is hidden, and hence called "*ʿolam*" and not that the root actually means eternity. See *BDB*, 761; *TDOT*, 11: 147–152, on "*ʿalam*." Hence, "*ʿilm*" also means knowledge, as it is knowing things that were unknown earlier. Similarly, the root for the term "*khuld*" in Qur᾽an 21:34 is presumed to mean eternity, but its root actually means to creep in and to penetrate, such as someone creeping into or penetrating through sleep (*khālid fil-nawm*). As such, when people leave this world and penetrate the world to come, it is called "*khuld*," and not that the root actually means eternity. See Ibn Manẓūr, *Lisān al-ʿarab*, 3: 164–165 on "*khld*." Also see *BDB*, 317. Although the *TDOT* does not identify a relationship between the meanings of time and creeping in the term "*khld*" (see *TDOT*, 4: 397–399, on "*ḥ l d*"), it is suggested that the meaning for eternity comes from creeping or penetrating time. The definition of eternity for "*khuld*" and "*ʿolam*" are presumed, but are not necessarily the literal root definitions of the word. This brings into question if either scriptures assert eternity and everlastingness in the world to come or if it is assumed by interpreters.
118 Qur᾽an 10:3–6.
119 Ibn Manẓūr, *Lisān al-ʿarab*, 4: 268–276 on "*d b r*." The Hebrew Bible also sometimes uses it in that definition (e.g., Ecclesiastes 7:14). See Koehler and Baumgartner, *The Hebrew and Aramaic Lexicon of the Old Testament*, 209–210.
120 Ibn Manẓūr, *Lisān al-ʿarab*, 4: 275 on "*d b r*." It is also used in the Hebrew Bible in that definition (e.g., Exodus 5:3). See *BDB*, 183.
121 Ibn Manẓūr, *Lisān al-ʿarab*, 4: 273 on "*d b r*."
122 Ibid., on "*d b r*." Also see *BDB*, 180–184.
123 Ibid., on "*d b r*." Also see *BDB*, 182–183.
124 *BDB*, 180–184. It has been suggested that the etymological root of "*d b r*" meaning back is also used for words or speech is that talking means putting words in motion after another. However, such a connection is not generally accepted by scholars. See *TDOT*, 3: 94–95, on "*d b r*."
125 *BDB*, 184–185.
126 Ibn Manẓūr, *Lisān al-ʿarab*, 4: 274–275 on "*d b r*."

127 *BDB*, 184.
128 As it is being argued that the six days of creation in the Qur'an are allusions to Genesis 1 and have a relationship with the Gospel of John, some scholars have identified John's prologue with an implicit portrayal of a new creation; see Brown, J. K., "Creation's Renewal."
129 The *TDOT* shows a relationship between the terms "*dbr*" and "*amr*." See *TDOT*, 3: 98–100, on "*dbr*." It is suggested that "*dbr*" has a more comprehensive sense of to speak or to converse. As such, it is usually followed by a finite verb form of "*amr*" (e.g., Genesis 19:14, Deuteronomy 20:2–3, Ezekiel 14:4). However, they can also be synonymous sometimes (e.g., Isaiah 40:27).
130 *Genesis Rabbah*, 2:4, 17.
131 Köstenberger, Andreas J. *Encountering John: The Gospel in Historical, Literary, and Theological Perspective* (Grand Rapids, MI: Baker Academic, 2002), 53–57. Nonetheless, Köstenberger compares John's prologue with Isaiah 55:9–11, which uses the term "*dbr*," but the Septuagint does not render it as "*logos*," but as "*rēma*."
132 See Ronning, *The Jewish Targums*. There is no consensus on the dating of the targums. Some scholars suggest they were written well post-Christianity, while others suggest that at least some targums were perhaps written as early as the first century. See Flesher and Chilton, *The Targums*; Hayward, *Targums*; Houtman and Sysling, *Alternative Targum Traditions*; McNamara, *Targum and Testament Revisited*. Nonetheless, this does not dismiss the relationship between Genesis' "*amr*" and Johannine Logos.
133 *TDOT*, 3: 116–125, on "*dbr*."
134 Ibid., 1: 333, on "*amr*."
135 For further uses of "*dbr*" as Word of God, see *TDOT*, 3: 111–112, on "*dbr*."
136 *TDOT*, 1: 338–341, on "*amr*."
137 Ibid., 1: 328, on "*amr*."
138 Ibid.
139 Ibn Manẓūr, *Lisān al-ʿarab*, 4: 32–33 on "*amr*."
140 *TDOT*, 1: 328–329, on "*amr*."
141 See Lincoln, A. T. *Black's New Testament Commentary: The Gospel According to Saint John* (Peabody, MA: Hendrickson, 2006), 94–95.
142 *Genesis Rabbah*, 3:2, 20.
143 Psalm 33:6.
144 *Genesis Rabbah*, 2:4, 17.
145 Exodus 3:14.
146 Exodus 6:2–3.
147 John 1:1–5.
148 *Genesis Rabbah*, 2:5, 19; also 3:6, 22.
149 The Babylonian Talmud makes a connection between the Messiah and the resurrection of the dead. According to a note, it states, "The Talmud treats as self-evident the link between the Messiah and the resurrection of the dead, but the Mishnah has not done so, indeed, has no [*sic*] introduced the Messiah-theme at all. The Talmud then wants to know how the Messiah's coming relates to the resurrection of the dead." In Neusner, *The Babylonian Talmud*, 16: 774.
150 Qur'an 2:116–117.
151 Qur'an 3:47.
152 *TSQ* uses past-tense "was" as a translation of "*yakūn*," but I keep it in the present tense to be consistent with the Arabic term.

153 Qur'an 3:59–60.
154 Qur'an 6:73.
155 There could be wordplay occurring in here with Qur'anic exposition of John's passage, as "*ḥaqq*" is a polysemous term that could mean both truth and law. See Ibn Manẓūr, *Lisān al-'arab*, 10: 49–58 on "*ḥ q q*."
156 *Genesis Rabbah*, 1:7, 4.
157 Psalm 119:160.
158 Qur'an 19:34–35.
159 Al-Ṭabarī, *Jāmi'*, 18: 193–194 on Q. 19:34. Al-Ṭabarī shows that "*al-ḥaqq*" is God; al-Ṭabarsī, *Majma'*, on Q. 19:34. Ibn 'Arabī interprets "*qawl al-ḥaqq*" in this passage as that Jesus is the word of "*al-ḥaqq*," or in other words, the Word of God, as God is "*al-ḥaqq*." Ibn 'Arabī, *Tafsīr*, on Q. 19:34.
160 Unlike the *TSQ* which uses "mankind" as a translation for "*al-nās*," I prefer "humankind."
161 Qur'an 16:38–40.
162 Qur'an 40:68.

Chapter 8: Allegorical Interpretation

1 See Perrine, Laurence, "Four Forms of Metaphor," *College English* 33, no. 2 (1971): 125–138; Crisp, Peter "Between Extended Metaphor and Allegory: Is Blending Enough?" *Language and Literature* 17, no. 4 (2008): 291–308.
2 This section is revised from Galadari, Abdulla, "Inner Meanings of Islamic Finance: Understanding the Theory Behind All Theories," in *Islam, Accounting and Finance: Challenges and Opportunities in the New Decade*, eds. Norhayati M. Alwi and Sherliza P. Nelson (Kuala Lumpur: IIUM Press, 2011), 1–18.
3 Kahf, M., "Islamic Economics: Notes on Definition and Methodology," *Review of Islamic Economics* 13 (2003): 23–38.
4 For the history of interest rates see Homer, S., *A History of Interest Rates* (New Brunswick, NJ: Rutgers University Press, 1996).
5 Iqbal, Z. and Mirakhor, A., "Progress and Challenges of Islamic Banking," *Thunderbird International Business Review* 41, nos. 4/5 (1999): 381–405.
6 See Lewison, M., "Conflict of Interest? The Ethics of Usury," *Journal of Business Ethics* 22, no. 4 (1999): 327–339; Rosly, S. A. and Abu Bakr, M. A., "Performance of Islamic and Mainstream Banks in Malaysia," *International Journal of Social Economics* 30, no. 12 (2003): 1249–1265.
7 See Rogers, R. A., "The Usury Debate, the Sustainability Debate, and the Call for a Moral Economy," *Ecological Economics* 35, no. 2 (2000): 157–171; Carrasco, I., "Ethics and Banking," *International Advances in Economic Research* 12 (2006): 43–50; Naughton, S. and Naughton, T., "Religion, Ethics, and Stock Trading: The Case of an Islamic Equities Market," *Journal of Business Ethics* 23, no. 2 (2000): 145–159; Sen, A., "Money and Value: On the Ethics and Economics of Finance," *Economics and Philosophy* 9 (1993): 203–227.
8 Al-Rāzī, *Mafātīḥ*, 7: 74 on Q. 2: 275; Al-Zuḥaylī, *al-Fiqh al-islāmī wa adillatuhu* (Damascus: Dār al-Fikr, n.d.), 5: 3708.
9 Naqvi, S. N. H., *Islam, Economics, and Society* (London: Kegan Paul International, 1994).
10 Siddiqi, M. N., *What Went Wrong?* Keynote Address at the Roundtable on Islamic Economics: Current State of Knowledge and Development of Discipline held in

Jeddah, Saudi Arabia on May 26–27, 2004, http://www.siddiqi.com/mns/Keynote_May2004_Jeddah.html (accessed August 14, 2010).

11 See Metawa, S. A. and Almossawi, M., "Banking Behavior of Islamic Bank Customers: Perspectives and Implications," *International Journal of Bank Marketing* 16, no. 7 (1998): 299–313; Hamid, A. H. and Nordin, N. Z., "A Study on Islamic Banking Education and Strategy for the New Millennium: Malaysian Experience," *International Journal of Islamic Financial Services* 2, no. 4 (2001).

12 Zaher, T. S. and Hassan, M. K., "A Comparative Literature Survey of Islamic Finance and Banking," *Financial Markets, Institutions & Instruments* 10, no. 4 (2001): 203–227.

13 Diamond, D. W. and Rajan, R., "Liquidity Risk, Liquidity Creation, and Financial Fragility: A Theory of Banking," *Journal of Political Economy* 109 (2002): 289–327.

14 Ibn Manẓūr, *Lisān al-ʿarab*, 14: 304–307 on "*r b y*." Also see *TDOT*, 13: 272–276, on "*rb*."

15 Ibn Manẓūr, *Lisān al-ʿarab*, 14: 304–306 on "*r b y*."

16 In the prophetic tradition (*ḥadīth*), "*al-Firdaws rabwat al-jannah*," which means "Paradise is the great (raised) part of heaven." See al-Ṭabarānī (d. 360/970), *al-Muʿjam al-kabīr*, ed. Ḥamdī al-Salafī (Cairo: Maktabat Ibn Taymiyyah, 1994), 7: 213 (#6886).

17 Ibn Manẓūr, *Lisān al-ʿarab*, 14: 306 on "*r b y*."

18 The bilateral root "*r b*" is expanded to "*r b b*" in West Semitic and "*r b y*" in East Semitic. See *TDOT*, 13: 273, on "*r b*."

19 Ibn Manẓūr, *Lisān al-ʿarab*, 14: 306 on "*r b y*." *Lisān al-ʿarab*, 1: 399–409 on "*r b b*." *BDB*, 913–914.

20 Ibid., 1: 399–401 on "*r b b*."

21 Ibid., 1: 442–443 on "*r y b*." Also see *TDOT*, 13: 473–479, on "*r y b*."

22 Ibn Manẓūr, *Lisān al-ʿarab*, 12: 119–130 on "*ḥ r m*." *BDB*, 355–356. *TDOT*, 5: 184, on "*ḥ r m*."

23 Ibn Manẓūr, *Lisān al-ʿarab*, 11: 166–171 on "*ḥ l l*." *BDB*, 320–321. *TDOT*, 4: 409–417, on "*ḥ l l*."

24 Qurʾan 2:265.

25 I translate "*bayʿ*" as "sale" and not "buying and selling," as suggested by the *TSQ*, since it is more loyal to the Arabic term.

26 Qurʾan 2:274–279.

27 Ibn Manẓūr, *Lisān al-ʿarab*, 9: 203–206 on "*ḍ a ʿf*." In Hebrew, the term means to double. See *BDB*, 858.

28 Qurʾan 30:39.

29 "The early church fathers condemned usury. Tertullian, Basil, Ambrose, Chrysostom, and Jerome used Luke 6:34–35 to support their arguments against the practice." "Usury was considered oppressive to the poor and, thus, a forbidden practice for leadership and laypeople alike, even though it was legal in society." In *Lexham Bible Dictionary* (Bellingham, WA: Lexham Press); Schaff, P. and Wace, H., eds., *A Select Library of the Nicene and Post-Nicene Fathers of the Christian Church* (New York, NY: Charles Scribner's Sons, 1900), 36–38.

30 Luke 6:34–35.

31 Ibn Manẓūr, *Lisān al-ʿarab*, 8: 26 on "*b y ʿ*."

32 Ibid., 8: 23 on "*b y ʿ*."

33 Ibid., 4: 89 on "*t g r*."

34 Keeping loyal to the Arabic, unlike the *TSQ*, which translates "*bi-bayʿikum*" as bargain, I translate it as sale instead.

35 Qurʾan 9:111.

36 Qurʾan 71:4.

37 Ibn Manẓūr, *Lisān al-ʿarab*, 13: 166–171 on "*d y n*." *BDB*, 192. *TDOT*, 3: 187–194, on "*d y n*." The *TDOT* shows the synonymity between "*dyn*" (to judge) and "*ryb*" (to bring forth a lawsuit/quarrel) *TDOT*, 3: 188, on "*d y n*." The *TDOT* also illustrates the term "*m d n*," as in "*madīnah*" is rooted in "*dyn*" meaning a judicial district or province, *TDOT*, 3: 190, on "*d y n*."
38 Qurʾan 82:17–19.
39 As before, unlike *TSQ*, I translate "*bayʿ*" as sale to be more loyal to the Arabic term.
40 Qurʾan 2:282.
41 Qurʾan 42:13–15.
42 Qurʾan 45:17.
43 I translate "*al-nās*" as "humankind" instead of "mankind" used by *TSQ*.
44 Qurʾan 3.9.
45 I translate "*khalaq*" as divided, based on my discussion in Galadari, "*Creatio ex Nihilo*."
46 I translate "*ʿalaq*" as clinging, instead of "blood clot" used by *TSQ*, as it appears to be perhaps more loyal to the original Arabic root meaning.
47 Unlike the *TSQ*, which translates "*al-insān*" as "man," I translate it as "the human."
48 Qurʾan 96:1–5.
49 Qurʾan 3:19.
50 For more on the sayings of jurists on the verses of "*muḥkamāt*" and "*mutashābihāt*" please see Al-Karamī (d. 1033/1624), *Aqāwīl al-thiqāt fī taʾwīl al-asmāʾ wal-ṣifāt wal-āyāt al-muḥkamāt wal-mushtabihāt*, ed. Shuʿayb al-Arnaʾūṭ (Beirut: Muʾassassat al-Risālah, 1986).
51 I translate "*al-nās*" as "humankind" instead of "mankind" used by *TSQ*.
52 Qurʾan 3:7–9.

Chapter 9: Conclusion

1 Wasserstrom, *Between Muslim and Jew*, 103.
2 Ibn Saʿd, *al-Ṭabaqāt al-kubra*, 2: 273–274; al-Bukhārī, *Ṣaḥīḥ al-Bukhārī*, 6: 182 (#4984). I wish to thank Ulrika Mårtensson for pointing this out to me.
3 I am indebted to Ulrika Mårtensson for pointing this out to me.
4 Al-Ṭabarī, *Jāmiʿ* [Q. 37:101–102], 21: 72–76.
5 Al-Rāzī, *Mafātīḥ* [Q. 37:102], 26: 346–349. Also, Ibn Kathir, *Tafsīr* [Q. 37:101–102], 7: 26–31.
6 Firestone, Reuven, "Abraham's Son," 115–116.
7 Qurʾan 27:76.
8 Meditation and low latent inhibition may have some neuropsychological associations; see Horan, Roy, "The Neuropsychological Connection Between Creativity and Meditation," *Creativity Research Journal* 21, nos. 2/3 (2009): 199–222. Since "*kashf*" may be understood as the power of intuition, individuals with low latent inhibition and high intelligence are usually very intuitive; see Sadler-Smith, Eugene, *Inside Intuition* (Abingdon: Routledge, 2008). For more on Sufi "*kashf*," see ʿAlī al-Hujwayrī (d. 465/1072), *Kashf al-maḥjūb* (Cairo: al-Majlis al-Aʿlā lil-Shuʾūn al-Islāmiyyah, 2004); Azadpur, Mohammed, "Unveiling the Hidden: On the Meditations of Descartes and Ghazzali," in *The Passions of the Soul in the Metamorphosis of Becoming*, ed. Anna-Teresa Tymieniecka (Berlin: Springer, 2003), 219–240. Also, you may compare with Saniotis, Arthur, "Mystical Mastery: The Presentation of Kashf in Sufi Divination," *Asian Anthropology* 6, no. 1 (2007): 29–51.

Bibliography

Abba, Raymond. "The Divine Name Yahweh," *Journal of Biblical Literature* 80, no. 4 (1961): 320–328.

Abdul-Raof, Hussein. *Schools of Qur'anic Exegesis: Genesis and Development*, Abingdon: Routledge, 2010.

Abdul-Raof, Hussein. *Theological Approaches to Qur'anic Exegesis*, Abingdon: Routledge, 2012.

Abrams, Meyer H. *Natural Supernaturalism: Tradition and Revolution in Romantic Literature*, New York, NY: W. W. Norton, 1973.

Abu al-ʿAbbās (d. 1224.1809). *al-Baḥr al-madīd fī tafsīr al-Qurʾān al-majīd*, ed. A. Raslān, Cairo: Dr. Ḥassan ʿAbbās Zakī, 1999.

Abu al-Muẓaffar (d. 471/1079). *al-Tabṣīr fil-dīn wa-tamyīz al-firqah al-nājiyah ʿan al-firaq al-hālikīn*, ed. K. Y. al-Ḥūt, Beirut: ʿĀlam al-Kutub, 1983.

Abū al-Walīd al-Bājī (d. 474/1082). *al-Muntaqa sharḥ al-muwaṭṭaʾ*, Cairo: Dār al-Kitāb al-Islāmī, 1914.

Abu Shuhbah, Muḥammad. *al-Isrāʾīliyyāt wal-mawḍūʿāt fī kutub al-tafsīr*, Cairo: Maktabat al-Sunnah, 1983.

Abu Zahrah (d. 1974). *Zahrat al-tafāsīr*, Cairo: Dār al-Fikr al-ʿArabī, n.d.

Abu Zayd, Nasr Hamid. *al-Ittijāh al-ʿaqlī fil-tafsīr: Dirāsah fī qaḍiyyat al-majāz fil-Qurʾān ʿind al-muʿtazilah*, Casablanca: Al-Markaz al-Thaqāfī al-ʿArabī, 1996.

Abu Zayd, Nasr Hamid. 1998. *Mafhūm al-naṣṣ: Dirāsah fī ʿulūm al-Qurʾān*, Ribat: al-Markaz al-Thaqāfī al-ʿArabī, 2014.

Abu Zayd, Nasr Hamid. "The Dilemma of the Literary Approach to the Qur'an," *Alif: Journal of Comparative Poetics* 23 (2003): 8–47.

Abu Zayd, Nasr Hamid. "The 'Others' in the Qur'an: A Hermeneutical Approach," *Philosophy Social Criticism* 36, no. 3/4 (2010): 281–294.

Abu-Deeb, K. "Studies in the Majāz and Metaphorical Language of the Qurʾān: Abū ʿUbayda and al-Sharīf al-Raḍī," in *Literary Structures of Religious Meaning in the Qurʾān*, ed. I. J. Boullata, 310–353, Abingdon: Curzon, 2009.

Adang, Camilla. *Muslim Writers on Judaism and the Hebrew Bible from Ibn Rabban to Ibn Hazm*, Leiden: Brill, 1996.

Ahlstrom, Gosta W. *Who Were the Israelites?*, Winona Lake, IN: Eisenbrauns, 1986.

Ahmed, Shahab. "Ibn Taymiyyah and the Satanic Verses," *Studia Islamica* 87 (1998): 67–124.

Al-ʿAskarī (d. 260/874). *Tafsīr*, Qom: Madrasat al-Imām al-Mahdī, n.d.

Al-Azharī, Abu Manṣūr (d. 370/981). *Tahdhīb al-lughah*, ed. M. ʿU. Marʿib, Beirut: Dār Iḥyāʾ al-Turāth al-ʿArabī, 2001.

Al-Baghawī (d. 526/1122). *Maʿālim al-tanzīl fī tafsīr al-Qurʾan*, Beirut: Dār Iḥyāʾ al-Turāth al-ʿArabī, 2000.

Al-Bāqillānī (d. 403/1013). *Tamhīd al-awāʾil fī takhlīṣ al-dalāʾil*, Beirut: Muʾassassat al-Kutub al-Thaqāfiyyah, 1987.

Al-Bayhaqī (d. 458/1066). *Shuʿab al-īmān*, Riyadh: Maktabat al-Rushd, 2003.

Albayrak, I. "Isrāʾīliyyāt and Classical Exegetes' Comments on the Calf with a Hollow Sound Q.20:83–98 / 7:147–155 with Special Reference to Ibn ʿAṭiyya," *Journal of Semitic Studies* 47, no. 1 (2002): 39–65.

Albayrak, I. "Re-Evaluating the Notion of Israʾiliyyat," *D. E. Ü. Ilahiyyat Fakültesi Dergisi* 14 (2001): 69–88.

Al-Biqāʿī (d. 885/1480). *al-Aqwāl al-qawīmah fī ḥukm al-naql min al-kutub al-qadīmah*, Cairo: Maktabat Jazīrat al-Ward, 2010.

Al-Biqāʿī (d. 885/1480). *Niẓam al-durar fī tanāsub al-āyat wal-suwar*, Cairo: Dār al-Kitāb al-Islāmī, n.d.

Al-Bukhārī (d. 256/870). *Ṣaḥīḥ al-Bukhārī*, ed. M. Z. N. Al-Nāṣir, Beirut: Dār Ṭawq al-Najāh, 2002.

Al-Dārmī (d. 255/893). *Naqḍ al-Imām Abi Saʿīd ʿUthmān ibn Saʿīd ʿAlī Al-Mrīsī al-Jahmī al-ʿanīd fima iftara ʿala Allāh ʿazza wa jall mina al-tawḥīd*, ed. R. Ḥ. Al-Almaʿī, Riyadh: Maktabat al-Rushd, 1998.

Al-Dhahabī, Muḥammad Ḥussain. *al-Isrāʾīliyyāt fīl-tafsīr wal-ḥadīth*, Cairo: Maktabat Wahbah, 1990.

Aleman, Andre, van Lee, Laura, Mantione, Mariska H. M., and de Haan, Edward. "Visual Imagery Without Visual Experience: Evidence from Congenitally Totally Blind People," *Neuroreport* 12, no. 11 (2001): 2601–2604.

Alexander, Irving A. "Personality, Psychological Assessment, and Psychobiography," *Journal of Personality* 56, no. 1 (1988): 265–294.

Al-Fahad, A. H. "From Exclusivism to Accommodation: Doctrinal and Legal Evolution of Wahhabism," *New York University Law Review* 79 (2004): 485–519.

Al-Ghazālī (d. 505/1111). *Iḥyāʾ ʿulūm al-dīn*, Beirut: Dār al-Maʿrifah, 2004.

Al-Hāshimī (d. 668/1269). *Takhjīl man ḥarraf al-tawrāt wal-injīl*, ed. M. A. Qadḥ, Riyadh: Maktabat al-ʿObaikān, 1998.

Al-Ḥijāzī, M. M. *al-Tafsīr al-wāḍiḥ*, Beirut: Dār al-Jīl al-Jadīd, 1993.

Al-Ḥowayzī (d. 1112/1700). *Tafsīr nūr al-thaqalayn*, unknown publisher, n.d.

Al-Hujwayrī, ʿAlī (d. 465/1072). *Kashf al-maḥjūb*, Cairo: al-Majlis al-Aʿlā lil-Shuʾūn al-Islāmiyyah, 2004.

ʿAlī ibn Abī Ṭālib, *Nahj al-balāghah*, ed. Fāris al-Ḥassūn, Qom: Markaz al-Abḥāth al-ʿAqāʾidiyyah, 1999.

Ali, Moch. "Rethinking the Semitic Texts: A Study of Intertextuality," *Studia Philosophica et Theologica* 8 (2008): 72–89.

Al-Jurjānī, Abdul-Qāhir (d. 471/1078). *Asrār al-balāghah*, Cairo: Maṭbaʿat al-Madanī, n.d.

Al-Juwaynī (d. 478/1085). *Shifāʾ al-ghalīl fī bayān mā waqaʿa fil-tawrāt wal-injīl min al-tabdīl*, ed. A. H. al-Saqqa, Cairo: Maktabat al-Azhariyyah lil-Turāth, 1978.

Al-Kalābādhī, Abu Bakr (d. 380/990). *al-Taʿarruf li-madhhab ahl al-taṣawwuf*, Beirut: al-Kutub al-ʿIlmiyyah, n.d.

Al-Kalbī (d. 204/819). *Kitāb al-aṣnām*, ed. A. Z. Pāsha, Cairo: Dār al-Kutub al-Miṣriyyah, 2000.

Al-Karamī (d. 1033/1624). *Aqāwīl al-thiqāt fī taʾwīl al-asmāʾ wal-ṣifāt wal-āyāt al-muḥkamāt wal-mushtabihāt*, ed. Shuʿayb al-Arnaʾūṭ, Beirut: Muʾassassat al-Risālah, 1986.

Al-Khālidī, Ṣalāḥ. A. *al-Qurʾān wa naqḍ maṭāʿin al-ruhbān*, Damascus: Dār al-Qalam, 2007.

Al-Khirāṭ, A. M. *ʿInāyat al-muslimīn bil-lughah al-ʿarabiyyah khidmah lil-Qurʾān al-karīm*, Riyadh: Mujammaʿ al-Malik Fahad li-Ṭibāʿat al-Muṣḥaf al-Sharīf, n.d.

Allen, Roger. *Arabic Literary Heritage: The Development of Its Genres and Criticism*, Cambridge: Cambridge University Press, 1998.

Allen, William Sidney. "Ancient Ideas on the Origin and Development of Language," *Transactions of the Philological Society* 47, no. 1 (1948): 35–60.
Al-Madinah International University, *al-Dakhīl fil-tafsīr*, n.d.
Almagor, E. "The Early Meaning of Majāz and the Nature of Abū ʿUbayda's Exegesis," in *Studia Orientalia Memoriae D. H. Baneth Dedicata*, Jerusalem: Magnes, 1979.
Al-Maḥmūd, ʿA. *Mawqif Ibn Taymiyyah min al-ashāʿirah*, Riyadh: Maktabat al-Rushd, 1995.
Al-Majlisī (d. 1111/1698). *Biḥār al-anwār*, Beirut: Muʾassassat al-Wafāʾ, 1984.
Al-Majlisī (d. 1111/1698). *Biḥār al-anwār, al-jāmiʿah li-durar akhbār al-aʾimmah al-aṭ-hār*, Beirut: Dār Iḥyāʾ al-Turāth al-ʿArabī, 1983.
Al-Majlisī (d. 1111/1698). *Mirʾāt al-ʿuqūl fī sharḥ akhbār āl al-rasūl*, ed. Jaʿfar al-Ḥusaynī, Tehran: Dār al-Kutub al-Islāmiyyah, 1990.
Al-Maqdisī (d. 355/966). *al-Badʾ wal-tarīkh*, Port Saʿīd: Maktabat al-Thaqāfah al-Dīniyyah, n.d.
Al-Masʿūdī (d. 346/956). *Murūj al-dhahab wa maʿādin al-jawhar*, Beirut: Dār al-Fikr, 1966.
Al-Maʿtūq, Aḥmad M. "Al-Alfāẓ al-Mushtarakah al-Maʿānī fil-Lughah al-ʿArabiyyah: Ṭabīʿatuhā, Ahammiyatuhā, Maṣādiruhā," *Majallah jāmiʿah umm al-qurā li-ʿulūm al-sharīʿah wal-dirāsāt al-islāmiyyah* 7, no. 21 (1997): 81–138.
Al-Māzandarānī (d. 1086/1699). *Sharḥ uṣūl al-kāfī*, eds. Abu al-Ḥasan al-Shaʿrānī and ʿAlī ʿĀshūr, Beirut: Iḥyāʾ al-Turāth al-ʿArabī, 2000.
Almond, Philip C. *Mystical Experience and Religious Doctrine: An Investigation of the Study of Mysticism in World Religions*, Berlin: De Gruyter, 1982.
Āl-Muʿammar, ʿAbdul ʿAzīz (d. 1244/1828). *Minḥat al-qarīb al-mujīb fil-radd ʿala ʿibād al-ṣalīb*, unknown publisher, n.d.
Al-Muḥammadī, F. A. *Salāmat al-Qurʾān min al-taḥrīf*, Markaz al-Abḥāth al-ʿAqāʾidiyyah, n.d.
Al-Muḥaqqiq al-Ḥillī (d. 676/1277). *al-Maslak fī uṣūl al-dīn wa talīh al-risālah al-mātiʿiyyah*, ed. Riḍa al-Ustādī, Mashhad: Mujammaʿ al-Buḥūth al-Islāmiyyah, 1994.
Al-Mūṣalī, *al-Khaṣāʾiṣ*, Cairo: al-Hayʾah al-Miṣriyyah al-ʿĀmmah lil-Kitāb, n.d.
Al-Nawawī (d. 676/1277). *Juzʾ fīh dhikr iʿtiqād al-salaf fil-ḥurūf wal-aṣwāt*, ed. A. Al-Dimyāṭī, Cairo: Maktabat al-Anṣār, n.d.
Al-Qaḥṭānī, S. *Kayfiyyat daʿwat ahl al-kitāb ila Allah taʿāla fi ḍawʾ al-kitāb wal-sunnah*, Riyadh: Muʾassassat al-Juraisi lil-Tawzīʿ wal-Iʿlān, n.d.
Al-Qarāfī, Shihāb al-Dīn (d. 684/1285). *al-Ajwiba al-fākhirah ʿan al-asʾilah al-fājirah fil-radd ʿala al-millah al-kāfirah*, ed. Bikr Zakī ʿAwaḍ, Cairo: Saʿīd Raʾfat, 1987.
Al-Qāsimī, M. J. *Maḥāsin al-taʾwīl*, ed. M. B. ʿUyūn al-Sūd, Beirut: Dār al-Kutub al-ʿIlmiyyah, 1998.
Al-Qummī, ʿAlī ibn Ibrāhīm (d. 329/942). *Tafsīr al-qummī*, Beirut: Muʾassassat al- Aʿlamī lil-Maṭbūʿāt, 1991.
Al-Qurṭubī (d. 671/1273). *al-Jāmiʿ li-aḥkām al-Qurʾān*, ed. A. Aṭfīsh, Cairo: Dār al-Kutub al-Miṣriyyah, 1964.
Al-Rāzī (d. 606/1210). *Mafātīḥ al-ghayb*, Beirut: Iḥyāʾ al-Turāth al-ʿArabī, 2000.
Al-Rūmī, F. *Ittijāhāt al-tafsīr fil-qarn al-rābiʿ ʿashr*, Riyadh: Idārāt al-Buḥūth al-ʿIlmiyyah wal-Iftāʾ wal-Daʿwah wal-Irshād, 1986.
Al-Saḥīm, M. *al-Islām: Uṣūluhu wa-mabādiʾuhu*, Riyadh: Ministry of Islamic Affairs, 2001.
Al-Salamī (d. 412/1021). *Ḥaqāʾiq al-tafsīr*, Beirut: al-Kutub al-ʿIlmiyyah, 2001.
Al-Ṣāliḥ, Ṣ. I. (d. 1407/1987). *Dirāsāt fī fiqh al-lughah*, Beirut: Dār al-ʿIlm lil-Malāyīn, 1960.
Al-Salmān, ʿAbdul ʿAzīz. *Mukhtaṣar al-asʾilah wal-ajwibah al-uṣūliyyah ʿala al-ʿaqīdah al-wāsiṭiyyah*, unknown publisher, 1997.

Al-Samarqandī (d. 373/983). *Baḥr al-ʿulūm*, unknown publisher, n.d.
Al-Saqqāf, ʿAlawī ʿA., ed. *al-Mawsūʿah Al-ʿaqdiyyah*, dorar.net, 2013.
Al-Saqqāf, ʿAlawī ʿA., ed. *Mawsūʿah al-firaq al-muntasabah lil-islām*, dorar.net, n.d.
Al-Shāfiʿī (d. 204/820). *al-Risālah*, ed. Aḥmad Shākir, Cairo: al-Ḥalabī, 1940.
Al-Shāfiʿī, Yaḥya ibn Abī al-Khayr (d. 558/1163). *al-Intiṣār fil-radd ʿala al-muʿtazilah al-qadariyyah al-ashrār*, ed. S. Al-Khalaf, Riyadh: Aḍwāʾ al-Salaf, 1999.
Al-Shahrastānī (d. 548/1153). *al-Milal wal-niḥal*, Beirut: Muʾassassat al-Ḥalabī, n.d.
Al-Shākrī, Ḥusayn, *al-Ṣādiq Jaʿfar ʿalayh al-salām, Mawsūʿah al-muṣṭafa wal-ʿitrah (9)*, Qom: Nashr al-Hādī, 1997.
Al-Shaʿrāwī, M. M. (d. 1419/1998). *al-Khawāṭir: tafsīr al-Shaʿrāwī*, Cairo: Maṭābiʿ Akhbār al-Yawm, 1997.
Al-Shīrāzī, M. *al-Amthal fī tafsīr kitāb Allāh al-munzal*, unknown publisher, n.d.
Al-Shīrāzī, M. *Nafaḥāt al-Qurʾan*, unknown publisher, n.d.
Al-Sijzī, Abu Naṣr (d. 444/1052). *Risālat al-Sijzī ila Ahl Zubayd fil-radd ʿala man ankar al-ḥarf wal-ṣawt*, ed. M. ba-ʿAbdullah, Medinah: ʿImādat al-Baḥth al-ʿIlmī bil-Jāmʿah al-Islāmiyyah, n.d.
Al-Simnānī (d. 736/1336). *al-Taʾwīlāt al-najmiyyah fī al-tafsīr al-ishārī al-ṣūfī*, Beirut: Dār al-Kutub al-ʿIlmiyyah, 2009.
Al-Suyūṭī (d. 911/1505). *al-Itqān fī ʿulūm al-Qurʾan*, ed. M. A. Ibrahīm, Cairo: Al-Hayʾah al-Miṣriyyah al-ʿĀmmah lil-Kitāb, 1974.
Al-Suyūṭī (d. 911/1505). *al-Wasāʾil fī musāmarat al-awāʾil*, Baghdad: Maṭbaʿat al-Najāḥ, 1950.
Al-Suyūṭī (d. 911/1505). *al-Mizhir fī ʿulūm al-lughah wa anwāʿihā*, ed. Fuʾād ʿAlī Manṣūr, Beirut: Dār al-Kutub al-ʿIlmiyyah, 1998.
Al-Ṭabarānī (d. 360/970). *al-Muʿjam al-kabīr*, ed. Ḥamdī al-Salafī, Cairo: Maktabat Ibn Taymiyyah, n.d.
Al-Ṭabarānī (d. 360/970). *al-Tafsīr al-kabīr*, Amman: Dār al-Kitāb al-Thaqāfī, 2008.
Al-Ṭabarī (d. 310/923). *Jāmiʿ al-bayān fī taʾwīl al-Qurʾān*, ed. Aḥmad Shākir, Damascus: Muʾassassat al-Risālah, 2000.
Al-Ṭabarī (d. 310/923). *Tarīkh al-rusul wal-mulūk*, Beirut: Dār al-Turāth, 1967.
Al-Ṭabarsī (d. 584/1153). *Majmaʿ al-bayān fī tafsīr, al-Qurʾān*, Beirut: al-Aʿlamī, 1995.
Al-Ṭabāṭabāʾī (d. 1402/1981). *al-Mīzān fī tafsīr al-Qurʾān*, Beirut: Muʾassassat al-Aʿlami lil-Maṭbūʿāt, 1997.
Al-Thaʿālbī (d. 429/1038). *Fiqh al-lughah wa sirr al-ʿarabiyyah*, ed. ʿA. al-Mahdī, Beirut: Iḥyāʾ al-Turāth al-ʿArabī, 2002.
Al-Thaʿlabī (d. 427/1035). *al-Ashbāh wal-naẓāʾir*, ed. Muḥammad al-Maṣrī, Damascus: Saʿd al-Dīn, 1984.
Al-Thaʿlabī (d. 427/1035). *al-Kashf wal-bayān ʿan tafsīr al-Qurʾān*, eds. Abī Muḥammad ibn ʿĀshūr and Naẓīr al-Sāʿidī, Beirut: Dār Iḥyāʾ al-Turāth al-ʿArabī, 2002.
Altschuler, Eric, "Did Ezekiel Have Temporal Lobe Epilepsy?" *Archives of General Psychiatry* 59, no. 6 (2002): 561–562.
Al-Ṭūfī, Najm al-Dīn (d. 716/1316). *al-Intiṣārāt al-islāmiyyah fī kashf shubah al-naṣrāniyah*, ed. S. M. al-Qarnī, Riyadh: Maktabat al-ʿObaikān, 1999.
Al-Tustarī (d. 283/896). *Tafsīr al-Qurʾān*, ed. Muḥammad ʿUyūn al-Sūd, Beirut: al-Kutub al-ʿIlmiyyah, 2003.
Al-ʿUthaymīn, Muḥammad Ṣ. *al-Uṣūl min ʿilm al-uṣūl*, Cairo: al-Maktabah al-Islāmiyyah, 2001.
Al-Wāḥidī (d. 468/1075). *Asbāb Nuzūl al-Qurʾān*, ed. ʿIṣām al-Ḥumaydān, Dammam: al-Iṣlāḥ, 1992.

Al-Yāzijī (d. 1324/1906). *Najʿat al-rāʾid wa shirʿat al-wārid fil-mutarādif wal-mutawārid*, Cairo: Maṭbaʿat al-Maʿārif, 1905.
Al-Zabīdī (d.1205/1790). *Tāj al-ʿarūs*, Alexandria: Dār al-Hidāyah, n.d.
Al-Zamakhsharī (d. 538/1143). *al-Mufaṣṣal fī ʿilm al-lughah*, Beirut: Iḥyāʾ al-ʿUlūm, 1990.
Al-Zarkashī (d. 794/1392). *al-Burhān fī ʿulūm al-Qurʾān*, Beirut: Dār Ihyāʾ al-Kutub al-ʿArabiyyah, 1957.
Al-Zuḥaylī. *al-Fiqh al-islāmī wa adillatuhu*, Damascus: Dār al-Fikr, n.d.
Ambrose (d. 397 CE). "Exposition of the Christian Faith," in *Nicene and Post-Nicene Fathers Second Series, Ambrose: Select Works and Letters*, trans. and ed. Phillip Schaff and Henry Wallace, New York, NY: Cosimo Inc., 2007.
Ambrose (d. 397 CE). *Seven Exegetical Works*, trans. Michael P. McHugh, The Fathers of the Church: A New Translation, vol. 65 (Washington, DC: Catholic University of America Press, 1972).
Amir-Moezzi, M. A. *The Divine Guide in Early Shiʿism: The Sources of Esotericism in Islam*, trans. D. Streight, Albany, NY: State University of New York Press, 1994.
Amsler, M. *Etymology and Grammatical Discourse in Late Antiquity and the Early Middle Ages*, Amsterdam: John Benjamins, 1989.
Anderson, Gary. "The Interpretation of Genesis 1:1 in the Targums," *Catholic Biblical Quarterly* 52, no. 1 (1990): 21–29.
Andreasen, N. C. and Glick, I. D. "Creativity and Mental Illness: Prevalence Rates in Writers and Their First-Degree Relatives," *American Journal of Psychology* 144 (1987): 1288–1292.
Antonovsky, Aaron. *Unraveling the Mystery of Health: How People Manage Stress and Stay Well*, San Francisco, CA: Jossey-Bass, 1987.
Aquinas, Thomas (d. 1274 CE). *Summa Theologica*, London: Burns Oates & Washbourne, n.d.
Arberry, A. J. *Revelation and Reason in Islam*, Abingdon: Routledge, 2008.
Aristotle (d. 322 BCE). *De Interpretatione*, trans. E. M. Edghill, Adelaide: University of Adelaide, 2015.
Asad, M. "Symbolism and Allegory in the Qurʾan," in *The Message of the Qurʾan* (appendix), Gibraltar: al-Andalus, dist. London: E. J. Brill, 1980.
Asani, Ali S. "Pluralism, Intolerance, and the Qurʾan," *The American Scholar* 71 (2002): 52–60.
Asani, Ali S. "So That You May Know One Another: A Muslim American Reflects on Pluralism in Islam," *The Annals of the American Academy of Political and Social Science* 588 (2003): 40–51.
Ashbrook, James B. "Neurotheology: The Working Brain and the Work of Theology," *Zygon* 19, no. 3 (1984): 331–350.
Athanasius (d. 373 CE). *Four Discourses Against the Arians*, n.p.: Fig Books, 2012.
Averroës (d. 595/1198). *The Decisive Treatise*, trans. C. E. Butterworth, Provo, UT: Brigham Young University Press, 2001.
Avis, P. *God and the Creative Imagination: Metaphor, Symbol and Myth in Religion and Theology*, Abingdon: Routledge, 1999.
Ayoub, Mahmoud. "Christian–Muslim Dialogue: Goals and Obstacles," *The Muslim World* 94, no. 3 (2004): 313–319.
Ayoub, Mahmoud. "Nearest in Amity: Christians in the Qurʾan and Contemporary Exegetical Tradition," *Islam and Christian–Muslim Relations* 8 (1997): 145–164.
Ayoub, Mahmoud. *The Qurʾan and Its Interpreters*, Albany, NY: State University of New York Press, 1992.

Ayoub, Mahmoud M. "Towards an Islamic Christology: An Image of Jesus in Early Shīʿī Muslim Literature," *The Muslim World* 66, no. 3 (1976): 163–188.
Ayoub, Mahmoud. "ʿUzayr in the Qurʾan and Muslim Tradition," in *Studies in Islamic and Judaic Traditions*, eds. W. M. Brinner and S. D. Ricks, 3–18, Atlanta, GA: Scholars Press, 1986.
Azadpur, Mohammed. "Unveiling the Hidden: On the Meditations of Descartes and Ghazzali," in *The Passions of the Soul in the Metamorphosis of Becoming*, ed. Anna-Teresa Tymieniecka, 219–240, Berlin: Springer, 2003.
Baker Encyclopedia of the Bible, Grand Rapids, MI: Baker Book House, 1988.
Baljon, J. M. S. "Qurʾanic Anthropomorphism," *Islamic Studies* 27, no. 2 (1988): 119–127.
Barlas, A. "Jihad, Holy War, and Terrorism: The Politics of Conflation and Denial," *American Journal of Islamic Social Sciences* 20 (2003): 46–62.
Barr, James. "The Question of Religious Influence: The Case of Zoroastrianism, Judaism, and Christianity," *Journal of the American Academy of Religion* 53, no. 2 (1985): 201–235.
Barr, James. *The Semantics of Biblical Language*, London: Oxford University Press, 1961.
Barrantes-Vidal, Neus. "Creativity & Madness Revisited from Current Psychological Perspectives," *Journal of Consciousness Studies* 11, no. 3/4 (2004): 58–78.
Barrett, Charles K. *Black's New Testament Commentary: The First Epistle to the Corinthians*, Peabody, MA: Hendrickson, 2000.
Baruch, Ilan, Hemsley, David R., and Gray, Jeffrey A. "Latent Inhibition and 'Psychotic Proneness' in Normal Subjects," *Personality and Individual Differences* 9, no. 4 (1988): 777–783.
Basri, Moshe. *Narratives of the Talmud: A Collection of Aggadot in the Babylonian and Jerusalem Talmuds and the Tosefta*, trans. Edward Levin, Jerusalem: Haktab Institute, 1994.
Bassler, Jouette M. "Mixed Signals: Nicodemus in the Fourth Gospel," *Journal of Biblical Literature* 108, no. 4 (1989): 635–646.
Bauckham, Richard and Mosser, Carl, eds. *The Gospel of John and Christian Theology*, Grand Rapids, MI: Wm. B. Eerdmans, 2008.
Bauer, W. *A Greek–English Lexicon of the New Testament and Other Early Christian Literature*, ed. F. W. Danker, Chicago, IL: The University of Chicago Press, 2000.
Beale, G. K. "Questions of Authorial Intent, Epistemology, and Presuppositions and Their Bearing on the Study of the Old Testament in the New: A Rejoinder to Steve Moyise," *Irish Biblical Studies* 21 (1999): 152–180.
Beaumont, M. I. *Christology in Dialogue with Muslims: A Critical Analysis of Christian Presentations of Christ for Muslims from the Ninth and Twentieth Centuries*, Carlisle: Paternoster, 2005.
Beaumont, M. I. "Early Christian Interpretation of the Qurʾan," *Transformation* 22, no. 4 (2005): 195–203.
Beekes, R. *Etymological Dictionary of Greek*, Leiden: Brill, 2010.
Beeston, A. F. L. "Himyarite Monotheism," in *Studies in the History of Arabia II: Pre-Islamic Arabia*, executive eds. Abdelgadir M. Abdalla, Sami Al-Sakkar, and Richard Mortel, 149–154, Riyadh: King Saud University, 1984.
Beit-Hallahmi, Benjamin. "Morality and Immorality Among the Irreligious," in *Atheism and Secularity*, ed. Phil Zuckerman, 113–141, Santa Barbara, CA: ABC-CLIO, 2010.
Beit-Hallahmi, Benjamin and Argyle, Michael. *The Psychology of Religious Behaviour, Belief and Experience*, London: Routledge, 1997.

Belfer-Cohen, Anna and Hovers, Erella. "In the Eye of the Beholder: Mousterian and Natufian Burials in the Levant," *Current Anthropology* 33 (1992): 463–471.
Bell, Richard. *Introduction to the Qur'an*, Edinburgh: Edinburgh University Press, 1953.
Bell, Richard. *The Origin of Islam in Its Christian Environment*, London: Frank Cass, 1968.
Bellamy, James A. "Textual Criticism of the Koran," *Journal of the American Oriental Society* 121, no. 1 (2001): 1–6.
Benedek, Mathias, Franz, Fabiola, Heene, Moritz, and Neubauer, Aljoscha C. "Differential Effects of Cognitive Inhibition and Intelligence on Creativity," *Personality and Individual Differences* 53, no. 4 (2012): 480–485.
Benedek, Mathias, Könen, Tanja, and Neubauer, Aljoscha C. "Associative Abilities Underlying Creativity," *Psychology of Aesthetics, Creativity, and the Arts* 6, no. 3 (2012): 273–281.
Bergen, Robert D. "Text as a Guide to Authorial Intention: An Introduction to Discourse Criticism," *Journal of the Evangelical Theological Society* 30, no. 3 (1987): 327–336.
Berger, Klaus. *Identity and Experience in the New Testament*, Minneapolis, MN: Fortress Press, 2003.
Berkey, Jonathan, P. *The Formation of Islam: Religion and Society in the Near East, 600–1800*, Cambridge: Cambridge University Press, 2003.
Beyenka, Mary M., trans. *Saint Ambrose Letters*, The Fathers of the Church: A New Translation, vol. 26, 437–447, Washington, DC: Catholic University of America, 1954.
Beyer, K. *The Aramaic Language: Its Distribution and Subdivisions*, trans. J. F. Healey, Göttingen: Vandenhoeck & Ruprecht, 1986.
Blanchard, Christopher M. "Al Qaeda: Statements and Evolving Ideology," *CRS Report for Congress*, Congressional Research Service, 2007.
Bloomfield, M. W. "Symbolism in Medieval Literature," *Modern Philology* 56, no. 2 (1958): 73–81.
Boismard, Marie-Émile. *St. John's Prologue*, Westminster: Newman, 1957.
Borgen, Peder J. "The Prologue of John—as Exposition of the Old Testament," in *Philo, John and Paul: New Perspectives on Judaism and Early Christianity*, Brown Judaic Studies, 131, 75–102, Atlanta, GA: Scholars Press, 1987.
Botterweck, G. J. and Ringgren, H., eds., J. T. Willis, trans., 1970. *Theological Dictionary of the Old Testament*, revised edn., Grand Rapids, MI: Wm. B. Eerdmans, 2011.
Bowker, J. W. *The Targums and Rabbinic Literature: An Introduction to Jewish Interpretation of Scripture*, Cambridge: Cambridge University Press, 1969.
Bowman, A. K. and Woolf, G. *Literacy and Power in the Ancient World*, Cambridge: Cambridge University Press, 1994.
Bowman, J. "The Debt of Islam to Monophysite Syrian Christianity," in *Essays in Honor of Griffithes Wheeler Thatcher*, ed. E. C. B. Maclaurin, Sydney: Sydney University Press, 1967.
Boyarin, Daniel. "The Gospel of the *Memra*: Jewish Binitarianism and the Prologue to John," *Harvard Theological Review* 94, no. 3 (2001): 243–284.
Braff, David L. "Information Processing and Attention Dysfunctions in Schizophrenia," *Schizophrenia Bulletin* 19 (1993): 233–259.
Brandt, P. Y., Clément, F., and Manning, R. R. "Neurotheology: Challenges and Opportunities," *Schweizer Archiv fur Neurologie und Psychiatrie* 161, no. 8 (2010): 305–309.
Brannan, Rick. *The Lexham Analytical Lexicon to the Greek New Testament*, Bellingham, WA: Logos Research Systems, 2013.

Bremmer, Robert H. *Giving: Charity and Philanthropy in History*, New Brunswick, NJ: Transaction, 2000.
Brenton, Lancelot Charles Lee, ed. *The Septuagint Version of the Old Testament, with an English Translation: and with Various Readings and Critical Notes*, London: Samuel Bagster, 1884.
Brock, Sebastian P. *The Bible in Syriac Tradition*, Piscataway, NJ: Gorgias Press, 2006.
Bromiley, G. W. *Theological Dictionary of the New Testament*, eds. G. Kittel and G. Friedrich, Grand Rapids, MI: Wm. B. Eerdmans, 1964.
Broome Jr., Edwin C. "Ezekiel's Abnormal Personality," *Journal of Biblical Literature* 65, no. 3 (1946): 277–292.
Brown, F., Driver, S. R., and Briggs, C. *Enhanced Brown-Driver-Briggs Hebrew and English Lexicon of the Old Testament*, Bellingham, WA: Logos Research Systems, 2000.
Brown, Jeannine K. "Creation's Renewal in the Gospel of John," *The Catholic Biblical Quarterly* 72, no. 2 (2010): 275–290.
Brown, Raymond E., "*Sensus Plenior* of Sacred Scripture," Ph.D. dissertation, St. Mary's University, 1955.
Brownlee, W. H. "The Ineffable Name of God," *Bulletin of the American Schools of Oriental Research* 226 (1977): 39–46.
Buber, Martin. *Moses: The Revelation and the Covenant*, New York, NY: Harper and Brothers, 1958.
Bultmann, Rudolf. *Das Evangelium des Johannes*, Göttingen: Vendenhoeck & Ruprecht, 1941.
Bultmann, Rudolf. "Die Bedeutung der neuerschlossenen mandäischen und manichäischen Quellen für das Verständnis des Johannesevangeliums," *Zeitschrift für die neutestamentliche Wissenschaft* 24 (1925): 100–145.
Burckhardt, T. *Introduction to Sufi Doctrine*, Bloomington, IN: World Wisdom, 2008.
Burton, J. "Notes Towards a Fresh Perspective on the Islamic Sunna," *Bulletin of the British Society for Middle Eastern Studies* 11, no. 1 (1984): 3–17.
Cairns, Earle E. *Christianity Through the Centuries: A History of the Christian Church*, Grand Rapids, MI: Zondervan, 1996.
Calder, N. "*Tafsīr* from Ṭabarī to Ibn Kathīr: Problems in the Description of a Genre, Illustrated with Reference to the Story of Abraham," in *Approaches to the Qur'an*, ed. G. R. Hawting and Abdul-Kader A. Shareef, 101–140, London: Routledge, 1993.
Camfield, David. "Neurobiology of Creativity," in *Neurobiology of Exceptionality*, ed. Con Stough, 53–72, New York, NY: Kluwer Academic/Plenum, 2005.
Campbell, Joseph. *Myths to Live By*, New York, NY: Viking Press, 1972.
Campbell, Joseph. *The Inner Reaches of Outer Space: Metaphor as Myth: Metaphor as Myth and as Religion*, New York, NY: Harper & Row, 1986.
Campbell, Joseph. *Thou Art That: Transforming Religious Metaphor*, Novato, CA: New World Library, 1996.
Canales, Arthur D. "A Rebirth of Being 'Born Again': Theological, Sacramental and Pastoral Reflections from a Roman Catholic Perspective," *Journal of Pentecostal Theology* 11, no. 1 (2002): 98–119.
Caplan, H. "The Four Senses of Scriptural Interpretation and the Mediaeval Theory of Preaching," *Speculum* 4, no. 3 (1929): 282–290.
Capps, Donald. *Jesus: A Psychological Biography*, Eugene, OR: Wipf and Stock, 2010.
Capps, Donald. *Jesus the Village Psychiatrist*, Louisville, KY: Westminster John Knox, 2008.
Carrasco, I. "Ethics and Banking," *International Advances in Economic Research* 12 (2006): 43–50.

Carroll, Bret E. *The Routledge Historical Atlas of Religion in America*, Abingdon: Routledge, 2000.
Carroll, John T. "Children in the Bible," *Interpretation* 55, no. 2 (2001): 121–134.
Carson, Shelley H. "Creativity and Psychopathology: A Shared Vulnerability Model," *Canadian Journal of Psychiatry* 56 (2011): 144–153.
Carson, Shelley H., Petersen, Jordan B., and Higgins, Daniel M. "Decreased Latent Inhibition is Associated with Increased Creative Achievement in High-Functioning Individuals," *Journal of Personality and Social Psychology* 85 (2003): 499–506.
Cartwright, Richard. "On the Logical Problem of the Trinity," in *Philosophical Essays*, 187–200, Cambridge, MA: MIT Press, 1990.
Casanova, Paul. "Idris et ʿOuzair," *Journal asiatique* 205 (1924): 356–360.
Catani, Marco, Dell'Acqua, Flavio, and Thiebaut de Schotten, Michel. "A Revised Limbic System Model for Memory, Emotion, and Behaviour," *Neuroscience & Biobehavioral Reviews* 37, no. 8 (2013): 1724–1737.
Ceccarelli, Leah. "Polysemy: Multiple Meanings in Rhetorical Criticism," *Quarterly Journal of Speech* 84, no. 4 (1998): 395–415. [Published online 2009.]
Chaika, E. "A Linguist Looks at 'Schizophrenic' Language," *Brain and Language* 1 (1974): 257–276.
Chaika, E. *Understanding Psychotic Speech: Beyond Freud and Chomsky*, Springfield, IL: Charles C. Thomas, 1990.
Chiappe, Dan L. and Chiappe, Penny. "The Role of Working Memory in Metaphor Production and Comprehension," *Journal of Memory and Language* 56 (2007): 172–188.
Chipman, L. N. B. "Adam and the Angels: An Examination of Mythic Elements in Islamic Sources," *Arabica* 49, no. 4 (2002): 429–455.
Chodkiewicz, M. *An Ocean Without Shore: Ibn Arabi, the Book, and the Law*, Albany, NY: State University of New York Press, 1993.
Cirrone, Steve. *Secular Morality: Rhetoric and Reader*, n.p.: SFC Publishing, 2015.
Claassens, G. H. M. "Jacob van Maerlant on Muhammad and Islam," in *Medieval Christian Perceptions of Islam*, ed. J. V. Tolan, 211–232, New York, NY: Routledge, 1996.
Clark, Matityahu. *Etymological Dictionary of Biblical Hebrew: Based on the Commentaries of Samson Raphael Hirsch*, Jerusalem: Feldheim Publishers, 1999.
Clarke, Ernest. G. "Jacob's Dream at Bethel as Interpreted in the Targums and the New Testament," *Studies in Religion* 4 (1975): 367–377.
Cockerill, Gareth L. "Hebrews 1:6: Source and Significance," *Bulletin for Biblical Research* 9 (1999): 51–64.
Coloe, Mary L. *God Dwells With Us: Temple Symbolism in the Fourth Gospel*, Collegeville, MN: The Liturgical Press, 2001.
Comprehensive Aramaic Lexicon Project. http://cal.huc.edu/. Hebrew Union College, Jewish Institute of Religion, Cincinnati, OH.
Condit, C. M., Bates, B. R., Galloway, R., Givens, S. B., Haynie, C. K., Jordan, J. W., Stables, G., and West, H. M. "Recipes or Blueprints for Our Genes? How Contexts Selectively Activate the Multiple Meanings of Metaphors," *Quarterly Journal of Speech* 88, no. 3 (2002): 303–325.
Corbin, Henry. *History of Islamic Philosophy*, trans. Phillip Sherrad, London: Kegan Paul, 1993.
Cortés, Juan B. and Gatti, Florence M. "The Son of Man or the Son of Adam," *Biblica* 49, no. 4 (1968): 457–502.
Coulter, J. A. *The Literary Microcosm: Theories of Interpretation of the Later Neoplatonists*, Leiden: Brill, 1976.

Crisp, Oliver D. *God Incarnate: Explorations in Christology*, London: Continuum, 2009.
Crisp, Peter. "Between Extended Metaphor and Allegory: Is Blending Enough?" *Language and Literature* 17, no. 4 (2008): 291–308.
Crone, Patricia. *Meccan Trade and the Rise of Islam*, Princeton, NJ: Princeton University Press, 1987.
Crone, Patricia. *Slaves on Horses: The Evolution of the Islamic Polity*, Cambridge: Cambridge University Press, 1980.
Crone, Patricia and Cook, Michael. *Hagarism: The Making of the Islamic World*, Cambridge: Cambridge University Press, 1977.
Cuypers, Michel. *The Composition of the Qur'an: Rhetorical Analysis*, London: Bloomsbury Academic, 2015.
D'Agostino, Armando, Castelnovo, Anna, and Scarone, Silvio. "Non-pathological Associations: Sleep and Dreams, Deprivation and Bereavement," in *The Neuroscience of Visual Hallucinations*, eds. Daniel Collerton, Urs P. Mosimann, and Elaine Perry, 59–89, Chichester: Wiley, 2015.
d'Aquili, Eugene and Newberg, Andrew. "Religious and Mystical States: A Neuropsychological Model," *Zygon* 28, no. 2 (1993): 177–200.
d'Aquili, Eugene and Newberg, Andrew. *The Mystical Mind: Probing the Biology of Religious Experience*, Minneapolis, MN: Fortress Press, 1999.
d'Aquili, Eugene and Newberg, Andrew. *Why God Won't Go Away: Brain Science and the Biology of Belief*, New York, NY: Ballantine Books, 2001.
D'Costa, Gavin. *Meeting of Religions and the Trinity*, New York, NY: Orbis Books, 2000.
Das, Sujit. *Islam Dismantled: The Mental Illness of Prophet Muhammad*, n.p.: Felibri Publications, 2012.
Daschke, Derek and Kille, D. Andrew. eds. *A Cry Instead of Justice: The Bible and Cultures of Violence in Psychological Perspective*, London: Bloomsbury Academic, 2010.
de la Potterie, Ignace. "Structure du Prologue de Saint Jean," *New Testament Studies* 30, no. 3 (1984): 354–381.
de Moor, Johannes C. *The Rise of Yahwism: The Roots of Israelite Monotheism*, revised edn., Leuven: Peeters, 1997.
de Ropp, R. S. "Psychedelic Drugs and Religious Experience," in *Magic, Witchcraft, and Religion*, eds. A. C. Lehmann and J. E. Myers, Mountain View, CA: Mayfield, 1993.
Deeks, David G. "The Prologue of St. John's Gospel," *Biblical Theology Bulletin* 6, no. 1 (1976): 62–78.
Demke, Christoph. "Der sogennante Logos-Hymnus im johanneischen Prolog," *Zeitschrift für die neutestamentliche Wissenschaft* 58, no. 1/2 (1967): 45–68.
Derrida, J. "Linguistics and Grammatology," trans. G. C. Spivak, *SubStance* 4, no. 10 (1974): 127–181.
Diamond, D. W. and Rajan, R. "Liquidity Risk, Liquidity Creation, and Financial Fragility: A Theory of Banking," *Journal of Political Economy* 109 (2002): 289–327.
Docherty, N. M., Hall, M. J., and Gordinier, S. W. "Affective Reactivity of Speech in Schizophrenia Patients and Their Nonschizophrenic Relatives," *Journal of Abnormal Psychology* 107 (1998): 461–467.
Dodd, Charles H. *Interpretation of the Fourth Gospel*, Cambridge: Cambridge University Press, 1953.
Donner, Fred. *Muhammad and the Believers: At the Origins of Islam*, Cambridge, MA: Harvard University Press, 2010.
Dressler, M. "Between Legalist Exclusivism and Mysticist Universalism: Contested Sufi Muslim Identities in New York," *The Muslim World* 100 (2010): 431–451.

Drewermann, Eugen. *Discovering the God Child Within: A Spiritual Psychology of the Infancy of Jesus*, trans. Peter Heinegg, New York, NY: Crossroad, 1994.

Driver, T. F. "The Case of Pluralism," in *The Myth of Christian Uniqueness: Toward a Pluralistic Theology of Religions*, eds. John Hick and P. F. Knitter, Eugene, OR: Wipf and Stock, 2005.

Drus, Marina, Kozbelt, Aaron, and Hughes, Robert R. "Creativity, Psychopathology, and Emotion Processing: A Liberal Response Bias for Remembering Negative Information is Associated with Higher Creativity," *Creativity Research Journal* 26, no. 3 (2014): 251–262.

Dunn, James D. G. *Christology in the Making: A New Testament Inquiry into the Origins of the Doctrine of the Incarnation*, Grand Rapids, MI: Wm. B. Eerdmans, 1996.

Dupré, L. K. *Symbols of the Sacred*, Grand Rapids, MI: Wm. B. Eerdmans, 2000.

Dvorak, James D. "The Relationship Between John and the Synoptic Gospels," *Journal of the Evangelical Theological Society* 41, no. 2 (1998): 201–213.

Ebstein, Michael. *Mysticism and Philosophy in al-Andalus: Ibn Masarra, Ibn al-ʿArabī and the Ismāʿīlī Tradition*, Leiden: Brill, 2014.

Edinger, Edward F. *The Bible and the Psyche: Individuation Symbolism in the Old Testament*, Toronto: Inner City Books, 1986.

Efthimiadis-Keith, Helen. *The Enemy Is Within: A Jungian Psychoanalytic Approach to the Book of Judith*, Leiden: Brill, 2004.

El-Badawi, Emran. *The Qurʾan and the Aramaic Gospel Traditions*, Abingdon: Routledge, 2013.

Eliade, Mircea. *The Sacred and the Profane: The Nature of Religion*, Orlando, FL: Harcourt Books, 1959 [republished 1987].

Ellens, J. Harold, ed. *Psychological Hermeneutics for Biblical Themes and Texts*, London: Bloomsbury Academic, 2012.

Ellens, J. Harold and Rollins, Wayne G. *Psychology and the Bible: A New Way to Read the Scriptures*, Santa Barbara, CA: Greenwood, 2004.

Elowsky, Joel C., ed. *Ancient Christian Commentary on Scripture: New Testament IVa, John 1–10*, Downers Grove, IL: InterVarsity Press, 2006.

Eltester, Walther. "Der Logos und sein Prophet: Fragen zur heutigen Erklärung des johanneischen Prologs," in *Apophoreta: Festschrift fur Ernst Haenchen*, eds. Walter Eltester and Franz H. Kettler, 109–134, Berlin: Verlag Alfred Töpelmann, 1964.

Erder, Yoram. "The Origin of the Name Idrīs in the Qurʾan: A Study of the Influence of Qumran Literature on Early Islam," *Journal of Near Eastern Studies* 49, no. 4 (1990): 339–350.

Eslinger, Lyle. "Inner-Biblical Exegesis and Inner-Biblical Allusion: The Question of Category," *Vetus Testamentum* 42, no. 1 (1992): 47–58.

Evans, Craig A. *Word and Glory: On the Exegetical and Theological Background of John's Prologue*, Sheffield: Sheffield Academic, 1993.

Eysenck, Hans J. "Creativity as a Product of Intelligence and Personality," in *International Handbook of Personality and Intelligence*, eds. Donald H. Saklofske and Moshe Zeidner, 231–247, Berlin: Springer, 1995.

Farrelly, M. John. *The Trinity: Rediscovering the Central Christian Mystery*, Lanham, MD: Rowman & Littlefield, 2005.

Fascher, Erich. "Christologie und Gnosis im vierten Evangelium," *Theologische Literaturzeitung* 93, no. 10 (1968): 721–730.

Fingelkurts, Alexander A. and Fingelkurts, Andrew A. "Is Our Brain Hardwired to Produce God, or Is Our Brain Hardwired to Perceive God? A Systematic Review on the Role of

the Brain in Mediating Religious Experience," *Cognitive Processing* 10, no. 4 (2009): 293–326.
Fink, Andreas, Slamar-Halbedl, Mirjam, Unterrainer, Human F., and Weiss, Elisabeth M. "Creativity: Genius, Madness, or a Combination of Both?" *Psychology of Aesthetics, Creativity, and the Arts* 6, no. 1 (2012): 11–18.
Firestone, Reuven. "Abraham's Son as the Intended Sacrifice (*Al-Dhabīḥ*, Qur'an 37:99–113): Issues in Qur'ānic Exegesis," *Journal of Semitic Studies* 34, no. 1 (1989): 95–131.
Firestone, Reuven. "The Qur'ān and the Bible: Some Modern Studies of Their Relationship," in *Bible and Qur'an: Essays in Scriptural Intertextuality*, ed. J. C. Reeves, Leiden: Brill, 2003.
Firro, K. M. "The Druze Faith: Origin, Development and Interpretation," *Arabica* 58, no. 1/2 (2011): 76–99.
Fishbane, Michael. *Biblical Interpretation in Ancient Israel*, Oxford: Oxford University Press, 1988.
Flaherty, Alice W. "Frontotemporal and Dopaminergic Control of Idea Generation and Creative Drive," *Journal of Comparative Neurology* 493, no. 1 (2005): 147–153.
Flesher, Paul V. M. and Chilton, Bruce D. *The Targums: A Critical Introduction*, Leiden: Brill, 2011.
Ford, David F. "Meeting Nicodemus: A Case Study in Daring Theological Interpretation," *Scottish Journal of Theology* 66, no. 1 (2013): 1–17.
Forrest, D. V. "Poiesis and the Language of Schizophrenia," *Psychiatry* 28 (1965): 1–18.
Forrest, Peter. *God Without the Supernatural: A Defense of Scientific Theism*, Ithaca, NY: Cornell University Press, 1996.
Förstel, Karl, ed. and trans. "Nicetas of Byzantium," *Schriften zum Islam*, Würzburg: Echter, 2000.
Fraade, S. D. "Rabbinic Polysemy and Pluralism Revisited: Between Praxis and Thematization," *Association for Jewish Studies Review* 31, no. 1 (2007): 1–40.
Frazier, J. G. *The Golden Bough*, New York, NY: Macmillan, 1950.
Fredericks, J. L. *Faith Among Faiths: Christian Theology and Non-Christian Religions*, Mahwah, NJ: Paulist Press, 1999.
Freedman, David N., general ed. *The Anchor Yale Bible Dictionary*, New York, NY: Doubleday, 1992.
Freedman, H. and Simon, M. *Midrash Rabbah*, London: The Soncino Press, 1969.
Freemon, Frank R. "A Differential Diagnosis of the Inspirational Spells of Muhammad the Prophet of Islam," *Epilepsia* 17 (1976): 423–427.
Freud, Sigmund. "A Religious Experience," *The Psychoanalytic Review* 20 (1933): 352.
Fried, Isaac. *The Analytic and Synthetic Etymology of the Hebrew Language*, Boston, MA: The Hebrew Etymology Project, 2004.
Galadari, Abdulla. "Behind the Veil: Inner Meanings of Women's Islamic Dress Code," *The International Journal of Interdisciplinary Social Sciences* 6 (2012): 115–126.
Galadari, Abdulla. "*Creatio ex Nihilo* and the Literal Qur'an," *Intellectual Discourse* 25 (2017): 381–408.
Galadari, Abdulla. "Inner Meanings of Islamic Finance: Understanding the Theory Behind All Theories," in *Islam, Accounting and Finance: Challenges and Opportunities in the New Decade*, eds. Norhayati M. Alwi and Sherliza P. Nelson, 1–18, Kuala Lumpur: IIUM Press, 2011.
Galadari, Abdulla. "*Layla al-Qadr*: Muḥammad Assuming Authority by Alluding to the Gospel of John," in *New Trends in Qur'anic Studies*, ed. Mun'im Sirry, Atlanta, GA: Lockwood Press, forthcoming.

Galadari, Abdulla. "Science vs. Religion: The Debate Ends," *The International Journal of Science in Society* 2 (2011): 1–8.

Galadari, Abdulla. "The Camel Passing Through the Eye of the Needle: A Qur'anic Interpretation of the Gospels," *Ancient Near Eastern Studies* (forthcoming).

Galadari, Abdulla. "The *Qibla*: An Allusion to the Shemaʿ," *Comparative Islamic Studies* 9, no. 2 (2013): 165–193.

Galadari, Abdulla. "The Role of Intertextual Polysemy in Qur'anic Exegesis," *International Journal on Quranic Research* 3, no. 4 (2013): 35–56.

Galadari, Abdulla. "The *Taqlīd al-Ijtihād* Paradox: Challenges to Qur'anic Hermeneutics," *Al-Bayān: Journal of Qur'ānic and Ḥadīth Studies* 13, no. 2 (2015): 145–167.

Gardner-Smith, P. *Saint John and the Synoptic Gospels*, Cambridge: Cambridge University Press, 1938.

Gargett, Robert H. "Grave Shortcomings: The Evidence for Neanderthal Burial," *Current Anthropology* 30, no. 2 (1989): 157–190.

Geiger, Abraham. *Was hat Mohammed aus dem Judenthume aufgenommen?* Bonn: F. Baaden, 1833.

Gesenius, William, *Gesenius' Hebrew-Chaldee Lexicon to the Old Testament*, Bellingham, WA: Logos Bible Software, n.d.

Gianotti, L. R. R., Mohr, C., Pizzagalli, D., Lehmann, D., and Brugger, P. "Associative Processing and Paranormal Belief," *Psychiatry and Clinical Neurosciences* 55 (2001): 595–603.

Gibbs Jr., Raymond W. "Authorial Intentions in Text Understanding," *Discourse Processes* 32, no. 1 (2001): 73–80.

Gibbs Jr., Raymond W., Kushner, Julia M., and Mills III, W. Rob. "Authorial Intentions and Metaphor Comprehension," *Journal of Psycholinguistic Research* 20, no. 1 (1991): 11–30.

Ginzberg, Louis. *Legends of the Jews*, Philadelphia, PA: The Jewish Publication Society, 2003.

Goss, James. "Poetics in Schizophrenic Language: Speech, Gesture and Biosemiotics," *Biosemiotics* 4, no. 3 (2011): 291–307.

Goss, James. "The Poetics of Bipolar Disorder," *Pragmatics & Cognition* 14, no. 1 (2006): 83–110.

Graf, D. F. and Zwettler, M. J. "The North Arabian 'Thamudic E' Inscription from Uraynibah West," *Bulletin of the American Schools of Oriental Research* 335 (2004): 53–89.

Grese, William C. "'Unless One Is Born Again': The Use of a Heavenly Journey in John 3," *Journal of Biblical Literature* 107, no. 4 (1988): 677–693.

Griffith, Sidney H. "Byzantium and the Christians in the World of Islam: Constantinople and the Church in the Holy Land in the Ninth Century," *Medieval Encounters* 3, no. 3 (1997): 231–265.

Grimshaw, G. M., Bryson, F. M., Atchley, R. A., and Humphrey, M. "Semantic Ambiguity Resolution in Positive Schizotypy: A Right Hemisphere Interpretation," *Neuropsychology* 24 (2010): 130–138.

Guo, L. "Al-Biqāʿī's Chronicle: A Fifteenth Century Learned Man's Reflection on His Time and World," in *The Historiography of Islamic Egypt, c.950–1800*, ed. Hugh Kennedy, 121–148, Leiden: Brill, 2000.

Gupta, Nijay K. "Which 'Body' Is a Temple (1 Corinthians 6:19)? Paul Beyond the Individual/Communal Divide," *The Catholic Biblical Quarterly* 72, no. 3 (2010): 518–536.

Guthrie, A. and Bishop, E. F. F. "The Paraclete, Almunhamanna and Aḥmad," *The Muslim World* 41, no. 4 (1951): 251–256.
Gyatso, Tenzin (Dalai Lama XIV). *Beyond Religion: Ethics for a Whole World*, New York, NY: Houghton Mifflin Harcourt, 2011.
Haight, Roger. *Jesus, Symbol of God*, Maryknoll, NY: Orbis Books, 1999.
Hall, S. G. *Doctrine and Practice in the Early Church*, Grand Rapids, MI: Wm. B. Eerdmans, 2003.
Halliday, W. R. *The Pagan Background of Early Christianity*, Whitefish, MT: Kessinger, 2010.
Halperin, David J. *Seeking Ezekiel: Text and Psychology*, University Park, PA: Penn State University Press, 1993.
Hamid, A. H. and Nordin, N. Z. "A Study on Islamic Banking Education and Strategy for the New Millennium: Malaysian Experience," *International Journal of Islamic Financial Services* 2, no. 4 (2001): 3–11.
Hanson, Anthony T. "John i. 14–18 and Exodus xxxiv," *New Testament Studies* 23, no. 1 (1976): 90–101.
Hanson, Anthony T. *The New Testament Interpretation of Scripture*, London: SPCK, 1980.
Hanson, Craig L. "Manuel I Comnenus and the 'God of Muhammad': A Study in Byzantine Ecclesiastical Politics," in *Medieval Christian Perceptions of Islam: A Book of Essays*, ed. John V. Tolan, New York, NY: Garland, 1996.
Ḥaqqī, Ismāʿīl (d. 1127/1715). *Rūḥ al-bayān fī tafsīr al-Qurʾān*, Beirut: Dār al-Fikr, n.d.
Haring, Nicholas M. "Commentaries on the Pseudo-Athanasian Creed," *Medieval Studies* 34 (1972): 208–252.
Harris, W. V. *Ancient Literacy*, Cambridge, MA: Harvard University Press, 1991.
Hawting, Gerald. "Review of Lüling," *Journal of Semitic Studies* 27 (1982): 111.
Hayward, C. T. Robert. "The Holy Name of the God of Moses and the Prologue of St John's Gospel," *New Testament Studies* 25, no. 1 (1978): 16–32.
Hayward, C. T. Robert. *Targums and the Transmission of Scripture into Judaism and Christianity*, Leiden: Brill, 2010.
Healey, J. F. "Lexical Loans in Early Syriac: A Comparison with Nabataean Aramaic," *Studi Epigrafici Linguistici* 12 (1995): 75–84.
Healey, J. F., ed. *The Nabataean Tomb Inscriptions of Madaʾin Salih, Journal of Semitic Studies, Supplement 1*, trans. S. Al-Theeb (Arabic section), Oxford: Oxford University Press, 1994.
Heath, P. *Allegory and Philosophy in Avicenna (Ibn Sînâ): With a Translation of the Book of the Prophet Muhammad's Ascent to Heaven*, Philadelphia, PA: University of Pennsylvania Press, 1992.
Heath, P. "Creative Hermeneutics: A Comparative Analysis of Three Islamic Approaches," *Arabica* 36, no. 2 (1989): 173–210.
Hecker, Bernice V. "The Biradical Origin of Semitic Roots," PhD Dissertation: University of Texas at Austin, 2007.
Hecker, H. M. "A Zooarchaeological Inquiry into Pork Consumption in Egypt from Prehistoric to New Kingdom Times," *Journal of the American Research Center in Egypt* 19 (1982): 59–71.
Heinrichs, W. "On the Genesis of the *ḥaqīqa–majāz* Dichotomy," *Studia Islamica* 59 (1984): 111–140.
Hess, Richard S. "Splitting the Adam: The Usage of ʾĀadām in Genesis I–V1," *Studies in the Pentateuch* 41 (1990): 1–15.

Hick, John. *A Christian Theology of Religions: The Rainbow of Faiths*, Louisville, KY: Westminster John Knox, 1995.

Hick, John. 2006. "Any Particular Religion?" in *The New Frontier of Religion and Science*, 146–153, Basingstoke: Palgrave Macmillan, 2010.

Hick, John. "Religion, Violence and Global Conflict: A Christian Proposal," *Global Dialogue* 2 (2000): 1–10.

Hick, John. "Religious Pluralism and Salvation," in *The Philosophical Challenge of Religious Diversity*, eds. P. L. Quinn and K. Meeker, 54-66, Oxford: Oxford University Press, 1988.

Hick, John. "The Next Step beyond Dialogue," in *The Myth of Religious Superiority: Multifaith Explorations of Religious Pluralism*, ed. P. F. Knitter, 1–12, Maryknoll, NY: Orbis Books, 2005.

Hick, John. "The Non-Absoluteness of Christianity," in *The Myth of Christian Uniqueness: Toward a Pluralistic Theology of Religions*, ed. J. Hick and P. F. Knitter, 16–36, Eugene, OR: Wipf and Stock, 2005.

Hinzen, Wolfram and Rosselló, Joana. "The Linguistics of Schizophrenia: Thought Disturbance as Language Pathology Across Positive Symptoms," *Frontiers in Psychology* 6 (2015): art. 971. http://dro.dur.ac.uk/15916/.

Hirschfeld, Hartwig. *New Researches into the Composition and Exegesis of the Qoran*, London: Royal Asiatic Society, 1902.

Hodge, Charles. *An Exposition of the First Epistle to the Corinthians*, New York, NY: Robert Carter & Brothers, 1857.

Hoffman, R. E. "Computer Simulations of Neural Information Processing and the Schizophrenia-Mania Dichotomy," *Archives of General Psychology* 44 (1987): 178–188.

Høgel, Christian. "An Early Anonymous Greek Translation of the Qur'an: The Fragments from Niketas Byzantios' *Refutatio* and the Anonymous *Abjuratio*," *Collectanea Christiana Orientalia* 7 (2010): 65–119.

Holman Illustrated Bible Dictionary, Nashville, TN: Holman Bible Publishers, 2003.

Homer, S. *A History of Interest Rates*, New Brunswick, NJ: Rutgers University Press, 1996.

Hooker, Morna D. "The Johannine Prologue and the Messianic Secret," *New Testament Studies* 21, no. 1 (1974): 40–58.

Hooper, Richard, ed. *Jesus, Buddha, Krishna, Lao Tzu: The Parallel Sayings—The Common Teachings of Four Religions*, Sedona, AZ: Sanctuary Books, 2007.

Horan, Roy. "The Neuropsychological Connection Between Creativity and Meditation," *Creativity Research Journal* 21, no. 2/3 (2009): 199–222.

Houtman, Alberdina and Sysling, Harry. *Alternative Targum Traditions: The Use of Variant Readings for the Study in Origin and History of Targum Jonathan*, Leiden: Brill, 2009.

Hurovitz, Craig S., Dunn, Sarah, Domhoff, G. William, and Fiss, Harry. "The Dreams of Blind Men and Women: A Replication and Extension of Previous Findings," *Dreaming* 9, no. 2/3 (1999): 183–193.

Ibn ʿAbdulsalām, Al-ʿIzz (d. 660/1262). *al-Imām fī bayān adillat al-aḥkām*, ed. Riḍwān Mukhtār ibn Gharbiyyah, Beirut: Dār al-Bashāʾir al-Islāmiyyah, n.d.

Ibn ʿAbdulwahhāb (d. 1206/1792). *al-Rasāʾil al-shakhṣiyyah*, eds. S. Al-Fawzān and M. al-ʿAilaqi, Riyadh: Al-Imam Muhammad ibn Saud Islamic University, n.d.

Ibn ʿAbdulwahhāb (d. 1206/1792). *Kashf al-shubuhāt*, Riyadh: Ministry of Islamic Affairs, 1998.

Ibn Abī al-Ḥadīd (d. 656/1258). *Sharḥ nahj al-balāghah*, unknown publisher, n.d.

Ibn Abī al-ʿIzz (d. 792/1390). *Sharḥ al-ʿaqīdah al-ṭaḥāwiyyah*, Riyadh: Ministry of Islamic Affairs, 1998.

Ibn al-ʿImād. *Kashf al-sarāʾir fī maʿna al-wujūh wal-ashbāh wal-naẓāʾir*, ed. Fuʾād Abdulmonʿim, Alexandria: al-Maktabah al-Miṣriyyeh, 2004.

Ibn al-Jizrī. *Manāqib al-asad al-ghālib mumazziq al-katāʾib wa muẓhir al-ʿajāʾib Layth ibn Ghālib amīr al-muʾminīn Abī al-Ḥasan ʿAlī ibn Abī Ṭālib*, ed. Ṭ. Al-Ṭanṭawi, Cairo: Maktabat al-Qurʾān, 1994.

Ibn al-Muthannā, Abū ʿUbaydah Muʿammar (d. 209/824). *Majāz al-Qurʾān*, Cairo: Maktabat al-Khānjī, 1961.

Ibn ʿArabī (d. 638/1240). *Tafsīr al-Qurʾān*, Beirut: Ṣādir, 2007.

Ibn ʿAsākir (d. 571/1175). *Tabyīn kadhb al-muftarī fīma nusiba ila al-imām Abī al-Ḥasan al-Ashʿarī*, Beirut: al-Kutub al-ʿArabī, 1984.

Ibn ʿĀshūr (d. 1973). *al-Taḥrīr wal-tanwīr*, Tunis: al-Dār al-Tūnisiyyah lil-Nashr, 1984.

Ibn Bābawayh (d. 381/991). *al-Tawḥīd*, ed. Hāshim al-Ḥusaynī al-Ṭahrānī, Qom: Manshūrāt Jamāʿah al-Mudarrisīn fil-Ḥawzah al-ʿIlmiyyah, 1978.

Ibn Baṭṭah (d. 387/997). *al-Ibānah al-kubra*, Riyadh: Dār al-Rāyah wal-Tawzīʿ, 1995.

Ibn Ḥanbal (d. 241/855). *al-Radd ʿala al-jahmiyyah wal-zanādiqah*, ed. Ṣ. Shahīn, Riyadh: al-Thabāt, 2002.

Ibn Ḥazm (d. 456/1064). *al-Faṣl fil-milal wal-ahwāʾ wal-niḥal*, Cairo: al-Khānjī, n.d.

Ibn Ḥazm (d. 456/1064). *al-Nāsikh wal-mansūkh fil-Qurʾān al-karīm*, ed. A. Al-Bindāri, Beirut: al-Kutub al-ʿIlmiyyah, 1986.

Ibn Hishām (d. 213/833). *Sīrah*, Cairo: Maktabat wa Maṭbaʿat Muṣṭafa al-Bābī al-Ḥalabī wa Awlādih, 1955.

Ibn Isḥāq (d. 151/768). *Sīrah*, Beirut: Dār al-Fikr, 1978.

Ibn Jinnī (d. 392/1002). *al-Khaṣāʾiṣ*, Cairo: al-Hayʾah al-Miṣriyyah al-ʿĀmmah lil-Kitāb, n.d.

Ibn Kathīr (d. 774/1373). *al-Bidāyah wal-nihāyah*, Beirut: Dār Iḥyāʾ al-Turāth al-ʿArabī, 1988.

Ibn Kathīr (d. 774/1373). *Tafsīr al-Qurʾān al-ʿaẓīm*, ed. Sāmī Salāmeh, Riyadh: Dār Ṭaybah, n.d.

Ibn Mājih (d. 273/887). *Sunan Ibn Mājih*, ed. M. F. Abdul-Bāqī, Cairo: Dār Iḥyāʾ al-Kutub al-ʿArabiyyah, n.d.

Ibn Manẓūr (d. 711/1311). *Lisān al-ʿarab*, Beirut: Ṣāḍir, 1994.

Ibn Qayyim (d. 751/1350). *al-Rūḥ fil-kalām ʿala arwāḥ al-amwāt wal-aḥyāʾ bil-dalāʾil min al-kitāb wal-sunnah*, Beirut: Dār al-Kutub al-ʿIlmiyyah, n.d.

Ibn Qayyim (d. 751/1350). *Hidāyah al-ḥayāra fī ajwibah al-yahūd wal-naṣāra*, ed. M. Al-Ḥāj, Jeddah: Dār al-Qalam, 1996.

Ibn Qayyim (d. 751/1350). *Ighāthat al-lahfān min maṣāʾid al-shayṭān*, ed. M. al-Faqī, Riyadh: al-Maʿārif, n.d.

Ibn Qudāmah al-Maqdisī (d. 620/1223). *Taḥrīm al-naẓar fī kutub al-kalām*, ed. A. M. S. Dimashqiyyah, Riyadh: ʿĀlam al-Kutub, 1990.

Ibn Saʿd (d. 230/845). *al-Ṭabaqāt al-kubra*, Beirut: Dār al-Kutub al-ʿIlmiyyah, 1990.

Ibn Sīdah (d. 458/1066). *al-Mukhaṣṣaṣ*, ed. Khalīl Ibrāhīm Jifāl, Beirut: Dār Iḥyāʾ al-Turāth al-ʿArabī, 1996.

Ibn Sulaymān, Muqātil (d. 150/767). *Tafsīr Muqātil ibn Sulaymān*, ed. A. M. Shaḥāteh, Beirut: Dār Iḥyāʾ al-Turāth, 2003.

Ibn Ṭāhir al-Baghdādī (d. 429/1037). *al-Farq bayn al-firaq wa bayān al-firqah al-nājiyah*, Beirut: Dār al-Āfāq al-Jadīdah, 1977.

Ibn Taymiyyah (d. 728/1328). *Al-Īman*, ed. M. al-Albānī, Amman: Al-Maktab al-Islāmī, 1996.

Ibn, Taymiyyah (d. 728/1328). *al-Jawāb al-ṣaḥīḥ liman baddal dīn al-masīḥ*, ed. ʿAlī ibn Ḥasan, ʿAbdul-Azīz ibn Ibrahīm, and Ḥamdān ibn Muḥammad, Riyadh: Dār al-ʿĀsimah, 1984.

Ibrāhīm, Muḥammad Zakī-al-Dīn. *'Iṣmat al-anbiyā'*, Cairo: Dār al-Naṣr, 1989.
Idel, Moshe. *Kabbalah: New Perspectives*, New Haven, CT: Yale University Press, 1988.
Iqbal, Z. and Mirakhor, A. "Progress and Challenges of Islamic Banking," *Thunderbird International Business Review* 41, no. 4/5 (1999): 381–405.
Isen, A., Johnson, M. Mertz, E., and Robinson, G. "The Influence of Positive Affect on the Unusualness of Word Associations," *Journal of Personality and Social Psychology* 48, no. 6 (1985): 1413–1426.
Isma'īl, M. B. *Dirāsāt fī 'ulūm al-Qur'ān*, Cairo: Dār al-Manār, 1999.
Izutsu, T. *Ethico-Religious Concepts in the Qur'an*, Montreal: McGill-Queen's University Press, 2002.
Jacobs, S. L. "The Last Uncomfortable Religious Question? Monotheistic Exclusivism and Textual Superiority in Judaism, Christianity, and Islam," in *Confronting Genocide: Judaism, Christianity, Islam*, ed. S. L. Jacobs, 35–46, Lanham, MD: Rowman & Littlefield, 2009.
Jaffer, A. and Jaffer, M. *Quranic Sciences*, London: ICAS Press, 2009.
James, William. *The Varieties of Religious Experience: A Study in Human Nature*, New York, NY: Longmans, Green & Co., 1902.
Jamieson, R., Fausset, A. R., and Brown, D. 1871. *Commentary Critical and Explanatory on the Whole Bible*, Hartford, CT: S. S. Scranton, 1997.
Janzen, J. Gerald. "What's in a Name? 'Yahweh' in Exodus 3 and the Wider Biblical Context," *Interpretation* 33, no. 3 (1979): 227–239.
Jeffery, Arthur. *The Foreign Vocabulary of the Qur'ān*, Baroda, India: Oriental Institute, 1938.
Jones, L. B. "The Paraclete or Mohammed: The Verdict of an Ancient Manuscript," *The Muslim World* 10, no. 2 (1920): 112–125.
Joseph, Rhawn. "Early Environmental Influences on Neural Plasticity, the Limbic System, and Social Emotional Development and Attachment," *Child Psychiatry and Human Development* 29, no. 3 (1999): 189–208.
Joseph, Rhawn. "The Limbic System and the Soul: Evolution and the Neuroanatomy of Religious Experience," *Zygon* 36, no. 1 (2001): 105–136.
Joseph, Rhawn. "The Neurology of Traumatic 'Dissociative' Amnesia: Commentary and Literature Review," *Child Abuse and Neglect* 23, no. 8 (1999): 715–727.
Joseph, Rhawn. *The Transmitter to God: The Limbic System, the Soul, and Spirituality*, San Jose, CA: University Press California, 2001.
Joseph, Rhawn. "Traumatic Amnesia, Repression, and Hippocampus Injury Due to Emotional Stress, Corticosteroids and Enkephalins," *Child Psychiatry and Human Development* 29, no. 2 (1998): 169–185.
Jung, Carl G. *Active Imagination*, Princeton, NJ: Princeton University Press, 1997.
Jung, Carl G. *Modern Man in Search of a Soul*, London: Kegan Paul, Trench, Trubner and Co., 1933.
Jung, Carl G. *Psychology and Religion*, New Haven, CT: Yale University Press, 1938.
Kahf, M. "Islamic Economics: Notes on Definition and Methodology," *Review of Islamic Economics* 13 (2003): 23–38.
Kahn, David. "From Chaos to Self-Organization: The Brain, Dreaming, and Religious Experience," in *Soul, Psyche, Brain: New Directions in the Study of Religion and Brain-Mind Science*, ed. Kelly Bulkeley, 138–158, New York, NY: Palgrave Macmillan, 2005.
Kamp, Albert H. *Inner Worlds: A Cognitive Linguistic Approach to the Book of Jonah*, Leiden: Brill, 2004.

Kaski, Diego. "Revision: Is Visual Perception a Requisite for Visual Imagery?" *Perception* 31, no. 6 (2002): 717–731.
Katz, Albert N. and Lee, Christopher J. "The Role of Authorial Intent in Determining Verbal Irony and Metaphor," *Metaphor and Symbolic Activity* 8, no. 4 (1993): 257–279.
Katz, Steven T., ed. *Comparative Mysticism: An Anthology of Original Sources*, Oxford: Oxford University Press, 2013.
Kaufman, James C. "Dissecting the Golden Goose: Components of Studying Creative Writers," *Creativity Research Journal* 14, no. 1 (2002): 27–40.
Kaufmann, Stephen A., ed. *Targum Lexicon: Comprehensive Aramaic Lexicon Project*, Cincinnati, OH: Hebrew Union College, n.d.
Kaye, A. S. "Arabic Morphology," in *Morphologies of Asia and Africa*, ed. A. S. Kaye, Warsaw, IN: Eisenbrauns, 2007.
Keddie, N. R. "Symbol and Sincerity in Islam," *Studia Islamica* 19 (1963): 27–63.
Kenawy, Salah. "A Linguistic Reading in the Disjointed Letters," *Islamic Quarterly* 42, no. 4 (1998): 243–255.
Kenett, Yoed, N., Anaki, David, and Faust, Miriam. "Investigating the Structure of Semantic Networks in Low and High Creative Persons," *Frontiers in Human Neuroscience* 8 (2014): art. 407.
Kéri, Szabolcs. "Genes for Psychosis and Creativity: A Promoter Polymorphism of the Neuregulin 1 Gene Is Related to Creativity in People with High Intellectual Achievement," *Psychological Science* 20, no. 9 (2009): 1070–1073.
Kerr, Nancy H. and Domhoff, G. William. "Do the Blind Literally 'See' in Their Dreams? A Critique of a Recent Claim that They Do," *Dreaming* 14, no. 4 (2004): 230–233.
Khalil, M. H. "Salvation and the 'Other' in Islamic Thought: The Contemporary Pluralism Debate," *Religion Compass* 5 (2011): 511–519.
Khoury, Adel-Théodore. *Les théologiens byzantins et l'islam: Textes et auteurs [VIIIe-XIIIe siècles]*, Leuven: Nauwelaerts, 1969.
Kiang, M. and Kutas, M. "Abnormal Typicality of Responses on a Category Fluency Task in Schizotypy," *Psychiatry Research* 145 (2006): 119–126.
Kieffer, B. "Herder's Treatment of Süssmilch's Theory of the Origin of Language in the *Abhandlung über den Ursprung der Sprache*: A Re-evaluation," *The Germanic Review: Literature, Culture, Theory* 53, no. 3 (1978): 96–105.
Kille, D. Andrew. *Psychological Biblical Criticism*, Minneapolis, MN: Fortress Press, 2001.
King, Karen L. *What Is Gnosticism?* Cambridge, MA: Harvard University Press, 2003.
King, Leonard W. *Legends of Babylon and Egypt in Relation to Hebrew Tradition*, Oxford: Oxford University Press, 1916.
Kischka, U., Kammer, T. H., Maier, S., Weisbrod, M. Thimm, M., and Spitzer, M. "Dopaminergic Modulation of Semantic Network Activation," *Neuropsychologia* 34, no. 11 (1996): 1107–1113.
Kister, Meir J. "Ḥaddithū ʿan Banī Isrāʾīla wa-la Ḥarajā: A Study of an Early Tradition," *Israel Oriental Studies* 2 (1972): 215–239.
Klein, Ernst *A Comprehensive Etymological Dictionary of the Hebrew Language for Readers of English*, Jerusalem: Carta, 1987.
Knauf, Ernst A. "Yahwe," *Vetus Testamentum* 34, no. 4 (1984): 467–472.
Koehler, L. and Baumgartner, W. *The Hebrew and Aramaic Lexicon of the Old Testament*, Leiden: Brill, 2000.
Koester, Craig R. *Symbolism in the Fourth Gospel: Meaning, Mystery, Community*, Minneapolis, MN: Fortress Press, 1995.

Koester, Craig R. *The Dwelling of God: The Tabernacle in the Old Testament, Intertestamental Jewish Literature, and the New Testament*, Washington, DC: Catholic Biblical Association, 1989.

Koh, Caroline. "Reviewing the Link Between Creativity and Madness: A Postmodern Perspective," *Educational Research Reviews* 1, no. 7 (2006): 213–221.

Kopf, L. "Religious Influences on Medieval Arabic Philology," *Studia Islamica* 5 (1956): 33–59.

Kosmala, Hans. "The Name of God (YHWH and HU')," *Annual of the Swedish Theological Institute* 2 (1963): 103–120.

Köstenberger, Andreas J. *Encountering John: The Gospel in Historical, Literary, and Theological Perspective*, Grand Rapids, MI: Baker Academic, 2002.

Kozbelt, Aaron, Kaufman, Scott Barry, Walder, Deborah J., Ospina, Luz H., and Kim, Joseph U. "The Evolutionary Genetics of the Creativity–Psychosis Connection," in *Creativity and Mental Illness*, ed. James C. Kaufman, 102–132, Cambridge: Cambridge University Press, 2014.

Krill, A., Alpert, H. J., and Ostfeld, A. M. "Effects of a Hallucinogenic Agent in Totally Blind Subjects," *Archives of Ophthalmology* 62, no. 2 (1963): 180–185.

Krippner, Stanley, Richards, Ruth, and Abraham, Frederick D. "Creativity and Chaos While Waking and Dreaming," *Lumina* 21, no. 2 (2010): 1–17.

Krueger, Robert. "The Origin and Terminology of the Athanasian Creed," *Western Pastoral Conference of the Dakota-Montana District*, October 5–6, 1976.

Langdon, R. and Coltheart, M. "Recognition of Metaphor and Irony in Young Adults: The Impact of Schizotypal Personality Traits," *Psychiatry Research* 125 (2004): 9–20.

Langkammer, P. H. "Zur Herkunft des Logostitels im Johannesprolog," *Biblische Zeitschrift* 9 (1965): 91–94.

Lapide, C. *The Great Commentary*, trans. T. W. Mossman, Edinburgh: John Grant, 1908.

Lapin, Hayim. *Rabbis as Romans: The Rabbinic Movement in Palestine, 100–400 CE*, Oxford: Oxford University Press, 2012.

Lehmann, A. C. and Myers, J. E., eds. *Magic, Witchcraft, and Religion*, Mountain View, CA: Mayfield, 1993.

Lenski, Richard C. H. *The Interpretation of St. John's Gospel*, Minneapolis, MN: Augsburg, 1961.

Lenski, Richard C. H. *The Interpretation of St. Paul's First and Second Epistles to the Corinthians*, Minneapolis, MN: Augsburg, 1963.

León, D. Muñoz. "El Pentateuco en San Juan," in *Entrar en lo Antiguo: Acerca de la relación entre Antiguo y Nuevo Testamento*, eds. I. Carbajosa and L. Sánchez Navarro, Presencia y diálogo 16, Madrid: Facultad de Teología "San Dámaso," 2007.

Leonhard, Dirk M. A. and Brugger, Peter. "Creative, Paranormal, and Delusional Thought: A Consequence of Right Hemisphere Semantic Activation?" *Neuropsychiatry, Neuropsychology, & Behavioral Neurology* 11, no. 4 (1998): 177–183.

Lewison, M. "Conflict of Interest? The Ethics of Usury," *Journal of Business Ethics* 22, no. 4 (1999): 327–339.

Lexham Bible Dictionary, Bellingham, WA: Lexham Press.

Lincoln, A. T. *Black's New Testament Commentary: The Gospel According to Saint John*, Peabody, MA: Hendrickson, 2006.

Lioy, Dan. *The Search for Ultimate Reality: Intertextuality Between the Genesis and Johannine Prologues*, New York, NY: Peter Lang, 2005.

Lobban, R. A. "Pigs and Their Prohibition," *International Journal of Middle East Studies* 26, no. 1 (1994): 57–75.

Lodge, Daniel J. and Grace, Anthony A. "Developmental Pathology, Dopamine, Stress, and Schizophrenia," *International Journal of Developmental Neuroscience* 29, no. 3 (2011): 207–213.

Lorenz, M. "Problems Posed by Schizophrenic Language," *Archives of General Psychiatry* 4 (1961): 603–610.

Louie, Kenway and Wilson, Matthew A. "Temporally Structured Replay of Awake Hippocampal Ensemble Activity during Rapid Eye Movement Sleep," *Neuron* 29 (2001): 1454–156.

Louw, J. P. and Nida, E., eds. *Greek–English Lexicon of the New Testament Based on Semantic Domains*, New York, NY: United Bible Societies, 1989.

Lubow, R. E. and Gewirtz, J. C. "Latent Inhibition in Humans: Data, Theory, and Implications for Schizophrenia," *Psychological Bulletin* 117, no. 1 (1995): 87–103.

Lubow, R. E., Ingberg-Sachs, Y., Zalstein-Orda, N., and Gewirtz, J. C. "Latent Inhibition in Low and High 'Psychotic-Prone' Normal Subjects," *Personality and Individual Differences* 13, no. 5 (1992): 563–572.

Lüling, Günter. *Über den Ur-Qurʾan: Ansätze zur Rekonstruktion vorislamischer christlicher Strophenlieder im Qurʾan*, Erlangen: Verlagsbuchhdlg, 1974.

Luxenberg, Christoph. *Die syro-aramäische Lesart des Koran: Ein Beitrag zur Entschlusselung der Koransprache*, Berlin: Verlag Hans Schiller, 2000.

Macdonald, Duncan B. *Aspects of Islam*, New York, NY: Macmillan, 1911.

Maçkali, Zeynep, Gülöksüz, Sinan, and Oral, Timuçin. "Creativity and Bipolar Disorder," *Turkish Journal of Psychiatry* 25, no. 1 (2014): 50–59.

Madelung, W. "Abū ʿUbayda Maʿmar b. Almuthannā as a Historian," *Journal of Islamic Studies* 3, no. 1 (1992): 47–56.

Makram, ʿAbdulʿāl Sālim. *al-Mushtarak al-lafẓī fī al-ḥaql al-Qurʾānī*, Beirut: Muʾassassat al-Risālah, 1997.

Malinowski, Bronislaw. *Magic, Science and Religion*, New York, NY: Doubleday, 1954.

Marshall, Howard. "Church and Temple in the New Testament," *Tyndale Bulletin* 40, no. 2 (1989): 203–222.

Martin, Richard C. "Createdness of the Qurʾān," *Encyclopedia of the Qurʾān*, ed. Jane D. McAuliffe, Leiden: Brill, 2005.

May, Eric. "The Logos in the Old Testament," *Catholic Bible Quarterly* 8, no. 4 (1946): 438–447.

Mazuz, Haggai. *The Religious and Spiritual Life of the Jews of Medina*, Leiden: Brill, 2014.

McCreery, Charles. *Dreams and Psychosis: A New Look at an Old Hypothesis*, n.p.: Oxford Forum, 2008.

McGrath, Alister E. *Historical Theology: An Introduction to the History of Christian Thought*, Chichester: Wiley-Blackwell, 2013.

McNamara, Martin. "*Logos* of the Fourth Gospel and *Memra* of the Palestinian Targum (Ex 12^{42})," *The Expository Times* 79, no. 4 (1968): 115–117.

McNamara, Martin. *Targum and New Testament: Collected Essays*, Tübingen: Mohr Siebeck, 2011.

McNamara, Martin. *Targum and Testament Revisited: Aramaic Paraphrases of the Hebrew Bible: A Light on the New Testament*, Grand Rapids, MI: Wm. B. Eerdmans, 2010.

Meissner, William W. *The Cultic Origins of Christianity: The Dynamic of Religious Development*, Collegeville, MN: Liturgical Press, 2000.

Melchert, C. "Qurʾanic Abrogation Across the Ninth Century," in *Studies in Islamic Legal Theory*, ed. B. G. Weiss, Leiden: Brill, 2002.

Melvin, David. "The Gilgamesh Traditions and the Pre-history of Genesis 6:1–4," *Perspectives in Religious Studies* 8, no. 1 (2011): 23–32.

Menken, Maarten J. J. " 'Born of God' or 'Begotten by God'? A Translation Problem in the Johannine Writings," *Novum Testamentum* 51 (2009): 352–368.

Menken, Maarten J. J. "Genesis in John's Gospel," in *Studies in John's Gospel and Epistles: Collected Essays*, Leuven: Peeters, 2015.

Merkur, Dan. *Gnosis: An Esoteric Tradition of Mystical Visions and Unions*, Albany, NY: State University of New York Press, 1993.

Metawa, S. A. and Almossawi, M. "Banking Behavior of Islamic Bank Customers: Perspectives and Implications," *International Journal of Bank Marketing* 16, no. 7 (1998): 299–313.

Mettinger, Tryggve N. D. *Namnet och närvaron: Gudsnamn och gudsbild I Böckernas Bok*, Örebro: Bokforlaget Libris, 1987.

Meyendorff, John. "Byzantine Views of Islam," *Dumbarton Oaks Paper* 18 (1964): 113–132.

Milik, J. T. "Inscriptions grecques et nabatéennes de Rawwafah," *Bulletin of the Institute of Archaeology* 10 (1971): 54–59.

Miller, Ed L. "The Johannine Origins of the Johannine Logos," *Journal of Biblical Literature* 112, no. 3 (1993): 445–457.

Miller, John W. *Jesus at Thirty: A Psychological and Historical Portrait*, Minneapolis, MN: Fortress Press, 1997.

Mingana, A., ed. "The Apology of Timothy the Patriarch Before the Caliph Mahdi," *Bulletin of the John Rylands Library* 12, no. 1 (1928): 137–298.

Mitchell, Basil. *Morality: Religious and Secular—The Dilemma of the Traditional Conscience*, Oxford: Oxford University Press, 1980.

Mitchell, R. L. C. and Crow, T. J. "Right Hemisphere Language Functions and Schizophrenia: The Forgotten Hemisphere?" *Brain: A Journal of Neurology* 128 (2005): 963–978.

Modarressi, H. "Early Debates on the Integrity of the Qur'an: A Brief Survey," *Studia Islamica* 77 (1993): 5–39.

Mohammed, K. "Assessing English Translations of the Qur'an," *Middle East Quarterly* 12 (2005): 58–71.

Mohr, C., Graves, R. E., Gianotti, L. R. R., Pizzagalli, D., and Brugger, P. "Loose but Normal: A Semantic Association Study," *Journal of Psycholinguistic Research* 30 (2001): 475–483.

Moloney, Francis. *Belief in the Word: Reading John 1–4*, Minneapolis, MN: Fortress Press, 1993.

Montgomery, James A. "The Hebrew Divine Name and the Personal Pronoun Hū," *Journal of Biblical Literature* 63, no. 2 (1944): 161–163.

Moody, D. "God's Only Son: The Translation of John 3:16 in the Revised Standard Version," *Journal of Biblical Literature* 72, no. 4 (1953): 213–219.

Morgenstern, Julian. "Deutero-Isaiah's Terminology for 'Universal God,' " *Journal of Biblical Literature* 62, no. 4 (1943): 273–274.

Moulton, J. H. and Milligan, G. *Vocabulary of the Greek Testament*, Peabody, MA: Hendrickson, 1930.

Mowinckel, Sigmund. "The Name of the God of Moses," *Hebrew Union College Annual* 32 (1961): 121–133.

Moyise, Steve. "Authorial Intention and the Book of Revelation," *Andreas University Seminary Studies* 39, no. 1 (2001): 35–40.

Muir, William, trans., *The Apology of al-Kindy: Written at the Court of al-Mâmûn (Circa A.H. 215; A.D. 830), in Defence of Christianity Against Islam*, London: Society for Promoting Christian Knowledge, 1887.

Murray, Evan D., Cunningham, Miles G., and Price, Bruce. "The Role of Psychotic Disorders in Religious History Considered," *The Journal of Neuropsychiatry and Clinical Neurosciences* 24, no. 4 (2012): 410–426.

Murtonen, Aimo E. *A Philological and Literary Treatise on the Old Testament Divine Names ʾl, ʾlwh, ʾlhym, and Yhwh*, Helsinki: Societas Orientalis Fennica, 1952.

Musa, A. Y. *Ḥadīth as Scripture: Discussions on the Authority of Prophetic Traditions in Islam*, London: Palgrave Macmillan, 2008.

Musa, A. Y. "The Qurʾanists," *Religion Compass* 4 (2010): 12–21.

Muslim (d. 261/875). *Ṣaḥīḥ Muslim*, ed. M. F. Abdul-Bāqī, Beirut: Iḥyāʾ al-Turāth al-ʿArabī, n.d.

Mutahhari, M. "Understanding the Uniqueness of the Qurʾan," *al-Tawḥīd* 1 (1987): 9–23.

Naʿnāʿah, R. *al-Isrāʾīliyyāt wa atharuhā fī kutub al-tafsīr*, Damascus: Dār al-Qalam, 1970.

Nanji, A. "Ismāʿīlism," in *Islamic Spirituality: Foundations*, ed. Seyyed Hossein Nasr, 179–198, London: Routledge & Keegan Paul, 1987.

Naqvi, S. N. H. *Islam, Economics, and Society*, London: Kegan Paul, 1994.

Nasr, Seyyed Hossein, ed., *The Study Quran*, New York, NY: HarperOne, 2015.

Naughton, S. and Naughton, T. "Religion, Ethics, and Stock Trading: The Case of an Islamic Equities Market," *Journal of Business Ethics* 23, no. 2 (2000): 145–159.

Nawas, John A. "A Reexamination of Three Current Explanations for al-Maʾmun's Introduction of the *Miḥna*," *International Journal of Middle East Studies* 26, no. 4 (1994): 615–629.

Neihardt, J. G. and Black Elk. *Black Elk Speaks*, Lincoln, NE: University of Nebraska Press, 1979.

Nelson, W. D., trans. *Mekhilta De-Rabbi Shimon bar Yoḥai*, Philadelphia, PA: The Jewish Publication Society, 2006.

Nestle-Aland (NA28). *Novum Testamentum Graece*, http://www.nestle-aland.com/en/read-na28-online/, n.d.

Netland, H. A. "Exclusivism, Tolerance, and Truth," *Missiology* 15 (1987): 77–95.

Netland, H. A. "Religious Exclusivism," in *Philosophy of Religion: Classic and Contemporary Issues*, ed. P. Copan and C. Meister, 68–69, Oxford: Blackwell, 2008.

Neusner, Jacob, trans. *The Babylonian Talmud: A Translation and Commentary*, Peabody, MA: Hendrickson, 2011.

Neusner, Jacob, trans. *The Jerusalem Talmud: A Translation and Commentary*, Peabody, MA: Hendrickson, 2008.

Neuwirth, Angelika. *Der Koran als Text der Spatantike: Ein europaischer Zugang*, Frankfurt: Verlag der Weltreligionen im Insel Verlag, 2010.

Neuwirth, Angelika. "The Qurʾan in the Field of Conflict Between the Interpretative Communities: An Attempt to Cope with the Crisis of Qurʾanic Studies," in *Fundamentalism and Gender: Scripture–Body–Community*, eds. Ulrike Auga, Christina von Braun, Claudia Bruns, and Jana Husmann, Eugene, OR: Pickwick Publications, 2013.

Neuwirth, Angelika. "The Two Faces of the Qurʾān: Qurʾān and Muṣḥaf," *Oral Tradition* 25, no. 1 (2010): 141–156.

Newberg, Andrew B. *Principles of Neurotheology*, Farnham: Ashgate, 2010.

Newberg, Andrew B. and Lee, B. Y. "The Neuroscientific Study of Religious and Spiritual Phenomena: Or Why God Doesn't Use Biostatistics," *Zygon* 40, no. 2 (2005): 469–489.

Newby, Gordon. *A History of the Jews of Arabia: From Ancient Times to Their Eclipse Under Islam*, Columbia, SC: University of South Carolina, 1988.

Newby, Gordon. "Observations About an Early Judaeo-Arabic," *The Jewish Quarterly Review* 61, no. 3 (1971): 212–221.

Newheart, Michael W. *My Name Is Legion: The Story and Soul of the Gerasene Demoniac*, Collegeville, MN: Liturgical Press, 2004.

Neyrey, Jerome H. "The Jacob Allusions in John 1:51," *Catholic Biblical Quarterly* 44, no. 4 (1982): 586–605.

Nielsen, Tore A. and Stenstrom, Philippe. "What Are the Memory Sources of Dreaming?" *Nature* 437 (2005): 1286–1289.

Norris Jr., Richard A., ed. *The Christological Controversy*, Philadelphia, PA: Fortress Press, 1980.

Nunn, J. and Peters, E. "Schizotypy and Patterns of Lateral Asymmetry on Hemisphere-Specific Language Tasks," *Psychiatry Research* 103 (2001): 179–192.

O'Connor, K. M. "The Islamic Jesus: Messiah-hood and Human Divinity in African American Muslim Exegesis," *Journal of the American Academy of Religion* 66, no. 3 (1998): 493–532.

O'Connor, M. "The Arabic Loanwords in Nabatean Aramaic," *Journal of Near Eastern Studies* 45, no. 3 (1986): 213–229.

O'Leary, De Lacey. *Comparative Grammar of the Semitic Languages*, Abingdon: Routledge, 2000.

O'Neill, J. C. "The Prologue to St John's Gospel," *Journal of Theological Studies* 20, no. 1 (1969): 41–52.

O'Reilly, Thomas, Dunbar, Robin, and Bentall, Richard. "Schizotypy and Creativity: An Evolutionary Connection?" *Personality and Individual Differences* 31, no. 7 (2001): 1067–1078.

Oppenheim, A. Leo, Reiner, Erica, and Roth, Martha T., eds. *The Assyrian Dictionary of the Oriental Institute of the University of Chicago*, Chicago, IL: The Oriental Institute, 1956–2011.

Osborn, E. *Tertullian: First Theologian of the West*, Cambridge: Cambridge University Press, 2003.

Pagels, E. H. "Exegesis of Genesis 1 in the Gospels of Thomas and John," *Journal of Biblical Literature* 118, no. 3 (1999): 477–496.

Painter, J. "Rereading Genesis in the Prologue of John?" in *Neotestamentica et Philonica*, eds. D. E. Aune, T. Seland, and J. H. Ulrichsen, Leiden: Brill, 2003.

Paloutzian, Raymond F. and Park, Crystal L., eds. *Handbook of the Psychology of Religion and Spirituality*, New York, NY: The Guilford Press, 2013.

Parke-Taylor, Geoffrey H. *Yahweh: The Divine Name in the Bible*, Waterloo, ON: Wilfrid Laurier University Press, 1975.

Patai, R. "The Shekhina," *The Journal of Religion* 44, no. 4 (1964): 275–288.

Pennacchio, Catherine. "Lexical Borrowing in the Qur'an: The Problematic Aspects of Arthur Jeffery's List," *Bulletin du Centre de recherché français à Jérusalem* 22 (2011). https://bcrfj.revues.org/6643.

Perrine, Laurence. "Four Forms of Metaphor," *College English* 33, no. 2 (1971): 125–138.

Peters, J. R. T. M. *God's Created Speech: A Study in the Speculative Theology of the Muʿtazili Qāḍī l-Quḍāt Abu l-Ḥasan ʿAbd al-Jabbār ibn Aḥmad al-Ḥamadānī*, Leiden: Brill, 1976.

Philo. *Philo*, eds. F. H. Colson and G. H. Whitaker, Cambridge, MA: Harvard University Press, 1929–1962.

Piel, Alexander K. and Stewart, Fiona A. "Non-Human Animal Responses Towards the Dead and Death: A Comparative Approach to Understanding the Evolution of Human Mortuary Practice," in *Death Rituals, Social Order and the Archaeology of Immortality in the Ancient World: Death Shall Have No Dominion*, eds. Colin Renfrew, Michael J. Boyd, and Iain Morley, 15–26, Cambridge: Cambridge University Press, 2015.

Pizzagalli, D., Lehmann, D., and Brugger, P. "Lateralized Direct and Indirect Semantic Priming Effects in Subjects with Paranormal Experiences and Beliefs," *Psychopathology* 34 (2001): 75–80.

Plummer, Robert L. "Righteousness and Peace Kiss: The Reconciliation of Authorial Intent and Biblical Typology," *The Southern Baptist Journal of Theology* 14, no. 2 (2010): 54–61.

Potts, Daniel P. "Trans-Arabian Routes of the Pre-Islamic Period," *Travaux de la Maison de l'Orient* 16, no. 1 (1988): 127–162.

Pourhamzavi, Karim. "How Jihadists Think and Act," *New Zealand International Review* 40 (2015): 15–18.

Pratt, Douglas. "Islamophobia as Reactive Co-Radicalization," *Islam and Christian–Muslim Relations* 26 (2014): 205–218.

Pratt, Richard L. *Holman New Testament Commentary: I & II Corinthians*, ed. M. Anders, Nashville, TN: Broadman & Holman, 2000.

Pregill, M. "The Hebrew Bible and the Quran: The Problem of the Jewish 'Influence' on Islam," *Religion Compass* 1, no. 6 (2007): 643–659.

Prentky, R. A. "Mental Illness and Roots of Genius," *Creativity Research Journal* 13, no. 1 (2010): 95–104.

Proudfoot, Wayne. *Religious Experience*, Berkeley, CA: University of California Press, 1985.

Prunet, J.-F. "External Evidence and the Semitic Root," *Morphology* 16, no. 1 (2006): 41–67.

Quddus, Munir, Bailey III, Henri, and White, Larry R. "Business Ethics: Perspectives from Judaic, Christian, and Islamic Scriptures," *Journal of Management, Spirituality & Religion* 6, no. 4 (2009): 323–334.

Radel, Rémi, Davranche, Karen, Fournier, Marion, and Dietrich, Arne. "The Role of (Dis) inhibition in Creativity: Decreased Inhibition Improves Idea Generation," *Cognition* 134 (2015): 110–120.

Rahman, Fazlur. "Some Key Ethical Concepts of the Qur'ān," *The Journal of Religious Ethics* 11, no. 2 (1983): 170–185.

Räisänen, Heikki. "The Portrait of Jesus in the Qur'ān: Reflections of a Biblical Scholar," *The Muslim World* 70, no. 2 (1980): 122–133.

Rashi (d. 1105 CE). *Torah with Rashi's Commentary*, ed. Y. I. Z. Herczeg, Brooklyn, NY: Mesorah, 1998.

Rawls, John. *Political Liberalism*, New York, NY: Columbia University Press, 1996.

Rawls, John. *Theory of Justice*, Cambridge, MA: Harvard University Press, 1971.

Reed, D. A. "How Semitic Was John? Rethinking the Hellenistic Background to John 1:1," *Anglican Theological Review* 85, no. 4 (2003): 709–726.

Reicke, Bo. "Traces of Gnosticism in the Dead Sea Scrolls?" *New Testament Studies* 1, no. 2 (1954): 137–141.

Reinhold, Frances L. "Exiles and Refugees in American History," *The Annals of the American Academy of Political and Social Science* 203 (1939): 63–73.

Reisel, Max. *The Mysterious Name of Y. H. W. H.: The Tetragrammaton in Connection with the EHYEH ašer EHYEH-Hūhā-and Šem Hammephôrăs*, Assen: Van Gorcum, 1957.

Renz, Gabi. "Nicodemus: An Ambiguous Disciple? A Narrative Sensitive Investigation," in *Challenging Perspective on the Gospel of John*, ed. John Lierman, Heidelberg: Mohr Siebeck, 2006.

Resnick, I. "The Falsification of Scripture and Medieval Christian and Jewish Polemics," *Medieval Encounters* 2, no. 3 (1996): 344–380.

Reynolds, Gabriel S. "On the Qur'anic Accusation of Scriptural Falsification (*taḥrīf*) and Christian Anti-Jewish Polemic," *Journal of the American Oriental Society* 130, no. 2 (2010): 189–202.

Reynolds, Gabriel S. *The Qur'ān and Its Biblical Subtext*. Abingdon: Routledge, 2010.

Richard, E. "Expressions of Double Meaning and Their Function in the Gospel of John," *New Testament Studies* 31, no. 1 (1985): 96–112.

Richards, Ruth. "A Creative Alchemy," in *The Ethics of Creativity*, eds. Seana Moran, David Cropley, and James C. Kaufman, 119–136, Basingstoke: Palgrave Macmillan, 2014.

Ricoeur, P. *Hermeneutics and the Human Sciences*, trans. J. Thompson, Cambridge: Cambridge University Press, 1998.

Ricoeur, P. *The Rule of Metaphor: The Creation of Meaning in Language*, London: Routledge, 2004.

Ridderbos, Herman N. "The Structure and Scope of the Prologue to the Gospel of John," *Novum Testamentum* 8, no. 2/4 (1966): 180–201.

Rippin, Andrew, ed. *Approaches to the History of the Interpretation of the Qur'ān*, Oxford: Clarendon, 1988.

Rippin, Andrew. "RḤMNN and the ḤANĪFS," in *Islamic Studies Presented to Charles J. Adams*, eds. W. B. Hallaq and P. D. Little, 153–168, Leiden: Brill, 1991.

Rippin, Andrew. "The Function of Asbāb al-Nuzūl in Qur'ānic Exegesis," *Bulletin of the School of Oriental and African Studies, University of London* 51, no. 1 (1988): 1–20.

Rippin, Andrew. "The Qur'an as Literature: Perils, Pitfalls and Prospects," *British Society for Middle Eastern Studies Bulletin* 10, no. 1 (1983): 38–47.

Risse, Günther. *Gott ist Christus, der Sohn der Maria: Eine Studie zum Christusbild im Koran*, Bonn: Borengässer, 1989.

Rissi, Mathias. "John 1:1–18 (The Eternal Word)," *Interpretation* 31, no. 4 (1977): 395–401.

Robson, James. " 'Islām' as a Term," *The Muslim World* 44, no. 2 (1954): 101–109.

Robson, James. "The Material of Tradition I," *The Muslim World* 41, no. 3 (1951): 166–180.

Robson, James. "Tradition, the Second Foundation of Islam," *The Muslim World* 41, no. 1 (1951): 22–33.

Robson, James. "Tradition: Investigation and Classification," *The Muslim World* 41, no. 2 (1951): 98–112.

Rochais, Gérard. "La formation du Prologue (Jn 1:1–18)," *Science et Esprit* 37, no. 1 (1985): 5–44; 161–187.

Rodinson, Maxime. *Muhammad: Prophet of Islam*, London: Tauris Parke Paperbacks, 2002.

Rofé, A. *The Book of Balaam: A Study in Method of Criticism and the History of Biblical Literature and Religion*, Warsaw, IN: Eisenbrauns, 1979.

Rogers, R. A. "The Usury Debate, the Sustainability Debate, and the Call for a Moral Economy," *Ecological Economics* 35, no. 2 (2000): 157–171.

Rollins, Wayne G. *Soul and Psyche: The Bible in Psychological Perspective*, Minneapolis, MN: Fortress Press, 1999.

Rollins, Wayne G. and Kille, D. Andrew. *Psychological Insight into the Bible*, Grand Rapids, MI: Wm. B. Eerdmans, 2007.

Rolls, Edmund T. "Limbic Systems for Emotion and for Memory, but No Single Limbic System," *Cortex* 62 (2015): 119–157.

Rominger, Christian, Weiss, Elisabeth M., Fink, Andreas, Schulter, Günter, and Papousek, Ilona. "Allusive Thinking (Cognitive Looseness) and the Propensity to Perceive 'Meaningful' Coincidences," *Personality and Individual Differences* 51, no. 8 (2011): 1002–1006.

Ronning, John L. *The Jewish Targums and John's Logos Theology*, Peabody, MA: Hendrickson, 2010.

Rosly, S. A. and Abu Bakr, M. A. "Performance of Islamic and Mainstream Banks in Malaysia," *International Journal of Social Economics* 30, no. 12 (2003): 1249–1265.

Rowland, Christopher. "John 1.51, Jewish Apocalyptic and Targumic Tradition," *New Testament Studies* 30, no. 4 (1984): 498–507.

Runyan, William M., ed. *Life Histories and Psychobiography: Explorations in Theory and Method*, Oxford: Oxford University Press, 1982.

Sachedina, Abdulaziz. "Advancing Religious Pluralism in Islam," *Religion Compass* 4 (2010): 221–233.

Sachedina, Abdulaziz. "Is Islamic Revelation an Abrogation of Judaeo-Christian Revelation?" *Concilium: International Review of Theology* 3 (1994): 94–102.

Sachedina, Abdulaziz. "Islamic Theology of Christian–Muslim Relations," *Islam and Christian–Muslim Relations* 8, no. 1 (1997): 27–38.

Sadler-Smith, Eugene. *Inside Intuition*, Abingdon: Routledge, 2008.

Sahas, Daniel J. " 'Holosphyros'? A Byzantine Perception of 'the God of Muhammad,' " in *Christian-Muslim Encounters*, eds. Yvonne Y. Haddad and Wadi Z. Haddad, Gainesville, FL: University Press of Florida, 1995.

Saleh, Walid A. "A Fifteenth-Century Muslim Hebraist: Al-Biqāʾī and His Defense of Using the Bible to Interpret the Qurʾān," *Speculum* 83 (2008): 629–654.

Saleh, Walid A. "The Etymological Fallacy and Qurʾanic Studies: Muhammad, Paradise, and Late Antiquity," in *The Qurʾān in Context: Historical and Literary Investigations into the Qurʾānic Milieu*, eds. A. Neuwirth, N. Sinai, and M. Marx, 649–698, Leiden: Brill, 2010.

Sanfilippo, L. C. and Hoffman, R. E. "Language Disorders in the Psychoses," in *Concise Encyclopedia of Language Pathology*, ed. F. Fabbro, 400–407, Oxford: Elsevier Science, 1999.

Saniotis, Arthur. "Mystical Mastery: The Presentation of Kashf in Sufi Divination," *Asian Anthropology* 6, no. 1 (2007): 29–51.

Sarna, N. M. *The JPS Torah Commentary: Genesis*, Philadelphia, PA: The Jewish Publication Society, 1989.

Sasson, J. M. "Circumcision in the Ancient Near East," *Journal of Biblical Literature* 85, no. 4 (1966): 473–476.

Saussure, F. *Course in General Linguistics*, trans. W. Baskin, eds. P. Meisel and H. Saussy, New York, NY: Columbia University Press, 2011.

Saver, Jeffrey L. and Rabin, John. "The Neural Substrates of Religious Experience," in *The Neuropsychiatry of Limbic and Subcortical Disorders*, eds. Stephen Salloway, Paul Malloy, and Jeffrey L. Cummings, 195–215, Washington, DC: American Psychiatric Press, 1997.

Sayadmansour, Alireza. "Neurotheology: The Relationship Between Brain and Religion," *Iranian Journal of Neurology* 13, no. 1 (2014): 52–55.

Schaff, Philip. *Creeds of Christendom*, Grand Rapids, MI: Baker Book House, 1977.

Schaff, Phillip, ed. *A Select Library of the Nicene and Post-Nicene Fathers of the Christian Church*, New York, NY: The Christian Literature, 1888.

Schaff, Phillip, ed. *Saint Augustine: Sermon on the Mount, Harmony of the Gospels, Homilies on the Gospels*, trans. R. G. MacMullen, New York, NY: Christian Literature, 1888.

Schaff, Phillip and Wace, H., eds. *A Select Library of the Nicene and Post-Nicene Fathers of the Christian Church*, New York, NY: Charles Scribner's Sons, 1900.

Schlier, Heinrich. "'Im Anfang war das Wort' im Prolog des Johannesevangeliums," *Wort und Wahrheit* 9 (1954): 169–180.
Schnackenburg, Rudolf. *Jesus in the Gospels: A Biblical Christology*, Louisville, KY: Westminster John Knox, 1995.
Schnackenburg, Rudolf. "Logos-Hymnus und johanneischen Prolog," *Biblische Zeitschrift* 1 (1957): 69–109.
Schnackenburg, Rudolf. *The Gospel According to St. John*, trans. Kevin Smith, New York, NY: Herder and Herder, 1968.
Schnackenburg, Rudolf. "Und das Wort ist Fleisch geworden," *Internationale Katholische Zeitschrift* 8 (1979): 1–9.
Schneemelcher, W., ed. *New Testament Apocrypha*, Cambridge: James Clarke, 1991.
Scholem, Gershom G. *Jewish Gnosticism, Merkabah Mysticism, and Talmudic Tradition*, New York, NY: The Jewish Theological Seminary of America, 1960.
Schuldberg, David. "Six Subclinical Spectrum Traits in Normal Creativity," *Creativity Research Journal* 13, no. 1 (2000): 5–16.
Schwarcz, H. P., Grün, R., Vandermeersch, B., Bar-Yosef, O., Valladas, H., and Tchernov, E. "ESR Dates for the Hominid Burial Site of Qafzeh in Israel," *Journal of Human Evolution* 17, no. 8 (1988): 733–737.
Schwyzer, E. *Griechische Grammatik: auf der Grundlage von Karl Brugmanns Griechischer Grammatik. Bd. 2: Syntax und syntaktische Stilistik, vervollständigt und hrsg. Von Albert Debrunner. Handbuch der Altertumswissenschaft*, München: C. H. Beck, 1950.
Seim, Turid K. "Descent and Divine Paternity in the Gospel of John: Does the Mother Matter?" *New Testament Studies* 51, no. 3 (2005): 361–375.
Sen, A. "Money and Value: On the Ethics and Economics of Finance," *Economics and Philosophy* 9 (1993): 203–227.
Sevrin, Jean-Marie. "Le quatrième évangile et le gnosticisme: questions de méthode," in *Communauté johannique et son histoire: La trajectoire de l'Evangile de Jean aux deux premiers siècles*, Geneva: Labor et Fides, 1990.
Shameli, N. A. "Mullā Sadrā and Interpreting the Quranic Keywords in a Polysemous Method," *Tahqiqat-e Ulum-e Quran wa Hadith* 3, no. 1 (2007): 5–32.
Shams al-Dīn Al-Safārīnī al-Ḥanbalī (d. 1188/1774). *Lawāmiʿ al-anwār al-bahiyyah wa-sawāṭiʿ al-asrār al-athariyyah li-sharḥ al-durrah al-muḍiyyah fī ʿaqd al-firqah al-marḍiyyah*, Damascus: Muʾassassat al-Khāfiqīn wa-ha, 1982.
Siddiqi, M. N. *What Went Wrong?* Keynote Address at the Roundtable on Islamic Economics: Current State of Knowledge and Development of Discipline held in Jeddah, Saudi Arabia on May 26–27, 2004. Accessed August 14, 2010 at: http://www.siddiqi.com/mns/Keynote_May2004_Jeddah.html.
Simelidis, Christos. "The Byzantine Understanding of the Qurʾanic Term *al-Ṣamad* and the Greek Translation of the Qurʾan," *Speculum* 86, no. 4 (2011): 887–913.
Sina, Ali. *Understanding Muhammad: A Psychobiography of Allah's Prophet*, n.p.: FaithFreedom Publishing, 2008.
Sinnott-Armstrong, Walter. *Morality Without God?* Oxford: Oxford University Press, 2009.
Sirriyeh, E. "Wahhabis, Unbelievers and the Problems of Exclusivism," *Bulletin of the British Society for Middle Eastern Studies* 16 (1989): 123–132.
Sirry, Munʾim. *Scriptural Polemics: The Qurʾān and Other Religions*, Oxford: Oxford University Press, 2014.
Smart, N. *The Religious Experience of Mankind*, New York, NY: Macmillan, 1969.
Smith, Dwight Moody. *The Theology of the Gospel of John*, Cambridge: Cambridge University Press, 1995.

Smith, Jane I. *An Historical and Semantic Study of the Term "Islām" as Seen in a Sequence of Qur'an Commentaries*, Missoula, MT: Scholars Press, 1975.
Smith, Jane I. *Muslims, Christians, and the Challenge of Interfaith Dialogue*, Oxford: Oxford University Press, 2007.
Smith, P. "Did Jesus Foretell Ahmed? Origin of the So-Called Prophecy of Jesus Concerning the Coming of Mohammed," *The Muslim World* 12, no. 1 (1922): 71–74.
Soloveitchik, Joseph B. *Worship of the Heart: Essays on Jewish Prayer*, ed. Shalom Carmy, New York, NY: Toras HoRav Foundation, 2003.
Soroush, Abdulkarim. *The Expansion of Prophetic Experience: Essays on Historicity, Contingency and Plurality in Religion*, trans. Nilou Mobasser, Leiden: Brill, 2009.
Staton, K. *Unlocking the Scriptures for You: First Corinthians*, Cincinnati, OH: Standard Publishing, 1987.
Steigerwald, Diana. "Ismāʿīlī Taʾwīl," in *The Blackwell Companion to the Qurʾan*, ed. Andrew Rippin, 386–400, Malden, MA: Blackwell Publishing, 2006.
Stein, George. "The Voices that Ezekiel Hears: Psychiatry in the Old Testament," *The British Journal of Psychiatry* 196, no. 2 (2010): 101.
Stern, D. "Midrash and Indeterminacy," *Critical Inquiry* 15, no. 1 (1988): 132–161.
Stern, D. *Midrash and Theory: Ancient Jewish Exegesis and Contemporary Literary Studies*, Evanston, IL: Northwestern University Press, 1996.
Stringer, C. B., Grün, R., Schwarcz, H. P., and Goldberg, P. "ESR Dates for the Hominid Burial Site of Es Skhul in Israel," *Nature* 338 (1989): 756–758.
Stubbs, M. *Words and Phrases: Corpus Studies of Lexical Semantics*, Oxford: Blackwell, 2001.
Stuckenbruck, L. T. *Angel Veneration and Christology: A Study in Early Judaism and the Christology of the Apocalypse of John*, Tübingen: Mohr Siebeck, 1995.
Szaluta, Jacques. *Psychohistory: Theory and Practice*, New York, NY: Peter Lang, 1999.
Talbert, Charles H. *Reading Corinthians: A Literary and Theological Commentary on 1 & 2 Corinthians*, Macon, GA: Smyth & Helwys, 2002.
Talbott, T. "The Love of God and the Heresy of Exclusivism," *Christian Scholar's Review* 27 (1997).
Tarakci, M. and Sayar, S. "The Qurʾanic View of the Corruption of the Torah and the Gospels," *The Islamic Quarterly* 49, no. 3 (2005): 227–245.
Taymūr, Aḥmad (d. 1348/1930). *Naẓrah tārīkhiyya fī ḥudūth al-madhāhib al-fiqhiyya al-arbaʿah: al-Ḥanafī, al-Mālikī, al-Shāfiʿī, al-Ḥanbalī, wa intishārihā ʿind jumhūr al-muslimīn*, Beirut: Dār al-Qādirī, 1990.
Tertullian (d. 225 CE). "Adversus Praxean," in *The Ante-Nicene Fathers*, eds. Alexander Roberts and James Donaldson, Buffalo, NY: The Christian Literature Company, 1885.
Thalbourne, Michael A. and Delin, Peter S. "A Common Thread Underlying Belief in the Paranormal, Creative Personality, Mystical Experience and Psychopathology," *The Journal of Parapsychology* 58 (1994): 3–38.
Thāwdhūrus Abū Qurrah. *Schriften zum Islam*, eds. and trans. Reinhold Glei and Adel T. Khoury, Würzburg: Echter, 1995.
The New Bible Dictionary, Leicester: Inter-Varsity Press, 1996.
The Oriental Institute, *The Assyrian Dictionary of the Oriental Institute of the University of Chicago*, Chicago, IL: The Oriental Institute of the University of Chicago, 1964.
Timmerman, John H. *Do We Still Need the Ten Commandments? A Fresh Look at God's Laws of Love*, Minneapolis, MN: Augsburg Fortress, 1997.
Tobin, Thomas H., "Logos," in *The Anchor Yale Bible Dictionary*, ed. D. N. Freedman, New York, NY: Doubleday, 1992, 4: 348–356.

Torrey, Charles C. *The Jewish Foundation of Islam*, New York, NY: Jewish Institute of Religion Press, 1933.
Tritton, A. S. "The Speech of God," *Studia Islamica* 36 (1972): 5–22.
Troeltsch, E. *The Absoluteness of Christianity and the History of Religions*, Louisville, KY: Westminster John Knox, 2006.
Twakkal, Abd Alfatah. "Kaʿb al-Aḥbār and the *Isrāʾīliyyāt* in the *Tafsīr* Literature", M.A. dissertation, Institute of Islamic Studies, McGill University, 2007.
Ushama, Thameem. "The Phenomenon of al-Naskh: A Brief Overview of the Key Issues," *Jurnal Fiqh* 3 (2006): 101–132.
Utley, B. *Paul's Letters to a Troubled Church: I and II Corinthians*, Marshall, TX: Bible Lessons International, 2002.
Valesius. *Life of Eusebius Pamphilus*, in *An Ecclesiastical History to the 20th Year of the Reign of Constantine*, trans. S. E. Parker, London: Samuel Bagster, 1847.
van Ess, Josef. *The Youthful God: Anthropomorphism in Early Islam*, Tempe, AZ: Arizona State University, 1988.
van Nuys, Kelvin. "Evaluating the Pathological in Prophetic Experience (Particularly in Ezekiel)," *Journal of Bible and Religion* 21, no. 4 (1953): 244–251.
van Os, Bas. *Psychological Analyses and the Historical Jesus: New Ways to Explore Christian Origins*, London: Bloomsbury Academic, 2010.
van Os, Bas. "The Problem of Writing a Psychobiography of Jesus," in *Psychological Hermeneutics for Biblical Themes and Texts: A Festschrift in Honor of Wayne G. Rollins*, ed. J. Harold Ellens, 84–96, London: T&T Clark, 2012.
VanSledright, Bruce A. "What Does It Mean to Think Historically . . . and How Do You Teach It?" *Social Education* 68, no. 3 (2004): 230–233.
Vellanickal, M. *The Divine Sonship of Christians in the Johannine Writings*, Rome: Typis Pontificiae Universitatis Gregorianae, 1976.
Versteegh, C. H. M. *Arabic Grammar and Qurʾānic Exegesis in Early Islam*, Leiden: Brill, 1993.
Virkler, H. A. and Ayayo, K. G. *Hermeneutics: Principles and Processes of Biblical Interpretation*, Grand Rapids, MI: Baker Academic, 2007.
Von Denffer, Ahmad. *ʿUlum al-Qurʾān: An Introduction to the Sciences of the Qurʾān*, Markfield, UK: The Islamic Foundation, 2011.
Voss, Ursula, Tuin, Inka, Schermelleh-Engel, Karin, and Hobson, Allan. "Waking and Dreaming: Related but Structurally Independent—Dream Reports of Congenitally Paraplegic and Deaf-Mute Persons," *Consciousness and Cognition* 20, no. 3 (2011): 673–687.
Wafī, ʿAlī ʿAbdulwāḥid, *ʿIlm al-lughah*, Cairo: Nahḍat Miṣr lil-Ṭibāʿah wal-Nashr, n.d.
Walhout, Edwin *Christianity Down to Earth: Where We Are and Where We Should Be Going*, 2nd edn., n.p.: Lulu Press, 2015.
Walker, John. "Who Is ʿUzair?" *The Muslim World* 19, no. 3 (1929): 303–306.
Wansbrough, John E. "Majāz al-Qurʾān: Periphrastic Exegesis," *Bulletin of the School of Oriental and African Studies* 33, no. 2 (1970): 246–266.
Wansbrough, John E. *Qurʾanic Studies: Sources and Methods of Scriptural Interpretation*, Oxford: Oxford University Press, 1977.
Wansbrough, John E. *The Sectarian Milieu: Content and Composition of Islamic Salvation History*, Oxford: Oxford University Press, 1978.
Wasserstrom, Steven M. *Between Muslim and Jew: The Problem of Symbiosis Under Early Islam*, Princeton, NJ: Princeton University Press, 2014.
Waterland, Daniel. *A Critical History of the Athanasian Creed*, ed. John R. King, Oxford: James Parker, 1870.

Watson, J. "South Arabian and Yemeni Dialects," *Salford Working Papers in Linguistics and Applied Linguistics* 1 (2011): 27–40.
Watt, William Montgomery. *Bell's Introduction to the Qur'an*, Edinburgh: T&T Clark, 1970.
Watt, William Montgomery. "His Name Is Ahmad," *The Muslim World* 43, no. 2 (1953): 110–117.
Weber, Samuel. "Saussure and the Apparition of Language: The Critical Perspective," *Modern Language Notes* 91, no. 5 (1976): 913–938.
Wengst, Klaus. *Christologische Formeln und Lieder im Urchristentums*, Gütersloh: Gerd Mohn, 1972.
Wensinck, Arent J. *The Muslim Creed: Its Genesis and Historical Development*, Cambridge: Cambridge University Press, 1932.
Westerlund, David. "Ahmed Deedat's Theology of Religion: Apologetics Through Polemics," *Journal of Religion in Africa* 33 (2003): 263–278.
Whittingham, Martin. *Al-Ghazālī and the Qur'ān: One Book, Many Meanings*, Abingdon: Routledge, 2007.
Whittingham, Martin. "The Value of *taḥrīf ma'nawī* (corrupt interpretation) as a Category for Analysing Muslim Views of the Bible: Evidence from *al-radd al-jamīl* and Ibn Khaldūn," *Islam and Christian–Muslim Relations* 22, no. 2 (2011): 209–222.
Wiles, M. F. *The Spiritual Gospel: The Interpretation of the Fourth Gospel in the Early Church*, Cambridge: Cambridge University Press, 1960.
Williams, A. "Milton and the Book of Enoch: An Alternative Hypothesis," *The Harvard Theological Review* 33, no. 4 (1940): 291–299.
Wilson, Andrew, ed. *World Scripture: A Comparative Anthology of Sacred Texts*, St. Paul, MN: Paragon House, 1998.
Wilson, Rodney. *Economics, Ethics and Religion: Jewish, Christian and Muslim Economic Thought*, New York, NY: New York University Press, 1997.
Wohlman, A. *Al-Ghazālī, Averroës and the Interpretation of the Qur'an: Common Sense and Philosophy in Islam*, trans. D. Burrell, Abingdon: Routledge, 2010.
Wolfe, Michael W. "The World Could Not Contain the Pages: A Sufi Reading of the Gospel of John Based on the Writings of Muḥyī al-Dīn Ibn 'Arabī (1165–1240 CE)," PhD dissertation, Columbia University, 2016.
Wrobel, J. *Language and Schizophrenia*, Amsterdam: John Benjamins, 1989.
Yamauchi, Edwin M. *Pre-Christian Gnosticism: A Survey of the Proposed Evidences*, London: Tyndale, 1973.
Yamauchi, Edwin M. "Pre-Christian Gnosticism in the Nag Hammadi Texts?" *Church History* 48 (1979): 129–141.
Yu, Calvin K.-C. "Toward 100% Dream Retrieval by Rapid-Eye-Movement Sleep Awakening: A High-Density Electroencephalographic Study," *Dreaming* 24, no. 1 (2014): 1–17.
Yung, Alison R. and McGorry, Patrick D. "The Prodromal Phase of First-Episode Psychosis: Past and Current Conceptualizations," *Schizophrenia Bulletin* 22, no. 2 (1996): 353–370.
Zaborski, Andrzej. "Etymology, Etymological Fallacy and the Pitfalls of Literal Translation of Some Arabic and Islamic Terms," in *Words, Texts and Concepts Cruising the Mediterranean Sea: Studies on the Sources, Contents and Influences of Islamic Civilization and Arabic Philosophy and Science*, eds. R. Arnzen and J. Thielmann, 143–148, Leuven: Peeters, 2004.
Zaehner, Robert C. "The Qur'ān and Christ," in *At Sundry Times: An Essay in the Comparison of Religions*, London: Faber & Faber, 1958.

Zaher, T. S. and Hassan, M. K. "A Comparative Literature Survey of Islamic Finance and Banking," *Financial Markets, Institutions & Instruments* 10, no. 4 (2001): 203–227.

Zayd ibn ʿAlī (d. 122/740). *Tafsīr gharīb al-Qurʾān al-majīd*, ed. M. Y. Al-Dīn, Hyderabad: Taj Yusuf Foundation Trust, 2001.

Zilhão, João. "Lower and Middle Palaeolithic Mortuary Behaviours and the Origins of Ritual Burial," in *Death Rituals, Social Order and the Archaeology of Immortality in the Ancient World: Death Shall Have No Dominion*, eds. Colin Renfrew, Michael J. Boyd, and Iain Morley, 27–44, Cambridge: Cambridge University Press, 2015.

Zimmermann, Heinrich. "Christushymnus und johanneischer Prolog," in *Neues Testament und Kirche*, ed. Joachim Gnilka, Freiburg: Herder, 1974.

Index of Qur᾿anic Verses and Passages

General Index

Printed in the USA
CPSIA information can be obtained
at www.ICGtesting.com
LVHW011921050824
787388LV00001B/151